17⁵⁰

SNOHOMISH • CENTRALIA
LAFAYETTE • SEASIDE

art Glass

Description Bool

Inventory No.

Space No. **164**

$ 17⁵⁰

SNOHOMISH • CENTRALIA
LAFAYETTE • SEASIDE

art Glass
Bool

Description

Inventory No.

Space No. **164**

$ 17⁵⁰

THE COLLECTOR'S ENCYCLOPEDIA OF

AMERICAN ART GLASS

JOHN A. SHUMAN III

A Vivid Color Guide to Numerous Art Glass Types

COLLECTOR BOOKS
A Division of Schroeder Publishing Co., Inc.

Searching For A Publisher?

We are always looking for knowledgeable people considered to be experts within their fields. If you feel that there is a real need for a book on your collectible subject and have a large comprehensive collection, contact us.

COLLECTOR BOOKS
P.O. Box 3009
Paducah, Kentucky 42002-3009

Dedicated to peace and love for all mankind.

Acknowledgments

My deepest appreciation to the following groups and individuals for their cooperation, interest, sharing of materials, time and knowledge, and granting permission to photograph glass art objects in their collections: M.B. Stauffer, Director, Milan Historical Museum; Dwight P. Lanmon, Director, The Corning Museum of Glass; Robert F. Rockwell, The Rockwell Museum; Thomas Gardner, Director, Houston Antique Museum; Dorothy G. Hogan, Curator, Sandwich Historical Society Glass Museum; Paul N. Perrot, Director, Virginia Museum of Fine Arts; Marjorie Hill Treat, Wayne County Historical Society; John G. Labanish, Director, The Historical Society of Western Pennsylvania; Kirk Nelson, Curator of Art and Decorative Arts, The Bennington Museum; Irene Lewis Lawrie, Registrar, Lightner Museum; Karen A. Fordyce, Curatorial Assistant, The Currier Gallery of Art; Bill Schroeder, Collector Books; Linda Kruger, Editor, *Collectors News;* Edward A. Babka, Publisher, *The Antique Trader Weekly*; Catherine Murphy, Editor, *The Antique Trader Price Guide*; Richard Wright Antiques; Charon Antiques; Minna Rosenblatt Limited; Antique Emporium; Shaner's Antiques; Mr. and Mrs. Robert Ebinger; Ed and Kay Winnick; Mr. and Mrs. Albert T. Yuhasz; Jo and Owen Hastings; Bob and Etta Henry; Claude and Bernice Brooks; Mr. and Mrs. Eugene Sussel; Earl and Louise Heiser; Ray J. LaTournous; Ron and Eileen Rhoades; Laura and Harry Sine; Dorothy S. Groff, the late Mr. Oliver Lewis Christman, and Private Stock.

Foreword

From its early conceptual stages until the appearance of this book, *American Art Glass*, I have traveled widely throughout the United States. In that interim, information has been gathered both at those sites and through the mail, and I have had the pleasure of handling and photographing a variety of American glass types. Numerous libraries, museums, historical societies, dealers and private collectors have been most kind in sharing their time, interest and expertise.

This format offers a fresh approach to a subject that has been discussed many times and much new information is offered to the reader. The majority of the glass factories' products have been alphabetized so that they may serve as a quick and easy reference too. Included are characteristics of each glass type, pertinent dates, the names of important contributing individuals, shapes likely to be found, and most importantly—facsimiles of company signatures.

The glass examples pictured in color were chosen with the readers' interests in mind. These representative objects illustrate what is collectible, appeals to individual tastes and is of varying price ranges. They are intended to illustrate textures, shapes and colors, and each article depicted is fully described and priced according to the current market. In most instances, measurements are volunteered for each example or a height is given for one of the objects as a reference.

In addition, numerous advertisements from old magazines and trade journals, an art glass catalogue, and postcard views of glass factories are all shown in color. They will offer the reader both pleasurable and informative reading and viewing.

Other sections of the text illustrate glass-making tools and how they were implemented, definitions of significant glass terminology and a discussion concerning principal agents used in creating colored glass. A list is provided giving the names of contemporary glass manufacturers and sellers. This will be invaluable in keeping up with the various trends and also make you aware of look-alike reproduced items.

Two very important sections list the names and show the logos used on silver plate fixtures accompanying art glass, and the locations of cut glass factories plus a multitude of signatures incorporated on their output. Although it is true that cut glass is often considered as one separate field, I have chosen to incorporate it in this text. The difficulties encountered in producing heavy brilliant, clear and colored blanks, plus the precision required to cut many complicated patterns is a refined art in itself. When studied in this light, finely executed cut glass examples become jewels of art just as numerous examples of art glass become fluid art forms.

Also, I have provided the reader with additional black and white illustrations showing glass advertisements, the steps required to manufacture glass and views of the Mount Palomar Mold and the Mirror (the largest piece of glass ever cast). The first casting cracked when cooling and is on display at the Corning Museum of Glass.

Finally, an alphabetical price guide will give the reader an edge in establishing values for a variety of forms not pictured in the text. A visual time line chart places in perspective historical and literary events that were occurring at the same time a particular glass factory was being established. An extensive bibliography is intended to encourage the reader to do continuous reading in this very interesting field of glass manufacturing.

The general purposes of this book are to inform in an interesting, educational and appealing way; to emphasize the quality of hand craftsmanship; and to strive toward an understanding of the artistic ability and experience required to fabricate glass.

Emphasis upon cooperation in each shop; carefully manufactured molds; accurate formulas; precision manipulation of each hot object until completed; time consuming etching, cutting and decorating; and finally the cooling and marketing of the glass types produced all come into play.

I sincerely hope this book will serve you well and clarify many misconceptions that exist on the subject. Treat this book as a friend that you can continually refer to for information, or when seeking advice on what to buy and/or sell.

Table of Contents

Introduction

Imagine a crisp and blusterous winter morning in New England late in the 1800s. The brisk footsteps of a glassworker at dawn can be heard as a thick mantle of snow covers the ground. A solitary squirrel scampers by, foraging for food, and long dagger-like icicles hang from the buildings' edges. The artisan has arrived at his intended destination. He is cold and wind-bitten by the harsh weather.

Inside, the crews of men are warming themselves as they chat and prepare to commence work. A giant conically-shaped furnace radiates heat outwardly to the workers scattered throughout the room. The coal-fed furnace is 22 feet in diameter and contains ten pots. The furnace gorges itself with five tons of coal in a 24-hour period. Fires are seldom allowed to burn out, as this would be expensive to the operation, and might crack the pots.

The melting pots withstand temperatures of 2600 degrees for periods of 36 hours while the batch is being cooked. Each pot is constructed of special Stourbridge, England fire clay and Missouri clay. Built entirely by hand, the pots are fabricated a portion at a time, while the clay is covered with cloths to absorb the moisture. This procedure continues until the four foot diameter vessel is completed. Each pot will hold about a ton of glass; the life of a pot may range from a few weeks to eight months. Glass ingredients may deteriorate and crack the clay, so that molten masses run through the furnace grating below. On some occasions the glass solidifies and seals the crack; most frequently, the batch must be bailed out and placed in new pots. The brick inside the furnace has also been constructed to withstand the intense heat, as common brick would soon crumble.

The glass ingredients in the pots are now fluid and at white heat; their contents are kept in perfect fluidity from ten to 30 hours. Once the bubbles disappear and all foreign matter is skimmed, the furnace will be cooled; the metal will become thick and adhesive, and then it will be worked quickly.

This batch has been meticulously mixed and measured by one of the men, gathering scoops of ingredients from wooden bathtubs. Into the trough he places fine, pure white sand that is soft as flour. It has been screened many times, and iron deposits have been removed by means of electric magnets. Layer upon layer of necessary materials are spread, and then the worker shovels them from one end of the trough to the other, mixing them completely. Wasted glass is also added, as this promotes proper fusion and the chemical union of silica and the mixed bases.

Men are divided into gangs and work two six-hour periods, with a six hour break between. The gang consists of the "gatherer," who works glass taken from a pot on the end of his blowpipe; the job of reheating is assigned to the "sticker up;" a "servitor" does the necessary preliminary steps; and the "gaffer" refines and completes the example.

Glass is demanding to fabricate, but in the hands of a skilled craftsman, it is a very responsive medium. His art has been learned through many years of education, experimentation, and trial and error. The tools are a mere dozen, with only three absolutely essential to form a simple piece. They are: the blowpipe, the pontil rod, and a tool for shaping. In a thousand years, there have been only minor changes and very few additions to the glassmaker's tools.

One artisan takes a bulb of molten glass, about the size of a baseball, on the end of his pipe. Working rapidly, he uses a "block" to shape the white hot glass. Now he introduces air into the bottle by placing his lips on the other end of the pipe and blowing. As the batch begins to take on a light pink hue, it must be reheated again in the glory hole.

Retracted white hot, one man turns the blowpipe, while another shapes the base and neck of the bottle with his tongs. The bottle, held by its neck, must be turned around to complete the formation of the neck. Another man, with a pontil rod having a small blob of glass at its end, applies his pipe to the base of the bottle and retrieves it from the first worker.

Heated once again in the glory hole, a craftsman takes it out and cuts the neck of the bottle with shears. The molten glass, the consistency of taffy, is now tooled and shaped to form the lip of the decanter. Another worker applies the finishing touches by adding a small amount of glass to the side of the bottle to form a well-shaped handle. The pontil rod is now carefully knocked off, and holding tongs are used to carry the piece to a long annealing oven. If the object is cooled too quickly, it may crack or show imperfections.

The 60-foot oven, provided with a conveyor belt, moves the glass from the hot to the cool end in a period of four days. Some heavy, larger examples might require a week in the oven. Once the goods are properly cooled and tempered, they are wrapped with care in padded layers, boxed and shipped to major distributors.

Envision the exciting display of Art Glass as each example is unpacked at a major showroom! Its colors are vibrant, its textures are many and its forms are sensuous. Some hues are vivid, while others blend and shade in a subtle fashion. A myriad of textures exist including: shiny, iridescent and satin finishes; finely cut and precision polished treatments; deep and shallow etched designs; applied decorative overlay, prunts and rosettes; stained, silvered, mercury, overshot and coralene surfaces; artistically rendered, colorful enameling and heavy gold work; marvered designs, threading, colored striped loops in swags; leaded and stained glass; glass in metal mounts; opalescent and opaque types; glass with canes, mica flecks and metal powders trapped between the layers; and even random and controlled bubbles in clear and colored glass. This table and decorative glassware often simulates materials other than glassware, such as china and porcelain.

The term "Art Glass," as one can see, is a broad and very tolerant one, taking in vast arrays of glass techniques and colors. Glassmakers were fabricating during the Victorian era and well into the Art Nouveau period, from around 1880 up until as late as the 1930s. Their experimentation with decoration, techniques and materials brought creativity in glass to its apex in the United States.

During the late Victorian period, double colors and numerous interesting shaded wares were produced, new mixtures of chemical compounds were used and heated objects were sprayed with various chemicals and gases. Decorations were ornate with applied work in contrasting colors; there was a revival of Venetian decorating techniques, and many fluted and ruffled rims were evident.

By the end of the Victorian movement, Art Nouveau came to the forefront. The glassmakers reacted violently to the previous ornateness. Many artisans turned to nature for their models; they sought inspiration through examples of ancient glass. Iridescent and pitted surfaces, Venetian lace techniques, and millefiori rods to create floral designs were just some of the trends that followed. Much inspiration, of course, was received from the 16th century Venetians, whose skill and art-istry in glass have never been surpassed. Fortunately, the Art Nouveau leaders only borrowed ideas; these, in turn, were implemented in many new and interesting fashions.

Some notables in the art glass school include: Louis Comfort Tiffany, Frederick Carder, Joseph Locke, Frederick S. Shirley, Nicholas Lutz, Emil J. Larson, Victor Durand, Arthur J. Nash, William S. Blake, Edward D. Libbey, Evan E. Kimble, Harry Northwood, Jacob Rosenthal, George W. Leighton, H. C. Fry, Philip J. Handel, Robert M. Gundersen, William Leighton, Jr., Thomas Pairpoint and Martin Bach, Sr., plus many others.

From the standpoint of art and craftsmanship, much of this beautiful glass is a lasting tribute to the ingenuity and resourcefulness of the American manufacturer. The hand craftsmanship needed to manufacture quality art glass required supreme artistry in design and execution; it was a very definite break with the established traditions that had been employed to create pressed glass. For the lover of fine glass, learning about Art Glass and the processes required in manufacturing designates this time period as unique—a span that can truly be called the Golden Age of glass in the United States.

Descriptive Glass Entries

Acid Cutback - Steuben

This Steuben production was being made in limited numbers during the 1920s. There are about 400 different designs, comprising a total output of around 1800 pieces. Vases, bowls, urns, plates and candlesticks are the predominate items found.

The colored crystal usually includes two glass layers, the inner being cut away. Some Acid Cutbacks, however, are just one homogeneous mass. One portion may be glossy, while the other is acidized. In some instances the entire body is a flat finish. Designs are usually floral; the most desirable are animal and aquatic forms.

Most pieces appear to be unmarked. However, examples have been discovered with either the Steuben Fleur-de-Lis at the bases, or signed "F. Carder."

Look for unique color combinations, massiveness, excellent sharp cutting, artistically conceived Grecian shapes, and Chinese and other motifs. Patterns were derived from negative etched glass plates that were inked and heated. The excess ink was scraped away. Then transfer paper was placed over the plate and rubbed carefully to pick up the designs. This moistened paper was peeled and applied to the glass object and pressed, giving the glass its intended pattern. After the transfer was peeled, the portions of the design not to be etched were coated with wax. The object was then dipped in acid for a limited time to achieve the proper cutting depth.

This art form is likely to command four figures because of its desirability and relative scarcity.

Agata - New England

Agata is a unique opaque ware that is a novelty in the art glass field; it was produced less than a year by the New England Glass Company. Patented by Joseph Locke in January of 1887, Agata has the coloration of New England "Wild Rose" Peach Blow, shading from a deep rose at the top to a cream white at the base. Pronounced "oil spots" or splotches cover a portion, or all of the object. These were created when the article was covered with a metallic stain; then naptha, alcohol or benzene was spattered over it. As the flammable liquid evaporated in a muffle, the surface mottling was fixed. The same stains employed on Pomona were also used on Agata. Most objects were finished with a glossy surface; matte pieces are very desirable. Some rare examples have opal linings, a gold spiderweb tracery, or were mold blown in a pattern. Premium examples have deep coloration and pronounced spots. This glass is not found signed.

Shapes include: pitchers; cruets; celery vases; assorted bowls, mugs, condiment sets, punch cups, spooners, whiskey and water tumblers; toothpick holders; stick, lily, and "Morgan" vases in a molded, five-headed, amber glass, griffin holder. Prices for Agata have escalated appreciably in recent years. This art glass makes an excellent addition to an advanced collection.

Agate - Steuben (Moss Agate)

Also called Moss Agate by Carder, this marbleized glass simulates colors of mineral origin. Ranking high as an important Steuben creation, powdered colored glass in many colors formed the object; then it was coated with a clear layer of crystal. These objects are reminiscent of Roman and Venetian types. Every color imaginable is possible in these scarce vases, which are constructed of striated glass. Manufactured from about 1910 through the 1920s, these pieces are sometimes signed.

Agate - Tiffany

Numerous layers of colored glass make up this choice ware, which is then cut and usually smoothed to a high polish. It is sometimes referred to as "Laminated." The glass was worked at low temperatures very quickly to prevent the batch from turning dark. This product is one of the earliest by Tiffany. Paper labels and/or engraved marks will be found on these examples, most often seen in the shapes of vases. The ware is scarce and resembles polished agate stone in hues of yellow, tan and brown.

Albertine - Mount Washington

The term "Albertine" appears to be the name of an opaque, decorated, shiny glassware whose name was eventually changed to Crown Milano. In the late 1800s, this glass was also advertised as "Dresden Decorated" and "Ivory Decorated." A mark, believed to be the Albertine trademark, shows a red, enameled, four-pronged crown surrounded by a laurel wreath with a bow. Early and later catalogs show the same glass as Albertine and then termed by its more exotic counterpart, Crown Milano. This ware occurs predominately in vases, although assorted tablewares were also manufactured.

Amber - Steuben

In a subdued color having an intensity of medium gold brown, many objects of both a decorative and functional nature were made. Hawkes also purchased blanks with this coloration. All transparent colored crystal will vary in depth of color, based upon the thickness of the wall or foot of the vessel.

Amberina - Flashed

Flashed Amberina was of a later origin and a less expensive method for creating Amberina. Pieces were formed of solid amber glass and then coated on the top section with a gold mixture which produced the ruby hue. In flashed Amberina, a sharp demarkation can be detected instead of the gradual blending of colors. This type of glass is not nearly as desirable as genuine Amberina.

Amberina - Libbey

In 1888, the New England Glass Works moved to Toledo, Ohio, where Edward D. Libbey changed the firm's name to Libbey Glass Company. Amberina was made there around 1900 and again in 1920. These ventures revived some interest, but only small quantities of blown and pressed wares (made in molds) were manufactured. Rich in color and equal to early examples, pieces might be marked, "Libbey" in script letters in the pontil area or have a round paper label with the logo,

"Libbey - Made in U.S.A. Trademark." Typical shapes include baskets, compotes, vases and assorted tableware.

Amberina - New England

The New England Glass Company developed this single layered glass in 1883. Joseph Locke perfected the ware, which conventionally shades from red at the top to amber at its base. Locke ranks as one of the greatest and most versatile contributors to the American art glass field. Other glass patents taken out by him included: Pomona (1885), Plated Amberina (1886), Peach Blow (1886), Agate (1887) and Maize (1888).

The earliest Amberina has a flint quality and an excellent resonance when tapped lightly. Such examples shade from ruby (deep fuchsia, sometimes verging on purple) to a delicate amber color. Small quantities of gold in solution were added to a batch of transparent amber glass. Cooling and reheating the top portions of articles created the shadings in the finished products.

Reverse Amberina is unusual because the red and amber are reversed on the ware. It is not found as often, since it was easier to reheat the top of an article in the "glory hole," particularly hollow objects such as tumblers, pitchers and vases.

Pieces were blown into patterns having swirls, ribs, thumbprints and diamond quilting (Venetian Diamond). These blown-molded pieces of Amberina should have a pontil mark where the object was attached to a pontil (puntie, punty, ponty or pontil).

Pressed examples in the Stork pattern (New England Glass), and those in imitation of cut glass designs will not have rough or polished pontil marks.

During the era of extravagant cut glass, the New England Glass Company manufactured cut Amberina. The method for producing the sensitive Amberina glass blanks was patented by Edward D. Libbey on July 29, 1884. These were shaped and reheated to create a deep ruby outer surface, and the design was cut through to reveal the amber color on the inner surface of the glass. Occasionally, the New England Glass Works' oval paper label will be discovered with "Amberina - N.E.G.W."

Almost every type of glass article was manufactured in Amberina, and today's collector has an unlimited variety from which to choose. The novice collector should study books on art glass, view museum examples, and attend antique shows and sales. Learn to recognize the quality workmanship and forms of the early wares. When buying, expect to pay a fair price for your acquisitions, and transact business with a reliable dealer, willing to guarantee the item(s) in writing. Many reproductions are on the market, waiting for the less knowledgeable individual.

Amberina - Painted

Painted Amberina is another classification of Amberina glass that shades from one hue to another. This was achieved by painting the glass with a mixture of copper oxide and yellow ochre, and fixing the paint with a high temperature. When the article had cooled, it was subsequently repainted and reheated. This type is easily detected since the painting wears away, and the glass surface has an iridescence from the metallic stains.

Ambero - Mount Washington Pairpoint

This art glass was manufactured about 1900 in fairly limited quantities. It is a heavy ware having a chipped glass surface texture on the exterior and a smooth interior. The clear crystal glass was tinted a light yellow, and then colorful designs were painted on the inside surfaces. Green, brown, pink, lavender and yellow are normally the colors that the artists used. Motifs include forest scenes with peasant people; hanging leaves with flowers, fruit and nuts; plus sailing scenes. The glass was made into vases, hurricane lamps on turned wooden bases and lamp shades. It is safe to assume that few examples are found signed. When marked, an example will be signed "AMBERO" with a "C" initial.

Brown Enameled

Amethyst - Durand

A quality violet purple, transparent crystal was converted into assorted vases, covered jars, wines, bowls, plates and compotes. Often mold-blown in the Optic Rib pattern, examples may be found signed in silver stylus within the ground pontil.

Amethyst - Pairpoint

This ware is transparent and a resonant crystal having a violet coloration. Covered jars, compotes, sherbets, deep bowls, cornucopias and drinking cups were some of the items manufactured in this color. Many pieces had the popular engraved grape design; some examples have rolled rims and clear controlled bubble ball connectors. This glass was not signed and is still available to collectors.

Amethyst - Steuben

This is a Steuben rich purple, colored crystal that is scarce. A variety of decorative and functional objects were made, including wine glasses, candlesticks, desert bowls, luncheon services and compotes. Some pieces are found signed with the acid-etched Steuben Fleur-de-Lis. Many objects are ribbed, have folded rims, or large disk bases. It is not uncommon to find copper wheel engraved initials or florals on examples. This glass possesses a bell-like tonal quality when tapped and pontils are ground and polished. The color is uniform throughout its varying thicknesses. Some Amethyst pieces have chemical residue within or on the surface of the crystal. This glass apparently was difficult to produce.

Antique Green - Steuben

Dark in color and scarce, Antique Green might be compared to the hue present in a spinch leaf. It is a subdued color that was manufactured in both decorative and functional items. Some examples were acid-etched.

Aurenes - Steuben (Gold, Blue, Brown, Red, and Green)

Gold Aurene was introduced in 1904, the name "Aurene" describing the golden sheen imparted to the glass surface. Any piece of Aurene examined under a high power glass will reveal thousands of minute fractures that both reflect and refract the light, giving iridescence. Tin and iron chloride sprays gave the surfaces a matte finish. Spots that were missed took on a high mirror gloss which was undesirable. This ware was popular and produced until about 1933. The base glass was often clear, amber or topaz. Some Gold Aurene has stretch marks, which occurred after the glass was sprayed and shaped further.

Blue Aurene, introduced around 1905, utilized the same Gold Aurene formula, with the addition of cobalt to the batch.

Engraved Marks

STEUBEN AURENE   AURENE

◯ Pontil

Other iridized, colored Aurenes include Brown, Red and Green. Brown Aurene is a colored and iridescent brown glass sprayed with tin chloride.

Red Aurene was an early factory production item made from Alabaster or Calcite glass. The examples have Aurene decoration with florals, leaf forms, feathers or trailing threads.

Green Aurene is similar to Red Aurene, where examples are constructed of Calcite or Alabaster glass and Aurene decorations are applied using feathers, trailing or millefiori techniques. This glass was first made in 1904. All of the Aurenes are very scarce, command high prices and are predominately in vase forms.

Aurora - Pairpoint

This reddish amber, transparent, colored crystal is very attractive when viewed. Manufactured during the Pairpoint-Gundersen era, the color is found in an array of shapes including: sugars and creamers, open and covered compotes, covered vases, console bowls, flip vases and other interesting shapes. Clear bubble ball connectors and finials were popular. Some engraved patterns are: grape, floral, Wexford, and berry and leaf design. A rarity would be to discover an example embellished with a silver foot and finial. This color makes a warm and hospitable addition to a collection.

Aventurine

This unusual colored glass has small powdered particles of metals suspended between the clear outer layer and the colored inner casing. Fine particles of iron, brass, bronze, goldstone or even gold were gathered on the hot glass to form the desired object.

A decorative process whereby sparkling particles form some type of pattern, this technique was revived in America during the Victorian era. Quality examples of this glass are seldom seen. Shapes would include pitchers, vases and tumblers. The Union Glass Company was one firm that manufactured this glass type.

Belle Ware

Belle Ware   Enameled in red and blue

BELLE WARE CVH

Signed Belle Ware with molded CVH initials

The Helmschmied Manufacturing Company of Meriden, Connecticut, in 1903 announced through one of their catalogs "The Belle Ware," a new line of novelties for the wedding and holiday gifts. The illustrated pamphlet with descriptions and prices by the dozen went on to say "THE WORKMANSHIP is of the highest character and all strictly HAND PAINTED." The ware was intended for show case and window displays to create attention and interest. The whole line could be seen in shades of pink, blue, and lavender with or without the frosted effect. This addition over the decoration reminds the viewer of thousands of tiny clear glass beads spread evenly over the surface and fired-on for permanency.

The Helmschmied line was for sale by George Borgfeldt and Company at their New York City showrooms located on 48 West Fourth Street. Carl V. Helmschmied also had a New York City office at 253 Broadway.

Constructed of opal glass with decoration, examples were mounted with very fine gold plated trimmings and lined with the best satin. Decorations included: violets, roses, pond lilies, chrysanthemums, blue flowers, girl in pink, girl in waves, girl swimming, dancing girl, rococo figure, cupid in clouds, lady and cupid, sweet sixteen, and boy on deep rose and gold.

Some typical shapes were lidded jewel and handkerchief cases; vases; open jewel trays; puffs, bon bons, and ash trays (not lined); brush and comb trays, cracker jars, salt and pepper shakers, and even pen, brush, and comb trays in china; plus paper cutters in bronze, antique copper, and aluminum.

This difficult glass to procure was named after Carl Helmschmied's sister-in-law, Mrs. Isabella van Goerschen. She was fondly called "Bella" by both Mr. Helmschmied and his wife, Lillian.

Large handkerchief cases originally cost from $4.20 to $9.50 each. Smaller ones ranged from $2.90 to $7.90. Cracker jars sold from $3.00 to $4.50 each, and trays varied from $4.00 to $6.00. Prices today, as then, will be determined by the quality of tinting and gold work. Frosted examples command the highest prices.

Black Amethyst - Pairpoint

Pairpoint in this color is very difficult to locate. The dense, translucent nature of the glass will betray its true coloration to be a very deep amethyst when held near an intense light source. It is often associated with very formal table dining. This ware may be further enhanced by silver overlay patterns or silver overlay feet. Some very rare examples merge Flambeau glass and Black Amethyst, a popular combination in vases and drinking vessels.

Black Amethyst - Steuben

Steuben's shiny Black Amethyst is a violet red under a concentrated and intense light source. Examples are signed with the acid-etched Steuben signature and were probably produced during the '20s and '30s. Attractive compotes, perfumes, vases and candlesticks are some items made of this glass. Black combined with Alabaster, Ivory or Ivrene creates an outstanding decorator item. Also called "Mirror Black," this glass was acid-etched and could have rims trimmed in pink, blue or white.

Bluerina - Sandwich

This particular art glass is certainly not very plentiful. Some schools refer to it as being controversial; other collectors simply accept this transparent shaded glass. Termed Bluerina or Blue Amberina when the glass changes from blue to amber, the same reheating process was employed as for Amberina. Do not confuse Bluerina with Alexandrite, three graduated shades of glass (citron yellow, rose and bluish purple), originating with Thomas Webb, England. Painted Amberina, a product of the Sandwich Glass Company in 1870, depended upon a blue surface stain for the color gradation. This stain was fired to set its color; there is a tendency for the blue to be splotchy. Decorative tablewares such as pitchers, punch cups, vases and dishes are the items found.

Boston Silver Glass Company

Located in Cambridge, Massachusetts, this firm specialized in the manufacture of assorted silvered objects. Founded in 1857 by A. Young, the glasshouse ceased operations in 1871.

Bristol Yellow - Steuben

Twisted, vertically ribbed, and threaded, complete table services were among the items manufactured in this Steuben crystal colored glassware. Its vivid golden yellow hue was exceedingly popular and brilliant in comparison to similar wares produced by competing companies. Silver was used in this blend to create this most unusual yellow cast.

Bubbly - Steuben

Bubbly (air trap glass) was an early Steuben production item that had great success. Manufactured in the '20s and '30s, the bubbles were used by Carder in a decorative and also controlled sense. Bubbles in the glass were achieved originally with spiked molds. When molten glass was rolled over the slab, the spikes left marks in the hot glass. A second applied layer of glass locked in the air, so that the controlled designs could be achieved.

Random bubbles in the glass could be created by introducing a willow branch into the pot and withdrawing it immediately. Gasses were released from the green wood, enabling the artisans to begin working this glass. This same process would also eliminate both greenish and pinkish tinges when the workers wished colorless glass.

All shapes and forms, including vases, bowls, colognes and even luminors, were manufactured. This ware was popular in clear crystal, Wisteria, French Blue, Topaz, Pomona Green, Antique Green and Bristol Yellow.

Burmese - Mount Washington

Burmese is a thin and brittle art glass, blending from salmon pink at the top to canary yellow at its base. Only the Mount Washington Glass Company, in the United States, produced this ware. A patent was applied for in Washington, D.C., on September 28, 1885; thirteen days short of two months, on December 15, 1885, the patent was granted to Frederick F. Shirley, agent. This very beautiful coloration was created by adding small quantities of uranium oxide, gold, feldspar and fluorspar to the batch and then they were mixed carefully. Mold and free-blown pieces turned a sulphur yellow color throughout. Upon reheating the top portion, a delicate pink shade developed. A yellow top edge indicates that the glassworker chose to reheat the piece a second time.

Some elegant techniques were the use of ruffled and turned down edges; the application of stems, leaves and flowers; and ornate snail, ribbed feet and applied handles in both the popular "plush," or satin finish and in its glossy, or natural state. Designs were executed by the skilled artists' department under the direction of their superintendent, Albert Steffin. Much of the decoration was accomplished with paint and pure gold enamel, reduced in acid. Popular motifs consisted of poetic verses; the fish in the net; florals and leaves; birds; and the "Egyptian" design—very exotic with rider, camel, palms and pyramids. The predominate patterns in both finishes are quilted diamond, ribbed and hobnail. A very few outstanding examples were signed by Albert Steffin, and artists Frank Guba, Adolf Frederick and Herman Knechtel. The foreman of this department was Timothy Canty. An artist's particular style can often be recognized in other types of glass made by the same factory.

Signed and authenticated pieces command outstanding prices. They are also an excellent aid to identify less known examples. Some of the items produced in this ware in assorted sizes include bowls, vases, pitchers, candlesticks, cruets, sugars and creamers, ewers, perfumes, plates, shades, parlor lamps, syrups, toothpick holders, and cups and saucers.

Burmese was well received after it was highly praised by Queen Victoria and her daughter, Princess Beatrix. The Queen acquired a gift service and the Princess was sent four vases. Four vases were also bestowed upon President Grover Cleveland's wife, who prized them highly.

Good colored reproductions of this glass type cannot be made, since uranium oxide in quantity is now restricted to use by the military. During Robert M. Gundersen's reign, Burmese was reissued. The last batch of Burmese produced in New Bedford was by Robert Bryden on July 4, 1956. The Pairpoint factory in Sagamore, Massachusetts, with Robert Bryden as its president, made limited amounts of Bryden Pairpoint Burmese from 1970.

 Paper Label

Calcite (On Blue and Gold Aurene) - Steuben

Developed by Frederick Carder in 1915, this cream white and ivory translucent glass was named for the mineral it resembles. The batch consisted of a carefully regulated formula containing calcium phosphate, which gives it transparency. Each glass object was made from three separate gatherings, the outside often being sprayed with tin chloride to give it an iridescence.

Calcite was predominately used in gas and electric lighting fixtures, tablewares, ornamental objects and table lamps. It was used mainly for fixtures, since it radiates a very soft light. A few examples were engraved or acid-etched. The patterns were further clarified by rubbing with an unfired brown oxide; when air dried, it gave a nice contrasting hue.

Calcite served as both an inner and an outer casing for Gold and Blue Aurene glass. It also became the body for applying Brown, Red, and Green Aurenes and embellishing them with spider, feather, and leaf decor. Calcite is rarely found signed with a Fleur-de-Lis. However, lined and decorated Calcite can be found signed in a variety of other ways.

Acid Etched

Cambridge

The Cambridge Glass Company was founded in 1901 in Ohio. This firm specialized in pressed wares, including their early heavy pressed products marked "Near Cut." Later wares include etched stemware and colored, crystal and Crown Tuscan designed by Arthur J. Bennett. Crystal animals, "Black Amethyst," "blanc opaque," and crystal or colored objects with satin nude figures are sought. The company closed in 1954, reopened, and closed for good in 1958. The letter "C" in a triangle was used as their identifying mark after 1920.

Cameo - Honesdale

Gold Script Mark

Under the guidance of Carl F. Prosch, the Honesdale Decorating Company of White Mills, Pennsylvania, made fine crystal, multi-colored cameo (etched) art glass. The crystal blanks were cased in transparent hues of red, green and yellow. Designs were acid-cut, with the exposed surfaces being matte or etched, and the raised surface shiny. Art Nouveau flowers and stems, birds and other nature views outlined with scrolls are typical motifs. These designs were further decorated by hand with fine lined gold tracery over the colored crystal. The ware is most commonly found in the forms of bowls and vases, very rarely in drinking glasses. Some examples also are lustred and slightly iridescent. Signed specimens are at a premium and infrequently offered for sale.

Cameo - Mount Washington

Cameo glass manufactured by Mount Washington is rare and desirable. Most shapes are in the form of ruffled bowls, bowls with smooth turned-in sides or lamps. Many bowls are complemented by quadruple-plated ornate stands.

Colors are pink, pale blue, yellow and green, which have been cased over an opal glass. The entire body of the ware is usually satinized.

The predominate designs include a wreathed side view of a female, roses and leaves, and winged rampant griffins facing each other. Patterns were acid-etched, with little additional carving and shading by tools.

This cameo is possibly the first made in America. Finished articles had to be annealed in the lehr furnace.

Cameo - Tiffany

The varying output of Tiffany glass in the true cameo tradition is referred to as being carved. Some objects were lightly engraved with a copper wheel; others were very finely detailed and took many days, or weeks to complete. This intaglio process reveals insects, dragons, florals, fruits, nuts, leaves and others. Every imaginable color combination was implemented. Colored glass applied to crystal and carved created a pleasing contrast. These objects are usually signed; they are genuine conversation pieces. Some examples are iridescent; others possess one, two and possibly three layers of glass cut to display great artistic prowess.

Canaria - Pairpoint

Manufactured by Pairpoint, this transparent colored crystal is best described as vaseline colored, having a yellowish hue with light green tints when viewed in bright light. All forms of utilitarian tableware were produced, some etched, having the clear controlled bubble ball connectors, or both. It is difficult to build a large collection in this scarce color.

Cape Cod Glass Works

Deming Jarves, upon retirement in 1858 from the Boston and Sandwich Glass Company, decided to build his own glass factory. Although he was 67 years old, he had a modern glass works fabricated ten miles from the original Sandwich plant. It was named the Cape Cod Glass Company and was really intended for his son, John, to take over at the father's demise. The company was a thriving and successful venture for a time. Thomas Williams headed the list of many skilled workers, and Jarves possessed the genius for making fine glassware. For almost eleven years, great quantities of opaque and colored glass were produced here, including "Sandwich Alabaster," gold-ruby and Peach Blow.

After John died in 1863, Deming lost interest, and the plant closed in 1869 when the elder Jarves died. The last fire in a furnace was extinguished upon his demise.

Carder, Frederick - Steuben (See also/Steuben)

Frederick Carder, who studied with Emile Galle', was an English glass designer and Stourbridge technician, learning modern glass manufacturing techniques. Carder designed for Stevens and Williams, Limited, from 1880 to 1903, leaving for the United States in the same year. He and others established the Steuben Glass Works to make blanks for Thomas G. Hawkes and Company, Corning, New York. Much ornamental and colored glass in the Art Nouveau style was made there. Sold in 1918, the firm became known as the Corning Glass Company. Carder, as Art Director until his retirement formally in 1933, created much new glass with assorted colors and surface effects. After 1933, he experimented with glass and the lost wax process in his studio office. Many advanced and one of a kind examples, some in the Art Deco vein, were created. Finally, in 1959, Carder retired to 249 Pine Street, Corning, New York; he continued to be socially active and admired by people all over the world. He died peacefully on December 10, 1963.

Engraved

Cardinal Red - Steuben

This rare shade is best described as a Strawberry Red,

13

transparent, with a subtle opalescence present. The addition of opalescent white glass possibly causes this delicately hued effect. Apparently, this color was not very well received at the time it was in production. The ware, if found, may be either signed or unsigned.

Celeste Blue - Steuben

Of the blue crystals made by Steuben, this appears to be the lightest shade, being both brilliant and iridized. A great variety of objects were produced, most commonly in the vertical ribbed and diamond quilted patterns. Celeste Blue is a homogeneous glass and is not cased with clear crystal. Blue was popular with the public; thus, it should be easy to locate many interesting shapes.

Cerise Ruby - Steuben

Cerise or Gold Ruby is a pinkish red almost identical to a Cranberry Red in color. Its color was affected by the amounts of heat, flashing and 22-karat gold used in the batch.

To produce Cerise Ruby was demanding upon the gaffer. All production steps had to be ideal for a successful end result.

The color was made in limited accessory items and console sets. Its cranberry color may be combined with clear crystal; some items are reeded. Both swirled and plain patterns were utilized. Acid-etched signatures are sometimes detected on this ware. Some tableware was cut and etched.

This formula made it a necessity that the colloidal gold not separate and collect in the bottom of the pot, for this would spoil the color and metallic beads would be formed. The gold dissolved in aqua regia could not be overbalanced with carbonate; thus, oxidation had to be properly maintained to keep the gold in suspension.

Other Gold Ruby hues tried, with the addition of coloring oxides to a ruby batch, were Cinnamon Ruby (gold and uranium), Purple Gold Ruby (gold and cobalt), Brownish-Yellow Ruby (gold and iron), and Amethyst Ruby (gold and manganese).

Chintz - Nash

(See also/Arthur D. Nash)

 Engraved

Chintz glass was developed by Arthur Douglas Nash while he worked for Tiffany. The glass was never produced there; later pieces were made at the A. Douglas Nash Corporation and called "Chintz."

The process for manufacture was patented on March 27, 1934, when Nash was working for the Libbey Glass Manufacturing Company. Because of the cost factor, Libbey never commercially introduced this product. Only experimental objects were fabricated.

Plates, bowls, lamp bases, compotes, vases, candlesticks, stemware and covered boxes are typical shapes found in an array of colors. Rose, blue, lavender and green ribs and/or stripes (broad and narrow) are found marvered into opaque, opalescent, transparent, colored and Aquamarine glass. Some objects were also lustred.

The glass was very difficult to make because of the soft quality

of the background glass; also, colors that were patterned into the molded glass ran together when they were being shaped and reheated.

Chocolate - Indiana Tumbler and Goblet Company

Chocolate glass, mistakenly termed carmel slag, is a variegated opaque glass shading from brown to a light tan. A mold-blown and pressed ware manufactured from 1900 to 1903, it is highly popular today and comes in a variety of patterns. Among the numerous designs are "Ruffled Eye," "Leaf Bracket," "Fleur-de-Lis," "Cactus," "Running Deer," "Squirrel," "Wild Rose With Bowknot," "Serenade," "Cut Glass," "Shuttle," "Cupid," "Strigil," "Dewey," "Austrian," "Chrysanthemum," "Greentown Daisy," "Scalloped Flange," "Orange Tree," "Herringbone Buttress," "Geneva," "Water Lily and Cattail," "Diamond Point Paneled," "Melrose" and "Cord Drapery." Some covered novelty items comprised the nesting robin, dolphin, cat in hamper, nesting hen and rabbit. The glass manufactured by the Indiana Tumbler and Goblet Company, Greentown, Indiana was produced in almost every imaginable shape.

Chrysopras - Pairpoint

This coloration consists of brown streaks manufactured by Mount Washington, Pairpoint and Gundersen.

Cintra - Steuben

Cintra was placed into production about 1917 and was made into the early '20s. On a rarity scale, this exotic glass ranks closely to the choice Acid Cutbacks.

Crushed colored glass in powdered form was laid out on the marver in random fashion, a vertical striped design, or in very rare instances, in a form that resembled a bird and florals. Molten crystal glass was rolled over the powders and formed into a desired shape. Finally, another covering of clear glass encased the design in a permanent suspension. Some specimens have either small random bubbles or controlled bubbles, while others have none at all.

Color combinations are pink and blue or blue and yellow; some are single colors with sculptured, Acid Cutback, applied rings and rims, or additional colored and painted decor. Some objects were satinized, while many remain shiny; both types are quite attractive.

Cire Perdue - Steuben

 Incised Monogram

In the early 1930's after months of experimentation, Frederick Carder revived the lost wax process for casting glass. His limited production output consisted of satinized clear crystal figures, usually 4½" to 9½" in height. Birds, animals, fish plaques, portions of the human anatomy and portraits of famous people comprised his repertoire. The largest piece he ever cast was a Pyrex glass Indian head, 46" high, with a nose 12" thick.

His work in the '30s is reminiscent of Lalique's, combining shiny and frosted clear crystal surfaces. In the '40s, his emphasis was upon action models of athletes and portraits of famous people and friends. In the '50s up until 1959, Carder executed his cast and sculptured work in color. All of his output originated in his factory-studio on the 5th floor at the Corning Glass Works.

The complicated eight-step process was as follows: 1) A model in great detail was fabricated in clay, 2) A replica of the original was formed with plaster-of-Paris, 3)A mold in reverse was formed of hot glue and glycerine made from the plaster-of-paris form; in two or more sections this was then held in place by an external shell of plaster, 4) Two or three wax castings were made from the gelatine mold (set 3), 5) An investiture consisting of thick cream (plaster-of-Paris and powdered clay) was poured over the wax; it set in about 15 minutes, 6) This ceramic mold was dried for 24 hours, then placed in boiling water to melt the wax. Any residue was fired out after the ceramic mold had dried, 7) The mold was now ready for the gradual insertion of lumps and rods of glass. The kiln temperature was critical to melt the glass and force it to run into every fissure of the mold. 8) Finally, the glass and mold were cooled very gradually, using electric heating elements. Depending upon the casting's size, this process took two or more days. After cooling, the mold was carefully broken to free the glass casting, hopefully still intact, a very detailed original of the clay model.

Cluthra - Kimble

This glass, similar to cirro-stratus cloud formations, slightly resembles Steuben's ware; however, there are generally fewer bubbles in Kimble's glass.

Colonel Evan E. Kimble produced this type of glass for a relatively short period. Some rare examples are comprised of two or three colors; many are found in white, blue, orange, pink, yellow or green. Most often this glass is signed in silver stylus within the ground pontil. The capital "K" stands for Kimble; other marks, such as "20177-8/Dec. 8," may be translated as shape "20177," 8″ high, in "Decoration 8" which is blue.

Pontil

Cluthra - Steuben

Mr. Carder's Cluthra, characterized as a cloudy glass permeated with varying sized bubbles, first appeared in 1920. Alabaster glass was rolled over the marver covered with fine colored or opaline glass. Tapioca was picked up from another marver; this gave the hot glass its bubbling effect.

Steuben's Cluthra includes a great majority of their colors. The product is attractive, scarce, highly sought; when marked, it will be with the acid-etched Steuben Fleur-de-Lis.

Most of the objects in this ware are quite large, thick and heavy. Vases, bowls, colognes, boudoir sets and lamp bases are generally the items found. Some pieces are sculptured, Acid Cutback or have applied handles or feet in a variety of colored crystals.

Cobalt Blue - Pairpoint-Mount Washington and Gundersen Color

This is a rich deep sky blue color found cut, engraved, with spiral bands, in an overlay twist, with silver overlay, and with clear controlled bubble ball connectors. Objects made were vases, candlesticks, pitchers, covered vases, console sets and others.

Cobalt Blue - Steuben

This color is the darkest of the blues produced by Steuben. The hue was achieved from a cobalt base. Objects were cased with clear crystal; drinking stems may be clear. The blue was made in a vertical ribbed and diamond quilted pattern, being both lustrous and brilliant. A great variety of decorative and functional objects in this color came from the plant.

Coin - Central Glass Company

The first United States Mint was established in Philadelphia, Pennsylvania by an Act of Congress in April, 1792. Our nation, encouraged by its newly won freedom from Great Britain, forged ahead, passing coinage laws and importing both silver bullion and machines to mint coins.

In 1892, the centennial year of the mint, the Central Glass Company of Wheeling, West Virginia, produced what came to be known as United States Coin Pattern Glass. Patterns for the glassware consisted of six silver United States coins reproduced in glass relief and placed on each example in a most desirable location. Medallion motifs individually recorded in the glassware were silver dollars, half dollars, quarter dollars, twenty-cent pieces, dimes and half dimes. The United States coin patterns represented both the obverse and reverse sides of the coin. The only exception is the half dime, where the dated 1892 side is not shown. The relief coin designs came in clear, frosted, amber and gold gilt; most are found frosted on clear glass. The number of coins shown will vary with the size of the example.

A full line of tableware was manufactured in this pattern; production of the coin motif was stopped after just five months. A federal law declared the glass pattern to be a form of counterfeiting, even though the patterns were not identical to the silver coins being minted.

South American motifs, using portraits of Christopher Columbus, Americus Vespucius and coats-of-arms of Spain and the United States, were still permitted. This particular type is termed Columbian Coin Glass, or "Foreign Coin."

The portraits and other basic forms may be all clear, clear and frosted, clear and red, clear and amber, and clear with gold. One type of milk glass kerosene lamp was made in two sizes; the base and the bowl of this lamp were threaded and screwed together, as is done with most metal connectors.

The United States Coin pattern is difficult to find because of its limited production; prices for these desirable pieces are quite high. This type of glass, an art form, makes a fine addition to a collection.

Reproduced coin glass frosting is poor, as are the designs and letters which tend to blur. Spooners and toothpick holders are the examples most frequently copied. Some coins on reproduced pieces are oval in shape.

Coralene - Mount Washington

Coralene is a method of decorating that was used predominately on Satin and Mother-of-Pearl glass of varying colors and patterns. This process involved applying (clear, colored or opalescent) glass beads to the piece in a design with an affixative, and then firing to make the beads permanent. Patterns include sheaves of wheat, Fleur-de-Lis, seaweed, coral branches and others. Typical shapes are vases, pitchers, mugs, ewers, bowls, perfume bottles, punch cups, tumblers and finger lamps. Many inferior and spurious Coralene examples are appearing on the market. Usually the glass beading is not fired on the glass and flakes easily with the application of any pressure from the thumb.

Cosmos - Dithridge and Sons

Probably produced around 1900 by Dithridge and Sons, New Brighton, Pennsylvania, this opaque milk glass has become quite collectible. The ware is pressed, having an overall trellis-like, small diamond pattern with a stylized band of raised daisies. Also referred to as Stemless Daisy, the flowers are stained with yellow, pink and blue. Bands at the top of examples also have the pink or blue matted effect. Accessible pieces are not signed and consist of: butter dishes, assorted sized lamps, castor sets, sugars and creamers, pitchers, salts and peppers, syrups, tumblers, cologne bottles, vases and spooners.

Crackle (Craquelle)

A colored or clear glass made by numerous glass factories, Crackle is also known as Craquelle, or Iced Glass. The effect is achieved by plunging hot molten glass into cold water; the object is then mold or free-blown to the desired shape after reheating. Noticeable spider web cracks appear on the outside of the article, while the interior is smooth. Mount Washington; Sandwich; H.C. Fry; and Hobbs, Brockunier and Company were notables producing this interesting glass in assorted shapes.

Cranberry

Terms often associated with this transparent type of glass are "Ruby" and "Rose Red." The glass possesses a clear, reddish pink color achieved in the early glass of this period by adding small amounts of gold oxide to the pot. Examples reheated at low temperatures cast a blue violet tint.

Cranberry was produced from the 1820s to the 1880s in wines, water sets, finger and rose bowls, chalices, decanters, whimseys, punch cups, pitchers, salt dips, smoke bells, vases, tumblers, covered boxes, syrups, sugars and creamers, cruets, compotes, pickle castors and toothpick holders.

Both free-blown and mold-blown types were manufactured. Patterns occurring in mold-blown specimens are: daisy and button, ribbed, melon ribbed, hobnail, diamond, swirl, ribbed swirl, thumbprint and inverted thumbprint. Samples may have either a rough or a ground pontil. Occasionally, a rare signed or dated piece turns up.

Notable factories that fabricated "Ruby Glass" were: T.G. Hawkes & Company, Sandwich Glass Company, Northwood Glass Company, T.B. Clark and Company, Incorporated and many others.

Some decorating techniques included: applied crystal and thorn handles, applied rims and feet, etching, enameling, cutting, threading, overshot and ruffled rims. Lustre lights were enchanced with clear, cut prisms; some examples may be contained within silver or silver plated holders.

Copper placed in a batch, in later years, took the place of the more expensive gold oxide method. Other cheaper and inferior imitations were produced by using both flashing and staining. Sight over the edges of an example in bright light to establish if the object is good old Cranberry glass. Contemporary American manufacturers are producing some fine Cranberry pieces; look for them in your better gift shops and jewelry stores.

Crown Milano - Mount Washington

Originally, Albert Steffin and Frederick Shirley were issued a trademark to fabricate an elaborate and sophisticated opal glassware with both shiny and acid finishes, named Albertine. When signed, this glass has an enameled crown within a wreath, plus the catalog number below. This ware was not received very well by the public.

On January 31, 1893, the Mount Washington Glass Company, New Bedford, Massachusetts, was issued trademark papers to produce the same glass, changing its name to the more exotic title of Crown Milano. This time the venture was much more successful. The ware's background colors are subdued earth tones, which contrast well against tasteful embellishments and heavy gold enameling. Jewel work, occasionally, enhances the already brilliant ornamentation.

Often pieces are not marked, while a few display an original round paper label having a double-headed eagle and the letters "MT.W.G.CO." under the eagle in a semi-circle. Some have the painted letter "M" overlapping "C" with, or without, a four-pointed crown above the initials.

Enameled

Paper Label

Stamped

A number also may appear on the base, and if silver plated fixtures were used, these often were numbered and stamped "M.W."

If we compare today's prices of Crown Milano with an 1894 catalog, we get some idea how the ware has escalated. Today, prices are quoted in three and four figures; a common range then was from $2.00 for a perfume atomizer to $54.00 for an ornate, double-dished centerpiece mounted on a very elaborate quadruple plated stand.

Shapes seen in this fine glass include bowls, tumblers, dishes, candlesticks, lamps, cracker and biscuit jars, syrups, jardiniers, pitchers, cups and saucers, sugars and creamers, salts and peppers, powder and ring boxes, card trays, vases, ewers, humidors and pin holders.

Custard

Custard glass has a wide range of colors, normally shading from a rich yellow to a bone white. A variant of milk glass, it may resemble egg custard and is sometimes termed Buttermilk glass. Uranium salts were usually used in its manufacture; it possesses fiery opalescence, is heavy for a pressed glass type, generally is opaque, has a pleasing ring when tapped, will set the needle of a geiger counter in motion, and reacts to a black light.

About 194 patterns are known, many of lesser or minor importance. Twenty-three patterns are classified as major including: Argonaut Shell, Beaded Circle, Beaded Swag, Cherry and Scale, Chrysanthemum Sprig, Diamond With Peg, Fan, Fluted Scrolls, Geneva, Georgia Gem, Grape and Gothic Arches, Intaglio, Inverted Fan and Feather, Louis XV, Maple Leaf, Northwood Grape, Prayer Rug, Punty Band, Ribbed Drape, Ring Band, Victoria and Winged Scroll (Ivorina Verde).

Custard glass was manufactured from 1890 to 1915 by the following companies: Northwood (credited with the largest number of patterns and the greatest output), Heisey, Fenton, Jefferson, Tarentum, Diamond, McKee, Cambridge, Greenberg, Adams and LaBelle. At the LaBelle Glass Company, Harry Northwood worked as an artistic designer and a meticulous mold maker. Many new processes, designs and colors were conceived as a result of Northwood's genius at this Bridgeport, Ohio, factory. Some wares were signed "Northwood" in script on the base, or an "N" underlined within a circle.

Northwood

(N)

Most examples were ornately decorated in gold enameling, and often flashing or painting in green, blue, brown, pink and red is found on some portion of the embossed design. Decorative tints tended to tarnish and fade with hard use and constant washing. Added decorations painted on the surfaces by hand were often in the forms of flowers and foliage on commemorative and historical examples. Names of towns, states, specific events, buildings and dates may also be seen.

Besides the utilitarian pressed Custard, there is the "art" glass type which is most often blown. Many overlay variations, cased, applied and hand-decorated enameled patterns and designs exist. Vases and rose bowls were common Custard art glass forms.

This collectible pressed glassware has escalated in recent years, especially the Argonaut Shell, Inverted Fan and Feather, Chrysanthemum Sprig, Ivorina Verde, and Diamond Peg. Custard is found primarily in table settings, service pieces, miscellaneous, and souvenir items, plus banana boats, bowls, covered butter dishes, candlesticks, compotes, sugars and creamers, cruets, dishes, nappies, mugs, pitchers and tumblers, rose bowls, salts and peppers, relishes, sauces, plates, spooners, toothpick holders, vases and wines.

Since 1969, Custard glass has been reproduced using old molds; colors are too milky white, and many examples do not have opalescence. Novelty items and old patterns, with or without decoration, are most prominent. Look for lack of true wear, light objects and company insignias ground from the bases.

Cut and Colored Cut (See also Cut Glass Marks)

The Egyptians practiced the art of cutting and engraving glass around 1500 B.C. Cut glass, incised and engraved, has designs which are sharp and precise, indicating that much skill and patience were needed in its production. The glass is quite heavy, cut on thick blanks, has a bell resonance, and will refract the colors of the rainbow when placed in direct sunlight.

In the United States, it is believed that Henry William Stiegel produced the first cut glass around 1765-1770 at the Elizabeth Furnace Glass House, Lancaster County, Pennsylvania. John Frederick Amelung's factory at New Bremen, Maryland, is also noted for making cut glasswares for table use in the early 1800s.

In America cut glass is divided into three periods: Early (1765-1829), Middle (1830-1870), and Brilliant (1871-1905). Early cut glass is rare; its English and Irish influence shows motifs with the pillar, prism, flute, single star, roundlet, sharp diamond, English strawberry diamond, and strawberry diamond and fan. In the Middle Period, simple American designs were created in reaction to European patterns. Flute cuttings, fine line cutting, engraved glass (mythological and historical scenes), plus cut colored glass (stained, cased, or flashed) were popular. The Brilliant Period, a flowering of American cut glass, came into vogue with a variety of glasshouses making and showing their wares during the Centennial Exhibition, which began in Philadelphia in May, 1876. Brilliant Period designs are complex and deep. Many new motifs were created such as chair bottom, hobnail, block, prism, notched prism, hobstar, curved miter split, fan and pin wheel. Thousands of variations exist.

Some notables showing at the Philadelphia Exhibition were the Boston and Sandwich Glass Company, Christian Dorflinger, Gillinder and Sons, Mount Washington Glass Company and the New England Glass Company. The glass of this period is both extremely bright and clear. This result was achieved through perfected techniques of fusion, annealing, cutting and polishing. Gas heat also became popular since it could be controlled more accurately than coal fuel, and great deposits of almost pure sand were discovered in the Great Lakes region.

In 1893, the E.D. Libbey Glass Company, Toledo, Ohio, spun twelve yards of glass cloth for their exhibition at the World's Columbia Exposition, Chicago, Illinois. The cloth was made into a dress for Georgia Cayven at the cost of $25.00 per yard. The dress proved to be impractical for wearing.

Only a small quantity of cut glass was marked in any way. Authentic signed examples assist the collector in identifying companies and dating similar examples made by the same firm. Some colored cut glass exists, especially ruby, emerald green, and deep blue, but it is rarely seen or offered for sale.

Literally thousands of cut patterns were produced, many later in pressed pattern glass. A few popular patterns are: Bull's Eye,

Chrysanthemum, Comet, Corinthian, Devonshire, Florence, Harvard Chair Bottom, Kimberly, Middlesex, Strawberry Diamond and Fan, and Venetian.

The first cut glass using pressed blanks was made in 1902 by H.C. Fry Glass Company, Rochester, Pennsylvania. Before this date, all cut glass blanks had been blown.

The care of cut glass is critical, and all examples of an unusual nature should especially be cherished. Wash cut glass with a mild detergent and warm water in a plastic container, scrubbing carefully with a soft brush and cloth. Rinse in warm water and dry with a lint free towel. This procedure should be carried out when necessary, but not on a weekly basis. Sudden changes in temperature and intense sunlight will crack the finest piece of cut glass. Do not take chances! Display your glass in well lighted, and dust-free cabinets and other areas of your home where they will not be affected by drastic temperature changes or by household traffic patterns.

Cut Velvet

This speciality type art glass is no longer exceedingly common. The glass is made of two fused layers blown into a mold, creating the raised outer surface design, not to be confused with Mother-of-Pearl. The pattern seen most often is the diamond quilted; however, others, such as ribbing and herringbone, may be found. Most examples are acid-finished; thus, they have a velvet texture. Glossy pieces are occasionally discovered. This glass was made by many firms, both in the United States and Europe, during the late Victorian era. It would be very difficult to attribute this type since it was not signed. Shapes you will see include: bowls, ewers, pitchers, tumblers and vases. Some items have ruffled tops, applied clear frosted handles and rigaree. Popular colors are apricot, butterscotch, tan, apple green, turquoise, pink, blue, amethyst and yellow. Seldom will you find a shaded example having a two-toned body; inner casings are usually white.

Cypriote - Tiffany

This opaque "Antique" glass was successfully developed by Arthur J. Nash while working for Louis C. Tiffany. Manufactured from 1897 to 1927, the ware is both lustrous and pitted. The product is an imitation of ancient Roman glass that had been found buried in the earth. A gather of transparent yellow glass was rolled over the marver, picking up ground flecks of the same metal. Its surface was then lustred to achieve many colors. The term "cypriote glass" was also loosely applied to other Tiffany types with antique finishes. Predominately structured in vases, some examples are found in metal stands. Gold, brown, tan, blue and green colors, some with a paperweight technique, are avidly sought by collectors. Commanding high prices, the forms are frequently signed.

Delft Ware - Pairpoint

This translucent white opal glass was both free and mold-blown at Pairpoint. It was decorated with sailboats, canals and windmills in shades of blue, rust and green predominately. Some examples are signed "DELFT" on the bottom in blue, in a stamped rather than a freehand form. The glass was manufactured in the 1880s and continued into the 1920s. Shapes include miniature kerosene lamps, bowls and a variety of tableware. Marked pieces are difficult to procure.

De Vilbiss

The De Vilbiss firm in Toledo, Ohio, did not make assorted types of perfume bottles; rather, they constructed the components, such as the collars, cords and bulbs. These collectible perfumes and atomizers may be found with their original paper labels intact or stamped in black on their bases, "De Vilbiss - Made in U.S.A." Many firms from about 1900 to 1925 supplied bottles in every imaginable shape and texture. It is known that Steuben, Durand, Cambridge and Fenton made some of the output. Look for opalescent, iridescent, frosted, sprayed, enameled, mercury, craquelle, gilded, clear and even acid cutback examples. Apparently, the earlier bottles were manufactured in the United States; cheaper bottles were acquired from European sources (Czechoslovakia, Italy and France) from 1925 to 1938.

Stamped In Black   MADE *De Vilbiss* IN U.S.A.

Diatreta - Steuben

Made personally in limited quantity by Frederick Carder between 1945 and 1959, these very elaborate vases and bowls simulate Roman glass from the 4th century. Ornamentation was created through the cire perdue process and then fused to the object in a caged fashion with small glass struts. Examples in a variety of colors were satinized, personally signed "F. Carder," and dated. This glass is probably not attainable. Figurals, faces and leaves interlocking like lattices are characteristic of this extremely difficult and advanced process.

F. Carder Engraved
1955

Diatreta - Tiffany

Tiffany's Diatreta is an overlay decorative technique applied to the body of an example in an open diamond-shaped pattern. The raised glass diamonds are joined as if they were a crossed lattice.

Dorflinger

One of the giants in the cut glass field was Christian Dorflinger, born March 16, 1828, in Alsace, France. He became a master at engraving, etching, enameling and gold decoration. At 24 years of age, his ability was already recognized and he was chosen to manage the Long Island Flint Glass Works. By 1860, just eight years after taking on his first management post, he established, in Brooklyn, the Green Point Flint Glass Works.

At this second glasshouse, presidential sets were made for the White House when Abraham Lincoln and Benjamin Harrison were in office. Dorflinger, in fact, made the tableware for every president from Lincoln to Wilson. The elaborate Benjamin Harrison Presidential set, made in 1890, consisted of 520 pieces at a cost of $6,000.00. Some other special sets were manufactured for W.K. Vanderbilt's wedding in 1899, former President Menacol of Cuba, and the former Prince of Wales.

So dedicated was Dorflinger to his art that his health deteriorated, and he went to White Mills, Pennsylvania, to live and recuperate in 1862. By the age of 37, his health sufficiently improved, Christian built a glass factory close to White Mills near the Delaware. A wilderness at first, business prospered; the settlement grew, additions were made, until over 75 houses were erected for workers at the height of his success. He achieved international fame in the 1876 Centennial by winning first prize for a decanter and 38 state glasses representing the states then part of the United States.

Dorflinger's four sons joined the firm in 1881, and its name was changed to C. Dorflinger and Sons. About 1900, Dorflinger's grandchildren, Dwight and Charles, (Louis's sons) also became supervisors at the plant.

Dorflinger, being a perfectionist, constantly sought choice ingredients, quality workmen, and aesthetic techniques that would yield consistency, excellence of design and grace. At the pinnacle of operation in 1903, the plant consisted of over 30 white buildings with more than 650 workers listed on the payroll.

The factory displayed and sold a multitude of exquisite cut patterns in clear, colored, cut, etched and engraved glass. A variety of types included: lamps and lamp chimneys (plain and colored), finger bowls, candlesticks, plates, decanters, water bottles, punch bowls with cups and ladles, stemware, cruets, paperweights, cologne jars and pharmaceutical items. Their trademark, a circular white paper label, depicted in black lettering a large decanter and a piece of stemware to its left, another to the right, with the word "DORFLINGER" arched above them. Noteworthy workers associated with Dorflinger's fine quality wares were: Carl Prosch, Charles Northwood, Ralph Barber, Nicholas Lutz and Emil J. Larson.

The C. Dorflinger and Sons catalog (The Honesdale Decorating Company), about 1914 showed colored illustrations of their reproduction Venetian glassware. Made in medium shades of amber, amethyst and turquoise, the glass was lightweight, gracefully structured, with rough pontils and came in many assorted shapes. The items included vases; goblets; roemers; champagnes; clarets; cocktails; wines; parfaits; tumblers; sherries; oyster cocktails; cordials; pousse cafes; whiskey tumblers; grapefruit sets, finger bowls, sherbets, all with underplates; comports; covered ginger jars; covered bon bons; basins; aquariums; ringed, barreled, and bell beakers, with applied rings, lions heads and raspberry prunts; candlesticks; tall ale glasses; fruit bowls; covered puff boxes; salad and service plates; flower pans (used to float flowers in water); beakers and aquariums (with applied trimmings in many colors); bottle vases with applied decorations, eight arm vases; and so on.

Also shown in the same catalog were clear crystal mixing tumblers and stemmed and footed cocktail glasses. Each depicted roosters and fighting cocks that were enameled, etched, and gilded. Specific names included Enameled Black and White Rooster, Enameled Rooster, Two Enameled Cocks, Gilded Rooster with cut stem and star cut foot, Gilded Rooster and Rising Sun, Two Gilded Fighting Cocks, and an Engraved Cock.

Another line depicted was their Opal glassware made in Lilac, Rose, Amber and Green colors. The ware was again in the Venetian style, without any applied decoration, but it was unusual since it was an opalescent flashed crystal. Shape 618 included goblets, saucer champs, clarets, cocktails, wines, and cordials (all with knobbed stems), candlesticks, an 8″ vase, and finger bowls and footed sherbets having underplates.

A great variety of workers held positions at The Honesdale Decorating Company during its thirty-one years of operation (1901-1932). Names of workers and their job description included: Francis Fritchie, Alexander Linke, Herman Neugebauer, Frank Milde and Joseph Hocky (engravers); Frank Leisel, Fred Martin, Nicholas Stegner, Hugo Papert, Adolph Linke, Joseph Bischop, Joseph Bischop, Jr., (his son), Gustave Kettel and John Johns (decorators); Thomas Jones, William Varcoe and Alfred Kretschmer (printed paper transfers used in the acid resist process); Alexander LaTournous, Andrew Cowles, William Maisey, John Villaume and Rudolph Bates (placed the transfers on the glassware); Fred Crist (gold and transfer helper); Mrs. Amelia Bartheimess, Carrie Hill, Millie Moules and Laura and Lillian Hoey (painted varnish resist designs on the glass); Miss Smith, Miss Bonham, Rose Haun, Florence Secor, Elsie Kretschmer, Mabel Secor, Ethel Hawker, Mary Van Driesen, Mary Bell, Mary Williams, Helen Williams, Mabel Reinhard, Mae Lewis, Anna Ordnung, Amelia Linke, Mrs. Yarnis, Mrs. Mae Dennis and Mrs. Mabel Spy (gold burnishers); Howard Miller and Harry DeReamer (acid dippers); Fred Miller, Frank Artman and Charles LaTournous (chore and acid dipper helpers); Charles Seward (china kiln fireman and acid dipper); Christopher Hook (glass polisher); George Rippel (shipping clerk); William Cunningham and Raymond Fryer (boys who unpacked glass blanks); Raymond Stegner, Robert Willer, George Copper and Edward Welsch (cared for and attended the decorating kilns); Emily Holland, Anna Rippel, Laura Pragnel and Carrie Novinenmacher (glass washers); and Elsa Prosch, (Carl Prosch's daughter), plus Mae Finnerty, Edna Hawker and Gertrude Stone (bookkeepers).

Christian Dorflinger died in 1915, and his sons carried on the business until 1921. The war, inability to acquire quality ingredients from abroad, prohibition, plus the fact that cut glass was no longer popular, forced the remaining Dorflingers to close the business. (See also Honesdale)

Durand

Born in Baccarat, France, in 1870, Victor Durand, Sr., was the fourth generation in his family to work in glass. Descendants before him had worked at the Cristalleries de Baccarat. Upon completing considerable training in glasshouses in the United States, Durand opened the Durand Art Glass Company in Vineland, New Jersey, in 1924. Both knowledgeable and skilled men like Martin Bach, Jr. and Emil J. Larson created fine hand-blown art glass in competition with Tiffany, Steuben and Quezal.

Much early glassware was not signed; instead, silver and black paper labels were affixed. Later, Durand used the engraved silver signature, "DURAND" in script, or "DURAND" in script within a large "V." Some examples have numbers indicating the heights and shapes of objects.

Production consisted of bowls, rose bowls, vases, candlesticks, cruets, compotes, jars, lamp bases, shades, plates and stemware. Most notable patterns found on the above articles would include: the controlled Bubble, the Peacock Feather design, Gold Lustre Spider Webbing, Heart and Clinging Vine, Lustred, King Tut decoration, Cameo, Acid Cutback,

Egyptian Crackle and Moorish Crackle glass.

Typical Durand colors are blue, green, cranberry, white, pumpkin, and even clear glass incorporated artistically within the object to form impressive and colorful motion. Durand Art Glass was sold by district representatives in the finer jewelry and department stores of that day. The glass was always fairly expensive; some patterns never met with much popularity. The factory was headed by his son, Victor Durand, Jr., in the 1920s. In 1931, Victor Durand, Sr., was fatally injured in an automobile accident; the impact threw him through the windshield so that he received deep cuts on the face and the throat. Fellow glassworkers donated blood, but Durand only lived for twenty hours. The production of Durand Art Glass was terminated soon after his demise.

Favrile - Tiffany

Louis C. Tiffany Furnaces Inc. Favrile

Etched

The name "Favrile" was registered in 1894; this iridescent Art nouveau glass was developed in 1892 by Louis Comfort Tiffany. Blue, green, gold and other surface hues were achieved by spraying the hot glass with metallic salts, which were absorbed. The lustred effect came about through the density and color of the metal. "Favrile" probably got its derivation from the old English word "fabrile," meaning "belonging to a craftsman." Numerous varieties of objects were made of this glass; the majority were vases of different shapes and sizes. Many nature motifs, either applied or embedded in multi-colors, were featured.

Fenton

FENTON ART GLASS

Original Paper Label

The Fenton Art Glass Company was founded in Martins Ferry, Ohio, in 1905. It was organized by Frank, John and Charles Fenton (all brothers); production began in 1907 after the factory was moved to Williamstown, West Virginia, in 1906. Cheap natural gas seemed to be the incentive for moving.

Their factory manager was Jacob Rosenthal (originator of Chocolate glass at Greentown), who made all of Fenton's output for 25 years. Later his son, Paul, carried on using his father's formulas for another 18 years.

The company's products included custard, carnival, opalescent, pressed, molded, stretch, slag, hobnail, overlay and their "Fenton Art Glass" line. In 1926, the firm advertised their Art Nouveau shapes in the forms of candlesticks, vases, urns, covered bowls footed bowls, and fan vases. Decorations included splotched red, green and yellow glass threading and the "Heart and Clinging Vine" decor, all with lustre finishes.

Paper labels designate this product as "Vasa Murrhina," or "Fenton Art Glass." Many early examples, when not marked,

would be difficult to attribute. The firm is currently producing many items that may be found in finer gift shops with their contemporary paper labels affixed.

Findlay Onyx - Dalzell, Gilmore, and Leighton Company

A patent was received by George W. Leighton on April 23, 1889, permitting the Dalzell, Gilmore, and Leighton Company to produce this most decorative glassware. The glass was extremely brittle, chipped and cracked easily, and at one point during its manufacture, the factory was closed in an attempt to resolve the problem. Characterized by its raised eight-petaled flowers and textured leaves on common stems, production was cancelled in less than six months due to costs and its unpredictable nature.

Silver, amber, orange, raspberry, orchid and purple are the colors that were used. In the case of Silver Onyx, a mold was used to bring the object to its true size; another mold aided in creating the floral pattern in relief. Platinum lustre stain applied to the ornamentation was fired to hold it in place on the outer surface. Harsh cleaning will gradually remove this stain. The other colors mentioned fluctuated in shading, since repeated heating and thermal changes varied from one example to the next. Some pieces are cased with an opal glass, and lustres applied to the patterns usually differ from the body of each specimen. Concentric rings are usually found on the base of each piece, seeming to be a definite characteristic of this glassware.

This glass was made originally for everyday usage, occurring in assorted table patterns (bowls, celery vases, pitchers, salt and pepper shakers, spooners, sugar shakers, toothpick holders, tumblers, syrups and vases). It is scarce and brings good prices when seen. This ware has not been reproduced. The rim on each example is ground and frequently has flakes or chips; these do not detract appreciably from the value of this unique glass form, which was not signed.

Fireglow - Sandwich

This translucent blown and molded art glass was manufactured by the Boston and Sandwich Glass Company and others. It might appear similar to Bristol glass but is of a superior quality. Tan in color, usually with an acid finish, it may possess enameled and gilded decor. Fireglow should transmit a reddish brown glow when held to a bright light, similar to the glow cast from a blazing fire in a fireplace. Vases, pitchers, tumblers, plaques, ewers and bowls were a few objects that were produced.

Flambeau - Pairpoint

Flambeau, or Flambo, is a tomato red opaque ware fabricated by Pairpoint in the early 1920s. The ware was made for the Christmas trade, was a difficult metal to work and was only in production for a brief duration. Vases and wine goblets blown in this color were contrasted with black feet and stems; some examples were further adorned with exquisite silver overlay.

Flemish Blue - Steuben

Flemish Blue is a dark cobalt blue; its color was achieved through a copper base. Many shapes were merchandised in this color. The brilliance of the hue will be dependent, in part, upon the thickness or the thinness of the ware.

Florentia - Steuben

Florentia is exceedingly rare and a unique type of Carder glass found mainly in major museums. On occasion, an example is offered for sale. Manufactured either in the late '20s or '30s, there was created within the acid white crystal a soft appearing leaf form. This five-petaled leaf, in green (Jade) or rose (Rosaline), is delicately veined; the points project upwards from the bases of hollow examples, like vases and goblets. On a deep bowl viewed from above, they radiate outward in a circle. Flecks of mica throughout the glass give the added illusion of shimmering morning dew. Existing examples display both the Fleur-de-Lis signature and air traps, ranging from a common nail head to the size of a dime.

Florette - Consolidated

Florette Blown Ware was manufactured by the Consolidated Lamp and Glass Company of Pittsburgh, Pennsylvania, from 1894. Satin and glossy finished items were fabricated in white, pink, blue, green and opaque yellow. The inset diamond quilts are sometimes gilded. Some objects were made in the scarce Pigeon Blood and apricot hues. Specific forms found in the ware are salts and peppers, toothpick holders, tumblers, syrups, covered butter dishes, sugar sifters, mustards, sugars and creamers, spooners, celeries, finger bowls, cruets, pitchers, bowls, nappies, sauces and cracker jars.

Floriform - Tiffany

These unique Tiffany vases were a very popular form, representing the Art Nouveau era at its finest. Each vase has a long and fragile, thin stem commencing from a variety of feet, some flat, others bell shaped, etc. Their tops are adorned with an unbelievable variety of floral designs in exquisitely blended colors. Most are signed and numbered. The vases are highly sought and were made in many types of glass. Sometimes portions of the bowls are lustred.

Fostoria

The Fostoria Glass Company was founded in 1887 in Fostoria, Ohio. Many fine wares, including colored, clear, pressed, etched and gilded, are now being avidly collected. The firm later moved to Moundsville, West Virginia, and today it is one of the largest factories producing hand-made glass in the United States.

A branch of this firm, the Fostoria Glass Specialty Company, was established in 1899 on Fourth and South Poplar Streets by J.B. Crouse, J. Robert Crouse, Harry A. Tremaine and B.G. Tremaine. Their first glass was produced in 1901. Two factories were in operation by 1907, employing 700 men and producing 10,000 pounds of glass daily (their capacity).

Lustred glassware had been in production since about 1904. A trademark for "Iris" glass was issued on August 6, 1912.

IRIS

Oval paper labels identified the ware: without these, their work would be readily confused with Tiffany or Steuben's Aurene.

The Fostoria Glass Specialty Company's major output was lamps and lamp shades. Some fancy vases, bowls, dishes and plates were also made. A complete line of lighting equipment included bulbs, chimneys, glass tubing and globes for arc lamps.

Iris glass was usually cased and always iridescent. Numerous shade patterns included leaf, leaf and tendrils, pulled threaded, pulled feather, Heart and Vine, Heart and Spider Webbing and lustred dot. Shades had both flat and ruffled tops, coming in a great assortment of shapes. The base glass is usually opal, the interiors having gold lustred highlights. Gold was used in each batch of Iris glass; thus, costs were high and this type ware was only in production for a short duration. A repertoire of iridescent colors consists of green, tan, white, blue, yellow and rose.

Other items included in their output were table and decorative cut glass items, and "Clear Cut" frosted shades for lights and lamps cut with bright designs. General Electric Company absorbed the firm, its patents and trademarks and moved the company to Cleveland and Niles, Ohio, around 1917.

Frances Ware - Hobbs, Brockunier

This very popular and mold-blown tableware was produced by Hobbs, Brockunier Company, Wheeling, West Virginia, in the 1880 era. Some examples have ground pontils and bases; the ware was not signed. Pieces have amber, fluted rims and hobnails on the bodies which run from the bases in a staggered, one-two positioning up to the amber ribbon. Exceptions have been seen where hobnails cover the entire body. Camphor stain was applied externally to the body of each item, giving it a dull finish, while the amber tint is both external and internal. Handled examples have a matte stain on their handles up to the stained amber. Typical forms in this ware are bowls, dishes, pitchers, trays, tumblers, celery holders, toothpick holders, sugars and creamers, spooners and salt and pepper shakers.

The pattern maker's molds were constructed of carved hardwoods in six separate sections. Clamped together and dipped in water, after continued use, the hobs became rounder; eventually, the old molds were discarded for new ones. Plaster models were made from the wooden molds. From this model the hinged metal molds were created. The metal mold formed the glass object. Look for varying appearances in this most collectible glass.

French Blue - Steuben

This transparent colored Steuben glass possesses a grayish blue hue. French Blue is listed in a 1932 Steuben catalog. The light blue shade was contrasted with other colors, such as an amber foot on a pilsner glass. The glass is found with bubbles, applied threading and in a ribbed swirl pattern—to name a few variations.

Fry

Henry Clay Fry (1840-1929) established the Rochester

Tumbler Company in 1872. A man of varying talents, his business produced 80,000 whiskey tumblers per week. Later, he perfected a heat-proof process that was used in the manufacture of home canning jars.

The H.C. Fry Glass Company was formed in Rochester, Pennsylvania, in 1900. Typically the finest of cut glass houses, the firm also manufactured a variety of pressed, blown, etched, enameled and silver deposit forms.

Early Fry cut glass is prized by collectors. The best ground quartz, extra lead in the formula, and high temperature fusion produced an extraordinary crystal. Original patterns, precise compositions and precision cutting make this some of the best cut glass made in the United States.

Much of Fry's cut glass is unsigned. Two signatures were employed from 1901 to 1934. They are: the word "Fry" in script; and "Fry" centered in a shield, having "Fry" above and the word "QUALITY" below the central name.

The firm produced a white pressed opalescent ovenware which is being collected. Examples usually have the name in raised letters around the bases of objects.

The H. C. Fry Glass Company is perhaps best known for their attractive opal ware made from 1922 to 1933; it is referred to as Foval or Pearl Art Glass. Pieces are confused with Dorflinger and Sons opalescent glass and the Steuben Glass Works jade glass. Generally, the bodies of this glass were made with a white opalescent glass; necessary additions, such as feet, knobs, spouts and handles were added in cobalt, green, blue, black, amber, lavender and pink. Steuben did the opposite by constructing the bodies in colors of jade and used the opal glass for additions.

Some rare examples were enhanced with the addition of ornate silver deposit work; some of this was done by the Rockwell Silver Company, Meriden, Connecticut. Occasionally their mounts are hallmarked. Additional decorations include a crackled glass with etching, enameling, applied colored glass and the use of threading over the body of Foval.

Fry's opal art glass line was expensive to produce. This endeavor, plus financial difficulties, helped contribute to the demise of the factory. One source related that when the firm closed in 1934, a complete warehouse was opened to the public and the remaining Foval was sold at the unbelievable sums of five and ten cents per item.

Gillinder

GILLINDER

William T. Gillinder (1823-1871) was born near Newcastle-upon-Tyne, England. He worked in Birmingham at George Bacchus and Son, learning the art of making paperweights. Gillinder worked in a glasshouse in Mexborough at seven years of age. He contributed much to glassmaking in England and was noted as one of their finest artisans. The National Flint Glassmakers' Society credited him with their reorganization and success.

He migrated to the United States in 1853. At age 31, he became superintendent of the New England Glass Company, where he also made some paperweights. This position proved unsatisfactory; he moved to a variety of factories in Pittsburgh,

then St. Louis, and finally came to Philadelphia in 1861. He purchased a glassworks, naming it the Franklin Flint Glass Works. Lamp chimneys and hand-blown glassware were fabricated there. Cut glass designs showing exceptional workmanship include single star, hobnail and block and strawberry diamond motifs. Edwin Bennett joined the firm in 1863, contributing capital; the firm then was known as Gillinder and Bennett. In 1867, Bennett retired. His interests were taken over by James and Frederick Gillinder; the establishment then became known as Gillinder and Sons.

Gillinder and Sons achieved national fame as a result of the Centennial Exposition held in Philadelphia starting in May, 1876. Over two million people viewed the latest innovations and watched glass melted and shaped into objects. A one-story shop (96' by 109') was constructed in Fairmount Park near the entrance of the Exhibition of Machinery Hall. Souvenirs consisting of glass hats and slippers were given away to those in attendance; an additional $96,000.00 in sales resulted. During the Centennial, the firm made pressed and blown glass and operated a glass-cutting shop. The cost of this ornate structure was a mere $3,000.00

Some famous patterns credited to them are the Stippled Star, Classic, Mellor, Westward Ho and Lion. Items such as chandeliers, lamps and lampshades were specialty items, while other wares including platters, assorted relish dishes, ornate vases, paperweights, statuettes, bread trays and candlesticks were undoubtedly sold at the Centennial. Pieces were often frosted; some are marked "Centennial, 1876" or "Gillinder and Sons, Centennial Exhibition" in raised letters.

After William's death in 1871, the company moved from Philadelphia to Greenburgh, Pennsylvania. The firm became affiliated with the United States Glass Company in 1892, known as Factory G. In 1912, three sons of James Gillinder started their own glasshouse, known as Gillinder Brothers, Incorporated in Port Jervis, New York.

Green #5 - Steuben

Green #5, a bright and vivid emerald color, was a popular production item. This eye-appealing hue was fabricated in both decorative and functional items. Signatures on this colored crystal will include all of the acid-etched varieties.

Green Opaque - New England

A Cambridge, Massachusetts firm, the New England Glass Company, produced this scarce green opaque ware. Copper oxide added to an opal glass batch was the secret in creating this homogeneous glass. Each article will be found decorated with a mottled blue, metallic stain either at a mid-section or around its top. The mottling is separated from the soft, acid green body by a fine, wavy band of gold. This ware appeared in 1887, being manufactured in both the satin and rare glossy finishes for less than one year. Green Opaque is not signed but on very rare occasions, an example appears with the original paper label.

Shapes likely to be encountered in this type of glass include the following: parlor lamps, sugars and creamers, lily vases, cruets, various assorted bowls, sauce dishes, punch cups, mugs, toothpick holders, water and whiskey tumblers, pitchers and condiment sets.

Prices for these two varieties of glass have escalated appreciably in recent years. This is the type of art glass usually found in a very advanced collection.

Greentown Agate - Indiana Tumbler and Goblet Company

The Indiana Tumbler and Goblet Company, Greentown, Indiana, produced this desirable, molded art glass between January and June, 1903. Also known as Golden Agate and Holly Amber, the ware is characterized by alternating translucent bands of rich golden amber with stylized holly leaves and berries, and marbleized onyx of an opalescent nature. The pattern was also pressed in clear glass, plus experimentally in cobalt, rose and opaque white.

Perfected by glass chemist Jacob Rosenthal, the Holly vine pattern was created by Frank Jackson. Greentown's mold department designed many molds; others were made at the Hipkins Novelty Mold Company in Martins Ferry, Ohio. Charles Beam had been the skilled foreman until he departed for Kokomo late in 1900. The formula perfected by Rosenthal remains a secret. Researchers have suggested many ways that the glass was manufactured to achieve the unusual coloration. Some point to the batch ingredients, the process by which the batch was melted and subjected to the mold; others say that reheating techniques, or possibly the way articles were cooled in the lehr brought about the end result.

Items made in this pattern include sauce dishes, round bowls, creamers, spooners, covered sugars, covered butter dishes, round and square plates, water pitchers and tumblers, round water trays, pickle trays, syrups, cruets, salts and peppers, sugar shakers, cake stands, handled nappies, toothpick holders, oval and rectangular bowls, covered compotes, mugs and even vases. The most desirable examples are those on pedestals, especially the toothpick holder, the oval bowl, sugar bowl and butter dish.

A tragic fire on the morning of June 13, 1903, was soon out of control and razed the plant. Jacob Rosenthal found work at the Evansville Glass Company; eventually, he was factory manager at the Fenton Art Glass Company, Williamstown, West Virginia. He remained there until his death in 1933.

Golden Agate is prized highly today; its short life in production cannot begin to fill the void for avid collectors seeking good examples. The glass was reproduced in the 1960s by the St. Clair Glass Company.

Grotesque - Steuben

This term refers to a free-formed glassware made in the '20s and '30s by the Steuben Glass Works. Most examples are in the forms of bowls and vases (with molded feet). The undulating and handkerchief tops may be found in rose, green, blue, amber, purple and yellow blending into shiny clear crystal bottoms. Grotesque ware also occurs in just clear crystal, in colored crystal or in opaque glass. Objects are classical shaped and symmetrical with ground and polished bases. Some examples were signed.

Gundersen

The Gundersen Glass Works, Incorporated, was formed in 1939 when J. & B. Kenner, Incorporated, sold the silverware and glass departments of the original factory to businessmen in New Bedford. The three new successors included Thomas A. Tripp, president; Isaac N. Babbitt, treasurer and general manager; and Robert M. Gundersen, manager. Gundersen's personal code of excellence, plus his own glassmaking and craftsman skills, helped to re-establish the firm's former esteemed rank.

Floyd F. Cary (designer), O. Carl Banks (master cutter and engraver), H. Gilly Gulbranson and Anders Theon (fine glassblowers) incorporated their knowledge with quality formulas to produce unsurpassed works during this era. Pieces were marked with either a round silver label or an oval dark blue one. The first was marked "Gundersen Masterpiece" around the edge and showed a glassblower; to his left was a goblet and on his right was a vase. The second read "Fine Crystal - Hand Made By Gundersen."

Glassware manufactured by Gundersen consisted of decanters, pitchers, compotes, bowls, vases, candlesticks and numerous other specialties. Heavier and thicker examples of the former Mount Washington's Peach Blow and Burmese were made. The firm filled orders for many retailers and also did specialty work for well-to-do clientle seeking replacements and matches in shape, color, quality and cutting.

Robert Gundersen died in 1952 and the Gundersen Glass Works became a portion of the National Pairpoint Company. The finest of glassware had been fabricated under Gundersen's tutelage, and the spectrum of their output was extremely broad. Today this glass is collected and appreciated for its form, clarity, and precision cutting and engraving.

Handel

 Scratched or painted on glass, impressed or cast in the metal bases

Philip J. Handel, born in 1866, estblished the glass firm Handel and Company, 381 East Main Street, Meriden, Connecticut in 1893; it carried this name until 1903. As a young boy, Philip showed promise in art and was schooled in this field. He had a printing business until he was fourteen, quit school and worked at the Meriden Britannia Company for one month, moving then to the Meriden Flint Glass Company. While at this firm, he learned the art of glass decorating.

Handel and Company was incorporated on June 16, 1903 and became The Handel Company, Incorporated, with Philip J. Handel, president and treasurer; Antone E. Teich as vice president; and Albert M. Parlow as secretary.

Upon Philip Handel's early demise on July 14, 1914, his widow, Fannie, took over the business. William F. Handel, his cousin, became manager in 1919, and eventually vice president in 1926. The Depression forced the closing of the factory in 1936.

Handel's production included: decorative lamps, their most important item; wooden wares; metal objects; decorated opal ware, china, and porcelain; lamp globes; cologne bottles; chipped, decorated and etched cameo glass and glazed pottery. A wide variety of lamps in assorted sizes and shapes were fabricated by Handel. Some artistic procedures used in shade manufacture were the chipped glass effect on the exterior and hand-decorated on the interior, leaded shades, bent glass inserts, reticulated metal shades with glass inserts, parchment shades with fired-on glass beads, and textured glass shades lustred with fired-on metallic stains. Most shades discovered today are the half-dome variety. It is not uncommon to find the shades and/or bases signed, some with the addition of even the decorator's signature.

Bases of many lamps were antiqued bronze or a composition of white metal plated in bronze, brass, or copper finished in an antique green hue. The variety of artistic renderings found on lamp bases staggers one's imagination.

Some of the artistic decorators whose names are listed may be discovered on Handel items: 1) lamps - Henry Bedigie, F. Gubisch; 2) glass and porcelain - George Palme, Albert M. Parlow, William Runge; 3) china and glass - Walter Wilson, Peter Broggi; 4) others - Emil Melchior, George Lockrow, Hans Hueber, John Bailey, Robert Godwin, Arthur Hall, Carl Puffee, Edith Owens, William Clark, Katherine Welch and Katherine Casey. Numerous designers who formulated the variety of themes completed by the decorators were: Elliott Gardner, Rowene Cheney, Ray Freemantle, Elsie Jordan and Harry Homan.

H. BEDIGIE
Henry Bedigie signature on reverse painted kerosene lamp shade, about 1906.

HANDEL Lamps
Stamped into the metal rim of Teroma shades.

Hawkes

For five generations the Hawkes and Penrose families of Dudley, England, and Waterford, Ireland, had been glass artisans and cutters. Thomas G. Hawkes, a descendant, came to Brooklyn, New York, in 1863, working as a cutter for J. Hoare Company. His friend, Amory Houghton, Sr., at Corning Glass Works provided Hawkes with blanks when he opened his own cutting shop in Corning, New York, in 1880.

The Grecian and Chrysanthemum patterns enabled T.G. Hawkes to win two grand prizes at the Paris Exposition of 1889. Some other noteworthy patterns (or variations) included Bull's Eye, Corinthian, Devonshire, Harvard Chair Bottom, Russian, Strawberry Diamond and Fan, and Venetian (ordered by Franklin D. Roosevelt for the White House).

Corning continued to supply blanks for Hawkes until 1903; then the Steuben Glass Works was established as a subsidiary of T.G. Hawkes Company. Frederick Carder left Stevens and Williams, Stourbridge, England, at forty years of age to manage the plant. His technical skill, experience and creative prowess made him the right choice for the job. Carder was assisted by Hawkes' son, Samuel.

T.G. Hawkes always used a heavy quality glass with great purity and a high lead content. Their cut glass possesses a bell-like tonal quality. The Steuben Glass Works made blanks for the firm until 1918, when Hawkes was sold to the Corning Glass Works.

The company was inherited by Samuel Hawkes; upon his death in 1959, the firm closed its doors for good. All assets were disposed of in December, 1962. Situated on Market Street in Corning, New York, is an original brick structure with partially obliterated white painted letters. The building proclaims with the name and logo that this was a portion of the Hawkes' firm.

Heisey
The A.H. Heisey Glass Company of Newark, Ohio, had a long and prestigious career manufacturing quality glassware from 1895 to 1958. Their wares ranged from clear to colored crystal, and also included custard and milk glass. Items could be completely frosted, partially frosted or shiny; they also cut and etched glass and coated examples with silver and/or gold trim. Much of their output was pressed into molds. This firm advertised widely in numerous women's magazines of the era. The trademark, when seen, is an "H" within a diamond in raised relief on the glass. Rectangular paper labels were also used; some items were not marked or the labels have simply been lost over the years. Molds and the firm's name were acquired by the Imperial Glass Company in 1958. Imperial has reproduced popular objects without the Diamond H; this is especially true of their pressed animals, recreated after July, 1964.

A great variety of pressed crystal animals in clear and colored glass were made between 1933 and 1957. They range in sizes from 1" to 12". Some rare examples have been seen with gold, blue, red and white enameled highlights. These novelties, well received then, continue to increase in value. Included are the following: chick (head up), (head down); bull; rooster and rooster vase; wood duck; ducklings (floating or standing); cygnet (a young swan); sparrow; Asiatic pheasant; goose (wings down), (wings up), (wings half-way up); Scottie dog; Airedale; elephant; gazelle; giraffe; piglet; pig; rabbit; fish; doe's head; donkey; pony kicking; rearing horse bookends; horse head bookends; show horse; Clydesdale horses; and filly horses (heads forward), or (heads back).

Some popular Heisey patterns are as follows: Banded Flute, Beaded Panel and Sunburst, Beaded Swag, Cabachon, Coarse Rib, Colonial, Colonial Panel, Columbia, Continental, Daisy and Leaves, Empress, Fancy Loop, Fandango, Fern, Flat Panel, Grape Cluster, Pillows, Revere, Rib and Panel, Ridgeleigh, Satellite, Saturn, Stanhope, Sunburst, Toujours, Twist, Urn, Victorian, Waldorf-Astoria, Wampum, Warwick, Whirlpool and Yeoman.

Among the shades of colors incorporated in some glassware are: emerald green, blue, cobalt blue, vaseline, amber, opal, marigold, heliotrope, tangerine, moongleam, sahara, flamingo, zircon, dawn, red and black.

Etching on objects includes these designs: Adam, Ambassador, Biltmore, Chintz, Cleopatra, Frontenac, Heisey Rose, Lafayette Plate, Mayflower, Monticello, Orchid, Pied Piper, Plantation Ivy, Pompeii, Trojan and Renaissance.

Cut patterns used on some Heisey glassware are American Beauty, Arcadia, Aurora, Barcelona, Botticelli, Churchhill, Comet, Danish Princess, Debutante, Festoon, Forget-Me-Not, Garland, Inspiration, Jungle Flower, Killarney, Maryland, Melody, Midwest, Moonglo, Peach Tree, Sheffield, Southwind and Wheat.

A tremendous variety of shapes to search for include:

ashtrays, banana boats, baskets, bobeches, bonbons, bookends, bottles, bowls, cake stands, candelabras, candleholders, candy dishes, celeries, champagnes, cocktails, compotes, console sets, cruets, cups and saucers, decanters, dishes, figurines, goblets, hair receivers, humidors, jugs, mugs, nappies, paperweights, parfaits, perfumes, pitchers, plates, punch sets, relish dishes, rose bowls, sauces, spooners, syrups, toothpick holders, trays, tumblers, vases and wines.

Many dealers specialize in only Heisey glass and should prove very helpful when you are seeking specific information pertaining to shapes, prices, patterns, colors and scarcity. The Heisey Collectors of America welcome new members to its gracious and expanding ranks. Their address is Post Office Box 27, Newark, Ohio 43055.

Hobbs, Brockunier and Company

This firm was founded in Wheeling, West Virginia, in 1845 by John L. Hobbs and James B. Barnes, former workers at the New England Glass Company. They purchased the Plunket and Miller Glasshouse and renamed it Hobbs, Barnes, and Company. The sons, John Hobbs and James Barnes, joined the company later. The name Hobbs, Brockunier and Company came about in 1863, when two of Hobbs' sons and Charles Brockunier took over the firm. They hired William Leighton, Sr., former superintendent of the New England Glass Company, to manage the glass production. The firm became a very important manufacturer of glass in that area. In 1864, an inexpensive formula for soda lime glass was formulated; it revolutionized the glass industry.

Some general types of wares were blown, pressed, iridized and etched colored and crystal glassware. Patents were issued for the production of Spangled glass to William Leighton, Jr., on January 29, 1884. In February, 1886, William L. Libbey and Son licensed the firm to manufacture pressed, or Daisy and Button, "# 101 Pattern," Amberina. Their shaded opalescent was patented on June 1, 1886. Other wares known to be produced by Hobbs, Brockunier and Company were colored Craquelle and "Coral" glass, commonly referred to as Wheeling Peach Blow. A great variety of tableware and decorative items were fabricated by this firm.

Honesdale

A branch of C. Dorflinger and Sons was the Honesdale Decorating Company of Honesdale, Pennsylvania. The Wayne County community of Honesdale was noted for its glassmaking in the early 1900s. Carl Francis Prosch, born April 28, 1866, in Vienna, Austria, was one gifted artisan who helped make Honesdale very successful. He had worked for Bawo and Dotter as a designer of their European glass and china. Mr. Prosch worked for the firm ten years and came to New York City in 1890. He was married to Miss Caroline Heney on December 15, 1892; their three daughters were Elsa, Frances and Hilda.

In 1900, Prosch and his family settled in Honesdale. On January 1, 1901, the firm was established and managed by Carl F. Prosch. The factory was located on Maple Avenue in Seelyville. Mr. Prosch purchased the business in 1916 and continued its operation until poor health forced him to retire. Mr. and Mrs. Prosch were living at 622 Church Street, Honesdale,

at the time of his death on June 25, 1937.

Typical wares incorporated etched, engraved, gilded, iridescent and enameled Art Nouveau types influenced by Islamic and Chinese designs. The company was also noted for its gold and silver banded crystal tableware. Marks used at Honesdale were paper labels showing a goblet with the initials H.D.C. overlapping it, " *Honesdale* "

in gold script, the letter "P" within a keystone shield, and occasionally "H" within a diamond on blanks supplied by A.H. Heisey and Company. Some lime glass blanks were provided by the Fostoria Glass Company.

Icicle - Sandwich

This very unusual glass type is attributed to the Boston and Sandwich Glass Company. Examples of the ware have been viewed in a vibrant blue, cranberry and amber in the forms of bowls and vases. The icicle decoration, in clear crystal with sharp, pointed forms covered with granules, hangs from the rim of each object, complimented by smooth ruffled rigaree overlay about the neck. Three applied icicle feet with projecting fingers often support each piece; the bases have smoothly ground pontils; they are not signed. Examples of this glass are certainly not common and command good prices.

Imperial

The Imperial Glass Company, Bellaire, Ohio, was organized in 1901 by five outstanding citizens of Wheeling, West Virginia, just across the river boundary. J.N. Vance was president and Ed Muhleman was secretary of the company. Vance served as elected president until his death in 1913, Muhleman's business prowess established the firm's reputation for making quality glass. Muhleman retired in 1910; his death occurred in 1924.

Victor G. Wicke then became president of Imperial, managing sales. Agencies were set up throughout the United States, and their glass was also exported to Germany, the West Indies, South America, Mexico, New Zealand, Australia and South Africa (British). Mr. Wicke died in 1929.

J. Morris Dubois followed as the fourth president when the Imperial Glass Company went into bankruptcy in February, 1931. It was reorganized in August, 1931, as the Imperial Glass Corporation. Dubois retired after the firm was incorporated.

Earl W. Newton, Imperial's fifth president, is recognized for creating two very popular patterns still in production, "Candlewick" and "Cape Cod." He also influenced the Quaker Oats Company into selling glass as premiums. Mr. Newton retired in 1940.

Carl Gustkey succeeded Mr. Newton as president in 1940. He had been the former chief executive officer at Imperial.

Wares produced by Imperial include Star Holly, 1900; their iridescent "Carnival" glass begun around 1910; "Imperial Jewels," 1916, a pressed and blown colored ware with iridescent finishes; and "Free Hand," 1923 in many colors, with the "Drag Loop" or leaf and vine design. Most objects were iridized; other colored and crystal glass had applied threaded decor. Nuart and Nucut were also manufactured.

Trademark signatures include the name "Imperial," the double pointed arrow  (1914), the "German" cross

, later (1921) the name with the cross

and a gold paper label with raised designs appeared.

Imperial's shapes include vases, bowls, candlesticks, dishes, baskets and jars. Molds and equipment acquired from Central, Heisey and Cambridge are being used and marked to differentiate the original forms from the reproductions.

Intaglio - Tiffany

Intaglio was used by Tiffany to cut or etch a design in reverse relief below the original surface. Imperfections in the glass structure could be disguised with this technique. (See also Cameo/Tiffany).

Intarsia - Steuben

Fred'k Carder

Engraved Facsimile Signature

Intarsia was Carder's personal favorite out of all the glass he created. Only about 100 pieces were made by Frederick Carder and a very skilled gaffer named John Janson. Each example was personally signed, engraved "Fred'k Carder" about the base, but not on the underside. Produced in vases, bowls and a few goblets and wines, the glass consists of three layers. The two outer layers of clear crystal have fused within them a third layer of blue, black or amethyst glass. Colored floral and Arabesque designs, by name were Vermicelli, Ivy, Chinese Floral, Geometric, Modern and others. The glass was made around 1930 and advertised for sale in the Steuben catalogs. Its name was derived from a 15th century Italian marquetry technique.

Intarsia was manufactured by plating a bulb of crystal glass with colored glass which was permitted to cool. The colored design was treated with wax; the rest of the glass was etched showing a shallow design in relief. This glass was reheated, covered with another layer of crystal and then blown carefully into its desired shape. Stems and feet were added to complete each item.

Intarsia ranges in thickness from ⅛″ to 1/16″ of homogeneous glass. The thicker the design, of course, the lighter would be the color of the design in the finished product. Generally, this glass is heavier than most of Steuben's output, ranking in overall weight with Cintra, Cluthra and Acid Cutbacks.

Iridescent - Tiffany

Arthur J. Nash, when working for Tiffany, developed ways to lustre glass, duplicating the finish on ancient specimens. The iridescence was used to a great degree, especially on tableware and decorative forms, after it was widely accepted by the public.

The lustred effect varied with the density and color of the metal. Thus, Tiffany was able to achieve many interesting iridescent hues of his basic gold and blue colors.

Tiffany's multicolored iridescent wares reveal inlaid decorations; this glass is known as "Textured Lustre Ware." These objects are sought by avid collectors and demand high prices. Combinations of pulled threads, loops, feathers, vines and marvered hearts were used.

Iris - Fostoria

This art glass, developed by the Fostoria Glass Company, was trademarked in 1912. It is an iridescent type occurring in black, white, tan, blue, rose, yellow and green hues. (See also Fostoria).

Iris - Mount Washington

A rare type of iridescent glass with a rainbow coloration, its surface is both shiny and smooth. Iris Glass looks much like Webb's Bronze glass, but can be identified through some typical Mount Washington shapes. The company also copied original and grotesque forms found in ancient excavated glass. This product was advertised by Mount Washington in late 1878 as "Bronze," "Iris" and "Rainbow" glassware.

Ivory - Steuben

Ivory glass, a product of the '20s and '30s, is translucent, somewhat resembling the color of pressed "Custard." It has a bell like quality when tapped and is thicker and heavier than many Steuben wares. Most objects will not have the Fleur-de-Lis, but originally were marked with oval, silver paper labels.

This glass should be readily recognized due to its distinctive color; its exterior is usually smooth. The glass was blown into common patterns and each piece will have a smooth ground pontil. Uranium (U_3O_8) was added to the batch as a coloring agent.

Vases, some with acid etching, plus console bowls and candlesticks may be found. The Ivory forms were often contrasted with black. Ivory was also employed as a trim in the form of threading on darker glass.

Ivrene - Steuben

Ivrene glass, like Ivory glass, is rare; it is translucent, snow white and has a soft look. Some examples have reeding, copper wheel engraving, trim in a contrasting color, or iridization much like Verre de Soie.

The glass was first made in the form of lamp shades; later it was manufactured in limited quantities in console sets and vases. Table services were not always in complete sets.

Paper labels and a script "Steuben" signature were used on this ware. The signatures are often difficult to detect, especially if the bases have much wear.

Flared and ribbed shapes are noteworthy in Ivrene. Check for correctness of shapes when buying this or any glass. Probably produced in the '20s, some examples, but certainly not all, are opalescent.

Jade - Steuben

Jade glass, by the Steuben Glass Works, resembles the appearance of the mineral stone. A colored transparent opaline by nature, it was produced in a variety of colors, including Alabaster (clam broth); Amethyst Jade (scarce, somewhat murky); Light Blue Jade (turquoise colored); Dark Blue Jade (scarce, cobalt hued); Yellow Jade (canary yellow, scarce); Mandarin Yellow (heat sensitive, cracks easily, glowing yellow); Rosaline (light rose, most common, combined with Alabaster glass); and Jade Green (a true jade green).

Noteworthy shapes in this glass include console sets, vases, compotes, perfumes, cornucopias, cups and saucers, sherbets, drinking vessels, salt dips, plates and a host of others.

The Jades, predominately, are free-blown, usually with polished pontils. Copper wheel engraving is very beautiful to view on any of the Jades. Shiny surfaces and ribbed patterns were used to a great degree. Signed Jades will have a Fleur-de-Lis, block "STEUBEN," or script "Steuben" mark.

Jarves, Deming

Born in 1790, Deming Jarves, the son of a Hugenot immigrant and a glass technologist, incorporated the New England Glass Company in 1818; he remained there until 1825. In that year, he founded the Boston and Sandwich Glass Company. The Mount Washington Glass Works was also founded by him for his son, George, in 1837. Deming Jarves and Hiram Dillaway perfected, in 1828, a process for mold pressed glass; many other patents followed. One type of glass for which he is famous is the lacy variety. Deming moved again in 1858, establishing the Cape Cod Glass Company, which closed at his death.

Jersey Rose

Millville paperweights, consisting of a pink or yellow rose, were made by Ralph Barber from 1905-1918. The rose is open and its petal tips are opalescent; sometimes there are also a bud and three green leaves accompanying the main flower. The decoration is enclosed in a crystal ball, supported by a footed base.

Emil J. Larsen also made a glass rose weight during 1934-1935 at the Vineland Flint Glass Works; it was fabricated of red and yellow glass, accompanied by four leaves. These weights, if authentic, make nice additions to a collection.

KELVA   Stamped

Kelva - C.F. Monroe

This decorated opal ware, both in shiny and satin finishes, was one of three C.F. Monroe's products, decorated in Meriden, Connecticut. The blanks were acquired from French factories and the Pairpoint Manufacturing Company, New Bedford, Massachusetts. The finely executed and artistically enameled designs were carefully and imaginatively completed.

Kelva's trademark was registered August 2, 1904; some pieces were signed. It would be difficult to distinguish Kelva from Wavecrest and Nakara without the stamped signatures.

This ware is not too plentiful; therefore, prices in recent years have escalated. Bedroom and boudoir examples consist of hair receivers, dresser boxes, powder jars, cuff and collar boxes, pin dishes and hinged jewelry and trinket boxes. Other forms include letter holders; cigar humidors; biscuit, cookie, and cracker jars; lamps; planters; condiments; toothpick holders; and vases.

Some objects had fixtures added in brass, bronze or gilded base metals. Hinged examples were often lined with colorful satin, velvet or silk; these tended to fade and deteriorate over the years. Metal parts were attached with plaster-of-Paris.

Kerosene and Electric Lamps

As the 18th century was ushered in, people were seeking an adequate fuel to illuminate their lamps. Vegetable and animal oils became too exorbitant to be used in a widespread manner. The 1830s found alcohol and turpentine being combined as a cheaper substitute; this mixture, unfortunately, proved to be quite explosive. Lard oil was also tried, but it was limited in popularity as a result of extreme costs.

The first oil well in the United States was sunk in Titusville, Pennsylvania, on August 28, 1859, by Colonel Edwin L. Drake. This revolutionary find, a derivative known as "carbon oil," or kerosene, became the leading illuminant. Climbing a long wick by capillary action, kerosene was both fairly safe and cheap.

Glass factories quickly began manufacturing numerous types, shapes and sizes of lamps as an added revenue source. They decorated the glass, while, in some instances, subsidiary firms pressed and molded the brass and iron accessories.

In 1859, over 40 lamps were patented. During the next 20 years, some 80 different models received patents. Double student lamps, "Harvard lamps," table lamps, miniature lamps, parlor or reception lamps and a myriad of others were sold, giving both glamour and lighting to homes.

Stores, shops and mail-order houses took up the pursuit, selling these articles for $1.50 to $5.00 each. Montgomery Ward and Company, and Sears Roebuck and Company led the distribution from the 1870s up until around 1920.

"Gone with the Wind," a term made popular by the famous Margaret Mitchell novel, proved to be a very suitable term for many kerosene lamp types. These lamps are difficult to find complete, as the top bulb or chimney could easily be cracked when removed to light the wick. Intense heat from a wick turned too high could also cause a crack.

Reproduced lamps have little or no wear on the metal fixtures, inferior glass and gaudy enameling. Original glass and metal bases on "Gone with the Wind" lamps often have replacement parts; most notable are the top shades, which may closely match the design on the base. No two artists paint in the same style, however, and mellowed hues, realistic shading and correct colors are very difficult to duplicate.

The beginning of the 20th century saw lamps being converted and new productions wired for electricity. Again, many firms took up the challenge, fabricating both beautiful and functional lamps in astounding sizes and shapes with artistic bases constructed from many materials. There were floor and table lamps, numerous desk varieties, candle lamps - just an endless array. All colors of glass were treated by almost every method mentioned in this book under specific glass categories and the many techniques that they conceived to enhance glass in each factory. Steuben, Durand, Tiffany, Bradley and Hubbard, Mount Washington, Pairpoint, Handel, Smith Brothers, Wave Crest, Cut, Satin, Burmese, Royal Flemish, Mother-of-Pearl, Phoenix, Sandwich, Consolidated, Frank Art, Quezal, Moe Bridges, Jefferson, Eclipse, Duffner and Kimberly, H. J. Peters, Miller, Pittsburgh, Fostoria, U.S. Art Bent Glass Company, Moran and Hastings, Frankel Light Company, Cincinnati Artistic Wrought Iron Works, The Albert Sechrist Manufacturing Company, Lion Electric Company, Royal Art Glass Company, and William R. Noe and Sons were just a few of the many lamp producers.

Duffner & Kimberly
New York, New York

Bradley & Hubbard
Meriden, Connecticut

The Pairpoint Corp'n

The Pairpoint Corporation
New Bedford, Massachusetts
Mark stamped on shades

Kew Blas

The Union Glass Company, Somerville, Massachusetts, under the superintendence of W(illiam) S. Blake, manufactured this decorated and iridescent art glass. Its trade name was a result of shuffling the letters in his name.

Predominately manufactured in vase forms, true examples will be engraved, not etched. This glass can be confused with the output of Durand, Quezal, Tiffany and Steuben. Colors generally are browns, greens, tans, cream and snow white, enhanced by leaf and pulled feather patterns. Some objects have been seen with applied glass trailings about their necks; others were one solid, gold lustred surface.

Kew Blas first appeared in the marketplace in 1893. Some forms are truly classical, while others appear to be poorly conceived. A scarce and fine art glass type, Kew Blas is worthy of a place in your collection.

Etched

Kimble (See also Cluthra/Kimble)

The Kimble Glass Company, Vineland, New Jersey, came about in 1931, when Colonel Evan F. Kimble took over the Vineland Flint Glass Works after the demise of Victor Durand, Jr. All other art glass was discontinued except for this popular, but limited, production type—mostly vases.

Cluthra glass made in many colors is in a glossy finish and tends to be heavy. Single brilliant colors predominate; double colors are desirable and scarce. The glass is embedded with cloud-like formations and air bubbles of varying sizes. It is dissimilar to Steuben's Cluthra in shape and coloration, and the bubbles are less obvious to the viewer.

Kimble examples are usually signed in silver stylus on the base in the large ground pontil. 20144-12 This code lists the

shape (20144), height (12″), K (maker/Kimble), Dec - 7 (Decoration - 7, color/salmon pink). The most common colors are yellow, white, blue, pink, and green.

Durand glass was also produced at this factory site; apparently at one time a partnership had existed, since pieces are infrequently found signed "Durand-Kimble."

Larsen, Emil J.

A noteworthy glass craftsman born in Sweden in 1878, he was the ninth child in a family of eleven. At the age of seven, he had duties in the Kosta Glassworks, holding and cooling molds with water between each use. Numerous glasshouses where he later worked included Dorflinger Glass Works; Pairpoint Manufacturing Company; H.P. Sinclaire and Company, Bath, New York; Quezal Art Glass and Decorating Company; and Vineland Flint Glass Works.

His creations were in numerous glass types, including colored and decorated iridescent glass, colored transparent crystal with bubbles, ribs, pulled peacock feathers, colored cut, whimseys, pieces in the Steigel tradition, stemware and paperweights. His output of works was never signed.

Lava - Mount Washington

A rarity in art glass, Lava was granted two patents, the first on May 28, 1878, and the second September 30, 1879, for an improvement in ornamenting.

According to the patent, Lava was blown and pressed, being made from the following ingredients: seven parts of clear flint, one part carbonate of potash and two parts of lava. Most articles are in the form of vases, some with handles. The black glass, lavender (very rare), and iridized (very rare) examples were left with a shiny and/or acid finish.

Designs or colored glass fragments of assorted hues and shapes were embedded or a flux was used so that they would adhere. Some rare examples are outlined in gold; (very rare) grotesque figures and animals were gilded according to an artist's special whim. Certainly this glass is a noteworthy addition to any collection; the ware was never signed.

Although in very limited supply today, "Sicilian Ware," received considerable positive comments when sold in leading stores, and at the Mount Washington showrooms at 20 College Place, New York City. William H. Lum, showroom director indicated that the glass was a success and that orders were being filled as soon as possible.

Lava - Tiffany

Louis C. Tiffany's Lava glass was once called "volcanic glass." Predominately manufactured in asymmetrical vase forms, its body is found spotted with iridescent purples, blues, greens and golds patterned in horizontal and vertical stripes or abstract designs. Its rough and smooth surfaces give the effect of flowing molten lava; the glass is frequently signed. For the advanced collector, this glass is most worthy of collecting.

Libbey

William L. Libbey, in 1878, leased the New England Glass Company, Cambridge, Massachusetts, changing the name to the New England Glass Works, W.L. Libbey and Sons, Proprietors. His son, Edward D. Libbey, took over the operation in 1883 after the death of his father. The factory was closed in 1888 and moved to Toledo, Ohio, where Edward Drummond Libbey set up a glass company, renaming it the Libbey Glass Company. It became the largest cut glass factory in the world during the Brilliant Period. A Glass Pavilion was operated at the Chicago World's Fair in 1893; 130 craftsmen blew and cut glass. Souvenirs sold there were marked "Libbey Glass Company, World's Fair 1893." During the 1883-1940 era, much colored and ornamental glass was made in numerous techniques developed by Joseph Locke, a glass technician and giant in the art glass field. Amberina, Pomona, Agata, Peach Blow and Maize were some of the types made.

After Libbey's death in 1925, J.D. Robinson took over until his death in 1929. His sons, Joseph W. and Jefferson D. Robinson, became President and Vice-President; they hired A. Douglas Nash, who in turn introduced the Libbey-Nash Series in 1933. (See also Nash)

In 1936, after suffering monetary setbacks, the firm was absorbed by Owen-Illinois, Incorporated. Designs by Freda Diamond and Edwin W. Feurst brought about contemporary styles and leaded crystal tableware from 1940 through 1957. The firm now produces all tableware by automation.

Light Green - Pairpoint

This is the lightest colored, transparent crystal produced in a green hue. Production included vases, console sets, compotes, candlesticks and other forms. This scarce color is found plain, with engraved designs (grapes, colias, etc.), and clear controlled bubble ball connectors.

Locke Art

Joseph Locke, undoubtedly, ranks as one of the greatest and most versatile contributors to the field of art glass. Patents for the following types of glass were taken out after being perfected by Locke: Amberina (1883), Pomona (1885), Plated Amberina (1886), Peach Blow (1886), Agata (1887) and Maize (1888). These specific categories are discussed in depth throughout the text.

Born in Worcester, England, on August 21, 1846, Locke's excellent artistic background left its indelible mark on the 19th and 20th centuries. He served his apprenticeship in 1858 at the Worcester China firm, gleaning knowledge from prominent artists' lectures. Joining Hodgetts, Richardson and Company in 1868, he acquired the arts for engraving and cutting to create cameo glass. His copy of the two-handled (Roman) Portland Vase won a gold medal in 1878 at an exhibition in Paris. Locke also worked at the Red House Glass Works and at Webb and Corbetts for a brief period.

In 1882 Locke arrived in America, where he was scheduled for employment by the Boston and Sandwich Glass Company.

Agents mistakenly journeyed to New York City, where they planned to meet him; he, however, arrived in Boston. The New England Glass Company in Cambridge, Massachusetts, took advantage of this error and quickly hired Locke.

From 1882 to 1888, he worked for the New England Glass Company. In 1888, Locke became the first superintendent of the Libbey Glass Manufacturing Company, Toledo, Ohio. He also served as chief designer for the United States Glass Company, Pittsburgh, Pennsylvania, before retiring.

At this point, Joseph Locke spent the next 40 plus years, from 1891, creating his famous acid-etched and engraved "Locke Art" glass. When signed, the words "LOCKE ART"

LOCKE ART   Etched

will be incorporated in minute letters, hidden among the design. Out of a total service, perhaps only a very few pieces will be signed.

His shop was located in Mount Oliver, adjacent to Pittsburgh, and produced exquisite tableware using glass blanks procured from C. Dorflinger and Sons. Locke's work might be confused with Dorflinger's Kalana series. Some subjects found include: (Vintage pattern), flowers, fish, children's stories ("Brer Rabbit"), mythology and themes from the Bible (Egyptian design and "Flight into Egypt").

Joseph Locke's knowledge of chemistry combined with his artistic ability are reflected in his unique art forms. Resist (stearin, bee's wax, paraffin and mutton fat) was used for coating objects to be decorated. Next, the use of free-hand sketches and copper stencils resulted in pleasing designs; steel needles and orange wood tools assisted, giving both fine and broad lines where necessary. Hydrofluoric acid, accurately timed, produced varying depths and textures in each glass article. Some examples were enhanced further, using ammonium carbonate and other salts.

These artistic masterpieces have become relatively scarce in recent years; prices continue to climb. To acquire one of Locke's treasured pieces (a goblet, pitcher, tumbler, etc.), especially signed and in tinted hues, would be a revelation for any collector of fine art. Locke died in 1936, leaving behind a beautiful legacy of his abilities.

Lusterless - Mount Washington

White Lusterless was the first art glass produced at Mount Washington in 1881. The glass appears like alabaster, having been given a hydrofluoric acid bath. The soft appearance and touch make this glass aesthetically pleasing to own.

Most examples are beautifully ornamented with maidenhair ferns, cornflowers, wild roses, pansies, tulips, wild roses, pond lilies, irises, clematises, apple blossoms, lake and forest scenes, figural and others. Worn or repainted examples should not be considered for purchase. This glass was rarely signed but should be very easy to recognize. Collectible shapes include vases, plates, platters, lamps, pickle jars, rose bowls, boudoir bottles, paperweights and novelties.

Lutz Type

Nicholas Lutz was born at St. Louis in Lorraine, France.

At ten he worked as an apprentice in the St. Louis factory, He became a skilled glassworker and upon his arrival in the United States took employment with the Boston and Sandwich Glass Company. Working there from about 1870 until they closed in 1888, Lutz became recognized for his filigree, threaded and striped glassware. This ware, with parallel and spiraling stripes of opaque white and colored glass, had fine thread-like canes embedded in the body. The term "vetro a retorti" referring originally to this type of glass made at Murano, Italy, best describes this work. Unless authentication is possible (Lutz glass), it would be best to refer to this ware as (Lutz Type glass). Mr. Lutz made colorless crystal examples with threading around the exterior of the body, colored examples, some with engraved designs, and other pieces having prunts with molded cherub heads as an added ornamentation.

A variety of his work, in numerous shapes, may be viewed at the Sandwich Historical Society, Sandwich, Massachusetts. After the Sandwich factory closed its doors, Lutz worked for both the Mount Washington Glass Company and later the Union Glass Company.

Today it would be virtually impossible to acquire a genuine piece of Lutz glass. The remote opportunity might exist through an heir, museum or other authenticated source to acquire an example of his work.

Maize - Libbey, New England

Joseph Locke developed this molded glass pattern shaped like sweet corn, with vertical rows of kernels and husks overlapping and rising from the bottom of the object. The glass was manufactured at the New England Glass Company and was patented in 1889. It was also produced by Libbey Glass Company, Toledo, Ohio, after the factory moved and its name was changed. The ware was advertised around 1890 as "Maize Art Glass."

The body of this glossy household ware is a single glass layer produced in shiny opaque white (milk glass), light green, pale yellow and stained transparent. The corn leaves are usually green, but sometimes occur in brown, blue or red. They have a flowing movement about them and the coloring on some examples may be spotty and worn. Pitchers, celeries, salt and pepper shakers, sugar shakers, syrups, toothpick holders, butter dishes, tumblers, berry bowls and sugars and creamers are some of the varied shapes produced in this glass of limited quantities. Maize was never marked.

Mandarin Yellow - Steuben

Frederick Carder's Mandarin Yellow was made about 1915-1916. This translucent and brilliant yellow color was inspired by the yellow Chinese porcelains of the Ming dynasty (14th to 17th centuries). Internal stresses in this apparently weak structured glass caused it to crack; around a dozen examples are known to exist today, mostly in the form of vases.

Marble - Tiffany

A glass similar in nature to Agate, this ware has not been cut, but finished with an irregular surface. Several colored layers with veins and streaks are seen running throughout the body of the form. A difficult example to procure and predominately found in vase forms, it is usually signed.

Marina Blue - Pairpoint

This light blue coloration produced by Pairpoint and Gundersen has a blue-grey tint to it, which is much more noticeable on thin walled objects held to a bright light.

Marina Blue - Steuben

This light blue Steuben glass has a color that somewhat resembles Aquamarine. Traces of green may be seen when the object is properly illuminated.

Mary Gregory Type

This glassware, both clear and in various colors, was decorated with well-controlled white enamel, showing a young boy (s) and/or girl(s) in Victorian garb. The figures depict such whimsical acts as: catching butterflies, carrying a basket, rolling a hoop, reclining on a swing, holding a floral bouquet, playing a stringed instrument and so on. Other silhouetted figures, such as cherubs, may be discovered.

The ware was very popular during the Victorian era and is found in numerous shapes. Some typical forms are vases, water sets, wine decanters, plates, covered boxes, colognes and perfumes, ewers, mugs, pill boxes, pitchers, tumblers and epergnes.

Mary Gregory, a decorator working at the Boston and Sandwich Glass Company from 1870-1880, is said to have decorated glass with children. It is known that she did live and work at the factory; many critics have refuted that the artist ever painted such scenes. The debate goes on; perhaps glass collectors will never learn the truth!

Numerous factories, including others in this country and abroad—England, Bohemia, (Venice) Italy and Czechoslovakia—make this a very difficult glass to attribute. It would be questionable to say that a certain example was made at Sandwich and decorated by Mary Gregory. The glass is well termed "Mary Gregory Type."

Matsu-No-Ke - Steuben

Steuben's Matsu-No-Ke is a clear crystal with unusual applied, transparent, colored decor and handles which was patented in 1922. Vases, pitchers, sugars and creamers, and perhaps other shapes were adorned with colored branches and veined oval cactuses. Sometimes the glass is referred to as "Cactus." Popular colored hues were pink (Rosa), rose, amber, green and blue. This product has not been found signed; variations in the decoration are evidenced by similar etched designs which are termed "Fircone" and "Matzu."

Mercury

Produced between the 1850s and the 1900s by glass houses in Ohio, Pennsylvania, Virginia and Massachusetts, this ware is extremely lightweight. Mercury glass tends to discolor and oxidize when the pontil plugs have been lost or removed. Signatures may be discovered on some objects.

Clear glass vessels in many forms, with a hollow between their inner and outer walls, had a solution of mercury, tin, lead or bismuth applied to coat their interiors. The excess liquid was poured out and the open pontil was plugged to seal out the air.

Pitchers, wig stands, curtain tiebacks, vases, compotes, mugs, salts and even statues were made. Many objects had gold and silver gilt on inner surfaces. Shallow engraving, colorful enamels and stains were also used in a decorative fashion on the exteriors.

Mica-Flecked - Steuben

Mica flakes varying in both size and density were used decoratively in some Steuben glass. The granular flakes were picked up from the marver on a gather of hot glass and covered with another layer before the object was shaped into the desired form. These examples made in the '20s are rare; the color of the silver flecks varies with the lighting and the tinted glass covering the mica. Footed vases and compotes were two shapes made in this manner.

Millefiori - Steuben

First produced about 1910, this glass was also called "Tessera," a particular type of tile work. Glass rods of numerous colors were cut into ¼" segments. Placed into a mold in a particular pattern, they were reheated until fusion occurred. This shape was then removed from the kiln and worked into another molded batch of glass to form a plate, bowl, or plaque. Sometimes the decoration was used at the center of flowers on sculptured bowls and vases of fine quality and workmanship. The pieces are very beautiful to look on with their myriad of colors. Produced into the mid '20s, Aurene glass also, on rare occasions, had slices of canes inserted in the decorative marvered work to create florals.

Millefiori - Tiffany

Tiny rods of glass in blues, whites, greens, reds and yellow were placed within the exterior surfaces of bowls and vases. These florettes, with the addition of leaves and vines, created a most appealing and very realistic allusion. The rods ranged anywhere from about ¼" to 5" in diameter. Many examples are signed.

The aquatic representations reveal what appears to be both flowers and animals embedded in clear crystal and colored iridescent glass. Predominately in vase forms, this glass type is very desirable, scarce and expensive.

Moonlight - Steuben

As the name Moonlight suggests, this rare, colored, transparent glassware possesses a very delicate shaded hue. Only by placing it next to clear crystal, is it really possible to detect the extremely pale lilac-like bloom. From a distance, such an object seems to have a tint of gray; but this is not really the case. Generally, objects made in this color were not signed.

Moresque - Steuben

On display at the Rockwell Gallery, Corning, New York, are examples of this very rare glassware, along with all the other types discussed in this book. The body of Moresque glass has a custard coloration with haphazard, dark gray-green or dark gray-blue swirls running in a vertical fashion about the shiny surface. Footed vases and possibly other shapes were manufactured.

Mother-of-Pearl Satin

Synonymous terms for a ware having two or more layers of glass depicting a pattern are Pearl Satin, Pearl Ware, and Mother-of-Pearl Satin. This mold blown satin glass has internal indentations that aid in trapping air bubbles between layers of glass, creating an interesting effect. Linings on some pieces may be other than white.

Mother-of-Pearl was produced by many factories in Europe and the United States. The word "Patent" is occasionally found on some English *Patent.* examples. Notable American producers were the Mount Washington Glass Company, the Phoenix Glass Company, the Steuben Glass Works (rare), and the Louis C. Tiffany Glass Works (shells set in metal pieces).

Frederick Stacey Shirley, Mount Washington Glass Company, received a patent on June 29, 1886, relating to the making of "Pearl Satin Ware" with an acid finish. Joseph Webb. as manager of the Phoenix Glass Works, Beaver County, Pennsylvania, also patented his process on July 6, 1886, calling for the use of two molds.

Colors found in this attractive glassware may range from the very colorful rainbow hues to a single color, or one color shading from brighter to darker and/or lighter tints. Typical Mount Washington colors are shaded blues, pink, yellow and violet.

Patterns most often found are diamond quilt, swirl, herringbone, raindrop, peacock eye, moire', zipper, flower and acorn, drape and Federzeichnung. The diamond quilted is common and has an overall diamond pattern; the swirl design has diagonally swirled parallel lines over the body; the herringbone pattern has lineal serrated lines running horizontally across the example. Both of the above are gradually becoming scarce. The raindrop is represented as a circular pattern resembling thumbprints; the peacock eye shows two semicircles, one below the other, over a spot which symbolizes the eye; moire' has a watery appearance with graduated, erratic, concentric rings. Lines run vertically along the body of the piece and have a zipper appearance in the pattern of the same name; flower and acorn shows mottled convex surfaces in cameo-like relief; the drape has rows of sagging horizontal lines supported by vertical dividers. Federzeichnung portrays intricate maze-like designs in gold enamel, surrounding opal serpentine paths; some of the paths end abruptly, while others meander over the surface of the article. The seven patterns mentioned above are fairly difficult to procure, especially the peacock eye, zipper, flower and acorn, and Federzeichnung.

Additional decoration on Mother-of-Pearl examples may include applied work, threading, cameo techniques, gold leafing, enameling and the use of coralene beads adhered in a particular design. (See also Coralene)

Some typical shapes are vases, ewers, rose bowls, finger bowls, pitchers, tumblers, baskets, cruets, lamps, punch cups and bride's bowls. Collect those patterns, shapes and colors that are appealing to you personally.

Mount Washington Glass Company

Deming Jarves, of the Boston and Sandwich Glass Company, founded the Mount Washington Glass Works in South Boston,

Massachusetts, in 1837 for his son, George D. Jarves. The first superintendent was Captain Luther Russell. In 1839, George D. Jarves and Henry Comerais had new furnaces constructed and the overall facilities were enlarged under the name Jarves and Comerais. William L. Libbey, bookkeeper, joined the firm in 1851 and worked with the firm up until it closed in 1861. In the same year, William L. Libbey and Timothy Howe purchased the company; Howe died in 1866, and Libbey became the sole owner.

The business was moved to New Bedford, Massachusetts, in 1870, taking on its original name, the Mount Washington Glass Works. The three-floor glasshouse had a ten-pot furnace. In the basement were a carpenter's shop, engines, and a mixing and packing facility. The first floor consisted of offices, kilns, selecting rooms and a mold room. Cutting rooms and a large machine shop occupied the second floor. Stock and chandelier rooms took up the third floor.

Captain Henry Libbey became associated with the firm providing additional capital, and William Libbey resigned in 1872 to work as an agent for the New England Glass Company.

The factory closed briefly in 1873 during the depression. In late 1874, the company opened again with A.H. Seabury, president, and Frederick S. Shirley, agent. Finally in April, 1876, after reorganization, the company became the Mount Washington Glass Company. This company merged with the Pairpoint Manufacturing Company in 1894.

Quadruple-plated wares and assorted glass types from this union became highly respected and praised. Unique and ornate Britannia wares were manufactured and glass workers took great pride in displaying their cutting and glass-blowing skills. Since the firm did not mass-produce items, its products may be best characterized as hand made.

Throughout the firm's gradual development, such items listed were produced: cut, Lusterless, Albertine, Crown Milano, Royal Flemish, Cameo, Burmese, Amberina (Rose Amber), Pearl Satin, Mother-of-Pearl Satin, Peach Blow, Lava, Iris, Napoli, Verona, Ambero, Twist glass, Tavern glass, paperweights, lamps, clear and colored crystal (often engraved or cut), plus a host of quadruple plated objects, gold and silver plated, some with engraving and ornate applied work. This list encompasses all types of parts and holders used in association with the glass: punch bowls and goblets, cigarette holders, flat tableware, teapots, sugars and creamers, cups and saucers, mugs, moustache cups, napkin rings, butter dishes, children's cups, coffee pots, soda tumbler holders, cigar cases, jewel caskets, picture frames, assorted trophies for all sports and so on. Pairpoint also manufactured other items in pewter and German silver.

Nakara - C.F. Monroe

NAKARA   Stamped

No trademark was ever registered for Nakara. It is sometimes signed "NAKARA" or "NAKARA C.F.M. CO." in stamped, block letters. (See also Kelva)

Napoli - Mount Washington

This unusual and novelty, transparent or colored, crystal glass with decoration was patented in 1894 by Albert Steffin.

The process, similar to reverse painting on glass, had the artist profusely decorate the inside surface with examples of flowers, birds and fish—all enameled. The exterior body has gold or silver tracery, usually outlining the objects with perhaps the addition of a web-like network running over the entire body, joining the various motifs together.

Vases, bowls, pitchers, compotes, urns and cookie jars are some of the shapes completed in this glass. The golds and enamels were all fired in one operation, thus saving both valuable time and labor expenditures.

When signed, silver plated tops will be impressed "M.W." This glass is not well known; when found signed, it commands premium prices. The signatures are in yellow or black enamel, sometimes followed by a number, such as "Napoli 829." Certainly a fine addition to your collection, if you can find it.

Nash, Arthur J.

Arthur John Nash (1849-1934) was originally associated with Sir Edward Webb and managed his White House Glassworks in Stourbridge, England, About 1900, Arthur and his sons, A. Douglas (died 1940) and Leslie began managing the Tiffany Glass Furnace at Corona, New York. Employed on a shareholder basis, they developed many outstanding formulas and decorating techniques. Leslie Nash was responsible for creating a "peacock green" color and the bronze and copper fittings on many decorative pieces. The threesome later formulated "cypriote," having an ancient iridescence and an erupted bubbly surface. This glass is very desirable today. (See also Cypriote)

In later years, Louis C. Tiffany used public money to keep the glassworks open, even though Tiffany Furnaces then occupied first place in fine glass production. Tiffany withdrew his support and finances in 1928, and the A. Douglas Nash Corporation was formed by Nash, his father, and other associates. They made art glass in the fashion of Tiffany until 1931, when the depression forced luxury firms out of business.

Some Nash pieces, when not signed, closely resemble Tiffany's work, while others are recognized fairly readily. One type is his Chintz glass, which has a spoked pattern radiating from the center of each flat piece. On objects such as vases, the rays run in a perpendicular fashion over the body. Light green, brown, orange and pink spatterings on transparent and colored iridescent backgrounds are dominant. Pieces having a red background are highly sought and prized. The work is extremely well done but lacks finesse in the true Tiffany tradition.

Other Nash types included: Gold Lustre, Mineral Stained Crystal Tableware, Single and Double Ring Glass, Opalescent Optic and Silhouette. Gold Lustre has an iridescent gold color with pink, blue and green highlights. Tinted tableware was made by pattern-molding crystal glass and then applying a permanent stain to the glass surface. This type was stained with various colors and named Alexandrite, Banded, Beryl, Blue Grotto, Smoke and Trylon. Single and Double Ring Glass was formed predominately into ewers and decanters. Single Ring Glass has a doughnut-shaped body, while Double Ring Glass has a second doughnut shape running the opposite direction on the neck of the piece. Patterns in Opalescent Optic are Optic Leaf, Optic Diamond and Optic Rib.

Signed pieces have ground pontils, with the Nash signature

in small crude block letters and often a crude number, such as "185 AD NASH." This signature was used after the firm incorporated in December, 1929. Early Nash glass examples have been seen signed "Corona," or "A.D.N.A." (the A. Douglas Nash Association).

Nash worked for the Libbey Glass Company from 1932 to 1935. His designs included colored and opalescent glass, cut crystal, threaded and pulled decorations, clear crystal with applied lily pads, and crystal tableware with animal forms as stems.

The Silhouette glass mentioned above was constructed on the finest lead crystal. An assortment of tableware shapes included: goblet, champagne, claret, sherry, cocktail, cordial, sherbet, vase, center bowl, compote and candlestick. The pressed glass animals in this menagerie came in either opalescent glass or black "Moonstone," attached to clear crystal bowls. The eleven animals in the set included the monkey, bear, rabbit, antelope, cat, kangaroo, squirrel, elephant, camel, greyhound and giraffe. The chart indicates which animal was included with a particular shape.

Monkey - sherry
Bear - claret
Rabbit - sherbet and 10" vase
Antelope - ?
Cat - goblet
Kangaroo - cocktail
Squirrel - champagne (conventional and hollow stem)
Elephant - center bowl (10" in diameter)
Camel - 6" candleholder
Greyhound - cordial
Giraffe - compote

The Libbey-Nash series was widely advertised in such magazines as *The New Yorker, Time, Town & Country, Vogue,* and *Vanity Fair* when it first came out in 1933. Silhouette glass was moderately priced at $10.00 a dozen, the center bowl was $7.50, and a pair of candlesticks sold for $7.00. The venture was a dismal failure; today, interestingly enough, serious collectors pay in excess of $100.00 for a single example. Frequently these objects will be found signed on their bases with the tiny acid-stamped Libbey signature within a circle.

New England Glass Company

The Boston Porcelain and Glass Company, founded in 1814 at East Cambridge, Massachusetts, was acquired in 1817 by Deming Jarves. The following year it was incorporated.

A six-pot furnace, with 40 employed at its inception, was increased by 1818 to 24 glass cutting mills and two flint glass furnaces. The first lead furnace in the United States was believed to be the Deming Jarves' one at the New England Glass Company.

This red lead furnace was capable of a two-ton output per week, producing a great variety of lacy, mold-blown, mold-pressed, cut and engraved lead glass in English and Venetian styles. Later, many new colored glass types were perfected by Joseph Locke. (See also Joseph Locke) Grecian, antique and transparent lamps; plates; paperweights; chandeliers; and vases were made for domestic uses and exported to South America and the West Indies. Amberina, Plated Amberina, Pomona, Agata and Maize were manufactured from 1883.

Deming Jarves left in 1825 to found the Boston and Sandwich Glass Company; he was succeeded by Henry Whitney, the new general manager. By 1853, 500 employees working with five furnaces and ten pots put out 20,000 pounds of glass a week. Louis F. Vaupel (1824-1903) was born in Schildhort, Germany, and worked with his father in a glasshouse at age 12. He became an engraver and glass blower in 1836. Migrating to the United States in 1850, he became a master engraver at the New England Glass Company in 1853 and remained for 32 years. His fine Bohemian style engravings were accomplished on commemorative and presentation examples. Early work was on crystal; later examples were finely engraved on flashed ruby and other colored glass.

William L. Libbey (1827-1883), agent from 1872, leased the factory in 1878 after it suffered setbacks from lime glass competition. Closed by strikes in 1888, William's son, Edward Drummond Libbey (1884-1925), relocated the business in Toledo, Ohio, dissolving it in 1890 and assigning Libbey Glass Company as its new name.

Northwood Glass Company

Harry Northwood, an English glass expert and son of a distinguished decorator, settled in the United States in the 1880s. He worked for the La Belle Glass Company and the Bridgeport Glass Works, both located in Bridgeport, Ohio. Later he founded several of his own factories, including Indiana, Pennsylvania; Wheeling, West Virginia; Martins Ferry, Ohio; and Elwood City, Pennsylvania. Custard and Carnival glass were produced. Some custard is identified in script by the word "Northwood" *Northwood*;

Carnival may be impressed Ⓝ Ⓝ Ⓝ N

Prior to 1910, a double circle surrounded the letter, after that date the logo was simplified. It should be noted that much of Northwood's production was not marked. Imperial Glass used an overlapping "I" and "G" as their mark. Many of the companies marked little if any of their Carnival glass. To identify pieces, it is often necessary to go by the shape, pattern and sometimes the color of the particular example. Many patterns have been reproduced and reissued in recent years. Make certain you know the piece you are buying!

Known by various names throughout the United States, Carnival glass has been referred to as "Taffeta," "Nancy," "Cinderella," "Iridescent Glass" and "Poor Man's Tiffany." Companies involved in its production included: the United States Glass Company, Millersburg Glass Company, Northwood Glass Company, Fenton Art Glass Company, Westmoreland Glass Company, Imperial Glass Company and possibly Diamond Glass Company.

Around 1900, labor and monetary problems plagued many glasshouses in the United States. To alleviate these problems, factories moved westward where better facilities and resource materials existed.

Harry Northwood and his famous father, John, toured England and learned how to apply iron oxide and iron chloride to the outer glass layers, giving them an inexpensive iridescence. Thus the inception of art glass commodities at a fair market price became a reality, and by 1910, many companies were eagerly producing carnival. Today some select examples in certain patterns and colors command as much as true art glass.

Carnival was given as premiums, sold in five and ten cent stores, could be won at carnivals and was also listed in glass trade catalogs up until about 1925. Pieces were sold individually and as sets in dozen lots at very nominal prices. Over 500 pressed patterns were produced, and many pieces had designs on both the inner and outer surfaces.

Some of the colors that can be found in this ware are: marigold, amethyst, green, ice green, helios green, clear white, cobalt blue, icy blue, azure blue, pastel blue, peach opalescent, holly amber, butterscotch and red.

Opaline

This slightly translucent glass, made with the ashes of calcined bones and colored metallic oxides, was both mold-blown and mold-pressed. Many objects are decorated with enameling. Although the glass resembles the color of an opal, it may be found shaded in green, blue, pink or other hues. It was manufactured in the United States by the Boston and Sandwich Company about 1830 and elsewhere here and abroad through the 1880s. In Europe, France was a major producer of Opaline glassware. Typical shapes include bowls, perfumes, cologne bottles, sugars and creamers, ring trees, pitchers, vases, goblets, tumblers and covered boxes.

Orchid - Steuben

One product by Steuben was a transparent colored glass in a very light shade of amethyst. A second line, called "Oriental Orchid," was orchid-hued with white vertical stripes; the entire object was opalescent and coated both inside and out with a light lustre. This second type of glass is scarce, not signed, and made mostly in the form of vases, perfumes and candlesticks.

Oriental Jade - Steuben

This Steuben "Clouded Glass" is green in color with vertical stripes. Each object is opalescent with a lustred finish. It is doubtful if the ware was signed.

Oriental Poppy - Steuben

This glass has the same characteristics as Oriental Jade (see above). It is a rose-colored glass with vertical opalescent stripes. Both Oriental Jade and Oriental Poppy were fabricated into candlesticks, compotes, perfumes and vases.

Overshot - Sandwich

Overshot, or Frosted Ware, was produced at Sandwich for a period of about 20 years—from 1870 onward. It probably originated as a way of hiding defects in the surface of the glass; later, great quantities were manufactured as a general production item. A great variety of forms were produced including colognes, punch bowls, finger bowls and plates, cheese dishes, ice cream trays, jellies, footed nappies, baskets, celeries, lamps, tankards and assorted pitchers (some with ice bladders).

Two methods were used to achieve this glistening and attractive glassware with an unusual surface texture. In the first, the hot metal was rolled over a steel plate covered with minute glass particles. The gather was reheated in the furnace, melting the sharp corners on the fragments; the example was then expanded to its correct size. As this procedure took place, the glass being stretched developed smooth meandering tributaries. These vary in thickness from one object to the next; they should not be confused with the popular pressed pattern, Tree of Life.

In the second process, the worker expanded the red hot mass into its final form, and then the example was rolled in the glass fragments. No avenues or inroads exist in this type, and the surface is much sharper to the touch, making it difficult to wash and dry.

True Sandwich Overshot has the following traits: it is blown; the surface fragments are always clear; there was never any blending of colors, the object either was totally colored or clear crystal; and no fluted rims or signatures were used.

Pairpoint (See also Mount Washington Glass Company)

The Pairpoint Manufacturing Company was established in 1880 in New Bedford, Massachusetts, on Prospect Street, adjacent to the Mount Washington Glass Company. Thomas J. Pairpoint was the superintendent; Alexander H. Seabury, treasurer; and Edward W. Mandell, president. The two firms merged in July, 1894, and Pairpoint took over the glass manufacturing.

Because of financial problems in 1900, the company was reorganized as the Pairpoint Corporation and continued under that name until 1938. At its peak, the factory employed over 300 men as cutters, decorators, gaffers and helpers. In addition to cut, etched, and blown art glass, the factory made quadruple-plated silver items, including casket hardware; assorted brushes; epergnes; match safes; wine coolers; candlesticks; card receivers; ice pitcher sets; casters; communion objects; until there was a line of more than 200 items.

H FISHER

Lampshade painter at Pairpoint about 1900, scratched on the interior of a painted shade.

The glass and silver departments were sold to J. & B. Kenner in May, 1938. They, in turn, resold to a New Bedford Group in June, 1939.

Isaac N. Babbitt bought the glass factory and employed as manager, Robert M. Gundersen, a master glassblower from Pairpoint. Reorganized as the Gundersen Glass Works from 1939-1952, the firm specialized in hand-blown wares. After the death of Robert Gundersen in 1952, the factory became known as the Gundersen-Pairpoint Glass Works (1952-1957), reintroducing colored, cut and engraved products.

Trainee Robert Bryden, joining the firm in 1950, was elevated to sales manager in 1952, later becoming its manager to the present day. Antiquated equipment and deteriorating chimneys forced the firm to move to new quarters in East Wareham, Massachusetts (October, 1957 - February, 1958), and is now called the Pairpoint Glass Company, Incorporated.

Upon closing in 1958, Robert Bryden moved the Pairpoint

Glass Company to Spain (1958-1970), leasing facilities to fill the backlog of orders. Its present location was established in 1970 at Sagamore, Massachusetts, on the banks of the Cape Cod Canal. The firm makes both free and mold-blown objects, reviving an art famous on Cape Cod. Beautiful cutting and engraving adorn some objects. The observer who journeys to this site during business hours may watch glass being fabricated and have the privilege of purchasing one or many fine objects.

The present staff includes Alstair Ross, Robert Mason, David McDermott, Guy Maxwell, Bruce Cobb, Ed Poore, Carl Schweidenback, Bryant Silva (1972-1975) and others. Many limited editions, museum reproductions, presentation pieces, one-of-a-kind items and special custom orders have been filled by the factory.

Some noteworthy colors placed in production over the long evolutionary years included: flambeau (an opaque red orange), amethyst (in many hues), green (several shades), Ruby (gold and selenium), Canaria (vaseline/greenish yellow), cobalt blue (dark), marina blue (light), rosaria (cranberry), black, chrysopras (brown), Burmese (lemon yellow to shades of coral), Camellia (dusty rose to plum), opal (shiny and acidized), Peach Blow (dusty rose to white or pale blue), pink, Rose Amber (Amberina), Alice Blue (powder Blue) and others.

Stamped In Green

One article of note, Pairpoint Limoges China is highly cherished for its superior quality and artistic merit. Pairpoint had Limoges blanks manufactured according to their specified designs. These French pieces were elaborately decorated in New Bedford with florals, birds and exotic scenes. This china was in production for about 13 years. Similar views to Limoges may be found on Burmese, Royal Flemish and Crown Milano. Signed examples will be stamped "PAIRPOINT LIMOGES," with a crown between the words; or "PAIRPOINT MINTON," with the same type crown. Enameled or impressed numbers also have been viewed, such as "$\frac{2301}{216}$." The ware was manufactured in complete table settings, vases and ewers.

During the Pairpoint Manufacturing Company's evolution from 1880 to 1894, a number of buildings were constructed as business increased. The first building, constructed of brick in the spring of 1880, was three stories, measuring 120' x 40'. In 1881 the second edifice, three stories high, constructed of wood, 120' x 30' in area, appeared. A four-story brick structure, 150' x 40', was completed in 1882. Two other brick buildings were erected in 1890 and 1891. The first, measuring 40' x 80', was four stories high; the other, also four stories, was 260' x 40' in area.

Shades, globes and beautiful decorative lamps in more than 150 varieties were introduced to the public. When the Edison incandescent light bulb became popular, Pairpoint quickly filled the need and kept 10,000 of these in stock at all times.

Wares encountered and considered highly collectible are: brides' baskets in quadruple-plated holders, candelabras, candlesticks, console bowls, sugars and creamers, cologne and perfume bottles, epergnes, lamps, cookie and cracker jars, condiment sets, pitchers, whimseys, vases, wines and paperweights.

Paperweight Technique - Tiffany

This beautiful and rare glass fabricated by Tiffany, mostly in the forms of vases, changed color when it was reheated. Internal decorations in many colors showing florals (gladiola, morning glory, narcissus and crocus) and organic forms (leaves and tendrils) give the effect of peering into the water, viewing the designs underneath. An iridescence was used on the exterior layers that trap the design, as well as internal lustre.

Rather than refer to the object as being a paperweight type, it is best to simply call the example "Reactive Glass." Inlaid decorations consist of brown, pink, green, blue and yellow with the body of the object being anything from a gold ruby opalescent shade to a colorless crystal. Many forms are fully signed; some even have their original paper labels. This glass may be included in the finest collections. Some contemporary forms by very skilled artists do exist in this glass.

Pate de Verre - Steuben

The technique of forming glass objects from melted powdered glass is known as Pate de Verre. As early as 1500 B.C., the Egyptians made glass resembling minerals and semiprecious stones. In the 1920s and 1930s, Frederick Carder successfully revived this process, manufacturing limited figures, heads and panels.

A ceramic mold, after being fired and cooled, was filled with pulverized colored glass of many shades. As the temperature of the furnace was raised, the glass melted and shrank. This necessitated the addition of glass, which was cold; thus, many molds cracked, but the new pulverized glass flow would melt into the fissures, giving a marble-like appearance.

Visible imperfections, like fins from the excess glass creeping through the mold cracks, were easily ground; the example was then given a matte finish. Cameo designs, variegated finshes and marbleized pieces were made.

For Carder, these trial and experimental objects aided in developing techniques that would later assist in creating Diatreta. Diatreta, of course, required much more skill and patience to produce a satisfactory example.

Peach Blow - Gundersen, Mount Washington, New England, New Martinsville, Sandwich and Wheeling

One of the most desirable and rarest of the American Art Glass products is Mount Washington Peach Blow. It is a solid glass of very limited quantity that was not appreciated for its color during the era it was being fabricated. Made in New Bedford, Massachusetts, from 1886 to 1888 (patented July 20, 1886), this opaque ware shades from a delicate rose pink at the top to a light bluish gray. The color was achieved by using cobalt or copper oxide in small quantities instead of the uranium oxide in the Burmese formula. Most examples have an acid finish, which gives a soft matte effect. Florals and old English verses (both rare) add greatly to the intrinsic worth of such pieces. This type of glass is also termed Peach Bloom, or Peach Skin. This ware was marked with paper labels, but it would be very unlikely to find one intact today. Some shapes consist of rose bowls, toothpick holders, vases, creamers, salt and peppers, and cups and saucers.

New England Peach Blow, or "Wild Rose," was patented by Edward D. Libbey on March 2, 1886; the formula was created by Joseph Locke. A single layered glass, shading from deep rose hues at the top to an opaque white at the bottom, was only made at Cambridge, Massachusetts, until the factory moved in 1888. Fabricated in both a satin and glossy finish which is seldom decorated, it occurs in such shapes as vases, bowls, pitchers, finger bowls and whimseys. This glassware is not identified by way of signatures.

Robert Bryden, in April, 1953, announced at the Gundersen-Pairpoint Glass Works that Mount Washington Peach Blow would be hand-blown again, according to the original formula. Many one-of-a-kind examples were created, including cornucopias, tulip vases, nut dishes, compotes, cups and saucers, creamers and sugars, candlesticks, bon-bons and hat cigarette holders. H. Gilly Gulbranson was one of the craftsmen. Selling prices ranged from $5.00 for a compote or bon-bon dish, to $2.50 for a saucer or a hat cigarette holder. These revival and experimental pieces are extremely collectible and highly cherished today.

In 1886, J.H. Hobbs, Brockunier and Company, began producing facsimiles of Mrs. Mary Morgan's Chinese vase (reign of K'ang Hsi, 1662-1722), which sold for $18,000.00 on March 8, 1886. The Wheeling glass is constructed of two layers—the lining being an opal white glass. The outer layer shades from a mahogany or fuschia red at the top to a yellow gold at the bottom. Occurring in both polished and acid finishes, some examples have a molded design called Wheeling Drape, which resembles perpendicular swagged curtain folds.

Sandwich Peach Blow, a single glass layer, has a delicate pale pink shading. Pieces often have a mold-blown swirl pattern, an acid finish, and sometimes applied work, like an acidized thorny branch bail handle. This work was never marked.

New Martinsville Peach Blow (Muranese) is a single layered glass that has been blown in a mold to create a pattern. Opal shading, iridescence, yellow, orange and coral coloration predominate. Many hues exist including: Sunburst (pink), Sunglow (yellow), Sunlite (white), Sunrise (rubina), Sunray (amber), and Sundown (blue). The glass is both brittle and fragile. Made into vases, pitchers, frilled bowls, and brides' baskets with silver plated holders, some examples were also decorated with ornate enameled designs. New Martinsville is not marked.

Facsimiles of Mount Washington Peach Skin and Peach Blow labels

Peacock-Feather · Tiffany

Formed into bowls, vases and plates of varying shapes, this iridescent glass was developed by Arthur J. Nash for Louis C. Tiffany. This rare and esteemed glass resembles the eye and overall design found in an iridescent peacock feather. The in-

volved process called for precision and skill, imbedding the colored pieces to form the eye. Through reheating, manipulating and enlarging the form, a combed feather effect was created that is both beautiful and convincingly conceived. Examples most frequently are signed and numbered.

Peppermint Stick · Mount Washington

This little known clear crystal glass has a flint quality, is acidized on the exterior and shiny on the interior. An outer lip of applied rosaria cut in a picket fence design appears on all examples; some wide diametered objects have a 24 pointed star cut on their bases. Examples may also be found with additional cutting (scarce); some attractive specimens are set in quadruple holders. Forms likely to be discovered are bowls, creamers and sugars. This glass was never signed.

Phoenix

Much confusion exists between the articles manufactured by the Phoenix Glass Company, Monaca, Pennsylvania, and the Consolidated Lamp and Glass Company, Coraopolis, Pennsylvania. Glass of the same type was made by Consolidated in 1926 and Phoenix in 1941.

Consolidated called their sculptured glass in crystal or blue satin finishes Martele'. Some designs occurring in vases, bowls and candlesticks are Owl, Pine Cone, Katydid, Fish, Love Bird, Martele', Dogwood, Sea Gull, Black Berry and Honeysuckle. Prices ranged from 60¢ each to $4.50. Both companies were influenced by French Lalique glass.

Another line created by Consolidated around 1940 was termed the Dancing Nymph Line. The glass was made in French Crystal (smooth satin with clear figures), and Satin (an acid finish all over). The assortment is known in clear, blue, pink and blue green. The set included 18 plates (6", 8", and 10"), 8 cups and 8 saucers, 8 sherbets, 10 bowls (4½" and 8"), 8 cocktails, 8 goblets, and 4 vases (5¼" and 5½"). There were 72 pieces in the set. Selling prices for the assorted French Crystal and Satin were $38.00 and $26.00, respectively.

The Phoenix Glass Company catalog of 1942 described their decorative sculptured artware as being produced by four different processes: 1) Sculptured Cameo (Series 300) raised white translucence and fused ceramic background colors, 2) Sculptured crystal (Series 200) crystal glass details and soft background hues, 3) Sculptured Pearl Lustre (Series 400) frosted milk white background and raised Mother-of-Pearl lustre, and 4) Sculptured Brilliante (Series 600) fine crystal figures on an etched field. Prices for colorful and well ornamented pieces have continued to rise in recent years. Occasional gold or silver foil paper labels intact designate these products as Phoenix Art Sculptured Ware. The logos consist of the Phoenix bird in flight, with the words "ART SCULPTURED WARE" above and the word "PHOENIX." A second variation has the word "PHOENIX" on the left side of the label, and "SCULPTURED GLASSWARE" to the right.

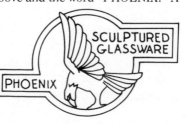

The third variety, an oblong white paper label marked "REUBEN WARE," was an example of a Martel'e mold produced by Phoenix and named for Reuben Haley.

Again, the shapes of this Phoenix line are mostly vases in assorted shapes; although bowls, dishes, covered boxes, candleholders and ash trays were also made. Some patterns are: Aster, Bachelor Button, Philodendron, Strawberry, Thistle, Dancing Girl, Zodiac, Freesia, Wild Geese, Daisy, Wild Rose, Madonna, Lily, Cosmos, Fern, Bluebell, Jonquil, Primrose, Star Flower, Pine Cone, Tiger Lily and Diving Girl.

One key, besides the differences in the two companies' molds to establishing the object's origin, is the stained color and how it was utilized. There are a few exceptions to this rule, but generally, Phoenix glass has a stained ground and raised white figures, while Consolidated colored their designs and left a white background.

Special fired stains found on some Phoenix glassware include: Taupe (dark brown), Coral (pale pink), Tan (light yellow brown), Cedar Rose (brownish red), Sea Green (deep green), Light Blue (light sky blue), and Slate Gray (deep gray). The quality and tone of each hue varies slightly from one example to the next.

Another valid way of separating the wares of the two firms is the color of the glass itself. Technicians at Phoenix did not possess the formulas or the ability to create unusual colors; thus, it may positively be assumed that custard, ruby, gold decorated and cased examples originated at Consolidated.

Pigeon Blood

A vivid and scarce transparent glassware produced at the end of the 1800s, Pigeon Blood is characterized as being blood red, having a red orange hue in bright light. One firm that produced this glass was the Consolidated Lamp and Glass Company. Production items, some molded in patterns, enameled, or in silver plated frames, include: bottles, brides' baskets, butter dishes, cracker jars, lamps, muffineers, pitchers, syrups, toothpick holders, wine sets, cruets, pickle castors, vases, compotes, salt and peppers, celery vases, candlesticks and goblets.

Production pressed patterns seen are Hobnail, Bulging Loop, Torquay, Diamond Quilt, Fine Rib, Vertical Rib and others. Examples may have scalloped and beaded edges. Most objects have a shiny finish; the glass is never signed, but one sample will aesthetically add to a collection.

Pink Slag - Indiana Tumbler and Goblet Company

Known as "Marble," "Slag," or "Agate," this opaque pressed glass was made by the Indiana Tumbler and Goblet Company, Greentown, Indiana. The rare pattern known as Inverted Fan and Feather shows a marbleized mixture shading from pink to white; deep colors command premium prices, dependent upon overall tone and density. Having been produced in a variety of tableware shapes from 1880 to 1900, one might discover bowls, pitchers, sugars and creamers, tumblers, butter and sauce dishes, compotes, cruets, punch cups, salts and peppers, spooners and toothpick holders. The miniature lamp in the shape of a swan is a great rarity for the advanced collector.

All examples have a raised scroll and floral pattern; some have the addition of four ribbed feet, such as the pitcher and the covered sugar and open creamer. Rims usually consist of large and small scallops, and ear-shaped handles have a beaded decoration.

This pattern was also executed in custard, opalescent (blue and yellow), and iridescent carnival (rare). Manufactured by the Northwood Glass Company, Indiana, Pennsylvania, 1898-1919, their colored and white mixture was called mosaic. The ware is very attractive in custard with its gilt relief on the raised designs.

Plated Amberina - New England

Plated Amberina, a rare art glass type, was of limited production. Patented on June 15, 1886, by the New England Glass Company, Cambridge, Massachusetts, it is characterized by vertical raised ribs running the length of the exterior. The glass has a glossy finish and is infrequently found with an original paper label affixed marked "N.E. Glass Co. 1886 Aurora." Examples, when found, vary somewhat in shading, although normally they shade from a deep fuchsia to a yellow gold at the base. Applied amber handles are plain. This ware is brittle and was difficult to manufacture; thus, little has survived in excellent condition. It is similar to Wheeling Peach Blow in appearance, but the molded ribs and creamy translucent opal lining (often with a bluish cast) aid in differentiating between the two.

Edward D. Libbey's patent called for an opalescent glass to be plated with a gold ruby. The pattern mold would create the vertical ribbed effect. A portion of the object was then reheated to yield the deep rose red hues. Items produced in this ware comprise pitchers, bowls, finger bowls, syrups, creamers, lemonades, punch cups, vases, tumblers, toothpick holders, spooners, and salts and peppers.

Unfortunately, this choice and expensive glass is being reproduced in an attempt to trick the anxious collector. Copies have rough pontils, contemporary shapes and poor coloration. Observe, especially, the lining color and its opalescence and the tendency for the fuchsia red top to run, not blend, into the rich yellow panels between the ribs, creating a murky raspberry swirl effect.

Pomona - New England

This feminine mold-blown and most delicate of the American Art Glass types was patented by Joseph Locke in 1885. Made only by the New England Glass Company, Cambridge, Massachusetts, the product utilized the goddess of fruit in mythology as its name.

Formed of this resonant glass crystal, "first grind/ground" was made for 13 months. The piece was covered with an acid-resist solution (wax), and then etched with concentric overlapping circles by hand, using a stylus needle. An acid bath quickly wore away the exposed surfaces, so they appeared like etched ice. Scalloped designs radiating from the top rims on most pieces have a gold metallic stain, which is a dilute nitrate of silver. Some blown examples also have patterns, such as diamond quilt and inverted thumbprint, upon which are etched stained, colored, nature motifs in amber, blue and vermillion. Etched patterns are: Pansy, Blueberry, Butterfly, Leaf, Cornflower, Strawberry, Fern, Rivulet, Bee, an Ear of Corn, or a Sheaf of Wheat, or a combination of these.

To save time and money, a quicker and cheaper method, termed "second grind/ground," was perfected and made after June, 1886, and well into the early 1900s. Acid-resist was affixed on the glass, and applied acid etched only the exposed surfaces, giving them a pebbly speckled effect like stippled ice.

Midwestern Pomona, about 1900, is a molded pattern glass like Pomona, with a frosted or sand-blasted finish. These shallow surface finishes were often done in a haphazard manner. Also termed pseudo-Pomona, examples will have gold stained surfaces, possibly enameled floral decors in many colors, and even twisted and frosted rope handles on some pitchers. Do not be fooled by this type of glass!

The quality of Pomona is determined by the condition of the original coloring and the artistry involved in the work. "First grind/ground" pieces with bright decorations usually prove to be more interesting and collectible. Stains will be removed easily with continued washing and the use of harsh and abrasive detergents. This glass is highly sought, especially decorated examples with unusual bright patterns. The glass is not signed and prices continue to climb.

Pomona Green - Steuben

A medium-hued green in the Steuben line, this color possesses an attractive brilliance and a rich bell quality when tapped. Oxide of uranium was used as a coloring agent to create a green, oily quality. Some Acid Cutback items, plus vases, bottles, candlesticks, sugars and creamers, and goblets were designed; some are found signed. Amber, Rosa, wisteria and amethyst were a few colors used as contrasts for handles, feet or other attachments.

Quartz - Steuben

Quartz glass, developed in the '20s by Frederick Carder for the Steuben Glass Works, has a satin finish; some objects display tiny bubbles throughout the metal (Cintra glass), while larger bubbles would indicate a batch of Cluthra glass.

The molten, colorless glass was plunged first into cold water, shattering the surface with a cracked effect. Reheated, the cracks would fuse to a degree; then the bubble, being heated again, was rolled over colored, powdered glass and cased with clear glass. Interesting variations occur with acid-etched, floral designs, sometimes complemented with the addition of handles, applied feet, leaves, trailing vines, etc. Highlights were produced by polishing all of the raised surfaces with a rotating buffer and pumice.

Some examples are found with rough pontils and the acid-etched Steuben Fleur-de-Lis mark on their bases or sides. The color of the glass determined such names as alabaster, amethyst, green, blue, peach, yellow and rose—all members of the Quartz family.

Quezal **Quezal**

The Quezal Art Glass and Decorating Company was founded in 1901 by Martin Bach, Sr., and Thomas Johnson at Brooklyn, New York. Both men had worked for Tiffany. Some of this fine art glass possesses dramatic iridescence with the colors blue, gold, white and green dominating. Striking designs were created on the outer surface and marvered into the body.

These forms are similar to Tiffany's Favrile and Steuben's Aurene Glass. Other lines included Gold Lustre glass; Agate glass; forms with pulled-up feather and peacock eye design; a pattern of leaves, flowers and trailing, applied shell decorations; heart and clinging vine; and advanced examples with well-engraved silver deposit embellishments.

Martin Bach, Sr., used the formulas he had learned while working for Tiffany to manufacture his Quezal glass. Some of his skilled gaffers and glassblowers included Thomas Johnson, William Wiedebine (gatherer), Percy Britton (decorator), James Gross (gaffer), Paul Frank (gaffer), Emil Larson, and T.C. (Conrad) Vahlsing (gaffer, and Bach's son-in-law).

The name "Quezal" was trademarked on October 28, 1902. Examples were numbered and had the word "QUEZAL" engraved in silver stylus block letters on the polished pontils. Some early pieces were not signed and are often confused with the work of Tiffany and Steuben. Around 1907, another trademark printed on a paper label was conceived. The colorful glass was named for the brilliant, long plumed Quetzal bird of Central America. Advertisements compared the lustred beauty of the glass to the exotic bird.

The factory, located at 1609 Metropolitan Avenue, Fresh Pond Road, Brooklyn, New York, had two furnaces that supplied 18 pots of glass daily—certainly a limited amount. Some production items included a great variety of vases and lamp shades, bowls, compotes, plates, nut dishes, salt dips, tumblers, candlesticks and baskets with twisted rope handles.

Between 1905 and 1918, the Quezal Art Glass and Decorating Company experienced monetary problems. In 1918, the officers of the Quezal works included Martin Bach, Sr., president; Conrad Vahlsing, vice-president; and Martin Bach, Jr., secretary. Mr. Bach, Sr., had bought out all other original incorporators by 1918.

In 1920, Conrad Vahlsing and Paul Frank departed to open a small shop near Elmhurst, New York, producing "Lustre Art Wares." The glass is exactly the same as Quezal and was fabricated until 1929.

With the demise of Martin Bach, Sr., in 1924, the firm was reorganized by Dr. John Ferguson and a group of philanthropists, who purchased the outstanding stock. Only one shop now produced Quezal art glass; the firm finally closed in 1925.

Martin Bach, Jr., journeyed to the Vineland Flint Glass Works in New Jersey. He was joined there by William Wiedebine, Percy Britton, and Emil Larson. At Vineland, they continued to make fancy Art Nouveau glassware, using Bach's formulas.

Rainbow and Rainbow Satin Mother-of-Pearl - Mount Washington (See also Iris, and Mother-of-Pearl Satin)

Occurring in both Mother-of-Pearl Satin and Satin glass, these types by Mount Washington display all conventional aspects, with the addition of alternating pink, blue and yellow stripes. Popular patterns represented in the Mother-of-Pearl variety include swirl, raindrop, herringbone, moire' and diamond quilted. The Rainbow shading may be either vivid or very subtle.

This rare glass, in the American variety, was never signed; some English examples may be marked, "Patent." A premium priced and fragile art glass with shapes likely to be seen are lamps, rose bowls, pitchers and tumblers, ewers, baskets, vases and covered boxes. Shiny and satinized, clear crystal was used for the application of feet, handles and ribbon edging.

Reading Artistic Glass Works

Some of this country's most collectible art glass was produced in the 1880s by a little known and short-lived glassworks in Reading, Berks County, Pennsylvania. The Reading Artistic Glass Works began operations on Saturday, October 18, 1884. Almost exactly two years later, it was out of business, a victim of economics; but during the two years of its existence, this company turned out clear and colored wares comparable to some of the best produced in much better known factories.

Utilitarian and decorative pieces were made in Amberina, opalescent wares, craquelle glass and clear flint. Although most pieces were free-blown, some were mold-blown. Patterns included Hobnail, Expanded Diamond, Bull's-Eye and Ribbed. The company made wine ewers; pitchers; two-handled vases; and jugs with ice bladders, similar in shapes and patterns to those made at the famed Boston and Sandwich Glass Works. Others featured spiral striping, looping, splashing and threading, associated with English Nailsea glass. Since none of the company's work was signed, it would be possible to mistake some items for those made at the Clichy and Baccarat sites in France and for some of the work done at Launay-Hautin. Recognizing the basic shapes is the key to identifying Reading's output.

The Reading Artistic Glass Works also manufactured gas shades, lamp globes and bases, spittoons, wine trays, flower pots, whimsical canes, chamber sets, handled baskets, fruit dishes, napkin rings and punch cups. The quality of its work, judged by contemporary standards, was high.

Lewis Kremp financed the building of the glassworks; he also owned the plot of ground where the building was constructed. Kremp was born October 26, 1820, in Saar-Union, Bas-Rhin, Alsace, France. He was active in branches of real estate, banking and insurance. The Kremps had five children and resided at 142 North Ninth Street, Reading, Pennsylvania.

Joseph P. Kremp, born September 17, 1854, worked for his father for a while; later he became notary public in Reading. He also served as treasurer during the organization of the glass company. Some sources contended that he was manager of the glassworks; this has never been verified.

This glasshouse employed Joseph and Adolph Bournique, emigrants from the Vosges Mountain district of Alsace-Lorraine, as its agents to hire employees, operate the factory and sell the finished products at a profit. Ten glassmakers and four helpers were also employed. Franklin Mourot was one of the glassblowers. Adolph Bournique, Joseph's son, was the superintendent.

Located at Ninth and Laurel Streets, the 65′ square building was two and one-half stories high, had a Mansard roof, and was part stone and part frame. There were three furnaces; one had a capacity of 15,000 pounds of glass in a 24 hour period. The crucibles were shipped from New York and installed on or about October 10, 1884. The "glory hole" furnace had six openings in which the glassblowers made colored glass objects. The "Lehr" furnace, used to temper articles, was 40′ long and 5′ wide.

Local sand was not used; instead fine white sand was shipped from Berkshire, Massachusetts. This sand was said to be one of the best deposits in the world.

The Reading Eagle, for September 10, 1884, reported that Joseph Bournique "had the reputation of being the best glass blower in the United States. He worked in factories in Boston; Connecticut; Philipsburg, Beaver County, Pennsylvania, and elsewhere." His method of manufacture was a lost art, known only by one other person - a manufacturer in Pittsburgh.

In an advertising circular dated November, 1884, Joseph Bournique and Company described their fine wares produced in all hues. Opalescent colors included violet, canary, turquoise, green, pink, white and sapphire; flint colors used were green, light blue, ruby, amethyst, amber gold, white, peacock blue and black.

A specialty type at Reading was a colored glass mottled on the surface with opaque white. Examples seen include black, and opalescent (pink, turquoise, and yellow). The factory also competed with the Boston and Sandwich factory by producing a novelty opalescent craquelle glass. Some examples may appear to have a slight overshot surface texture, but this is not always true of Reading's production. The wares were handled by distributors in Boston, Philadelphia, New York and Baltimore.

Some bases had rough broken-off pontils; others were ground and polished. None of the productions were gilded or enameled, although gas shades were often acid-etched with fine designs. Occasional examples were cased internally with an opal finish.

Rosa - Steuben

Produced in limited quantities in the '20s, this Carder color is a very subtle, pale, shaded rose amber. It was used predominately in conjunction with clear crystal and Pomona Green. Wines and goblets might be clear with the addition of Rosa stems; sugars and creamers in Rosa have Pomona Green handles, and candlesticks and bowls with the added feature of Pomona green feet make an attractive contrast. Selenium added to amber glass yielded this scarce color. An object entirely in Rosa, like a perfume bottle or powder jar would be a pleasing find.

Rosaline - Steuben

This pink jade glass having a soft rose color was almost without exception, accentuated with Alabaster. Rosaline has a cloudy appearance and yet is quite appealing to the eye. Paper labels or acid-etched Fleur-de-Lis signatures are the ones to seek. Examples may be further decorated with copper wheel engravings or the application of finials, feet, handles, rings, etc. in Alabaster glass. Complete dinner services, vases, console sets, covered jars, bowls and even acid cutback items may be discovered.

Rosaria - Gundersen-Pairpoint

During the Gundersen-Pairpoint era, a very attractive, transparent, colored crystal appearing much like Cranberry, was produced. This glass appears in the shapes of compotes, low and footed console bowls, covered vases, candlesticks and even paperweights. Some examples were blown in a diamond quilted pattern; others include clear feet, swirled or controlled bubble ball connectors, and objects cased in Rosaria, then cut in the Adelaide or other designs.

Rose Amber - Mount Washington, New England (See also Amberina)

Amberina, originating through the efforts of Joseph Locke at the New England Glass Company, was patented on July 24, 1883. The highly successful, shaded transparent glass was copied by the Mount Washington Glass Company. This patent infringement resulted in a lawsuit, whereby Mount Washington peacefully settled, thus they termed their product Rose Amber.

This glass was patented on May 25, 1886, and a paper label was designed to be attached to each example. Today, it would be a rarity to find an example with its label still intact.

Rose Amber shades from a ruby hue to a delicate amber. The batch contained oxide of gold and the metal in the pot was an amber shade. It is not until the glass is reheated, after being blown into a desired shape, that the transformation occurs, and the ruby coloration appears. Some desirable forms to consider are vases, syrups, spooners, pitchers, mugs, tumblers, cruets, sugars and creamers, bowls, covered butter dishes, condiment sets, toothpick holders and punch cups.

Rose Du Barry - Steuben

This subtle and delicate violet hue, not to be confused with Rosaline, was utilized as a liner to either crystal or Alabaster glass. Table service, boudoir items, threaded examples and an occasional acid cutback piece might be discovered in this scarce technique.

Rouge Flambe' - Steuben

This rare art glass type, consisting of fewer than one hundred examples, was produced by Frederick Carder about 1916-1917. Its color, ranging from tomato red to orange, and even coral pink, has a bright surface texture and was not acidized or iridized.

The color was inspired by decorations on Chinese famille rose porcelains, and the bowl shapes are copies of Chinese ceramic pieces. The most exacting controls of the batch were required to create this brilliant color, which proved to be fragile, causing straining and cracking of the glass.

Cadmium sulphate and selenium were used to produce this little known product; the addition of minute, metallic flecks of chrome oxide gave the ware a pearly finish. A constant temperature proved to be the critical factor in the making of this glass. Two extremely rare examples exist with Gold Aurene decorations about the bodies of the items.

Royal Flemish - Mount Washington

Royal Flemish, manufactured by only one firm, the Mount Washington Glass Company, New Bedford, Massachusetts, is a semi-transparent glass with an acid finish. Albert Steffin patented this unique method for decorating glass on February 27, 1894. Characteristic of this glass are the exotic and heavy, gold relief designs done in the random ribbed panels, to imitate the divisions of a stained glass window. Stained, transparent tans, browns and maroons are the predominate colors incorporated in the various divisions. All enameling is extremely fine and in high relief.

Exceedingly beautiful designs include Coin and Roman Head medallions, Guba ducks, Fish and Shell, Camel and Rider, Floral designs, Coats of Arms, Rampant Lions, Scrolls and others. Glass of this nature is for the advanced collector and is highly prized. Royal Flemish is found in the following shapes: pitchers, ewers, vases, cracker jars and occasionally in lamps.

Most pieces are not signed, but the glass is so easily recognized that this fact should cause little concern; also, the ware has not been reproduced because of the cost and artistry involved. When signed, the capital letters "R" and "F" are found enclosed within a dark red diamond. The two letters have a common main stem and a number may be located directly below the diamond. Some few examples may still have a paper label intact, showing a double-headed eagle in its center, with the wording "ROYAL FLEMISH" above in a circular fashion, and "MT.W.G.CO." below the eagles.

Paper Label   Red Enameled Mark

Rubina

Rubina, or Rubina Crystal, also spelled Rubena, is a shaded glassware that was very popular in the 1880s. Shading from ruby or deep cranberry at the top to clear crystal at its base, this ware was produced by numerous American firms using a variety of techniques. Rubina was first manufactured by George A. Duncan and Sons, Pittsburgh, Pennsylvania, in 1885. It is also believed that the Dorflinger Glass Works, White Mills, Pennsylvania, made this type of glass.

An already formed, clear, crystal object was flashed on its inner surface to achieve this effect. Some examples show a very gradual blending from the color to the clear; others reveal an abrupt line of demarcation.

Numerous artistic forms may be found including vases, bowls, biscuit jars, carafes, candlesticks, brides' baskets, boxes, covered butter dishes, cruets, pitchers, syrups, tumblers, sugar shakers, perfumes, celeries and jam jars. Some examples have enameled decor; some are set in quadruple-plated holders; still others have glass patterns, including Inverted Thumbprint, Honeycomb, Diamond Quilt and Ribbing. Overshot glass of this nature is rather difficult to locate. Rubina glass was not signed.

Rubina Verde

Like Rubina, Rubina Verde was manufactured in competition with Amberina, which was reheated to achieve its colorful shading. This glass shades from a ruby or deep cranberry, at its top to an aqua (green), or a greenish yellow, at its base. Made in the same fashion as Rubina, this type was fabricated by the Sandwich Glass Company, while Hobbs, Brockunier and Company is credited with being the first to make it in the late 1880s. Typical forms include brides' baskets, cruets, bowls, decanters, pitchers, tumblers, vases, syrups, salts and peppers, sweetmeat dishes and finger bowls.

Examples may have been mold-blown and then expanded further, or pattern-molded. Basic patterns consist of swirls, ribbing, Inverted Thumbprint, Hobnail, Diamond Quilted, Honeycomb, Coin Spot, Daisy and Button, Royal Ivy and Royal Oak. Some decorative forms were enameled florals, applied techniques, opalescence, ruffled rims, cutting, and silver or quadruple-plated holders, on occasion.

Ruby - Gundersen-Pairpoint

An intensely brilliant red, transparent and of flint quality, this color is difficult to collect in assorted shapes since it is scarce. Ruby was utilized for handled urns, cornucopia vases, footed and covered compotes, vases, swan-shaped dishes, plates and others. Controlled bubble ball and swirl connectors, applied feet and finials, all in clear crystal, present a pleasing contrast to the viewer. Their Ruby Twist glass, showing alternating ribbons of red and clear glass swirling from the centers of hollow and flat objects, is indeed striking and uncommon. This type of glass was made from the 1920s. Most Ruby glass examples have finely ground pontils, but are never signed.

Sandwich

When we think in terms of beauty, charm and variety, the famous Boston and Sandwich Glass Company comes to mind. Founded at Sandwich, Cape Cod, Massachusetts, as the Sandwich Glass Manufactory in 1825 by Deming Jarves, the firm was incorporated in 1826 as the Boston and Sandwich Glass Company.

Molded glass from the 1825-1840 era became known as Early Sandwich Glass. Under Hiram Dillaway, lacy glass was manufactured, plus paperweights, Venetian and English type wares, and (after 1830) some opaline wares were fabricated. Jarves left the firm in 1858, and the factory was closed in 1888 when the union urged management to share more profits with the workers, and the management locked out the workers on January 2, 1888.

During its active 63 year history, the firm averaged 100,000 pounds of glass per week. Other firms to manufacture glass on the Cape would include the Cape Cod Glass Works (1859-1869), Vasa Murrhina Art Glass Company (1883-1885), Sandwich Co-operative Glass Company (1888-1891), Electrical Glass Corporation, the Boston and Sandwich Glass Company II, the Boston and Sandwich Glass Company III, the Sandwich Glass Company and the Alton Manufacturing Company (1907-1908), known for its Trevaise glass. All of these factories, including the original Sandwich firm, went out of business for one or more of the following reasons: labor disputes, cheaper glass competition from the midwest, the glass was not well received by the public, glass cracking problems, financial problems, poor management, freight charges, raw material costs and furnace failures.

Blown three-mold, early pressed and lacy, cup plates, salts, miniatures, candlesticks and lamps, vases, water and wine sets, pattern glass, paperweights, cut, engraved, etched, threaded, frosted, overshot, fancy art glass types, and miscellaneous wares were produced. "Lacy Sandwich," a pressed pattern flint glass, was perhaps the choice of all their products. This fine quality glass is usually heavier than other types, and refracts light through the stipples that serve as a background for the main design. Over 1,000 patterns and variants have been listed.

Some names associated with the Boston and Sandwich Glass Company included: C.C.P. Waterman (geologist); C.E.L. Brinkeroff (salesroom supervisor - 1876); George L. Fessenden (director); Henry Francis Spurr (manager - 1882); George Franklin Lapham (glassblower); James Shevlin (glassworker); Francis Kern (glassworker); Nicholas Lutz, Michael Grady, James Grady (glass workers and threaders); and Thomas Dean (glassworker). Other glass artisans were: Charles E. Brady, Ezra G. Hamblin, John B. Louvet, Patrick F. Mahoney, John McNamee, Richard J. Murphy, John Murray, Peter Rosenberg and John Swansey.

Individuals interested in this type of glass should tour the very fine Sandwich Glass Museum located in the town of the same name in Massachusetts. Actual on-site viewing will allow for the authentication of any doubtful glass; otherwise, it should perhaps be correctly referred to as "Sandwich type."

Satin

An opaque glass coming in a variety of shapes, forms and colors, Satin glass may be found in both mold and free-blown designs. Some examples are in the forms of milk and opal glass; colored examples may have a white lining. All types have a pleasant velvet touch. A treatment of hydrofluoric acid was used to achieve this effect. Few pieces are ever found with a signature.

This attractive finishing technique, found on many glass wares, was especially popular during the 1880s and through the turn of the century. Much Satin glass was manufactured in this country by several West Virginia, Pennsylvania, New England and New York State factories. A variety of useful and decorative pieces include: brides' baskets, bowls, bottles, handled baskets, vases, lamps, biscuit jars, compotes, sugars and creamers, cruets, ewers, salts and peppers, rose bowls, pitchers, tumblers, toothpick holders, muffineers and epergnes.

Applied glass decorations, mold blown-out figures, intricate enamelings, silver mountings, ruffled edges, and occasional candy-striped designs are the major garnishments that may be viewed. Colors can be in the form of one basic tone, or in two or more subtle shadings of any of the following: rose, salmon, blue, pink, white, apricot, black, cranberry, orange, lime, lemon, brown, lavender and others.

Reproduced as early as 1930, examples are coming from England and Italy. English pieces of a better quality are lighter than their Italian counterparts. Definite indications of a reproduction are chalky linings, rough pontils, small reeded handles and poorly crimped edges. Some item are very rough to the touch, while others may have a satin feel very close to that found on authentic objects.

Sculptured - Steuben

The term "Sculptured" ware, in the sense that Frederick Carder intended, was glass types formed by investiture casting. These include Cire Perdue, Diatreta and Pate de Verre. (See these categories)

Sea Foam Green - Steuben

This rare hue by Steuben is an unusual and delicately tinted green with escaping overtones of blue. Viewed from several feet, the glass actually appears to suggest a wisp of blue, but under full light and closer inspection, its true nature will be revealed.

Selenium Red - Steuben

This color suggests a vibrant red used by Carder for vases and drinking vessels; sometimes it is ribbed or engraved in the Vineyard pattern. Selenium combined with cadium sulphide or zinc sulphide aided in producing this beautiful and very scarce transparent lead crystal. Some examples are found with a "Steuben" acid script signature.

Silver Deposit

During its era of popularity, Silver Deposit was referred to as Solid Deposit, Silver Overlay, Silver Inlay or Silver-Electroplated glass. In style from 1890 until the 1920s, this art glass technique involved the deposit of thick metallic silver on glass by means of electrolysis.

The glass object was painted with the intended design by coating it with a wash. The mixture consisted of borax, oxide of lead, sand, nitrate of potash, white arsenic and phosphate of lime added to powdered silver flux and then mixed with turpentine to form the wash.

Placed in a kiln, the piece was fired and thus the conductive material was set. Silver could now be deposited on the coated areas by submerging the object in an electroplating bath.

After the silver had been deposited, it was buffed and polished. Often objects were also handsomely hand-chased with attractive designs. Some articles are marked (impressed) listing the silver content and the manufacturer's name. Signed examples likely to be discovered include Alvin Manufacturing Company, Rockwell and Gorham.

Colored Silver Overlay in green, ruby and cranberry glass commands premium prices. Some typical shapes include colognes, perfumes, bottles, vases, cruets, pitchers, compotes, tumblers, whiskey decanters, salt dips, covered honey jars and liqueur sets.

Silvered

This heavy and decorative quality glassware resulted when a solution of silver nitrate was placed between the two walls of an object and then capped at the base. In the case of European examples, a metallic disk sometimes exists stamped "Hale Thomson, Patent, London," or "Varnish & Co., London, Patent."

Next the outer crystal covering was plated with a shade of red, blue, green, yellow or purple glass. This outer layer was then cut away to reveal artistic workmanship and the eye-appealing silver beneath. A noteworthy London manufacturer of this glass was E. Varnish and Company who patented the process on December 19, 1849.

William Leighton at the New England Glass Company, Cambridge, Massachusetts, patented on January 16, 1855, their process for making silvered glass door knobs. Union Glass Works, Somerville and the Boston Silver Glass Company, Cambridge, (both in Massachusetts) patented on April 4, 1865, their process for making hollow silvered glass items.

Other American factories known to have manufactured this type of ware were the Mount Washington Glass Company, New Bedford, Massachusetts; Dithridge and Company, Pittsburgh, Pennsylvania; the Brooklyn Flint Glass Company, Brooklyn, New York; and the Boston and Sandwich Glass Works, Sandwich, Massachusetts.

This glassware was produced in a variety of shapes, will not discolor, is of a fine quality and relatively difficult and expensive to acquire.

Silverina - Steuben

Silverina glass, a product of the '20s, involved covering transparent colored or crystal glass with mica flecks. Blown into a diamond-shaped mold which created indentations, the object was covered with a clear crystal layer and given its final form.

The mica flakes vary in size and density giving the glass a favorable radiance in any type of lighting. The flecks of mica take on the same hue as the glass covering them.

Occurring in bowls, fan and footed vases, compotes, candlesticks, goblets and other decorative examples, this glass may be signed. A matte finish was used on occasion and some pieces have a lightly lustred finish. This glass is relatively scarce.

Sinclaire

The incorporation of the H.P. Sinclaire Company, Corning, New York, was announced on May 14, 1904. Henry Purdon Sinclaire had been associated with T.G. Hawkes Glass Company since 1883, serving as its secretary and vice president. His father was an original stockholder of the Corning Glass Works, and his brother, William Sinclaire, was secretary of the same firm.

The two-story brick factory measured 60' wide by 120' long. It was completed around September, 1904, employing about 200 workers. Marvin Olcott, Sr., vice president of the company was also a principal investor. All blanks were purchased from the Corning Glass Works, Dorflinger, Pairpoint, Baccarat and others in the early years.

A specialty of the firm was their engraved glass of highest quality; cut glass was also produced. Sinclaire's love of nature is aptly shown in the intaglio fruit and flower patterns. Early examples were sharp and closely cut; later to save costs, large areas were left uncut revealing the clarity and quality of the glass.

Onward from 1920, Sinclaire manufactured its own colored and crystal blanks; about 1926 engraving was replaced by acid-etched designs. An acid-etched stamp showing an "S" surrounded by a laurel wreath interrupted by two shields was their insignia. This mark was only placed on perfect examples.

Colors most often found associated with this glass are ruby, blue, green, amber, and of course—their fine clear crystal.

Since shapes and colors used by Sinclaire and Steuben may be very similar or even identical, it becomes rather difficult to distinguish between the two. Steuben used an "S" trademark engraved with a diamond point after 1932; this should not be confused with Sinclaire's acid stamp. While much of Steuben's and Sinclaire's outputs were never signed, the pontils on the two types of glass should help solve the dilemma. Carder relied upon a varied number of pontil marks to complete his work (rough, waffle, pad and polished). This last type is usually about ½" in diameter, while Sinclaire's concave pontils range from 1" to 1½" in diameter.

Collectors of engraved patterns should seek the following: Number 1023; Bengal; Queens; Adam; Westminster; Baronial; Apples, Pears and Grapes, and Flute and Panel Border. Signed examples are valued as much as 50% above unsigned examples.

Many of Sinclaire's patterns appear like other glass cutting firms of that era. However the following designs were patented: Palm Leaf and Rosettes, Holly, Bird in a Cage, Wreath and Flower and Greek Key with variations. Cutting produced by this company varies from the simple interlacing motifs to rich and deeply incised patterns. Additional cut patterns include Medallion and Diamond, Hobstar, Intaglio Grape, Engraved Roses, Floral Leaf and Buds, and Strawberry Diamond and Fan.

Many outstanding articles may be located in the shape of bowls, vases, console sets, boxes, candlesticks, pitchers, tumblers, plates, cordials, relish dishes, trays and teapots. A choice example of signed Sinclaire glass is a worthwhile part of a collection.

Smith Brothers

A very exclusive decorating department was set up at the Mount Washington Glass Works in 1871. Through a contract with William L. Libbey, the New Bedford, Massachusetts, firm hired the brothers, Harry A. and Alfred E. Smith. Their name and artistic ability became synonymous with fine quality throughout the world; only the best artisans from abroad were hired.

A limited amount of their output, especially lamps and vases, were mounted in silver-plated holders made by the Meriden Britannia Company and Reed and Barton. Articles manufactured for sale included: lamps, shades, vases, bowls, plaques, toothpicks, muffineers, pickle jars, mustard pots, jardinieres, cuspidors, cracker and cookie jars, syrup jugs, powder boxes, tobacco jars, salt and pepper shakers, and sugar and creamer sets.

Many of the above mentioned articles were constructed of a shiny opal milk-white glass. This was blown or mold-blown, creating melon ribbed, swirled and cylindrical shapes. A flat satin finish was applied and further enhanced with enameling, gold tracery and highlights. Vases and bowls are frequently found with carefully controlled decorative beaded tops. The work was very fine and delicately done. A signed Smith Brothers addition to your collection would prove to be most pleasant and a wise investment.

Some of the flowers incorporated into the designs included roses, pansies, chrysanthemums, daisies, water lilies, violets and columbines. Popular birds used in decorating were gulls, storks, robins, finches, cranes, bluebirds and hummingbirds. Other decor consisted of butterflies, autumn leaves, winter scenes and the historical "Santa Maria" ship. Colors associated with the Smith Brothers included peach, rust, burmese, cream, tan, apricot, mauve, pink, blue, yellow, green and orange.

In 1874, the brothers opened their own shop at 28 & 30 William Street in New Bedford, Massachusetts. The original edifice is still standing. Some cut and engraved glass was also turned out by them. After the Smiths broke away from the Mount Washington Glass Company, a portion of their opal blanks were still supplied by this firm.

Smith Bro's.

Tiny enameled mark

TRADE MARK

Stamped rust colored mark

Facsimile of an original paper label

Copyrighted 1893 by A.E. SMITH

Minute brown enameled mark incorporated in the decoration, on the front of a Lusterless plate showing the "SANTA MARIA" ship.

Spangle

In manufacturing this glass, the first gather of transparent colored or opaque white was rolled on the table to pick up scattered flecks of mica or biotite. This gather was then cased with a clear or amber crystal, locking in the effect. The bubble was now expanded into any desired form. Hobbs, Brockunier and Company was issued a patent on January 29, 1884, in William Leighton, Jr.'s name. Pieces are not signed but a number of shapes were manufactured including vases, pitchers, handled baskets, brides' baskets, candlesticks, finger bowls, whimseys, cracker jars, lamps, mugs, perfume bottles and tumblers.

The variety of colors and shapes may also be ornamented with twisted and thorn handles (clear and colored), applied reeded handles, tooled feet, overlay crimped designs and even enameled work. Most objects have a shiny surface; some have mold-blown designs, ground pontils and ruffled edges. Many firms in the United States made this version of glass including the Vasa Murrhina Art Glass Company. (See Vasa Murrhina Art Glass Company)

Spatter

Confusion often arises with the term "End-of-Day" glass, as it was formerly believed that glassblowers daily took the remains of the colored glass pots to blow and mold frigger objects. This fact is incorrect as articles were produced in quantities for sale to the public. In recent years, the term Spatter has taken precedence and come to mean a spotted or multicolored glass usually having a white inner casing and a clear outer casing, often in a mold-blown pattern.

In England and the United States, frigger or whimsey objects were made during the late 18th and 19th centuries which included such objects as glass canes, jugs, hats, bells, rolling pins, tobacco pipes, animal figures, ship models, candlesticks and musical instruments. The variety of forms fabricated at a factory on a non-working day were paraded through the villages (on Sundays) stopping at public houses. Here they were judged, votes were cast, and the best items received prizes—which was good for the factory's future success in producing saleable goods.

Some ornate objects manufactured in this ware include handled baskets, vases, tumblers, pitchers, rose bowls, covered jars, candlesticks, covered boxes, decanters, cruets, salt dips and other assorted shapes. The same embellishments used on Spangle glass were also incorporated on Spatter glass. It is rather difficult to attribute glass of this nature to any one firm, although it is known that many American firms produced such a line.

Star Holly - Imperial

This scarce and relatively expensive milk glass pattern was made experimentally at the beginning of the twentieth century (about 1902) by the Imperial Glass Company of Bellaire, Ohio. It was an attempt to duplicate English Wedgwood in pressed glass. Each example has the raised factory mark, an ornate "I" overlapping the "G", appearing on its base. All pieces have intertwined holly leaves in high relief; tall hollow examples have tapered vertical columns. Some objects, when the form permits, also have a slightly raised central medallion consisting of eight holly leaves - hence, the derivation of the name "Star Holly."

Portions of each example, including the leaves, interiors, feet, handles and some borders retain their glossy milk glass finish. The background colorations in coral, green and blue vary in density from one piece to the next. Only one hue was employed per example. This colored matte finish, mostly on the surface, proved very complex and demanding to manufacture. Star Holly was decorated by hand and the tints had a tendency to blur. It is doubtful whether this pattern glass ever went into full production. Only a very limited number of pieces was ever offered for sale. Typical shapes include: goblets, wines, bowls, sugars and creamers, cups and saucers, sauce dishes and spooners. This glass would be an excellent addition to an advanced collection.

Raised factory mark

Steuben (See also Frederick Carder and individual Steuben glass categories)

Frederick Carder was born in Staffordshire, England on September 18, 1863. His early schooling was filled with in-

cidents where he lost his temper, although he gradually outgrew this trait to some degree. His determination and intense study of art and chemistry were put to use at the Leys Pottery owned by his father.

In 1878 after a disagreement, he left the pottery and made a visit to John Northwood's studio to view his great achievement in glass, the Portland Vase. Northwood tutored the young Carder and helped him secure a job designing glass for Stevens and Williams in Brierley Hill.

By 1881, Northwood agreed to close his art studio and work for Stevens and Williams. Carder and Northwood, working together, achieved many fine designs and completed numerous glassmaking endeavors. Northwood remained with the factory as manager and art director up to his death in 1902.

Carder continued studying, attending evening classes after regular working hours. His knowledge and ability enabled him to earn numerous awards. In 1888 at the national Competition, he won a silver medal; a year later he won another award—this time it was the coveted gold. In 1891, he set up his own school instructing talented workers in glassmaking, drawing, painting and sculpturing. Through his tireless efforts, the Stourbridge glasshouses greatly increased the number of highly skilled glassworkers available to them.

Carder was sent on tours in 1902, visiting glass centers in Germany and Austria. These published tours were so significant and informative that he was asked to visit the United States during the winter of 1903.

Arriving in Corning, New York, he was met by officials and taken on a tour of the Corning Glass Works. Later that day, he met Thomas Hawkes, president of T.G. Hawkes and Company. Apparently the two men got along well, for on March 11, 1903 the Steuben Glass Works was conceived, certainly against the wishes of Stevens and Williams who were very unhappy about losing Carder. This new firm would change the entire glassmaking industry, and etch Frederick Carder's name forever in the annals of gifted glass masters.

Frederick Carder was trouble shooter for this firm, and made many daily tours of the various departments handling all aspects of production. The Hawkes Company was sold in 1918 since the government considered it a "nonessential industry." The firm was incorporated as a division of the Corning Glass Works, and Carder, at age sixty-nine, served as its art director. Many challenges were accepted and conquered by Carder while he held this position.

Steuben glass, named for the county in New York, was manufactured with the needs of the public in mind. Its production was vast and included a variety of sizes, shapes and colors. Often types of glass were discontinued after little more than a year in production, to be replaced by something innovative and different that would attract attention and buyers.

Much of the glass produced by the firm was marked in some manner. A great variety of markings were included over the years. Numerous paper label types either of a circular, triangular, or octagonal nature were affixed to the pieces. The most common signature is a matte acid Fleur-de-Lis with the word "STEUBEN" in block letters. This form was used from 1903 to 1932. Some pieces will be found with an etched Fleur-de-Lis having either the word "CALCITE" or "STEUBEN" as part of their insignia. About 1929, a matte acid signature

"STEUBEN" in block letters or "Steuben" in script was employed. Aurene pieces are engraved, often in a shaky fashion with either "AURENE" or "STEUBEN AURENE." After 1932, a diamond-point etching is found using the letter "S" or the word "Steuben." Frederick Carder's signature and his monogram were also used on rare pieces and on those examples brought to him for identification. An Intarsia example of 1930 would have his signature engraved. Diatreta pieces were engraved with abrasive wheels on a flexible shaft—some with dates. From 1903 to 1932 Carder identified and signed examples by engraving his name.

Intarsia Signature

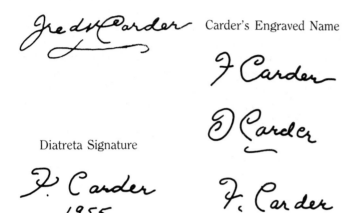

Carder's Engraved Name

Diatreta Signature

1955

Tavern - Pairpoint

During the 1920s and 1930s, the Pairpoint Corporation made a series of assorted tableware which they named Tavern or Tourist Ware. The glass has a clear or light grey cast with many bubbles, some being round while others are elongated. The bubbles tend to feel sharp at various locations on the interior and exterior of the object. Eight and 12" plates, 8" flip vases, 8" bulbous vases, glasses and goblets were decorated with heavy multi-colored enameling and transfers were also employed. A variety of decors include a basket of fruit, whale, donkey, elephants, musical notes, grapes, a boy with a balloon, Spanish galleon, a vase of flowers, a fox and other animals. The addition of potatoes to a batch of lime glass was the secret used to create this scarce bubbly glass.

Distribution of these articles was carried out through branch sales offices at the following locations: 43-47 West 23rd Street, New York City; Hammond Building, 278 Post Street, San Francisco, California; and 228 Coristine Building, St. Nicholas Street, Montreal, Canada. Enameled designs were completed in black, white, yellow, blue and red. The rims of plates are sometimes outlined with a narrow black line, and a wavy or scalloped black enameled line just inside the first one. Other plates have just the scalloped line. Tapered flip glasses and vases also received the same treatment on their top edges; near the bases, there is a single line of black running around the circumference. Bulbous vases have two narrow black lines near their tapered bases, two additional lines at the tapered necks;

and the same variable found on the rims of plates is also seen on the necks of vases. Most examples have a ground pontil and are numbered there. The list provided will assist you when checking for the white enameled numbers.

Whale decor, 8" vase, D1511/281
Galleon decor, 8" vase, D1511/282
Floral decor, 8" vase, D1511/285
Whale decor, 8" flip vase, D1513/281
Galleon decor, 8" flip vase, D1513/282
Floral decor, 8" flip vase, D1513/285
Whale decor, 8" plate, D1521/281
Whale decor, 12" plate, D1522/281
Galleon decor, 8" plate, D1521/282
Galleon decor, 12" plate, D1522/282
Floral decor, 8" plate, D1521/285
Floral decor, 12" plate, D1522/285

Threading and Reeding - Steuben

One interesting method of decorating Steuben glass was to apply glass threads to the exterior surfaces. Some threading was manipulated over the entire body, but generally only a portion of the object was covered. When the spirals are fairly regular and close together, the decor was accomplished by machine and is correctly termed "threaded" decoration. On objects where the application is both irregular and haphazard, we say that the piece possesses a "reeded decoration."

The hand-threading method (reeding) was achieved by the gaffer rotating the object attached to the pontil rod over the arms of his chair. Molten glass threads were carefully applied to the example in this fashion.

Reeding may be very fine, almost hair-like threads to those up to ¼" in thickness. Used on crystal and iridescent wares, the threads may also run up and down overlapping each other. Sometimes the reeding is marvered into the base glass to varying depths.

Both threaded and reeded glass are often found with damage—either slight or severe. It is not uncommon to find spaces between the reeding and the object itself. Seek and purchase a threaded or reeded example for your collection that either has minimal damage or none at all. Glass of this nature is often coated with dust and dirt if it has not been cared for properly. The example acquired will need to be washed, rinsed, and dried properly to prevent further damage.

Tiffany, Louis Comfort

Synonymous with the Art Nouveau period and the luxurious tastes of that era is the name Louis Comfort Tiffany. Louis, born in 1848, dedicated his life to the greater appreciation of the aesthetics, especially the utilization of colors in all forms of art. Known as a painter, decorator, landscaper, architect and designer, Tiffany is perhaps most fondly remembered as the person behind the manufacture of much beautiful art glass. Capitalizing upon his independent nature, he created a dynasty of unique freshness and individuality.

Louis visited Spain and Africa at the age of twenty and took a liking to Islamic, African and Moorish art, which was reflected in his later works. Numerous other trips germinated interests in ancient Roman and Greek glass that had achieved iridization as a result of surface decomposition. He became very interested in glass and sought to learn all he could about its reactions to various chemicals and how decoration could be incorporated into the body of the glass.

Much of Tiffany's success was in his ability to design and personally supervise the production of glass made by his skilled staff. The rest of the credit was due to Arthur J. Nash for his artistic prowess and technical skill in perfecting glass formulas, decorating processes and his insistence, along with Tiffany's, that all objects had to be perfect in their manufacture.

Nash was assisted by his sons, A. Douglas and Leslie Nash, Dr. Parker McIlhiney, a chemist, and even Tiffany whose input of ideas were often successful, but sometimes a failure even after experimenting for years.

Both men (union workers) and boys worked together in groups or shops headed by a gaffer and aided by a blower, gatherer and decorator at Corona, New York. The factory was located at the corner of Main and Irving Streets and the men took extreme pride in their abilities.

Some known workers' names include: gaffers—James A. Stewart, Thomas Manderson, James H. Grady, August LeFevre and Joseph Matthews. Blowers, decorators, and gatherers consisted of: Victor Lilequist, Thomas Heather and Morris Cully (blowers); James Stewart, David McNichol, "Big Florrie" Sullivan, Harold Britton and William Saas (decorators); and John Nelson, Anthony Sterling, Victor LeFevre, Robert Hicks, and Dave McNichol (gatherers). All workers received both encouragement and very adequate compensation. Some men including Harry Britton, John Hollingsworth and James Grady worked at Corona until its demise in 1928.

The following guide may be used to date examples. The years 1892-1893 were recorded as 1-9999. Prefix letters A-Y, excluding X (experimental) indicate the object was made from 1894-1905. Suffixes A-W, excluding X and Y, date the piece from 1906-1928. Other marks were the prefixes "S"-Glass Shades and Globes, "EX" - Exhibition, small "o" - Special Order, "P" - Pottery, "BP" - Bronze Pottery, "EL," "EC," and "SG" describe Enamels; the suffix "A-COLL" indicates the glass was in Tiffany's Private Collection. To pinpoint a prefix year use A and B for 1894, C and D for 1895, and so on. For the suffixes, each letter is a year—thus A is 1906, B is 1907, and the progression continued through the suffix W which is 1928.

Some other engraved signatures found on Tiffany include: "L.C.T. Favrile"; "L.C. Tiffany Favrile"; "Louis C. Tiffany"; "Louis C. Tiffany, Furnaces, Inc."; "Louis C. Tiffany, Inc., Exhibition piece"; and "Tiffany Studios, New York."

The variety of glass fabricated was quite remarkable when one considers that around 5,000 colors and varieties (no two alike) were created each year. A variety of types called by the following names were offered to the public: Paperweight, Millefiore, Lava, Cypriote, Diatreta, Agate, Marbleized, Cameo, Intaglio, Single Iridescence, Decorated Iridescence and the Peacock Feather. (See also each separate category)

Representing a beautiful natural form in iridescent blue, gold and green, the Peacock Feather design is extremely realistic. The "evil eye" center in some feather designs adds a mystical quality to this very desirable art form.

Other contributions by Tiffany included sterling silver tableware, jewelry, enamels, pottery, tiles, mosaics, rugs, stained glass windows, and intricately designed floor, table lamps, and hanging shades.

Tiffany died in 1933 at the age of 85. What had been considered fashionable art, that which he had influenced and changed, now was an oddity or eccentricity. A new transitional art movement was forming which he had not understood or approved.

Laurelton Hall, his summer home on Oyster Bay, Long Island, (Cold Spring Harbor), built and furnished with his firm's creations, was later converted to an Art Foundation for students in 1919. Many artists, later well-knowns, benefited from this opportunity to study in such beautiful surroundings. Until his death, Mr. Tiffany devoted the majority of time and interest to the Tiffany Art Foundation.

During the war, the Foundation could not function normally. The estate was offered to the government and operated as the office of Scientific Research and Development from 1942 to the end of 1945.

Increasing operating costs deterred the true purposes of encouraging and educating art students. Finally the Trustees secured permission of the courts to reorganize the Foundation. The contents of Laurelton Hall were offered for sale by Parke-Bernet Galleries, Incorporated, 30 East 57th Street, New York City on September 24-28, 1946.

Proceeds of this sale were added to a capital fund; the income was given in cash grants to worthy art students enabling them to travel and study.

Tortoise-Shell · Sandwich

This glass commodity, as the name implies, was manufactured in imitation of the unusual natural coloration found in the shell of the hawksbill, a small sea turtle. Before the invention of plastics, this turtle was almost to the point of extinction. The shell, through an involved series of steps, was utilized, cut into thin layers, steamed into shape, carved and polished. From these pieces, workers and artists made fine hair combs, covered boxes, mirrors, tea caddies, bracelets and cigar cases; many were ornamented with inlaid Mother-of-Pearl, gold, sterling silver, ivory and miniature portraits.

Its glass counterpart has a deep, rich, brown and amber mottling between two layers of clear glass. Tortoise-Shell glass is translucent and was manufactured in Germany, other European countries, and at the Sandwich Factory on Cape Cod, Massachusetts. Bottles, bowls, cruets, pitchers, vases, plates and tumblers are some of the types of items to be found. Pieces may have mica flecks throughout the ware, and infrequently gold or enameled decorations were employed. The glossy glass was fabricated from about 1880 to 1900. Articles, unless they are signed, are very difficult to attribute to a particular glasshouse.

Clumsy, heavy and oddly shaped forms, very dissimilar to the originals, are presently being imported from Italy as Tortoise-Shell glass. Many such objects may be seen on display in the glass and china section of the better department stores and in gift and card shops. Bases have been viewed with both rough and ground pontils. The texture of the glass is extremely thick, and when held to a bright light, will reveal a rather light and transparent pinkish brown hue.

Trevaise - Alton Manufacturing Company

In 1907, the Alton Manufacturing Company became the last firm to produce glass in Sandwich, Massachusetts. Patrick J. McCarthy was its superintendent and Gardenio F. King was the factory's manager.

It was King who called his art glass in the Art Nouveau style, Trevaise. An advertisement in the weekly newspaper stated "The Alton Manufacturing Company is receiving orders for its various lines of goods including the new and beautiful 'Trevaise' ware, an artistic product which may well lay claim to the highest place in the glassmakers art and which it is believed is destined to become of world-wide repute." The claim, however, did not materialize and by 1908, this decorative, iridescent art glass was made no more. The factory doors closed to repair their boilers and the output of the Alton Manufacturing Company ceased forever.

Trevaise glass was made by former Tiffany employees and certainly only limited quantities of it exists. Characteristically the glass resembles Tiffany's Favrile, Carder's Aurene, and the Union Glass Company's Kew Blas.

All examples possess mainly pulled leaves, swirls or a combination of the two marvered into the glass surfaces. Blue, green and amethyst colors were not signed, are opaque, and have soft muted surfaces.

To date, only vases without feet or handles have been documented. Their rims are plain and the center of each object is the widest diameter. All vases had a glob of glass applied to their bases for added strength; this was polished and resembles a donut shape. The exterior surfaces often were inferior showing numerous pock marks that penetrated the finish. Most examples are thick and heavy giving an almost clumsy appearance. This glass would be relatively difficult to acquire in today's marketplace.

Tyrian - Steuben

Few examples of this rare art glass were made at Steuben between 1916-1917 since the workers had difficulty in its production. Most examples have a greenish gray or blue hue at the top shading to a grayish purple at their bases. This opaque glass when first gathered and formed was green. The unstable metal upon reheating under oxidizing conditions turned purple. The longer the object was reheated, the deeper became the color toward the base. Most objects have gold Aurene leaves and trailing threads marvered into their bodies, with the addition of an iridescent sheen created by spraying with stannous chloride. All objects were in the shapes of large classical formed vases signed "TYRIAN" and numbered. Some few vases either were created with trailed threading in relief or a hooked decoration of Aurene over white embedded in the glass. Frederick Carder assigned the name Tyrian to this glass since its color suggests the purple used in fabrics at Tyre, the capital of ancient Phoenicia. This noted seaport on the Mediterranean Sea derived their dyestuff from the bodies of certain mollusks.

Union Glass Company (See also Kew Blas)

Founded in 1851 on Webster Avenue in Somerville, Massachusetts, the Union Glass Company thrived until 1860. Reorganized under Mr. Dana, its new owner, the firm prospered for 15 years from 1870, producing silvered glass, pressed glass and cut glass blanks. Its new officers were Charles Chafflin, president; Amory Houghton, treasurer; and John Gregory, company agent.

At Mr. Dana's death, about 1900, Julian de Cordova, his son-in-law managed the plant, improving facilities, and produced the famous "Kew Blas" glass and Venetian forms which brought about the company's real recognition. Production continued until 1924—the date that the factory closed. Some typical forms were vases, tumblers, decanters, rose bowls, candlesticks, wines, creamers, finger bowls, salts, compotes, plates and pitchers.

Vasa Murrhina Art Glass Company

Idle from the death of Deming Jarves in April, 1869, the Cape Cod Glass Company was purchased by Charles W. Sparr on September 18, 1882. John Charles DeVoy and Dr. R.C. Flower of Boston leased the furnaces and working glass areas in May, 1883. Their intent was to manufacture an art glass called Vasa Murrhina; the firm's name would be the Vasa Murrhina Art Glass Company. Charles Sparr had the furnaces and buildings repaired at his expense. In June the factory was ready for occupancy.

The furnaces were lit on June 28th; a celebration followed on July 4th with speeches and respected citizens of Sandwich in attendance. Reverend Joseph Marsh, 88 years of age, produced on July 17, 1883, at the site, the first piece of Vasa Murrhina glass.

This new glass process made possible more than 3,400 colored combinations. The procedure was recorded in the patent office on July 1, 1884. Any colored or clear glass could be ornamented by coating it with mica. A thin sheet of mica was submerged for 48 hours in a bath of silver, nickel, gold or copper. Next, the sheet was taken out and dried. A hot ball of metal was attached to the glassblower's pipe and rolled over the mica to pick up the metallic sprinkles and/or colored glass particles. When the batch was subjected to heat, the glass flowed freely adhering to the mica. Blown and pressed wares in the shapes of vases, tumblers, decanters, bulbous and cylindrical lamp bases, plates, handled letter seals and toy books (whimsies) were some of the objects manufactured.

Production included several hundred pieces of glass per week by August 1, 1883. Frequent visitors from Boston graced the site in late August, viewing the creation of many beautiful glass objects. Fair exhibits were also held in Louisville, Kentucky, and Boston, Massachusetts. Encouraging responses and increased demands caused the firm to place additional furnaces in operation.

Unfortunate finances and glass cracking in the annealing ovens forced Mr. DeVoy, the superintendent, to close the factory briefly late in 1883. Stocks were sold, gaining an additional $300,000.00 in working capital. Upon the resumption of operations, some flint glass was also manufactured, but it had no appeal. The serious cracking problem in their Vasa Murrhina brought production to a final closing in the winter of 1884. Only 30% of each batch was successfully marketed. Few examples with handles or spouts are in existence, and no fluted edges exist on this rare and desirable glass made in Sandwich. At no time was any of the production signed.

Other firms noted for the creation of Vasa Murrhina were Hobbs, Brockunier and Company, Wheeling, West Virginia; Farrall Venetian Art Glass Manufacturing Company, Brooklyn, New York; William Webb Boulton, England; Rice William Harris, Islington Glass Works, Birmingham, England; and Arthur John Nash, manager of the Whitehouse Glass Works, Stourbridge, England. These patents occurred from 1878 to 1884.

Venetian · Steuben

Around the 1918-1920 era, Frederick Carder decided to place in production glass items which were similar to the techniques used by Venetian glass artisans for centuries.

Carder, while in the employment of Stevens and Williams, had revitalized certain forms as a result of his travel and study on the continent. At Steuben, certain of these characteristics were again used liberally on some lines. Their period of production was for a very limited endurance.

Venetian traits included folded rims and bases; hollow stems; a wafer applied between the base and the stem; ball stems; the application of prunts, handle rings and edges trimmed in a different color from the body of the example; plus the liberal use of silver and gold mica flecks on scarce objects.

Some typical colors used both singly and in pairs were Amber; Topaz; Amethyst; Marina, Flemish and Celeste Blue; Wisteria; Pomona Green; Verre de Soie; Aqua Marine (an iridized greenish tint); and Cyprian (a pale green iridescence with applied Celeste Blue at the rims).

Perhaps the most appealing adornment was the application of delicate and colorful blown fruits (especially pears and apples) and flowers. The straited fruit is usually in shades of red, green and yellow with stems and leaves. They were attached by a wafer of glass and appeared as finials, part of the stem, or attached to the outside walls (such as on a compote).

By studying the typical shapes and noting the specific characteristics mentioned, the collector might be fortunate to discover an example of Steuben's Venetian glass with or without the acid-stamped signature.

Verona · Mount Washington

A little known glass type, produced by the Mount Washington Glass Company starting in 1894, was the introduction of transparent colored and crystal blanks. Few examples are ever found with the word "VERONA" in enamel on their bases. The limited output in this poorly received glassware was finely enameled and veined. Thin washes were outlined in gold on the exterior surfaces and gold spatterings also occurred about the necks of objects. Free and mold-blown vases were the major items produced—some with turned-out ears or ruffled tops. Many examples were outlined with wax where a particular pattern was desired and then sprayed in a dustry rose or smoky tan coloration. After removing the wax, assorted floral, court scenes, or others were artistically fulfilled.

Verre de Soie · Steuben

Verre de Soie was a clear crystal which has an iridized hue created by spraying each object with stannous chloride. Produced throughout the Carder era and originally called Flint Iridescent, Stevens and Williams manufactured it as early as 1885-1886. At the Corning factory, it was called "V.D.S."

Having a distinctive smooth surface like silk, the glass was delicately frosted and reflected a rainbow spectrum of hues. Widely acclaimed by the populace, Carder ranked Verre de Soie as his favorite iridized glass, and ranked it next to Intarsia overall in the products he created. Popular names like "Glass of Silk," "Angel's Breath," and "Angel Skin" have been connected with this ware. The descriptive French term Verre de Soie is correctly pronounced "V-air da Swa."

Beginning collectors may confuse this product with White Carnival glass which was pressed and had raised patterns on either or both sides. Some glass originating in Europe plus reproductions may cause some consternation. Often on such objects, harsh hues of green or purple predominate with the blue and yellow gold lacking. When the texture is rough to the touch, assume that the article was not made by Steuben.

Shapes in this very collectible glass run the gamut to include: vases, stemware, plates, perfumes, colognes, compotes, candlesticks, bowls, salt dips, sherbets and underplates, creamers and sugars, nut dishes, and gas shades—to name just a few. Many objects are in the same forms as Aurene with the presence of ruffled edges, ribbed and diamond quilted patterns, and even the addition of copper wheel engraving and silver overlay. Shape, therefore, is another critical aid in determining whether the piece is Steuben or not.

Another iridized form of glass which does not appear misty white is the green hued variety. Much rarer and called Aqua Marine, the glass cannot be mistaken when compared with Verre de Soie.

Finally, between 1915 and the 1920s Carder also produced this same green iridescent glass with blue rings of Celeste blue applied to the lip of a rim or foot. Some few items in all three types had the addition of prunts, threading, applied handles, a signature, or an original paper label.

Wave Crest · C.F. Monroe

A trademark was issued to the C.F. Monroe Company granting them permission to produce "Wave Crest Ware" on May 31, 1898. It is the oldest of the three types manufactured. (See also Kelva and Nakara) Most opal blanks were first dipped in acid to give them a smooth finish before decorating commenced. Careful and imaginative art renderings plus scrolls, ribs and puffy pillow shapes add to the overall illusion. This glassware is very collectible in addition to Kelva and Nakara, especially if you are artistically minded and enjoy finely executed designs. Examples of Wave Crest have been seen signed "C.F.M. Co.," "WAVE CREST WARE," and "Wave Crest, Trademark" with the stamped red banner mark.

J G FARRIS   Wave Crest American artist

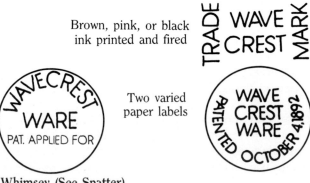

Brown, pink, or black ink printed and fired

Two varied paper labels

Whimsey (See Spatter)

Color Photographs and Prices

TOP LEFT: Left to right: Agata cruet, New England Glass Company, 5½", $2,880.00; Agata tumbler, 4¾" high, $1,368.00, New England Glass Company, privately owned.

BOTTOM LEFT: Agata lily vase, 6" high, New England Glass Company, $2,520.00, privately owned.

TOP RIGHT: Agata tumbler, ground pontil, New England Glass Company, 3½" high, Milan Historical Museum, $1,116.00.

BOTTOM RIGHT: Castor set, Rose Amber, Mount Washington Glass Company, silverplate frame marked "The Acme Silverplate Co., Boston, No. 725," vinegar and oil bottles with applied amber handles and amber facet cut stoppers and pair of salt and pepper shakers with pewter tops, Inverted Thumbprint pattern, $1,728.00 set, privately owned.

TOP LEFT: Hobbs, Brockunier pressed Amberina dish, Daisy and Button pattern, scalloped edge, 5½" diameter, $252.00, privately owned.

TOP CENTER: Amberina crackle pitcher, applied ribbed amber handle, ground pontil, 7¾" high, $540.00, Milan Historical Museum.

TOP RIGHT: Libbey Amberina Jack-in-the-pulpit vase, ground pontil, enameled florals and "World's Fair - 1893" on the turned down rim, 6¾" high, $720.00, privately owned.

BOTTOM LEFT: Amberina decanter, amber cut stopper, ground pontil, 12" high, Inverted Honeycomb pattern, $720.00, privately owned.

BOTTOM RIGHT: Amberina toothpick, Kate Greenaway figural holder, signed "James W. Tufts, Boston, Quadruple Plate," 4¾" to top of holder, $540.00, Milan Historical Museum.

Amberina flint goblet, 6¼" high, slight twist pattern, $252.00, privately owned.

OPPOSITE PAGE

TOP: Reverse Amberina pitcher, Quilted Diamond pattern, probably New England Glass Company, East Cambridge, Massachusetts, circa 1880s, 5" high, $338.00 privately owned.

BOTTOM LEFT: Mount Washington cruet with amber faceted stopper, deep coloration, unusual swirled pattern, 6½" high, $720.00, privately owned, Amberina.

BOTTOM RIGHT: Inverted thumbprint syrup, silverplated top numbered "1954," 5¾" high, New England Glass Company, $900.00, privately owned. An accompanying round silverplated tray (not shown) is also numbered "1954" and is engraved "Mother." The plate has the same ribbed edge as the collar on the syrup, and is marked "James W. Tufts Boston Warranted Quadruple Plate," privately owned, Amberina.

TOP: Rose amber miniature ewer, Mount Washington Glass Company, applied amber handle and wishbone feet, berry prunt, 4½" high, $504.00, privately owned.

BOTTOM: Sandwich Amberina tankard pitcher, 10" high, applied amber twisted collar and handle, rosettes at the base of the handle, $1,080.00, Houston Antique Museum.

TOP LEFT: Belle Ware jewelry box with hinged ormolu brass collar, coralene finish, rose motif, signed in blue, $720.00, privately owned.

TOP RIGHT: Plated Amberina tumbler, good color, ground pontil, 3¾" high, Milan Historical Museum, $2,448.00, New England Glass Company.

BOTTOM: Plated Amberina water pitcher, amber handle, deep coloration, 7" high, circa 1886, New England Glass Company, Houston Antique Museum, $8,640.00

TOP LEFT: Mount Washington glossy lemonade, 4½" high, Diamond Quilted pattern, $324.00, privately owned, Burmese.

TOP RIGHT: Shiny Burnese sugar and creamer, ground pontils, applied ear handles, excellent coloration, 5½" to top of the creamer, $1,440.00 set, Milan Historical Museum, Hobnail pattern number 131.

CENTER LEFT: Two pieces of matte finished Mount Washington Burmese, both have ground pontils, sugar is 3¼" in diameter, and the creamer is 3½" high, $540.00 pair, privately owned.

BOTTOM RIGHT: Mount Washington shiny Burmese pitcher, applied handle, ground pontil, 6½" to the top of the spout, $1,044.00, Milan Historical Museum.

BOTTOM LEFT: Mount Washington satin Burmese vase, scalloped top, applied neck rigaree, 4" high, $468.00, privately owned.

TOP LEFT: Burmese matte finish grouping. Left, lily vase, 8¼" high, center, Diamond Quilted toothpick, 2" high; cruet, 6½", ribbed, $1,152.00, $468.00, $1,130.00, all privately owned.

BOTTOM LEFT: Decorated Burmese vase, 4¾" high, acid exterior with glossy interior, enameled bird and floral decor, $2,520.00, privately owned.

BOTTOM RIGHT: Mount Washington decorated Burmese bowl, satin finish, 3½" diameter, 1¾" high, $504.00, privately owned.

TOP LEFT: Bluerina goblet, flint quality, 8" high, clear base and six sided cut stem, attributed to the Boston and Sandwich Glass Company, Inverted Thumbprint pattern, $180.00, privately owned.

BOTTOM LEFT: Blue Amberina ribbed pitcher, applied blue handle, gilded top, ground pontil, 6¾" high. The tumbler is engraved and in the Inverted thumbprint pattern. A very unusual coloration, $410.00 set, Milan Historical Museum.

TOP RIGHT: Floral decorated Mount Washington Burmese vase, 10" high, $1,008.00, privately owned.

BOTTOM RIGHT: Mount Washington Burmese stick vase with handles, floral decor, 12" high, $3,024.00 privately owned.

57

Burmese lamp, base and shade acid-etched, decorated with fish and net decor, gilted mounts, Mount Washington Glass Company, circa 1885–1900, 19" high, $13,680.00, "Collection of The Corning Museum of Glass, gift in part of William E. Hammond."

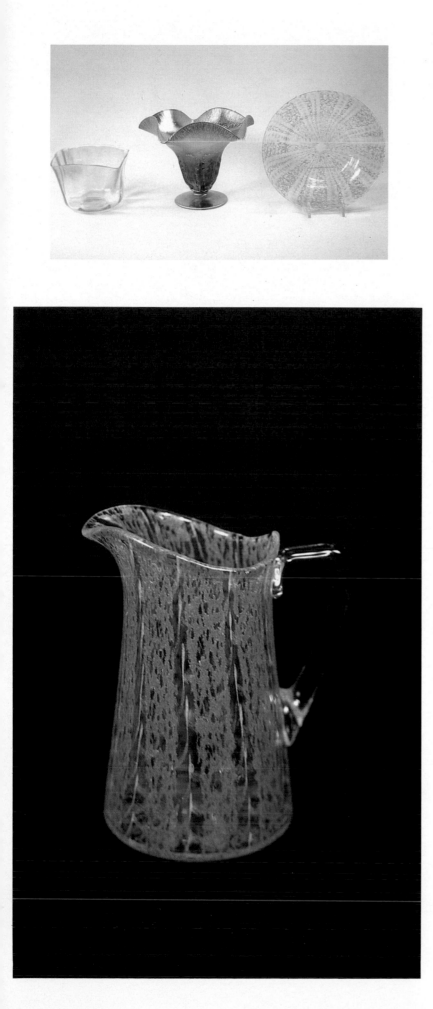

TOP LEFT: Nash grouping: left, molded crystal "Smoke" finger bowl, 3" high, 1¼" ground pontil, signed "A. 129 NASH," $144.00; blue iridescent flower form vase on a foot, five-paneled top, ground pontil, 5" high, flint glass, $900.00; Chintz flint glass plate, 6½" diameter, $223.00, green and rose spattering on clear, small ground pontil, signed "1985 AD NASH," privately owned.

BOTTOM LEFT: Nash Chintz miniature creamer, applied clear handle, ground pontil, 4⅛" high, $338.00, Milan Historical Museum.

TOP RIGHT: Consolidated Custard vase, molded with raised Dogwood flowers and branches that are tinted, 10½" high, $144.00, privately owned.

BOTTOM RIGHT: Coralene vases: left, apricot snowflake Mother-of-Pearl with blue Coralene, $936.00; right, pink and green turned-down top, applied amber beading and amber feet, 5½" high, $1,080.00, Milan Historical Museum.

TOP LEFT: Chocolate glass covered cracker jar, Cactus pattern, 7¾" to top of the finial, $504.00, privately owned.

TOP RIGHT: Hobnail cranberry bowl opalescent applied candy ribbon edge, flint, ground pontil, 3¼" high, 8¾" in diameter, $252.00, Milan Historical Museum.

BOTTOM: Spatter bride's basket satinized and ruffled, Coralene floral decor, 11" diameter and 12" to the top of the Meriden quadruple-plated holder, $828.00, Milan Historical Museum.

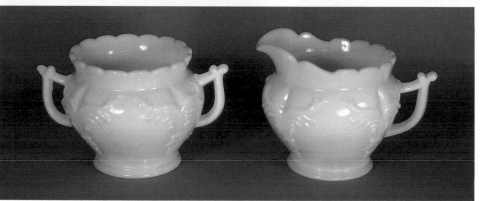

TOP LEFT: Cosmos covered butter dish, 5½" to the top of the finial, $288.00, privately owned.

TOP RIGHT: Cosmos miniature kerosene lamp, enameled flowers on milk glass, 7¾" high, $396.00, Milan Historical Museum.

CENTER: Winged Scroll (Ivorina Verde) sugar and creamer, 3¾" to the top of the creamer's spout, $216.00 set, Milan Historical Museum.

BOTTOM: Custard covered sugar and creamer, Argonaut Shell, both signed "Northwood" on the base, creamer, 4½" high, sugar bowl, 6½" high, $396.00 set, privately owned.

TOP: Cranberry colored satin grouping with decorations: left, Mount Washington salt and pepper fig-shaped shakers, $504.00 set; center, pickle castor in a quadruple-plated holder attributed to Mount Washington, $540.00, 11¼" to the top of the handle; right, pewter-topped salt and pepper shakers, $144.00 set, privately owned.

BOTTOM: Enameled Cranberry grouping: salt and pepper on the left are in the Honeycomb pattern, the quadruple-plated holder is stamped "Rogers & Bro. Quadruple Plate," $216.00 set: center, Inverted thumb print pickle castor, $468.00; right, squat salt and pepper shakers, $180.00 set, privately owned.

LEFT: Vase, green shaded cut to clear, trumpet shape, 12" high, Middlesex pattern variation, $1,728.00, privately owned.

TOP RIGHT: Colored cut plate, 9" diameter, Cranberry to chartreuse, all cutting is on the reverse side, edge made up of 16 scalloped panels, center has a 16 sided cut star, $504.00, attributed to the New England Glass Company; bowl, 5½" high, deeply cut emerald green to clear, diameter 5¾", attributed to Dorflinger, $468.00, privately owned.

BOTTOM: Claret glass, cut green to clear, 1895, 4⅝" high, Napoleon pattern (also called Monarch pattern). Patented by John Hoare, Corning, New York, at a later date. Cut at the John S. O'Connor factory, Hawley, Pennsylvania. O'Connor had worked for Dorflinger, $122.00, Wayne County Historical Society.

TOP: Part of a set including cut pitcher and five tumblers, gilded, attributed to Linke, Krantz and Sell, Honesdale, Pennsylvania, pitcher, 10½" high to the top of the lip, tumblers, 4" high, $1,440.00 set, Wayne County Historical Society.

BOTTOM: Sixteen-point colored cut dish, Russian cut panels are interspersed with Daisy and Button panels, 8" diameter, $252.00, privately owned.

Pair of wine glasses, ruby overlay, circa 1918, C. Dorflinger and Son, White Mills, Pennsylvania, $576.00 pair, "Collection of The Corning Museum of Glass, gift of Kathryn H. Dorflinger."

TOP LEFT: Cut Velvet stick vase, 9" high diamond quilting exterior with cased white interior, robin's egg blue, $266.00, privately owned.

TOP RIGHT: Ribbed Cut Velvet vase, butterscotch color, applied frosted handles, 5" high, $540.00, Milan Historical Museum.

BOTTOM: Cut Velvet matte finish vase, ruffled top, deep rose, white lining, diamond pattern, 7" high, $540.00; Cut Velvet glossy cruet, clear cut stopper, clear applied handle, diamond quilted, 6" high, white lining, brilliant rose color, $1,080.00, privately owned.

DeVilbiss grouping of perfumes, all signed: central example is 9½" high, $180.00, $158.00, $216.00, $288.00 set, all privately owned.

Wine glass, circa 1890, C. Dorflinger and Son, White Mills, Pennsylvania, spiral cut, $288.00, "Collection of The Corning Museum of Glass, gift of Kathryn H. Dorflinger."

TOP LEFT: Dorflinger gold ruby lamp chimney, 11½" high, $158.00, privately owned.

TOP RIGHT: Green loving cup with 3 clear applied handles, 7½" high, 6" diameter at the top, scratched on the bottom, "Made by Axel Larson, 1897," $432.00, Wayne County Historical Society.

CENTER: Clear flint cocktail glass made at the Dorflinger factory by Emil J. Larson. Etched with a fighting cock, also note the fused glass cherry, 4¼" high, $216.00, privately owned.

BOTTOM RIGHT: Hock goblet made at Dorflinger, designed by Carl Prosch, 7¼" high, gold decoration, cut stem, and the original paper label (beige lettering on a bluish charcoal background), diamond-shaped, shows a drawing of a goblet with the initials "HDC" superimposed over the goblet, and the names "HONESDALE" at the bottom, $144.00, Wayne County Historical Society.

TOP: Durand, left to right: green iridescent vase with gold lustre King Tut decoration, 5¼" high, $1,728.00; Cranberry Peacock Feather design on a clear vase, intaglio cut flower, 8¾" high, $1,296.00; cut overlay decanter, green to clear, 11¾" high, $1,008.00; Egyptian Crackle vase, opal body with gold and green overlay, lustred, 5¼" high, $1,800.00, privately owned.

BOTTOM LEFT: Durand amethyst ribbed vase, ground pontil, signed in silver stylus "V DURAND - 1986 - 6," 5¾" high, $288.00, privately owned.

BOTTOM RIGHT: Two out of a set of six Durand goblets, blue and white pulled feather design, iridescent gold stems and bases, 7" high, $216.00 each, privately owned.

TOP LEFT: Two Durand vases: left, 8¼" footed vase with green King Tut decor, ground pontil, $1,224.00; right, 4½" opal vase with blue and gold lustred Hearts and Vines and gold Spider Webbing, flat ground bottom, $972.00. Both vases have gold interiors and are privately owned.

TOP RIGHT: Durand footed bowl, gold King Tut swirl, lustred foot, 5½" high, signed "DURAND" within a "V" and numbered "2001-h," $936.00, Milan Historical Museum.

BOTTOM: Grouping of blown art glass: circa 1900–1935, Durand, Vineland, New Jersey, and the Union Glass Works, Somerville, Massachusetts, tallest example is 8½" high, $180.00, $648.00, $576.00, $1,188.00, and $1,008.00, "Collection of The Corning Museum of Glass."

TOP LEFT: Durand ginger jar with lid, blue lustre with Heart and Clinging vine decoration, 9" high, signed "DURAND 1964-8," $2,160.00; right, blue lustre glass trumpet vase with gold lustre King Tut decor, 13½" high, gold iridescent lining, $1,512.00 privately owned.

TOP RIGHT: Left, blue iridescent vase with opal King Tut designs, 9¾" high, $1,260.00; right, gold iridescent vase, 6¾" high, signed "DURAND" within a "V" and numbered "1990-6," $792.00, privately owned.

BOTTOM LEFT: Durand Moorish Crackle vase with Lava decoration, 11¾" high, signed in silver "DURAND" in a "V," $972.00, Milan Historical Museum.

BOTTOM RIGHT: Durand grouping: left, gold iridescent vase, green and ivory pulled feather design and random gold threading, ground pontil, 8½" high, $1080.00; gold iridescent vase, 6" high, green King Tut decor, $936.00; right, blue lustred vase with white Heart and Clinging Vine decoration, 6½" high, signed "V-DURAND 1716-6," $1,224.00, all privately owned.

TOP LEFT: Pale pink Findlay Onyx muffineer, raspberry flowers, yellow stems, platinum beards, 5¼" high, privately owned, $2,160.00.

TOP RIGHT: Findlay Onyx syrup 6½" high, applied opalescent handle and silverplated top; creamer has an applied opalescent handle; $1,080.00, $576.00, privately owned.

BOTTOM: Findlay Onyx syrup with silverplated metal flip top and applied opalescent handle, 6¾" high, $1,080.00, privately owned.

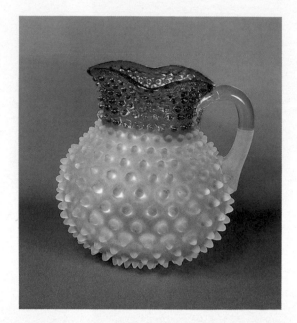

TOP LEFT: Findlay Onyx spooner, satin finish, raspberry colored 3⅞" high, $612.00, Milan Historical Museum.

TOP RIGHT: Frances Ware pitcher, applied handle, ground pontil, 7½" high, frosted hobnail with amber rim, $288.00, privately owned.

BOTTOM: Frances Ware syrup, pewter top, applied handle, 6¾" high $122.00, Milan Historical Museum.

TOP LEFT: Fry Foval basket, opalescent, applied cobalt handle and wafer attaching the foot, ground pontil, circa 1920s, 8½" high, $612.00, Antique Emporium.

TOP RIGHT: Fry Foval handled vase, opalescent, applied cobalt blue handle, 1920s era, 7¾" high, $612.00, Antique Emporium.

BOTTOM: Fry Crackle glass lemonade set, pitcher, 10¾" high, ground pontil, applied cobalt handle and foot; 6 glasses have applied cobalt feet, 5½" high, $576.00 set, Antique Emporium.

TOP LEFT: Fry Foval cup and saucer, flint glass, polished pontils, cup is 3½" across, saucer is 5" across, height of both pieces together is 2½", $144.00 set; Foval perfume, jade green foot and stopper lid, $180.00. Both the lid and the body of the perfume are engraved with flowers and leaves, privately owned.

TOP RIGHT: Divided Fry opalescent plate, one of 6, signed in raised block letters, "FRY'S HEAT RESISTING GLASS," $14.00 each, privately owned.

BOTTOM: Golden Agate covered dolphin, Greentown, 4½" high, $1080.00, Milan Historical Museum.

TOP LEFT: Gone with the Wind lamp, 23½" high, circa 1880, brass fittings and cast iron base, $828.00, privately owned.

TOP RIGHT: Miniature milk glass lamp, 9" to the top of the chimney, pink flowers and green leaves, marked "Acorn - the P. & A. Mfg., Co.," $252.00, privately owned.

BOTTOM LEFT: Green Opaque tumbler, 3½" high, $1,116.00, Milan Historical Museum.

BOTTOM RIGHT: Green Opaque punch cup, 2½" high, New England Glass Company, $864.00, privately owned.

TOP LEFT: Dome shaped Handel lamp 25½" to the top of the finial, shade painted in reverse with leaves and daffodils, also signed "HANDEL 7/22," $1,440.00, Milan Historical Museum.

BOTTOM RIGHT: Handel leaded lamp, 24" high, Dogwood pattern, shade's diameter 19¼", shade's rim impressed "HANDEL 1908," brass base signed in raised letters, "HANDEL 1908," $3,600.00, privately owned.

BOTTOM LEFT: Chipped Teroma/Handel crystal vase painted with a woodland scene, 10¾" high, artist signed, "John Bailey," $2,160.00, Milan Historical Museum.

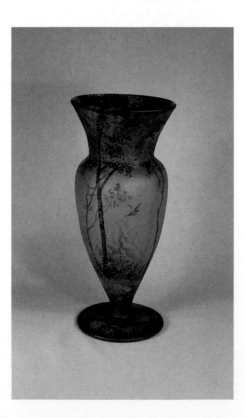

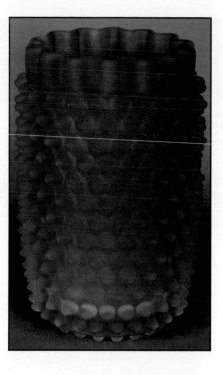

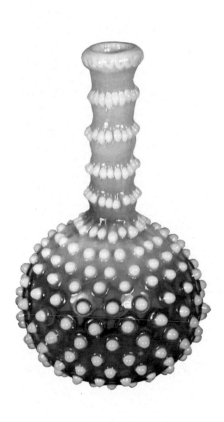

TOP: Pink frosted hobnail vase, 6½" high, ruffled top, possibly Hobbs, Brockunier and Company, Wheeling, West Virginia, $216.00, Milan Historical Museum.

LEFT: Opalescent hobnail barber bottle, apple green coloration, 7½" high, $266.00, Milan Historical Museum.

BOTTOM: Blown molded flint glass creamer, opalescent with hobs, white opalescent handle, ground pontil, circa 1885, 4¾" high, $144.00, privately owned.

Opalescent, ruffled, diamond-shaped bowl with hobnails, shaded pink to white, 4 footed quadruple-plated base is marked, "MERIDEN & COMPANY 131," attributed to the Mount Washington Glass Company, 9½" high, $360.00, privately owned.

TOP: Holly Amber bowl and tumbler: left, 7½" diameter; right 4" high, bowl, $576.00, tumbler, $554.00, Milan Historical Museum.

BOTTOM: Three crystal pieces made at Dorflinger and gilded at Honesdale: Left, sherbet glass, Cornflower pattern, 1900–1932, 3½" high, $216.00; center, flower bowl, Biltmore pattern, large ground pontil, 3⅜" high by 8½" diameter on the base, $288.00; right, Water Lily goblet with raised gold and enamel, $216.00, Wayne County Historical Society.

A portion of a water set consisting originally of a pitcher and 6 tumblers, today the pitcher and 4 tumblers remain. The pitcher is 8¾" high, and the tumblers are 3¾" high. This enameled and gilded set was originally given to Frank W. Schuerholtz by E. A. Lindsey, the chickens depicted are Silver Campines. Two other sets were made: one for Morris Delano with Buff Orpingtons, and the other for John Nixon with White Leghorns. The three sets were made from T. B. Clark glass blanks, 14 K gold trim was added by the Honesdale Decorating Company, the initials "FWS" are on the pitcher, the enameled chickens were executed by Gustave Kittel, $936.00 set, Wayne County Historical Society.

Large Honesdale acid-etched vase with gold decor, 12" high, Regeletto pattern and 905-1014 (also called St. Regis), stippled panels are iridized, large ground pontil, $325.00, Wayne County Historical Society.

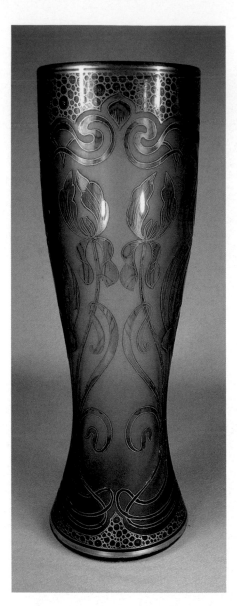

LEFT: Signed "Honesdale" cameo vase with Art Nouveau whiplashes and stylized iris flowers, green cased over clear crystal, acid-etched background, 12¼" high, $648.00, privately owned.

CENTER: Two color cameo vase signed "Honesdale," frosted background with the green and yellow skillfully cut and gilded to reveal a pastoral setting with trees in bloom and the sun rising over the distant hillside, $684.00, Wayne County Historical Society.

RIGHT: Corset-shaped crystal vase cased with cranberry, etched background, gilded cranberry Art Nouveau designs, extremely deep cutting, 10⅜" high, signed "Honesdale," $792.00, Wayne County Historical Society.

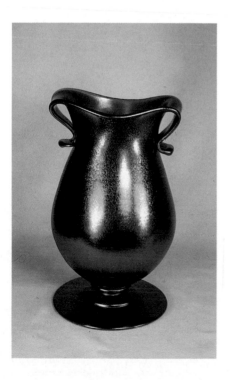

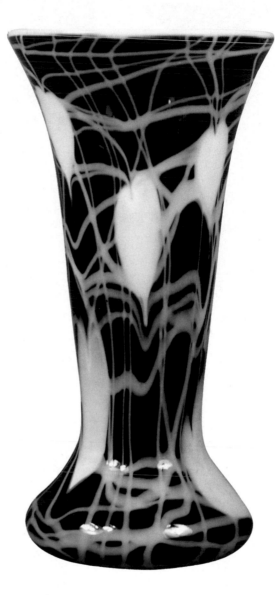

TOP LEFT: Imperial orange iridescent vase with blue leaves and vines, ground pontil, 9⅛" high, $338.00, Milan Historical Museum.

BOTTOM LEFT: Imperial vase with its original label, turned down top, 9" high, lustrous iridized highlights, $216.00, Milan Historical Museum.

RIGHT: Cobalt blue Imperial vase with white marvered leaves and vines, original gold paper label in the ground pontil reads "FREE HAND MADE IN U.S.A." around the edge, and the word "IMPERIAL" separated into groups of 2 letters by the German cross, 7½" high, $288.00, privately owned.

TOP LEFT: Signed "Kew-Blas" gold trumpet vase, 12" high, $1,440.00, privately owned.

TOP RIGHT: Pair of Kew Blas swirled and iridescent candlesticks, 8" high, ground pontils, signed "KEW-BLAS," $684.00 pair, Milan Historical Museum.

BOTTOM RIGHT: Green Kimble Cluthra vase with ribs and bubbles, 6" high, signed "K 20177-6 Dec. 09" in silver stylus in the ground pontil, $324.00, privately owned.

BOTTOM LEFT: Large 3 color Kimble Cluthra vase with applied handles, 11" high, ground pontil, signed "K 20144-12 Dec - 7," $612.00. Variegated orange and white mottling with bubbles and charcoal handles, privately owned.

TOP: Libbey compote, white bowl with pink marvered flower, clear applied stem and base, signed "Libbey," 6⅛" high, $554.00, Milan Historical Museum.

RIGHT: Optic Diamond crystal vase with blue marvered threading, ground pontil, 8" high, Libbey Glass Company, circa 1932, $360.00, privately owned.

BOTTOM: Signed "Libbey" covered jar, has Libbey circular cut glass trademark marked "LIBBEY CUT GLASS TOLEDO, O." around the edge with a central eagle, wings outspread, head to the left. The satin jar is melon ribbed with enameled daisies, 3" high, $432.00, Milan Historical Museum.

TOP: Etched Locke Art water glasses, flint, water lily and cattail decor, 3½" high, $86.00 each, privately owned.

BOTTOM: Locke Art Vintage Grape corset shaped pitcher, 8½" high, lower portion of the handle etched, also 13-petaled flower under the top portion of the handle where applied, 24 point cut star on base, signed, flint glass. Shown are 2 matching tumblers from the set of 6, 5 are signed and all have 16 ribs, 4½" high, $1008.00 set, privately owned.

TOP: Signed "LOCKE ART" vessel with concave foot, 2¾" high, flint glass, used for eating cherries, the pits were placed in the concave foot, Pansy decoration, $288.00, privately owned.

BOTTOM: Locke Art pitcher, engraved Geisha girl, apple blossom design on the back, cut applied handle and foot, 10¼" high, $684.00, Milan Historical Museum.

TOP LEFT: Ruby glass Lutz decanter, Sandwich, engraved flowers and leaves, $720.00, courtesy of Sandwich Historical Society Glass Museum.

TOP RIGHT: Pair of Lutz Ruby glass chalices, Sandwich, $720.00 pair, courtesy, Sandwich Historical Society Glass Museum.

BOTTOM LEFT: A portion of a threaded table set made by Nicholas Lutz for his wife, clear with pink threading. Tumbler, $108.00; covered jar, $216.00; threaded jug, $216.00, courtesy of Sandwich Historical Society Glass Museum.

BOTTOM RIGHT: Clear threaded cranberry lemonade tankard pitcher and 2 glasses, etched upper half gives a crackled appearance, pitcher, $216.00; glasses, $122.00 each, courtesy Sandwich Historical Society Glass Museum.

TOP LEFT: Electric blue dish, gilded edge, polished back, Mary Gregory type enameled decor, etched "Hannah - Atlantic City - 1898," $144.00, privately owned.

TOP RIGHT: Emerald green tankard pitcher, applied handle, ground pontil, 6¼" high, highlighted gold rim, Mary Gregory type decor showing a young girl catching butterflies, $338.00, privately owned.

BOTTOM: Black Mary Gregory type vase, the young boy has a toy cow tied to a stick, 13" high, circa mid-1800s, $360.00, privately owned.

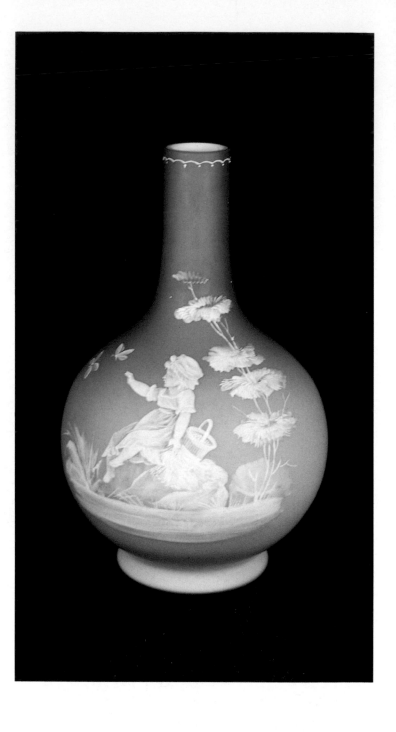

LEFT: **Rubina satin vase, Mary Gregory type enameling, attributed to the Boston and Sandwich Glass Company, inverted thumbprint, rough pontil, gold around the ruffled top, 9¼" high, $360.00, privately owned.**

RIGHT: **Unusual pink satin Mary Gregory type vase, 9" high, $576.00, Milan Historical Museum.**

TOP LEFT: Maize syrup with pewter top, applied handle, 7½" high, $367.00, Milan Historical Museum.

TOP RIGHT: Mercury glass creamer, silver quadruple-plated top, clear applied handle, cut variation of the Roman Key design, circa 1870, 6" high, attributed to the Boston Silver Glass Company, $137.00, privately owned.

BOTTOM: Miniature mercury glass creamer and footed toothpick holder, creamer has clear applied handle; both examples have white enamel decoration and gold liners; the toothpick holder is 3¾" high. Creamer, $86.00, toothpick, $58.00, Milan Historical Museum.

TOP: Box signed "KELVA" with hinged ormolu collar, original lining, swivel beveled mirror on the interior, 6-sided with lily decoration, 3¼" high, 5" diameter, $648.00, privately owned.

BOTTOM: Nakara blown-out hexagonal box, original lining, ormolu collar, 3" high, $518.00, privately owned.

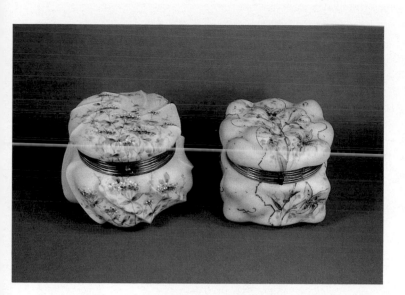

TOP: Two Wave Crest boxes: right puffy egg crate decorated with lilies, 4¼" high, $612.00; left Helmschmied Swirl, delicate florals, 4½" high, $648.00; both have plain ormolu collars, privately owned.

BOTTOM: Wave Crest vase, 23" to the top of the handles, iris decor, ornate ormolu handles and dolphin feet, $1,368.00, privately owned.

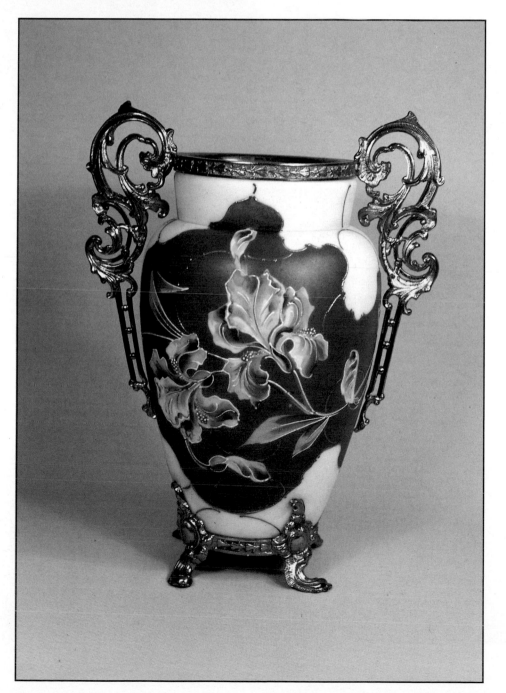

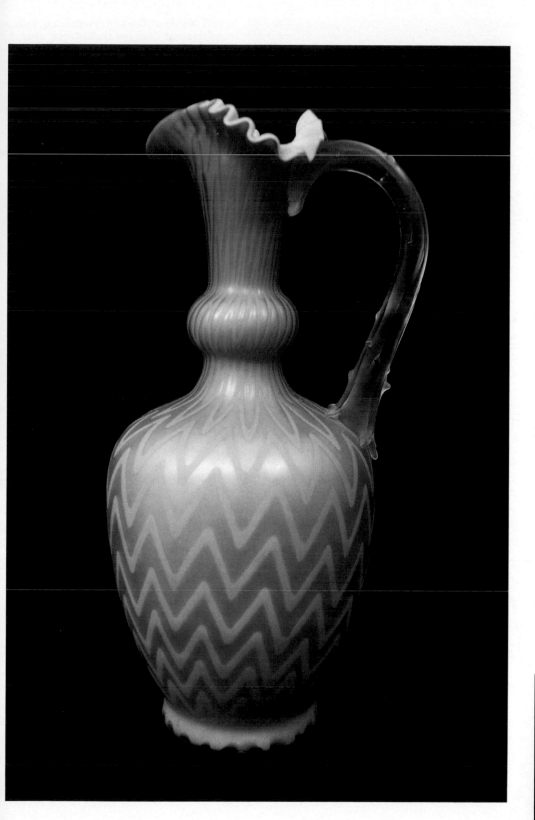

OPPOSITE PAGE TOP: Wave Crest sugar, jam jar and creamer with quadruple plated tops and handles, Helmschmied Swirl (Erie Twist), wild rose motif, 6½" top the top of the jam jar finial, $936.00 set, privately owned.

OPPOSITE PAGE BELOW: Wave Crest cigarette and match holder, apple blossom decoration, 3¾" high, 7" long, $576.00, privately owned.

TOP: Pink to white ewer, Mother-of-Pearl Satin, Herringbone pattern, clear frosted thorn handle, tri-cornered ruffled spout, bulbous neck, ground pontil, 11¾" high, $468.00, privately owned.

BOTTOM: Satin Mother-of-Pearl vase, raised Hobnail pattern, ground base, 6 sided pinched-in top, apricot to white shading, white interior casing, 5¼" high, $324.00, privately owned.

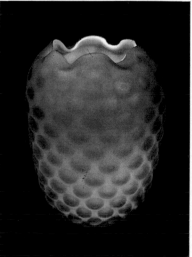

TOP: Mother-of-Pearl grouping: left to right, tri-cornered Diamond Quilted vase, shaded hues of turquoise, ground pontil, enameled floral and leaf decor, white interior, 5¾" high, $338.00; 8-sided melon ribbed vase, Diamond Quilted, ground pontil, interior cased in white, shaded pink to white exterior, 10" high, $432.00; ruffled pink to white rose bowl with white interior, Herringbone pattern, rough pontil, $252.00, privately owned.

BOTTOM LEFT: Two color rainbow Mother-of-Pearl vase, enameled in gold, crimped and turned down top, Raindrop pattern, ground pontil, 10¾" high, $1,130.00, Milan Historical Museum.

BOTTOM RIGHT: Rainbow Mother-of-Pearl examples: left, Diamond Quilted cruet, clear frosted handle and stopper, 6¼" high, $1,260.00; right, Herrigbone ewer, ruffled top and clear frosted handle, 6½" high, $1,368.00, privately owned.

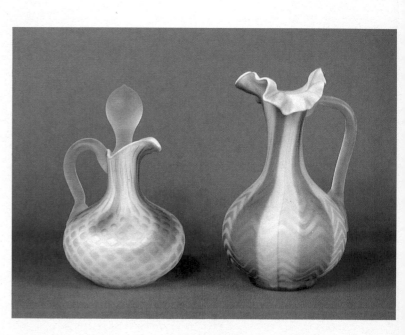

TOP: Right, Moiré pattern Mother-of-Pearl ruffled basket with frosted ribbon, applied thorn handle and tooled feet, ground pontil, 9" high, shades blue to white, $612.00; left, bulbous apricot Mother-of-Pearl pitcher, applied clear frosted and reeded handle, ground pontil, Diamond Quilted with diamond shaped spout, 4½" high, $468.00, privately owned.

RIGHT: Three-color Mother-of-Pearl Diamond Quilted vase, ground pontil, applied frosted reeded handles and ruffled ribbon edge, white lining, 7" high, $3,600.00, Milan Historical Museum.

BOTTOM: Blue Mother-of-Pearl bride's basket in a quadruple plated holder, crimped top with applied ribbon edge, Herringbone pattern, white lining, quadruple plated holder has grape and vine decor, stamped "Reed & Barton," 11" to the top of the handle, $792.00, Milan Historical Museum.

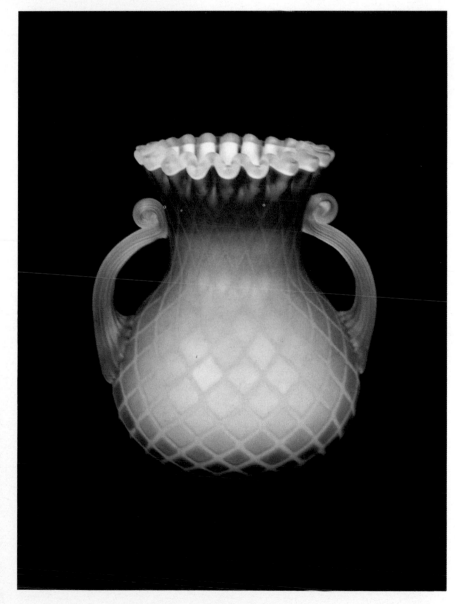

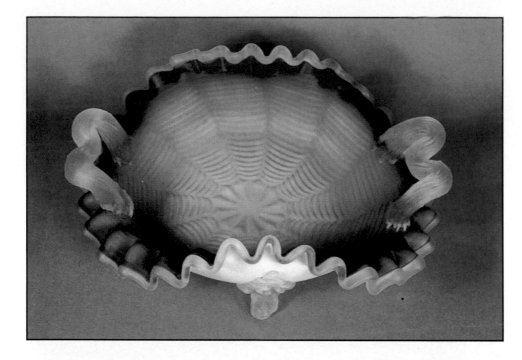

TOP: Mother-of-Pearl footed and handled basket, Spider Web design, ruffled with applied frosted ribbon edge, M-shaped handles and ruffled feet, pink hued, 11" diameter, $612.00, Milan Historical Museum.

BOTTOM: Root beer colored Mother-of-Pearl vase with 4 sided turned out top, Flower and Acorn design, ground pontil, white interior, satinized with ribbon edge, 3¾" high, $1,224.00, Milan Historical Museum.

OPPOSITE PAGE: Shiny Albertine (early Crown Milano) ewer, applied and gilded thorn handle, florals, scrolls and net decoration, signed in red enamel with a laurel wreath around a crown and the number "1011," 9¼" to the highest part, $1,800.00, Milan Historical Museum.

BOTTOM: Long neck shiny Albertine vase, applied spiral thorn ribbon gilded with raised leaves and spider mums, silver tracery over some petals, 13" high, ground pontil, red enameled signature consisting of red laurel wreath with bow surrounding a crown, number "1018" appears below the bow of the wreath, $1,728.00, privately owned.

RIGHT: Shiny Albertine vase, 11½" high, 5½" diameter at the top, embellished with entwining thorny ribbon, russet enameling inside and out highlighted with gold, rose and leaf decor, numbered in red in the ground pontil, "60/1208," $1,656.00, privately owned.

OPPOSITE PAGE: Blue Mount Washington Cameo bride's basket in a quadruple-plated holder, winged griffin motif, fruit design on the holder, marked with a "P" within a diamond, 10" high to the top of the holder, $1,224.00, privately owned.

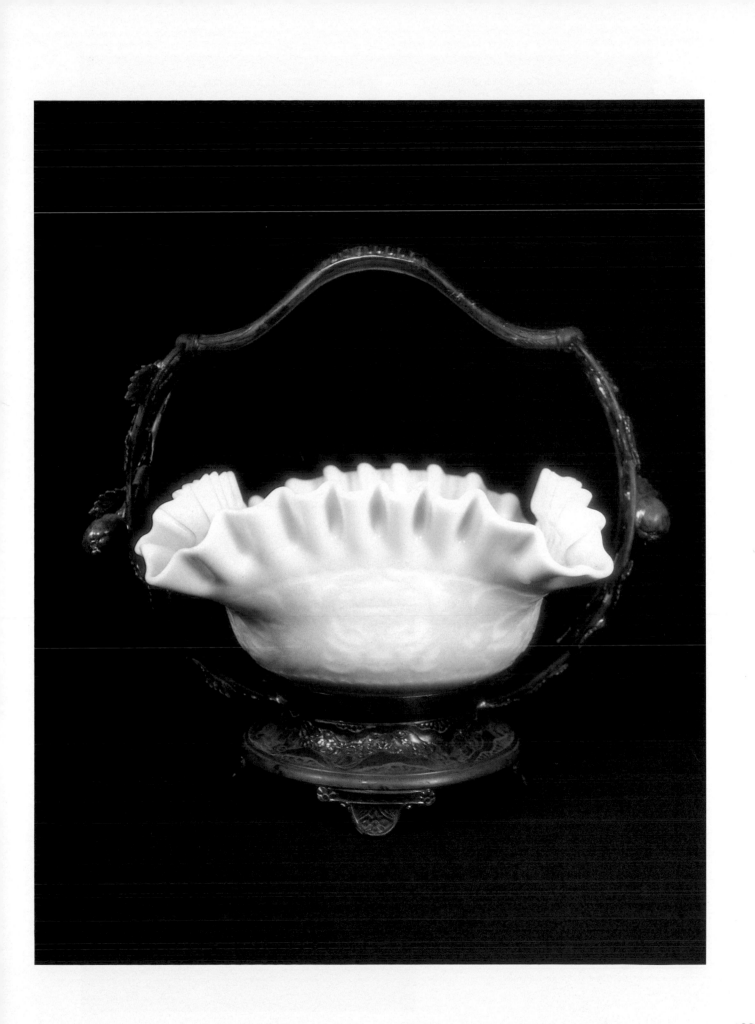

TOP: Amber Craquelle vase attributed to Mount Washington, iridescent, gilded collar, enameled with a brown lobster on the front and a reddish pink crab on the back, both are outlined in gold, hollow ground base, 5¼" high, 6" diameter, $216.00, privately owned.

BOTTOM: Mount Washington Coralene vase, ruffled top, inner milk white casing, ground pontil, satinized Peach Blow coloration, 7¼" high, yellow Seaweed design beading, $504.00, privately owned.

TOP LEFT: Ruffled Crown Milano bride's basket in a Pairpoint quadruple-plated stand with handles, circa 1890–1895, 10½" high, $1,188.00, "Collection of the Corning Museum of Glass."

TOP RIGHT: Satin Crown Milano pitcher on a Royal Flemish blank, twisted handle, decor done in earth tones, spider mums and leaves outlined in gold, numbered "506" with a crown over "CM" in gray black enamel, 8½" high, $1,008.00, privately owned.

BOTTOM: Two Crown Milano lidded jars; left, circa 1894, bulbous with pansy decor, lid marked "M.W 4419/c," base signed with enameled crown, overlapping "CM" and number "520," $936.00; right, jeweled with mottled background and applied gold threading, circa 1890s, original paper label on the base marked "Crown Milano MT. W.G. Co.," lid stamped inside "M.W 4413/f," $1,440.00 privately owned.

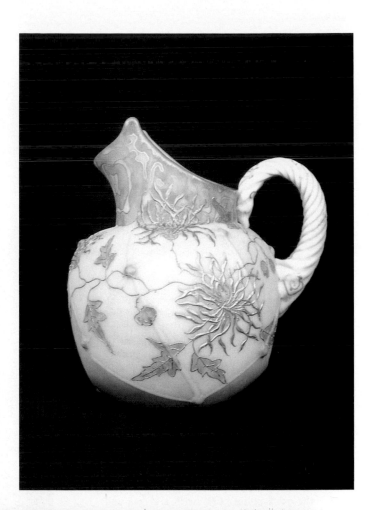

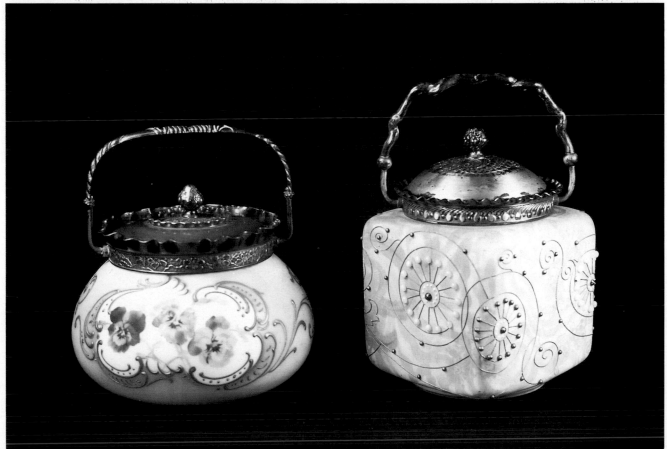

TOP LEFT: Multi-hued floral Crown Milano cracker (biscuit) jar, quadruple-plated top, interior of the lid stamped "MW 4419/c," signed in violet on the base with a crown above an overlapping "CM," 6" to the top of the final, $1,260.00, privately owned.

TOP RIGHT: Crown Milano vase with applied handles, ground pontil, gilded panel with blue violet figures, 5¾" high, $1,728.00, Milan Historical Museum.

BOTTOM: Crown Milano ewer, applied twisted handle, matte finish, heavy gilding and floral designs, 10½" high, signed with the overlapping "CM" with a crown and numbered "559" $2,448.00, Milan Historical Museum.

TOP: Mount Washington Lava vase, satin finish, ground pontil, 8¾" high, $4,320.00, Milan Historical Museum.

BOTTOM: Shiny Mount Washington lava vases and fragments: fragments were acquired from Miss Eleanor Bowman, New Bedford, Massachusetts, a retired bookkeeper at Pairpoint for 25 years who also dug fragments on the original glass site; left, vase with applied handle and ground top, inserts of green, blue, pink, white and lavender are outlined in gold, 4¾" high, $1,152.00; right, conical vase with multi-colored panels, ground top, 6" high, $792.00, privately owned.

TOP LEFT: Mount Washington Lusterless plate, 11" diameter, original painting depicts leaves and iris, $144.00, privately owned.

TOP RIGHT: Pair Lusterless boudoir bottles with blown stoppers, blown 2 mold, rough pontils, enameled dogwood and leaves, 9¼" high, $324.00 pair, privately owned, Mount Washington.

CENTER: Two Mount Washington Lusterless pitchers: left, highlighted blue handle with gilding, fern decoration, ground pontil; right, clear acid etched handle, rough pontil, 8" high to the top of the square spout, decorated with a flower and leaves, $432.00 each, privately owned.

BOTTOM: Lusterless Mount Washington plate, 7½" diameter, illustrated is the "Santa Maria" in brown tones, signed on the front "copyrighted 1893, A. E. Smith," $576.00, privately owned.

TOP: Squat footed Napoli compote, flint glass, ground pontil, gilding outlines the edges of the foot and the ruffled bowl, hued leaves and cherries are on the underside of the bowl, gold outlining is on the top surface, 3½" high, $252.00, privately owned, Mount Washington.

BOTTOM: Napoli nappy, serrated turned down handle, ground pontil, Palmer Cox Brownies playing musical instruments and a baying dog, a gold network divides the ground, $468.00, Milan Historical Museum, Mount Washington.

TOP LEFT: Mount Washington overlay ewer, serrated spout, ground pontil, 9" high, white, interior, shaded robin's egg blue to white, interior, applied amber thorn handle, tooled leaves, and molded pink, yellow and blue flowers, $648.00, privately owned.

TOP RIGHT: Mount Washington Rainbow pitcher, clear applied ribbed handle, Inverted Thumbprint pattern, ground pontil, 7½" high, $540.00, Milan Historical Museum.

BOTTOM: Three examples of Mount Washington's Peppermint Stick, cranberry ribbon edges with Picket Fence cutting, each is acidized, two have additional cutting, all are in quadruple-plated holders: left, creamer, $144.00; center, bowl, $288.00, holder stamped "HARTFORD SILVER PLATED CO. QUAD. PLATE"; right, open sugar bowl, $144.00, privately owned.

TOP: Royal Flemish vase, 6¼" high, raised gold lines segment the Indian Red, Burnt Sienna, and green tones, 5 coin medallions are spaced over the body of the vase including Roman soldier, rampant lion, dancing graces, an elderly gentleman and a sunburst, $2,880.00, privately owned.

BOTTOM: Royal Flemish vase with handles, gold and silver coin medallions are superimposed over the raised gold dividing segments, 4½" high, $3,744.00, privately owned.

TOP LEFT: Elaborate Royal Flemish ewer, applied twisted rope handle encircles the neck, muted earth tones and heavy gilding cover the surface, rampant lion decoration, shields, and scrolled leaves, 15¼" high, $5,760.00, Milan Historical Museum.

TOP RIGHT: Royal Flemish vase with dragon decoration, obverse mythological beast's head, 7½" high, $3,744.00, privately owned.

BOTTOM: Signed Royal Flemish pitcher, applied rope handle, 9" high, raised gold segmented panels, fish and shell decor, both tinted and acid-etched divisions, $5,040.00 privately owned.

TOP LEFT: Pair of Mount Washington Verona bottle vases, ribbed, ground pontils, 9¾" high, enameled front and back, sacred Ibis in flight, $1,440.00 pair, Milan Historical Museum.

BOTTOM LEFT: Verona pitcher, ribbed, floral decoration front and back, applied ribbed claw handle, ground pontil, 7¾" to the top of the handle, $972.00, Milan Historical Museum, Mount Washington.

RIGHT: Ribbed Verona vase, pinched in top, ground pontil, delicately tinted flower and leaves, highlighted with gold, 8" high, $648.00, privately owned, Mount Washington.

LEFT: Pair of Ambero hurricane lamps, tinted on the interior with chestnut leaves and burrs, exterior has a rough chipped ice effect, glass shades held in place by brass liners, turned walnut bases, 21" high, $720.00 pair, privately owned, Pairpoint.

RIGHT: Pairpoint Ambero vase, fruit and leaf decor, 8⅛" high, stamped "The Pairpoint Corp'n," also artist signed by Frank Guba, " *F.H.GUBA* "

$1,368.00, Milan Historical Museum.

TOP LEFT: Burmese tinted cracker jar, gold plated top and handle, interior of the lid numbered "3930" with the "P" within a diamond, the base is marked "3930/232," colorful floral enameling, 9" high to the top of the bail handle, $540.00, privately owned.

TOP RIGHT: Pairpoint Tavern Glass vase, bubbly, 8" high, ground pontil, numbered in white enamel "D_{281}^{1513}," Whale decoration, $144.00, privately owned.

BELOW: Two Pairpoint footed compotes with clear bubble ball connectors; left, Auroria color etched with flowers and leaves and butterflies in a spider web (Colias Design), flint quality, 6" high, $194.00; right, black amethyst, 7½" high, bowl 7¾" diameter, $216.00, privately owned.

Pairpoint grouping: left, and center, blown rose stoppers by Charles Kaziun, decanter by Gundersen. Pear is a paperweight, controlled bubble, applied stem, original paper label — "P" within a diamond — "Pairpoint, Made in U. S.A." Decanter has engraved rose and buds by Otto Carl Banks, ground pontil label with a glassblower standing surrounded by the words, "GUNDERSEN MASTERPIECE," 10¾" to the top of the stopper. $864.00, $1,332.00, $108.00, Milan Historical Museum.

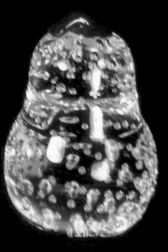

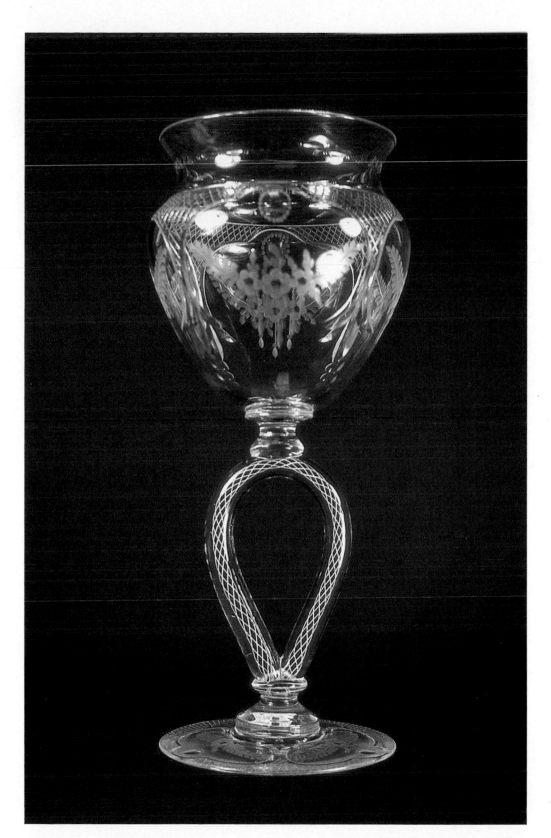

Pairpoint vase, number "1818," pink and white air traps in the twisted stem (Veneti Design), 12" high, bowl and foot engraved with garlands of flowers, $684.00, Milan Historical Museum.

TOP RIGHT: Pairpoint lamp painted on the reverse, pastoral field and mountain scene, shade stamped "The Pairpoint Corp'n," embossed silver plated base with column stamped "PAIRPOINT E3056," with the capital "P" within a diamond, $1,728.00 Milan Historical Museum.

BOTTOM RIGHT: Three heavily cut and covered topaz compotes with ball finials, Pairpoint, ground pontils. Left and right examples, 6½" high, $216.00 each; central, 8¾" high, $360.00, privately owned.

BOTTOM LEFT: Pairpoint porcelain Limoges ewer, 6¼" high, 9" long, triangular spout, applied and gilded 2 lotus branch handle, molded and tinted green leaves, highlighted with gold enameled lotus blossoms and leaves, has the green Pairpoint/Limoges stamp with crown, impressed "2028," also marked in green "2028/56," $1,152.00, privately owned.

Pairpoint Puffy lamp, blown-out grapes and leaves decorated on the reverse side, grape motif carried through on the pewter type base, 18½" to the top of the shade, marked on the inside rim in gold capital letters, "PAT APPLIED FOR," $6,480.00, privately owned.

TOP: Pairpoint Delft Ware ewer-type handled vase, opalescent white, rough pontil, 8¾" high, shaded blue windmill scene, $108.00, privately owned.

BOTTOM: Pair of Ruby Gundersen-Pairpoint vases, the feet are connected by clear bubble balls, ground pontils, 13" high, $396.00 pair, privately owned.

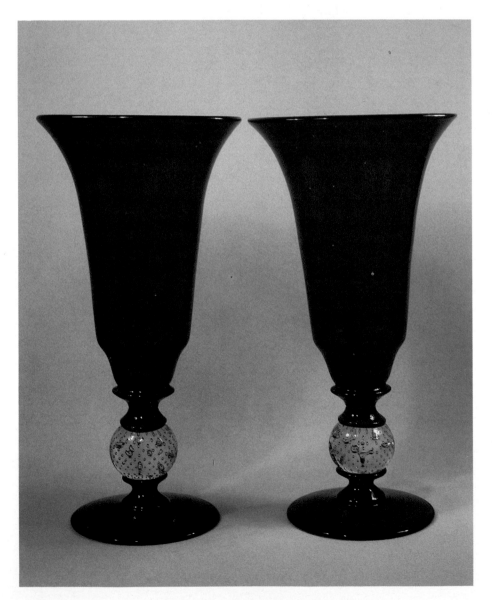

TOP LEFT: Gundersen-Pairpoint crystal perfume bottles, polished bases: left, large bubble ball, straight bird tail stopper with bubbles, 10" high; bubble ball base and stopper, ground optic bottle, 8½" high, $144.00 each, privately owned.

TOP RIGHT: Pair of crystal Gundersen-Pairpoint perfume bottles manufactured for Irving W. Rice and Company, New York: left, 8 ribbed bottle with polished base, tooled leaves and petals topper, 3" high, $94.00; right, heavy 4 lobed paperweight style base, ornate tooled leaves and petals stopper, 8" high, $194.00, privately owned.

CENTER: Gundersen-Pairpoint crystal perfumes: left, 6 cranberry ribs on the bottle, tooled leaf stopper with cranberry edges, 7¼" high, $180.00; right, 8 ribbed crystal base with applied amber wafer, finial has tooled cranberry flower and 4 tooled crystal leaves, 5¾" high, $216.00, privately owned.

BOTTOM: Crystal paperweight cologne bottle, internal finial decoration, Masonic symbol inside the bottle with the wording "Holiness to the Lord," 10 sided bottle, faceted and polished, ground pontil, 5½" high, $252.00, privately owned.

TOP: Footed Gundersen Peach Blow vase, matte finish, 9½" high, $288.00, Milan Historical Museum.

BOTTOM LEFT: Gundersen Pairpoint cup and saucer, applied white reeded handle, Peach Blow, original wholesale price for the set was $7.75, 3¼" high, saucer has ground base, cup has rough pontil, $216.00 set, privately owned.

BOTTOM RIGHT: Gundersen Peach Blow wine, 1950s vintage, applied stem and base, ground pontil, 4½" high, $194.00, privately owned.

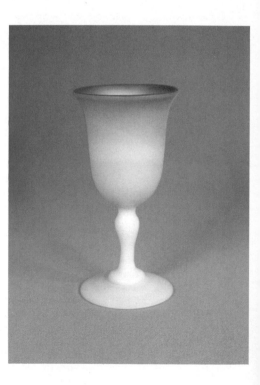

TOP LEFT: Siamese rosebowls, Mount Washington Peach Blow, ribbed with applied white floral prunts, 3⅛" high, $1,080.00, Milan Historical Museum.

TOP RIGHT: Mount Washington Peach Blow vase, crimped tri-cornered top, 3 applied shell feet, applied berry prunt, 6¾" high, $5,040.00, Milan Historical Museum.

BOTTOM: Three-piece set of Mount Washington Peach Blow, Queen's decoration, all have original paper labels, vases are 8" high; bowl has tri-cornered top and applied berry prunt, applied and tooled feet, 7" high, $21,600.00.

"On waste and woodland, rock and plain,
Its humble buds unheeded rise;
The rose has but a summer reign,
The daisy never dies!"

Mount Washington Peach Blow creamer, 5½" high, decorated with a verse by James Montgomery, $5,328.00, Houston Antique Museum.

TOP LEFT: Bulbous Peach Blow vase, satinized pink, ground pontil, molded left hand swirl, tooled top with clear acidized ribbon edging, attributed to Sandwich, $864.00, privately owned.

TOP RIGHT: Iridescent ruffled bride's basket, flint, yellow and orange sunburst interior, pink exterior, circa 1900, 8½" diameter, $216.00, privately owned, New Martinsville.

BOTTOM LEFT: New England Peach Blow: left, glossy trumpet vase, 9¾" high, $1,152.00; right, acid finish toothpick holder, $540.00, Milan Historical Museum.

BOTTOM RIGHT: New England Peach Blow grouping: left and right, matte and shiny tankard pitchers, with applied reeded handles, 9" high, $1,440.00 each; foreground, ruffled bowl, $1,008.00, Houston Antique Museum.

TOP LEFT: Glossy Wheeling Peach Blow examples: left, tumbler, 3¾" high, $480.00; right, cruet with stopper and applied amber handle, 6½" high, $1,872.00, Milan Historical Museum.

TOP RIGHT: Acid-treated Wheeling Peach Blow stick vase, deep mahogany top, white lining, 8½" high, $1,440.00, Milan Historical Museum.

CENTER: Wheeling Peach Blow classic stick vase, glossy finish, white lining, ground pontil, 10" high, $1,728.00, privately owned.

BOTTOM LEFT: Wheeling Peach Blow pitcher, Drape pattern, glossy, applied amber reeded handle, opal lining, Hobbs, Brockunier and Company, 4¾" high, $936.00, Milan Historical Museum.

BOTTOM RIGHT: Shiny Wheeling Peach Blow Morgan type vase, pressed 5 griffins, amber base acidized, white liner, Hobbs, Brockunier and Company, Wheeling, West Virginia, circa 1886–1891, 10" high, $1,872.00, "Collection of The Corning Museum of Glass."

126

TOP: Phoenix pillow-shaped vase, flying geese decor in white on a blue ground, 9⅛" high, 11" diameter, $288.00, privately owned.

BOTTOM: Pigeon Blood grouping, Torquay pattern: left, lidded jar with handles, 8½" high, $684.00; bride's basket, 11" diameter, $914.00; lidded jar, 8½" high, $684.00, all have quadruple-plated fixtures, Antique Emporium.

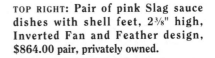

TOP RIGHT: Pair of pink Slag sauce dishes with shell feet, 2⅜" high, Inverted Fan and Feather design, $864.00 pair, privately owned.

LEFT: Pink Slag tumbler, Inverted Fan and Feather pattern, 4" high, $576.00, Milan Historical Museum.

BOTTOM RIGHT: Two second-grind Pomona pitchers: New England Glass Works, both have excellent staining and are in the Inverted Diamond pattern; left, tankard with clear applied handle and blueberries and leaves design, 8½" high, $504.00; right, creamer with stained handle, 6¾" high, $360.00, Houston Antique Museum.

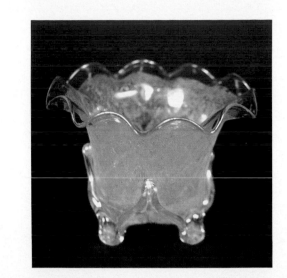

TOP LEFT: **Pomona first-grind cruet, applied foot, ground pontil, cornflower decor, ball stopper, 7" high, $410.00, privately owned.**

TOP RIGHT: **Pomona vase, stained wishbone feet and ruffled top, first-grind, Expanded Diamond pattern, 3¾" high, $288.00, Milan Historical Museum.**

CENTER: **Pomona second-grind creamer and sugar, applied handles, 4" high, Butterfly and Pansy pattern, gold and blue staining $864.00 set, Milan Historical Museum.**

BOTTOM RIGHT: **Left, Pomona first-grind tumbler, Acanthus Leaf decor, 3⅝" high, $180.00; right, punch cup, second-grind, applied handle, Blueberry and Leaf decoration, stained red, blue and gold, $194.00, Milan Historical Museum.**

Three clear inkwells, faceted and with stoppers, internally cased with colorful wine glasses, circa 1830, manufactured in the Pittsburgh area, 7⅞" to the top of the blue example, $540.00 set, Milan Historical Museum.

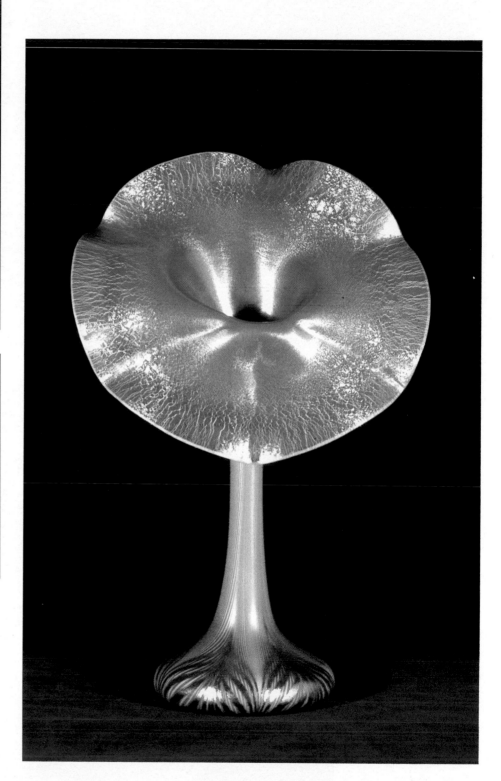

TOP LEFT: Quezal gourd-shaped vase, opal glass, pulled and applied decoration, brown toned with blue, gold and pinkish lavender highlights, signed and numbered, 7¾" high, $3,600.00, Milan Historical Museum.

RIGHT: Jack-in-the-pulpit Quezal vase, opal glass with pulled green leaf decoration, gold lustre lining, engraved "Quezal," $2,160.00, The Historical Society of Western Pennsylvania.

BOTTOM LEFT: Left, iridescent peacock blue Quezal vase, 6" high, signed "Quezal," $936.00; right, opal with green Coiled design, gold at the base, gold and pink iridescent lining, signed "Quezal, S 879," $1,368.00, privately

132

OPPOSITE TOP LEFT: Three gold lustred Quezal vases, all signed and numbered: left, 6½" high, opal glass with pulled decorations; center, corset-shaped, opal glass, pulled green and gold decor; right, gold lustre vase having pink highlights, engraved silver deposit decoration; $1,440.00, $1,728.00, $2,160.00, Milan Historical Museum.

OPPOSITE TOP RIGHT: Iridescent Quezal goblet and ruffled top flower form, both are signed and numbered, pulled and marvered leaf designs; left, 8⅛" high, $396.00; right, 5¾" high, $792.00, retains the original distributor's label (—A. STOWELL & CO. INC. WINTER ST. BOSTON), Milan Historical Museum.

OPPOSITE BOTTOM: Quezal opal glass basket, twisted rope handle, leaf pattern in green and gold lustre, guilloche decoration above in gold lustre, signed "Quezal," 6¼" to the top of the handle, $1,584.00, privately owned.

TOP LEFT: A colorful assortment of Reading Artistic Glass Works fragments donated by the late Miss Marie Ada Miler Kremp whose grandfather Lewis Kremp was the founder of the factory.

TOP RIGHT: Opalescent rose pink Reading pitcher, 9¼" high, fiery opalescent reeded handle, rough broken pontil, bulbous portion of the pitcher is 7" wide, $396.00, privately owned.

BOTTOM: Reading clear Craquelle pitcher with overshot effect, faint tan tint, 10" high, applied clear reeded handle, 6" at its greatest diameter, rough pontil, $360.00, privately owned.

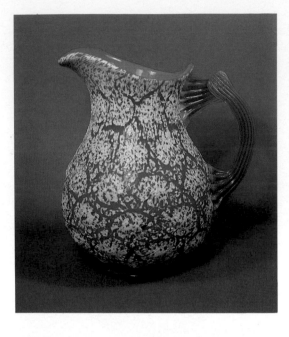

TOP LEFT: Pink opalescent Reading pitcher, raised Coin Spot design, 9½" high, white opaque mottling, applied opalescent base and most unusual 2 piece applied fiery opalescent reeded handle, rough pontil, 6" at its widest portion, $432.00, privately owned.

TOP RIGHT: Pair of Reading opalescent baluster-shaped pitchers, clear applied handles, rough pontils, both 11½" high; left, opalescent Coin Dots, $396.00; right, opalescent vertical Ribbed pattern, $396.00, privately owned.

BOTTOM LEFT: Shiny black baluster vase with white opaque surface mottling, made at Reading, 14" high, ruffled 4 sided top, rough pontil, a most unusual example, $576.00, privately owned.

BOTTOM RIGHT: Left, 14" white opalescent baluster vase with Craquelle finish and slight overshot texture, Reading, white opalescent ring at the neck, rough pontil, $396.00; right, Reading 12" white opalescent pitcher with overshot effect, opalescent handle, rough pontil, $360.00; both privately owned.

TOP: Rubina crystal pickle castor, ornate quadruple plated holder, marked "Derby Silver Co.," 11" to the top of the handle, $554.00, Milan Historical Museum.

BOTTOM: Rubina Verde pitcher, Inverted Thumbprint, colored applied reeded handle, ground pontil, enameled butterfly and flowers, 6¾" high, $324.00, Milan Historical Museum.

TOP LEFT: Cranberry champagne pitcher with overshot and bladder, clear applied handle, 11" high, 6" diameter, 1870–1887, $540.00, courtesy of Sandwich Historical Society Glass Museum.

TOP RIGHT: Blue overshot pitcher, Sandwich, applied amber reeded handle in scalloped shell design, 8" high, 8" diameter, circa 1870–1887, $432.00, courtesy of Sandwich Historical Society Glass Museum.

BOTTOM RIGHT: Cranberry Sandwich overshot pitcher, tooled feet, applied thorn handle and icicles, 13" high, $648.00, Houston Antique Museum.

BOTTOM LEFT: Sandwich amber overshot pitcher, clear applied reeded handle, 9" high, $410.00, courtesy of Sandwich Historical Society Museum.

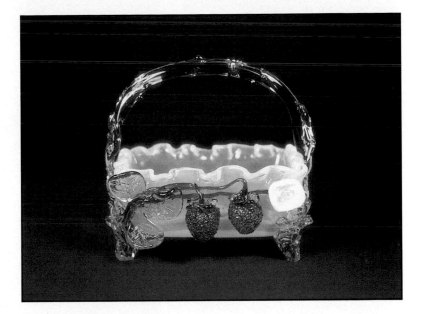

TOP LEFT: Sandwich opalescent creamer, pink top, applied overshot strawberry, tooled leaves, applied amber thorn handle and feet, ground pontil, 5" high to the top of the spout, $612.00, Milan Historical Museum.

TOP RIGHT: Rectangular opalescent ruffled Sandwich basket, ground pontil, applied amber thorn handle and 4 feet, overlay strawberries, leaves, stems and blossom, 7" high, 6" wide, 4" deep, $756.00, privately owned.

BOTTOM RIGHT: Black amethyst rectangular lidded box, ormolu collar and feet, white enameled Mary Gregory type decoration, 5" high, attributed to the Boston and Sandwich Glass Company, $1,008.00, Milan Historical Museum.

BOTTOM LEFT: Six-sided Tortoise-shell finger bowl, ground pontil, silver flecks scattered throughout the glass, 2¾" high, circa 1890, attributed to the Boston And Sandwich Glass Company, $180.00, privately owned.

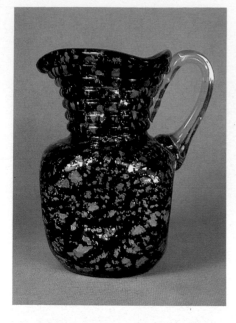

TOP LEFT: Unusual cobalt creamer, Spangle glass with mica flecks, clear casing, pinched in sides, clear applied handle, ground base, 5" high, $252.00, Milan Historical Museum.

TOP RIGHT: Paperweight on white latticino, red 10 petaled clematis, green stem with 3 leaves and a bud, center of the flower is a cane, attributed to the Boston and Sandwich Glass Company, $1,584.00, Milan Historical Museum.

BOTTOM: Latticino paperweight with tinted fruit on green leaves, 2½" diameter, $1,440.00, attributed to the Boston and Sandwich Glass Company, Milan Historical Museum.

TOP: Sandwich Cranberry icicle vase, clear applied neck rigaree, ground pontil, 9" high, $1,224.00, Milan Historical Museum.

BOTTOM: Left, 8 ribbed smoky topaz vase, clear rim rigaree, 8 clear overshot icicles, 1¼" ground pontil, 5½" high, $396.00; electric blue ribbed bottle shaped vase, 12" high, 3 applied free formed clear overshot feet, ground pontil, 16 assorted length clear overshot icicles, clear applied rigaree at the neck over the icicles, $1,224.00; both manufactured by the Boston and Sandwich Glass Company, privately owned.

TOP LEFT: Amber tankard pitcher, 7½" high, 4¾" diameter, amber handle and amber threading, copper wheel engraved heron among water lilies and cattails, $396.00, courtesy of Sandwich Historical Society Glass Museum, Sandwich.

TOP RIGHT: Sandwich glass fragments dug at the factory site in September, 1938, by E. Karl and Caroline Houck, also Isabel and Geier Freehafer, donated by Mr. and Mrs. Albert T. Yuhasz.

BOTTOM RIGHT: Pair of clear flint horn glasses (megaphone shaped) with ruby threading, ground pontils, engraved with an "H," 5¼" high, 2" diameter. Part of a set of 6, ordered engraved for a librarian named Miss Hooper from Brookline, Massachusetts, $108.00 each, privately owned, Sandwich.

BOTTOM LEFT: Creamer attributed to the Boston and Sandwich Glass Company, white overlay cut to clear crystal, clear applied handle, 3⅛" to the top of the handle, $468.00, Milan Historical Museum.

TOP LEFT: Overlay cologne bottle with stopper, ruby glass cased with white and cut away, cut designs outlined in gold, ground pontil, 6½" high, $216.00, privately owned.

TOP RIGHT: Mold blown vase, acorn bottom, crimped petal top, opalescent, shades like a vivid sunrise, red-orange to yellow, 2⅞" high, possibly Sandwich, $216.00, Milan Historical Museum.

BOTTOM RIGHT: Sandwich Fireglow vase, 9" high, bulbous base, narrow tapered neck, enameled floral and leaf decoration, $252.00, privately owned.

BOTTOM LEFT: Sandwich Fireglow, lidded jar with white fiery opalescent liner, 5¼" high, $288.00, gilded with enameled bird and leaf decor, Milan Historical Museum.

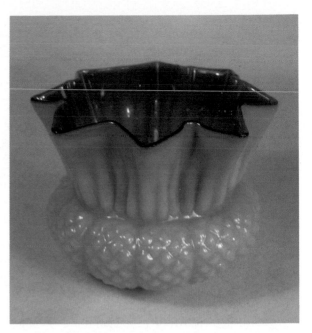

TOP: Ruffled satin bride's basket, internal enameling, in a quadruple-plated silver holder, footed and handled with a full figure, signed "Meriden," 11½" to the top of the figure, $554.00, Milan Historical Museum.

BOTTOM RIGHT: Mount Washington rose to pink satin cookie jar, Venetian Swag pattern, enameled flowers and leaves with gilding, quadruple-plated silver top with bail handle, lid stamped "M.W 4413/b," 7" high, $432.00, privately owned.

BOTTOM LEFT: Ribbed and swirled pink and white opalescent vase, ruffled top, in a signed "PAIRPOINT" quadruple-plated presentation holder, engraved "Withers Div. U.R.K. of P. to W.B. Lawrence Capt. Jan. 8-95," 9" high with the holder, $504.00, privately owned.

LEFT: White Satin "Gone with the Wind" lamp, blown-out hanging grape motif, brass fixtures, cast iron base with raised grape design, circa late 1880s, 26½" high, $936.00, privately owned.

TOP RIGHT: Pair of shaded opalescent syrups: left, Blue, Daisy and Fern pattern, applied blue handle, tin top, 5½" high, $166.00; right, light Cranberry Spanish Lace syrup, clear applied reeded handle, silver-plated top, 5½" high, $252.00, privately owned.

BOTTOM RIGHT: Red Satin "Gone with the Wind" lamp, raised poppy flowers, stippled background, brass fittings, cast iron base with claw feet, circa late 1890s, 25½" high, $1080.00, privately owned.

TOP LEFT: Ruby overlay silvered glass spooner, cut through in a pattern, footed, 5" high, engraved "Presented to ELLEN A. SWINERTON BY ELISABETH CROCKER," $288.00, courtesy of Sandwich Historical Society Glass Museum, Sandwich.

TOP RIGHT: Ten inch silver deposit clear glass pitcher, Iris design with well executed hand chasing, impressed "999/1000 FINE, PATENTED 3850," at the base of the handle, engraved dates "1854–1904" appear opposite the handle on the front of the pitcher, probably a 50th wedding anniversary present, 24 point cut star on the bottom, attributed to the Alvin Silver Decorating Company, New York, $432.00, privately owned.

BOTTOM RIGHT: Ruby silvered glass footed salt, ruby cut through to a pattern in the silvered glass, plated with a tiny layer of clear glass, broken off pontil that is sealed, 3" high, attributed to the Boston and Sandwich Glass Company, $252.00, privately owned.

BOTTOM LEFT: Signed and ribbed Sinclair green crystal vase, 3" ground pontil, 12" high, rim is gilded, decor consists of 3 acid-etched and gilded butterflies, acid-etched poppies and leaves, stained and gilded, referred to as "Pearl" ware, $360.00, privately owned.

TOP: Pair of conical vases with gilded body rings, both signed in small enameled script, "Smith Bro's," left, 8" high, tinted tan with hummingbird and floral design, $202.00; right 5¾" high, light blue ground, 2 round panels, one showing reeds against a mountain background, the other depicts 2 birds perched on a branch in blossom, $180.00, privately owned.

CENTER: Smith Brothers melon-ribbed covered jar, satin finish, decorated with pansies, 3½" high, signed with the rampant lion mark in red, $540.00, privately owned.

BOTTOM: Satin melon-ribbed covered jar, quadruple-plated collar and twisted handle, enameled floor decor, 3¾" high, Smith Brothers, rampant lion trademark, $468.00, privately owned.

LEFT: Shiny milk glass parlor lamp, brass fittings, cast iron claw-footed base, enameled pansies and leaves, attributed to the Smith Brothers, 18" high, $612.00, privately owned.

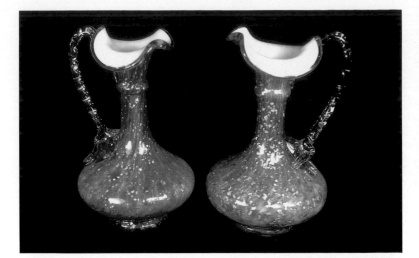

TOP LEFT: Pair of Victorian Spangle ewers, white liners, clear outer casings and ornate applied clear handles, ground pontils, 9½" high, $1080.00 pair, Milan Historical Museum.

CENTER LEFT: Spangle grouping: left, green basket, clear applied and twisted thorn handle, fluted top, ground pontil, 7" to the top of the handle; center, red and white water tumbler in Acanthus Leaf pattern, clear outer casing; right, multi-colored basket, clear twisted and applied reeded handle, ground pontil, $238.00, $144.00, $209.00, Milan Historical Museum.

BOTTOM LEFT: Spatter baskets with ruffled tops: left, heart shaped, applied clear thorn, bail type handle; right rectangular, clear twisted thorn handle, 8" to the top of the handle. Both have white linings, clear outer casings and ground pontils, $223.00, $252.00, Milan Historical Museum.

TOP RIGHT: Spatter and spangle creamer, square top, swirled rib exterior, clear outer casing, white interior, applied clear reeded handle, 5¾" high, circa 1880s, $238.00, Antique Emporium.

BOTTOM RIGHT: Spatter pitcher, tri-cornered ruffled top, green with opalescent white spattering, 7½" high, clear applied reeded handle, ground pontil, $194.00, Antique Emporium.

TOP LEFT: Star Holly coral tinted footed stemware, 3¾" high, raised factory mark on the base, $266.00, Milan Historical Museum.

TOP RIGHT: Wedgwood blue Star Holly goblet, Imperial Glass Company, 5" high, finely stippled base with the intertwined "IG" mark in the center, $288.00, privately owned.

BOTTOM: Steuben Verre de Soie trio: left, three-pronged thorn vase, Fleur-de-Lis signature, 6½" high; center, three-piece condiment set, applied and tooled blue stem and leaf; right, footed glass, applied pink threading, $216.00, $288.00, $209.00, Milan Historical Museum.

OPPOSITE TOP: Steuben three-piece Ivory console set, applied black feet, circa 1930, candlesticks, 11⅛" high, gift of Dr. Nordberg, $1,728.00 set. "The Rockwell Museum Collection, courtesy of The Corning Museum of Glass."

OPPOSITE BOTTOM: Black glass Steuben grouping, circa 1920s: left to right, pair of candlesticks, acid etched vase, two covered jars with gold tops, tallest example 12" high, $1,440.00, $3,600.00, $576.00, $720.00, "The Rockwell Museum and The Corning Museum of Glass Collection, courtesy of The Corning Museum of Glass."

TOP: Three-pronged Ivrene lily vase, Steuben, late 1920s, 11¾" high, $1,800.00, "Courtesy of The Corning Museum of Glass, gift of Frederick Carder."

BOTTOM LEFT: Steuben Alabaster vases with applied black glass decoration, probably about 1925, center example, 8" high, $504.00, $576.00, $540.00, "The Rockwell Museum Collection, courtesy of The Corning Museum of Glass."

BOTTOM RIGHT: Console set and vase, Rose over alabaster, Steuben, copper wheel engraving, candlesticks 14½" high, $684.00, $936.00, $576.00, "The Rockwell Museum Collection, courtesy of The Corning Museum of Glass."

TOP LEFT: Venetian-styled Steuben Cyprian covered compote, iridescent, applied blue edging with blue handles and free standing rings, rough pontil, apple finial, 11" high, $324.00, privately owned.

TOP RIGHT: Steuben Verre de Soie grouping, about 1905–1930s, covered vase, 12¼" high: left to right, $238.00, $288.00, $338.00, $410.00, $302.00, "The Rockwell Museum Collection, courtesy of The Corning Museum of Glass."

BOTTOM: Nine Steuben drinking glasses, assorted shapes and glass types, circa 1920s, tallest goblet 8" high, prices vary, $144.00 – 432.00, "The Rockwell Museum Collection, courtesy of The Corning Museum of Glass."

TOP: Diatreta vase, signed "F. Carder 1955," inscribed "Life Is Short, Art Is Long," 9" high, amethyst shades, $28,800.00+, "Collection of The Corning Museum of Glass, Bequest of Gladys C. Welles."

BOTTOM: Frederick Carder Diatreta vase, 6⅜" high, singed "F. Carder 1953," varying amethyst shades, $28,800.00, "Collection of The Corning Museum of Glass, gift of Frederick Carder."

TOP: Mandarin Yellow vases, Steuben, about 1916, tallest example, 6¼" high, $14,400.00+ per example, Collection of The Corning Museum of Glass, Bequest of Gladys C. Welles, Gift of Frederick Carder, and Gift of Gillett Welles."

BOTTOM: Steuben Rouge Flambé bowl, circa 1926, bequest of Frank and Mary E. Reifschlager, 6!/3" high $11,520.00+, "The Rockwell Museum Collection, courtesy of The Corning Museum of Glass."

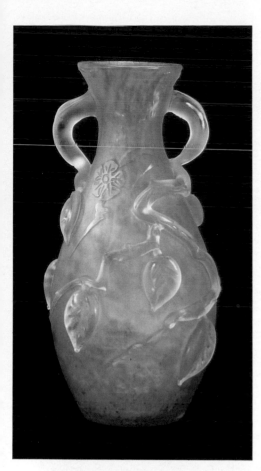

TOP LEFT: Steuben Rose quartz vase, late 1920s, 11¼" high, cut flower, satinized clear applied handles, leaves, and stems, $4,320.00+ "Reifschlager bequest, The Rockwell Museum Collection, courtesy of The Corning Museum of Glass."

TOP RIGHT: Cintra grouping, two vases and a bowl, about 1917, Steuben, tallest example, 15/½: high, $1,152.00+ for each, "The Rockwell Museum Glass Collection, courtesy of The Corning Museum of Glass."

BOTTOM: Left to right, green Florentia vase, pink ruffled bowl, compote and pair of candlesticks, Steuben, late 1920s, bowl, Reifschlager bequest, vase 13" high, $7,200.00+, $8,600.00, $7,200.00, $4,320.00+ pair, "the Rockwell Museum Collection, courtesy of The Corning Museum of Glass."

Steuben Tyrian Glass vase, number "2422", 10½" high, dated "1917", $11,520.00+, "Collection of The Corning Museum of Glass, Bequest of Gladys C. Welles."

TOP: Crystal bowl, Steuben trial piece, 3¼" high, enameled floral decor in green, yellow and blue. This type of decoration was not used on production items, no price comparison available, "Collection of The Corning Museum of Glass, gift of Corning Glass Works."

BOTTOM: Steuben Plum jade vase, 11¾" high, acid-etched Peking pattern, 1920s, $3,600.00, "The Rockwell Museum Collection, courtesy of The Corning Museum of Glass."

Rose Quartz etched vase, Steuben, variant number "6650," 12½" high, acid finished, circa 1920s, $2,160.00. "Collection of The Corning Museum of Glass, gift of Otto Hilbert."

TOP LEFT: Copper wheel engraved dragon on black, signed "Hawkes," ground pontil, 8⅛" high, circa 1920, Corning glass Works blank, $324.00, Milan Historical Museum.

TOP RIGHT: Cluthra vase with applied crystal handles, Steuben Glass, 10" high, shaded green to white, number 6870, late 1920s, $1080.00, "The Rockwell Museum Collection, courtesy of The Corning Museum of Glass."

BOTTOM: Steuben Glass Millefiori bowls, 1915-1930, center example. 11¼" diameter, $1,728.00 per example. "The Rockwell Museum and The Corning Museum of Glass Collection, courtesy of The Corning Museum of Glass."

TOP: Cire Perdue, puma killing a snake, Frederick Carder, Steuben Glass, 1941, 8" long, $5,040.00+, "Collection of The Corning Museum of Glass, Gift of Corning Glass Works."

BOTTOM LEFT: Frederick Carder signed self portrait, 1951, no price comparison available, frosted glass, animal masks below, around the ring is the wording "ENGLAND - 1864-1902 FREDERICK CARDER. 1864-1950 USA - 1903-1950. GLASS MAKING," "Collection of The Corning Museum of Glass, gift of Corning Glass Works."

BOTTOM RIGHT: Frederick Carder, Pate de Verre classical figure and dancing fawn panel, 1930s, Steuben Glass, 9¼" long, varies from ¼" to ½" in thickness, $2,880.00+, "Collection of The Corning Museum of Glass, Bequest of Gladys C. Welles."

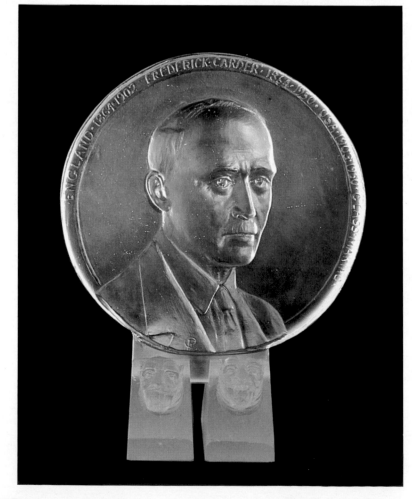

Steuben Gold Aurene vase, black and white collar, probably 1910-1920, Reifschlager bequest, 10!/3" high, $4,320.00+, "The Rockwell Museum Collection, courtesy of The Corning Museum of Glass."

Decorated Gold Avenue vases with millefiori flowers, Steuben, circa 1905-1910, tallest vase 12¼" high, $3,600.00 each, "The Rockwell Museum Collection, courtesy of The Corning Museum of Glass."

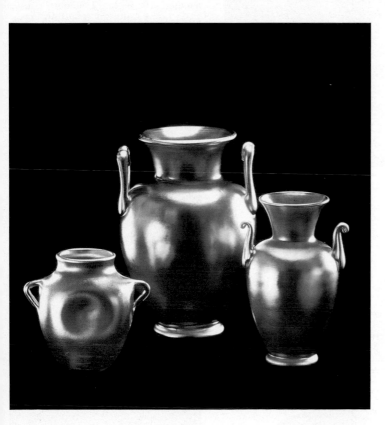

TOP LEFT: Gold Aurene grouping, Steuben, all three signed: left, swirled decoration; center, pink and green highlights, 6¼" high; right, ribbed body and three ribbed feet, $1,728.00, $2,160.00, $828.00, privately owned.

TOP RIGHT: Steuben millefiori Green and Gold Aurene vases: left, signed "AURENE 211" 4" high; right, signed "AURENE 573," 4¾" high, both have ground pontils, $2,520.0, $2,160.00, Milan Historical Museum.

BOTTOM RIGHT: Three Steuben Aurene perfumes, all signed, tallest example is 6½" high: left, Blue Aurene with applied handles; center, pinched in sides; right, melon ribbed, shape number "1455," $720.00, $7565.00, $684.00, privately owned.

BOTTOM LEFT: Iridescent Steuben Gold Aurene vases with applied handles, circa 1940 to early 1930s, tallest vase, 10½" high, $720.00, $756.00, $684.00, "The Rockwell Museum Collection, courtesy of The Corning Museum of Glass."

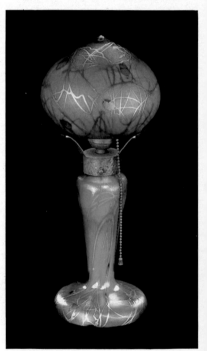

TOP: Red, Green and Brown Aurene vases with applied Gold Aurene decorations and linings, about 1910-1915, center vase, 10¼" high, Steuben Glass, $6,480.00+, $3,312.00+, $5,472.00+ "The Rockwell Museum Collection, courtesy of The Corning Museum of Glass."

BOTTOM RIGHT: Steuben boudoir lamp, Green Aurene with Gold Aurene decor, 15½" high, about 1916, $4,320.00+, "Reifschlager bequest, The Rockwell Museum Collection, courtesy of The Corning Museum of Glass."

BOTTOM LEFT: Three-footed Blue Aurene examples, circa 1905-early 1930s, iridescent, tallest example with applied handles, 10" high, all Steuben Glass, $504.00, $1,008.00, $720.00, "The Rockwell Museum Collection, courtesy of The Corning Museum of Glass."

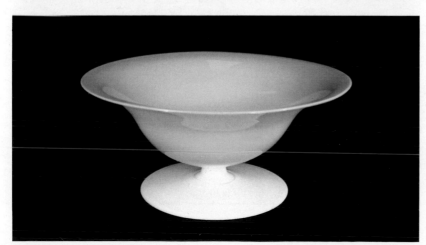

TOP LEFT: Steuben Yellow Jade iridescent vase, Blue Aurene overlay branch and leaf decor, 11" high, $2,592.00, Milan Historical Museum.

TOP RIGHT: Steuben Alexandrite console set, 1920's, candlesticks, 12" high, private collection, $720.00 set, "Courtesy of The Corning Museum of Glass."

CENTER: Jade Green Steuben nappy and swirled mug, applied Alabaster handles, nappy has a ground pontil; mug is signed with the Fleur-de-Lis signature, mug is 5¾" high, $122.00, $144.00, Milan Historical Museum.

BOTTOM: Steuben Blue Jade compote, Alabaster foot, ground pontil, 4¾" high, 10¼" diameter, $360.00, Milan Historical Museum.

OPPOSITE TOP: Yellow Silverina bowl and blue candlesticks, Diamond Optic pattern, circa late 1920s, Steuben, diameter of bowl, 11", $936.00, $720.00 pair, "The Rockwell Museum Collection, courtesy of The Corning Museum of Glass."

OPPOSITE BOTTOM: Topaz grouping, six examples with applied decoration, height of covered jar, 12¾", The Rockwell Museum Collection, 3 pieces gifts of Gratia R. Montgomery: left to right, compote $216.00; vase with rings, $144.00; covered jar, $252.00; bowl and underplate, $144.00; decanter with stopper, $252.00; and footed vase, $180.00, "Courtesy, The Corning Museum of Glass."

TOP: Steuben Selenium Ruby grouping: left, ribbed vase with ground pontil, Fleur-de-Lis mark, $216.00; right, swirled candlestick, copper wheel engraved with grapes and leaves, block signature, 12" high, $288.00, Milan Historical Museum.

BOTTOM; Five-piece Intarsia grouping, Steuben, late 1920's and early 1930's. The Rockwell Museum and The Corning Museum of Glass Collection: left to right, square footed crystal bowl with blue decoration; number "7051" bowl, black and crystal, Modern design; blue and crystal vase, 6 sided foot; amethyst and crystal vase, 6 sided foot; amethyst decorated and crystal compote, square footed base. All pieces have the engraved "Fred'k Carder" facsimile signature at their bases about the foot and stem; black and crystal bowl unsigned, $ 8,352.00+, $7,920.00+, $9,360.00+, $8,640.00+, $8,928.00; tallest example 9¾" high, "Courtesy of The Corning Museum of Glass."

Steuben amethyst cased, cut and engraved glassware, 1920s, center goblet, 10" high, $216.00 each, "Collection of The Corning Museum of Glass."

TOP LEFT: Amethyst Steuben ribbed goblet, clear stem and finger bowl, both 16-ribbed with ground pontils, flint quality, bowl signed with the acid-stamped "STEUBEN" signature within a Fleur-de-Lis, goblet, 6" high, bowl, 2¼" high, 4¾" diameter, $50.00, $236.00, privately owned.

TOP RIGHT: Pair of Steuben colognes: left, Bristol Yellow, 7: high, flat ground, pink swirled stopper with mica flecks, crown shaped body cut from a globular exterior wall, $396.00; right, black square bottle, tooled floral jade Green stopper, $275.00, Milan Historical Museum.

CENTER: Steuben 16-ribbed crystal vase, applied Wisteria colored filigree and prunts, 7" high, 6½" diameter, signed "STEUBEN" in block letters, $396.00, privately owned.

BOTTOM: Steuben Bristol Yellow three-piece perfume set, black lids and applied black threading. Large jar has the Fleur-de-Lis signature, a ground pontil, and measures 6½" high, $588.00 set, Milan Historical Museum.

TOP: Steuben Paperweight or heavy cut cologne bottles with internal colored decorations, bottle on left with bubbles, 7½" high, circa 1920s, $1,440.00 each, "The Rockwell Museum Collection, courtesy of The Corning Museum of Glass."

BOTTOM: Steuben drinking vessels, five from a set of 49 pieces, clear bowls, Rosa stems and feet, copper wheel engraved, all signed with the Fleur-de-Lis, tallest glass is 8½" high, $6,480.00 set, privately owned.

OPPOSITE PAGE: Four shaded crystal Grotesque vases and a bowl, Steuben Glass, in amethyst, Flemish Blue and ruby, circa late 1920s - early 1930s, tallest vase is 18" high, private collection and The Rockwell Museum Collection. Left to right, amethyst vase, $338.00; Flemish Blue bowl, $432.00; tallest ruby vase, $864.00; Flemish Blue vase, $720.00; ruby vase, $432.00, "Courtesy of The Corning Museum of Glass."

Top: Pair Steuben cut crystal pheasants, variant of number 6504, 12" long, flat ground tails and bases, circa late 1920s, $1,224.00 pair, Milan Historical Museum.

BOTTOM: Steuben Oriental Jade and Oriental Poppy grouping, late 1920s, vase on the left, 7" high, "The Rockwell Museum Collection; left to right, vase, $540.00; cologne with stopper, $576.00; rectangular cologne with flower stopper, $540.00; tapered cologne, $504.00; vase, $468.00, "Courtesy of The Corning Museum of Glass."

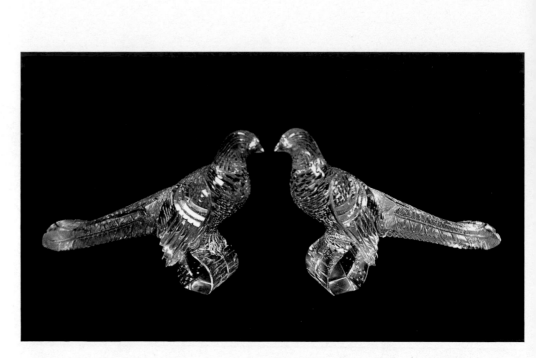

TOP LEFT: Iridescent Tiffany trumpet vase, applied dome base, green heart-shaped leaves and vines, 11¾" high, signed "1534 - 640 M L.C. Tiffany Favrile," $1,800.00, Milan Historical Museum.

RIGHT: Iridescent blue Tiffany candle lamp, ruffled shade, twisted base, pink and yellow highlights, signed "L.C.T. Favrile," 13¼" high, $1,728.00, Milan Historical Museum.

BOTTOM LEFT: Greenish gold Tiffany bowl and footed sherbet, bowl 2½" high, glazed bottom iridescent inside, signed "L.C.T.," $1080.00; sherbet, 3¼" high, Artichoke pattern, elephant foot, three layers of glass, signed "L.C.T. Favrile," $1,224.00, Milan Historical Museum.

TOP RIGHT: Two intaglio-cut Tiffany pieces, grapes and leaves, gold iridescent, pink and blue highlights: bowl signed "L.C. Tiffany - Favrile," $648.00; goblet marked "L.C.T.," $360.00, privately owned.

CENTER RIGHT: Three gold iridescent Tiffany vases, all signed "L.C.Tiffany Favrile,": left, miniature flower form with green heart shaped leaves, $1,800.00; ribbed central flower form, 8½" high, $1,368.00; right, vase in Moravignian design, $1,224.00, privately owned.

BOTTOM: Tiffany, Egyptian decorated vase, gold lustre body, green lustre neck decor, signed "L.C. Tiffany Favrile," 5" high, $4,032.00; ribbed brown iridescent vase with delicate feather design, "L.C.T.," 9¾" high, $3,600.00, numbered "F537,"; gourd vase, lustred, brown leaf decor, marked "V632 L.C. Tiffany Favrile," 5¾" high, $3,880.00; blue and gold iridescent vase, mold blown embossed designs, signed "N1688 L.C. Tiffany Favrile, " 5¼" high, $2,304.00, all privately owned.

Tiffany iridescent blue Jack-in-the Pulpit vase, Art Nouveau design, circa 1900-1912, Corona Furnace, Long Island, New York, 18¾" high, $4,320.00, "Courtesy of The Corning Museum of Glass."

Tiffany iridescent orange vase, applied threaded and hooked wavy horizontal stripes, carmel colored liner, signed "A2843," 3⅛" high, $2,448.00, Milan Historical Museum.

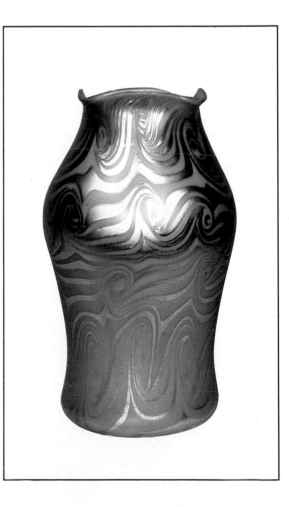

OPPOSITE PAGE TOP LEFT: Opalescent onion-shaped Tiffany vase with green vertical ribs and long narrow neck, 12¼" high, signed "L.C.T.N7391," $7,200.00, Milan Historical Museum.

OPPOSITE PAGE TOP RIGHT: Two delicate Tiffany flower forms with slender stems: left, opalescent ruffled open flower with green leaf decoration, 12¼" high, $3,456.00; right, opal glass with green combed and pulled leaf decor, the same design is carried through on the foot and the vase resembles a bud about to open, $2,880.00. Both examples are signed "L.C. Tiffany Favrile," the one on the right also has a paper label, privately owned.

OPPOSITE PAGE BOTTOM RIGHT: Pair of Tiffany pieces: left, Jack-in-the Pulpit vase, green pulled leaf decoration, gold lustred interior, stretched edge, lavender highlights, 7¼" high, signed "L.C.T. 926," $1,800.00; right, iridescent gold vase with green and white pulled feathers, gold lustred ruffled top, stretch edge, marked "L.C.T.56B," $1,224.00, privately owned.

OPPOSITE PAGE BOTTOM LEFT: Tiffany ribbed and pastel butterscotch flower form, 10" high, possesses its original paper label and is signed, "L.C.Tiffany - Favrile," $3,744.00, privately owned.

TOP LEFT: Tiffany lustred pastel colored glass: left, iridized footed sherbet, $360.00; right, stemmed wine, 6¼" high, $324.00, both signed and numbered, Milan historical Museum.

TOP RIGHT: Tiffany Lava glass vase, blown glass, circa 1900, 5⅜" high, 7" diameter, inscribed "L.C.Tiffany-Favrile 22 A-Coll," K. Wetzel Photo, Virginia Museum of Fine Arts, The Sydney and Frances Lewis Art Nouveau Fund, $23,760.00.

BOTTOM: Green and light blue iridescent Tiffany vase, button pontil, signed "L.C.Tiffany - Favrile," Damascene decoration, square top, 9" high, $1,080.00, privately owned.

TOP: **Pair of Tiffany candlesticks, opalescent Reactive Star pattern, both signed and numbered, plus original paper labels in green and gold, 3¾" high, $1080.00 pair, Milan Historical Museum.**

BOTTOM: *A grouping of Tiffany Favrile vases, circa 1893-1920; left to right, vertical ribbed gold iridescent amber glass with green and white florals, 9⅝/8" high, engraved "L.C.T. 1908"; gold iridescent amber glass with green leaf and vine decoration, 2¾" high, signed "2907 E L.C.Tiffany - Favrile"; gold iridescent amber glass with green flower decor, 14⅜" high, marked "691 E L.C. Tiffany - Favrile,"; calyx floriform, engraved "7188D L.C. Tiffany - Favrile," 9" high, gold iridescent amber glass with green leaf and vine decoration; Floriform, 11⅜" high, signed "385 L.C. Tiffany - Favrile," translucent white with blue and red outer layer pulled near the top, applied translucent white foot with pulled green threading and gold iridescent bottom; floriform, engraved "8054 L.C.T.," 16" high, iridescent amber glass with red and white pulled feather decor, white threading around the bottom edge; 2¾" high iridescent cobalt blue vase, green leaf and vine decoration, signed "4305 K L.C.Tiffany - Favrile; gold iridescent vertical ribbed pattern, amber glass, 13¾" high, marked "9121 M L. C. Tiffany - Inc - Favrile"; vase in brass stand, iridescent amber glass with green and white pulled feather decoration, 15¼" high, glass engraved "L.C.T.," brass base stamped "TIFFANY STUDIOS NEW YORK 1043"; and gold iridescent amber glass vase with iridescent scrollwork and panel decoration, engraved "L.C.T. H1552" 6&/8" high. Values $2,016.00, $720.00, $3,024.00, $2,304.00, $3,600.00, $3,168.00, $756.00, $1,728.00, $2,448.00, $3,360.00, Currier Gallery of Art.*

TOP LEFT: Reactive paperweight vase with internal and external surface iridescence, signed "L.C. Tiffany-Favrile - 375 F," circa 1925, ground pontil with original green ground and gold lettered circular label, 6¼" high, flowers, stems and leaves decor, $8,928.00+, privately owned.

BOTTOM LEFT: Blown Lava glass vase, circa 1907, Louis C. Tiffany, Corona, Long Island, New York, 8' high $19,440.00, "Collection of The Corning Museum of Glass."

RIGHT: Two Tiffany vases, left to right: ruffled flower form, opalescent Reactive glass with combed green leaf effect, iridescent gold interior, enameled base signed "LOUIS C. TIFFANY FURNACES, INC. 150, " 10½" high, $2,304.00; alabaster vase with red and gold pulled feather design, 7½" high, signed "L. C. Tiffany Favrile B218," $4,032.00, Milan Historical Museum.

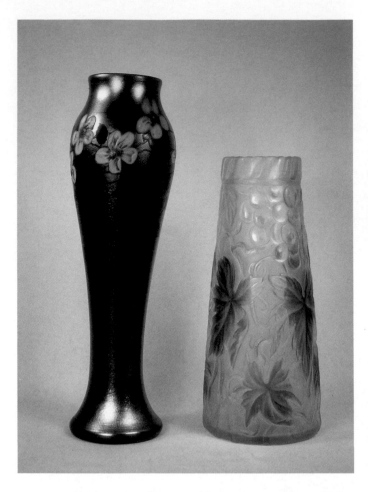

TOP LEFT: Blue green iridescent Tiffany vase, signed "6410 M Louis C. Tiffany Inc. Favrile," intaglio leaves and vines, millerfiori flowers, 15" high, $4,320; right, carved crystal vase, cameo decoration, green padded leaves, frosted grapes, leaves and tendrils, 11¾" high, signed "5438 C L.C. Tiffany Favrile," $4,608.00, privately owned.

BOTTOM: Lustred pastel blown bowl with applied decoration, circa 1904, designed by L. C. Tiffany, 2¾" high, $936.00, "Collection of The Corning Museum of Glass."

TOP RIGHT: Tiffany Marquetry vase, cut overlay decoration, circa 1900, 5" high, $8,640.00, "Collection of The Corning Museum of Glass."

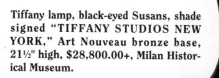

Tiffany lamp, black-eyed Susans, shade signed "TIFFANY STUDIOS NEW YORK," Art Nouveau bronze base, 21½" high, $28,800.00+, Milan Historical Museum.

Tiffany Daffodil table lamp, 26" high, 20" shade, base and shade signed "Tiffany Studios New York," Minna Rosenblatt Limited, $17,280.00.

180

Tiffany Pond Lily lamp, circa 1906, leaded glass, bronze base, 26½" high, 19" diameter, $100,800.00+, Virginia Museum of Fine Arts, Gift of Sydney and Frances Lewis, K. Wetzel Photo.

Tiffany Fish Lamp, circa 1906, leaded glass, bronze, copper, mosaic-glass tiles, 18" high, 16" diameter, $74,880.00+, K. Wetzel Photo, Gift of Sydney and Frances Lewis, Virginia Museum of Fine Arts.

Tiffany Gould Peacock Lamp, before 1914, blown glass, enamel on copper, 40½" high, 13" diameter, $129,600.00+, Virginia Museum of Fine Arts, gift of Sydney and Frances Lewis Foundation, K. Wetzel Photo.

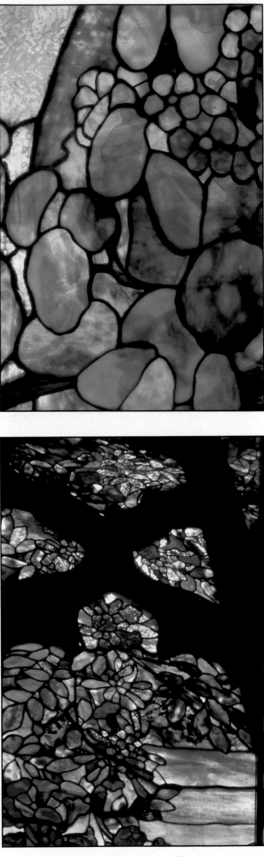

LEFT: Landscape window, designed by Louis C. Tiffany, Corona, Long Island, New York, about 1900, 6'10" high, Gift of Seymour Koehl and Michael Cronin, $14,400.00+, "Collection of The Corning Museum of Glass."

TOP RIGHT: Tiffany Studios' leaded glass window, detail shows flowers and leaves, circa 1905, "Collection of The Corning Museum of Glass."

BOTTOM: Details showing flowers and sky area in leaded glass window, Louis C. Tiffany, Tiffany Studios, New York, 1905, "Collection of The Corning Museum of Glass."

TOP: Four Tiffany vases: left to right, green, gold lustre leaf decor, intaglio carved bees, button pontil, stamped "CORONA," 3¾" high, $2,880.00; Samian Red, silver gray threaded decoration, signed "L.C.T. F 2303," 4¼" high, $6,912.00; deep blue iridized vase, silver bat wing motif, original black paper label + signature "L.C.T. B 2270," 5½" high, $2,880.00; gourd-shaped green over opal glass, gold lustre leaf decoration, original green paper label + signature "L.C. Tiffany - Favrile," 8¼" high, $3,888.00, privately owned.

BOTTOM RIGHT: Alton Manufacturing Trevaise vase, pulled feather design, iridescent with soft green, yellow and lavender hues, 3⅝" high, 4" diameter, gold lining, $1,188.00, courtesy of Sandwich Historical Society Glass Museum.

BOTTOM LEFT: Trevaise vase, Alton Manufacturing Company, 1907–1908, 5⅜" high, 6¼" diameter, iridescent amethyst, silver and gold, donut-shaped wafer on the base, $1,260.00, courtesy of Sandwich Historical Society Glass Museum.

Tiffany iridescent blown glass punch bowl, silver gilt with three ladles, circa 1900, bowl 14¼" high, 24" diameter, ladles 10" long, 2½" wide. Fabricated by Tiffany Studios for the Paris Exposition of 1900, considered one of the finest examples of Art Nouveau made in America, $144,000.00+, Virginia Museum of Fine Arts, K. Wetzel Photo, The Sydney and Frances Lewis Art Fund.

TOP LEFT: Ribbed Union Glass Company vase, ground pontil, 4⅝" high, circa 1885, amber base with silver and blue vertical flecks throughout, $360.00, Milan Historical Museum.

TOP RIGHT: Blue Vasa Murrhina tumbler-like vase, a mixture of colored glass and gold colored mica, plated with colorless glass, $144.00, courtesy of Sandwich Historical Society Glass Museum.

CENTER RIGHT: A deep amber whimsey in the shape of a charging bull, free-blown and tooled nostrils, marbleized forelock and horns, cloven hooves, hump, beard, genitals and tail are shown in detail, possibly a South Jersey product, 7¾" high, 10½" long, $180.00, privately owned.

BOTTOM RIGHT: Deep sapphire blue Vasa Murrhina decanter with stopper, gold mica flecks, cased in clear glass, $288.00, courtesy of Sandwich Historical Society Glass Museum.

BOTTOM LEFT: Vasa Murrhina Art Glass vase, 1883–1884, 5¾" high, rough pontil, ground top, black glass with colored splotches and gold mica marvered into the exterior surface, $252.00, privately owned.

Art Glass Catalogue in Color

The 31 views are from an original catalogue dated February 16, 1910. Shown are water color renderings of art glass church windows, rose window and transom lights, church window emblems, leaded Art Nouveau, leaded colored art, leaded colored Art Nouveau, and art lamps and shades. Also shown but not illustrated are other assorted glass types offered by The Foster-Munger Company, Chicago, Illinois. Pictured in black and white in their catalogue number 101 were glass sheets embedded with ribbed and/or polished wire; plain ribbed; prism glass; enameled, chipped and textured glass; fancy chipped lettering and designs for doors; sand-blasted door lights; stock lace door lights; special lace transom lights; beveled plate glass with mitre cutting; leaded beveled plate; leaded clear double strength; name and number door plates; bank and office signs; chipped signs; colored lodge emblems; colored advertising hanging signs; small hanging signs; outside chipped signs; outside chipped column signs; chipped wall or hanging signs; window display electric signs; and double sided jeweled electric signs for outside.

The final pages in the catalogue show mirrored hall trees and coat racks, framed mirrors, plate glass towel bars and shelves, paints and varnishes, wood fillers, furniture polish, stains, putty, glass cutting glaziers' diamonds, ladders and church pulpits.

All of the colored windows were listed as being "made up in rich and well blended colors of Opal and Opalescent." Some backgrounds were "of light Variegated Cathedral tints," other had "painted figures burned in glass."

Following is a paragraph quoted directly and addressed "To The Trade:" which I found of great interest.

"We call particular attention to the variety of high grade church window designs shown at prices very much lower than usually charged for inferior windows by our competitors. Now, there is a reason for it. To begin with we do not have to depend upon our Church Window Department to make our business pay. The making of church windows is a most important branch of our business, but not our sole business. Any firms devoting themselves exclusively to making church windows have to pay high salaried artists when business is slack and then make it up in their prices for the work they do. Our employees have all they can do all the time; if not on church windows, on similar equally high grade art glass work. We are the largest concern in this line in America and buy material in the biggest quantities and save in original cost, securing prices that smaller concerns cannot possibly do. These are some of the reasons why we are able to cut down the fancy prices ordinarily charged by our competitors."

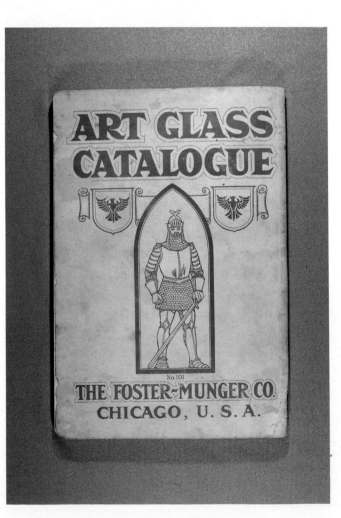

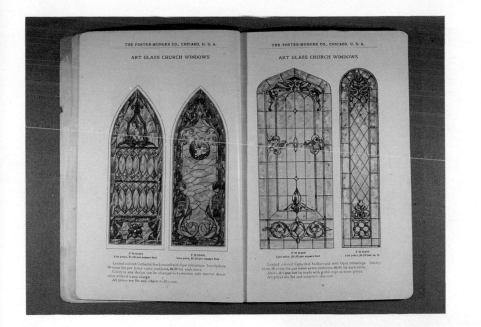

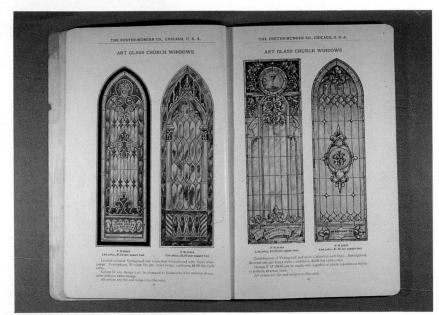

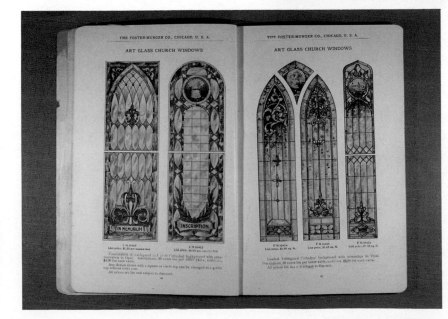

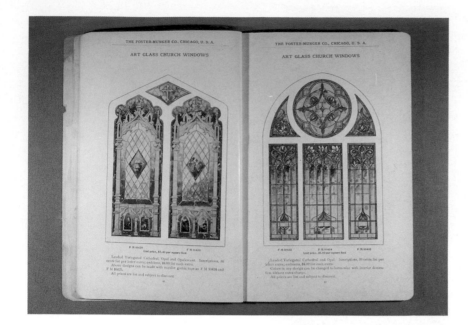

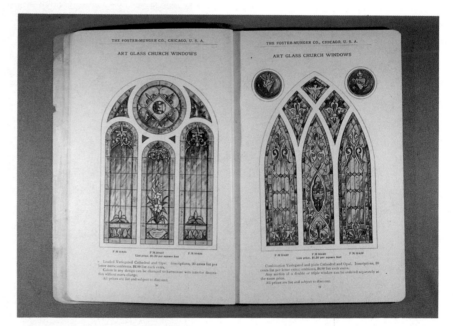

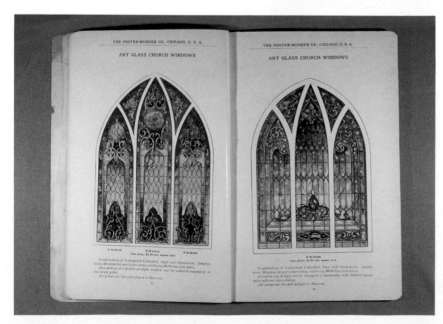

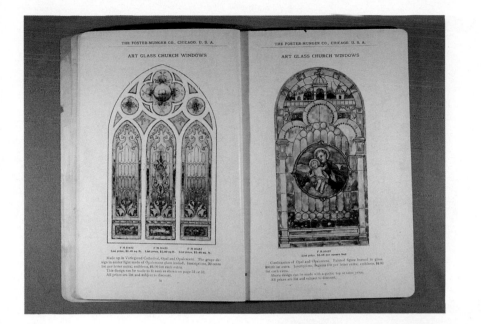

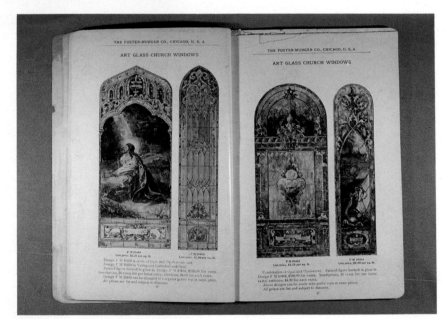

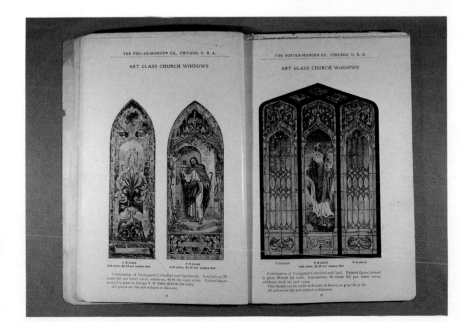

191

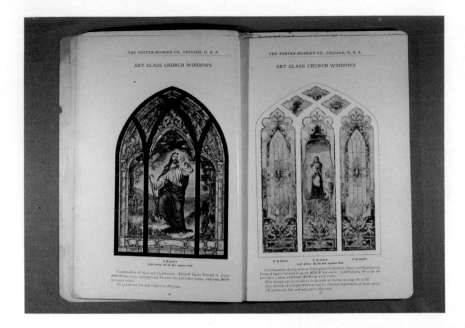

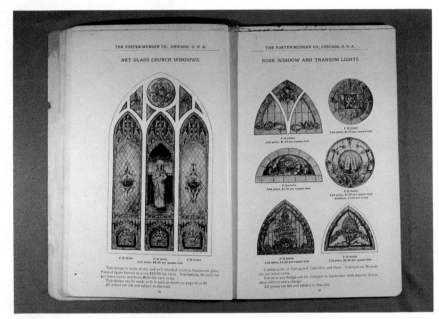

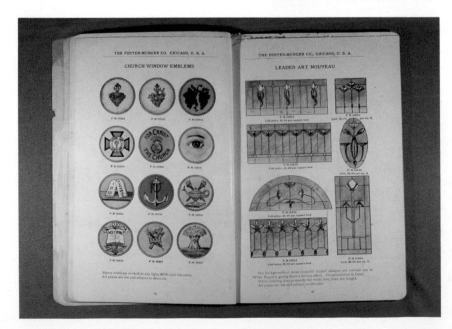

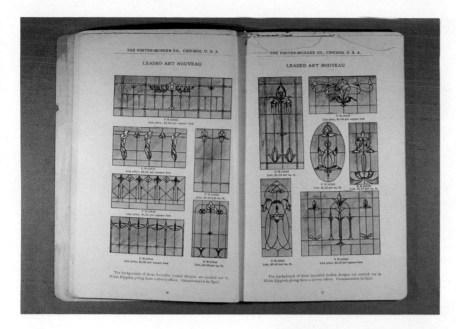

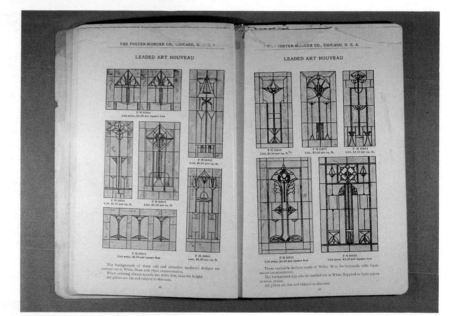

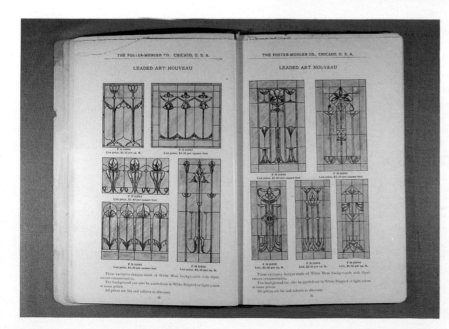

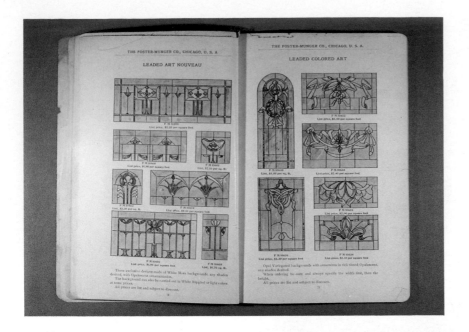

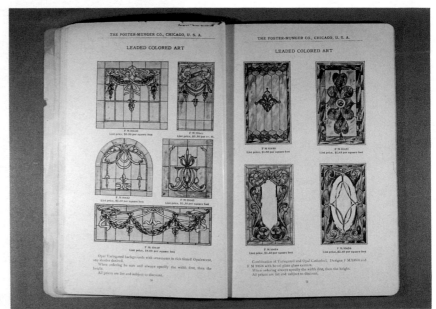

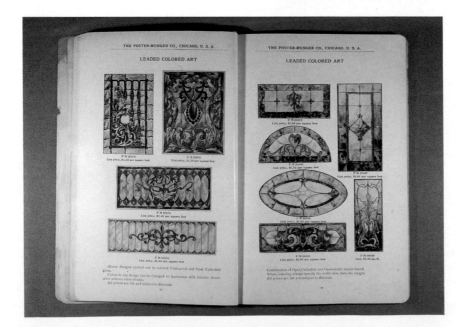

194

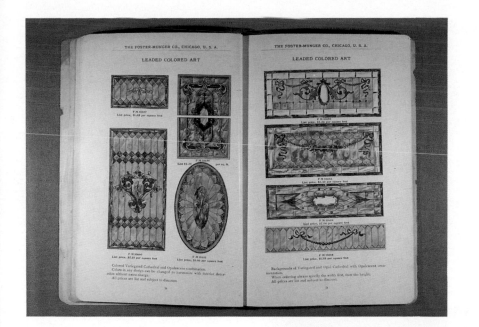

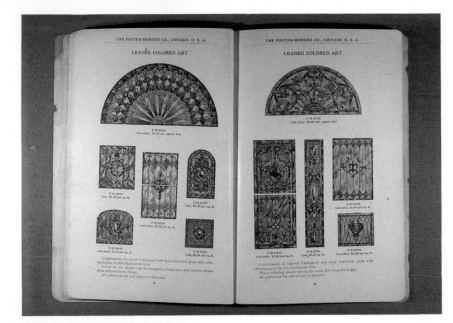

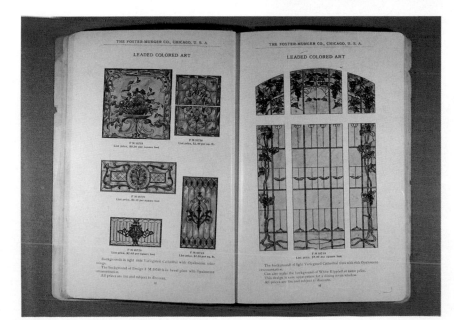

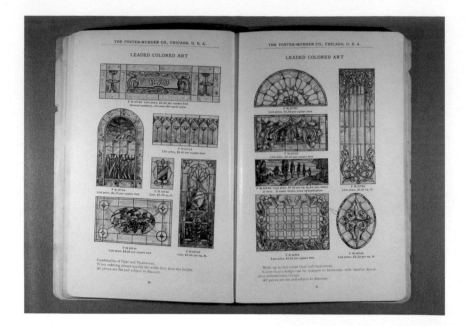

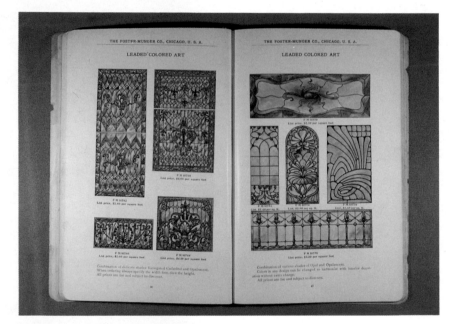

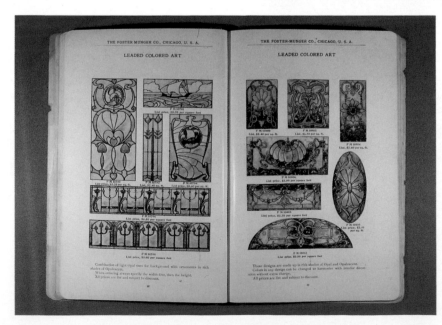

196

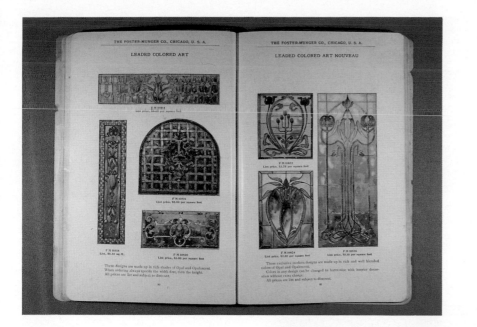

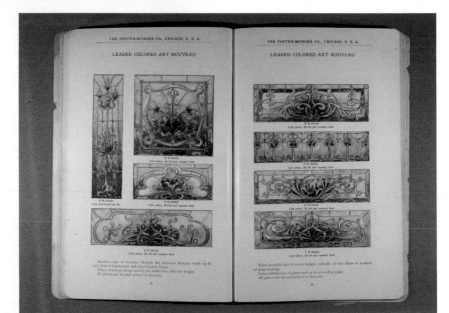

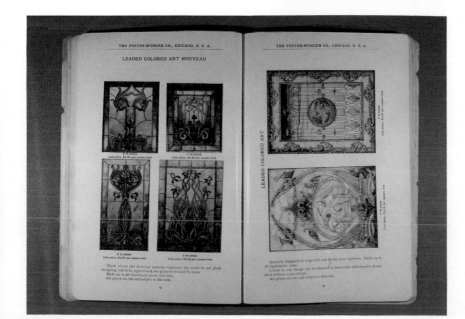

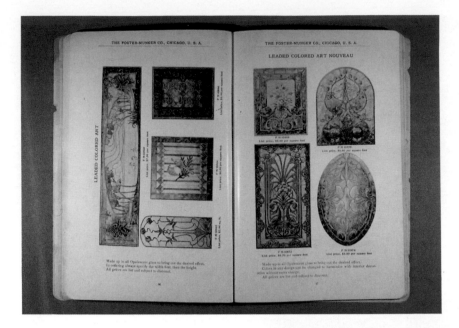

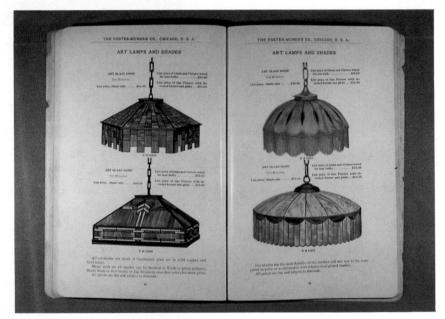

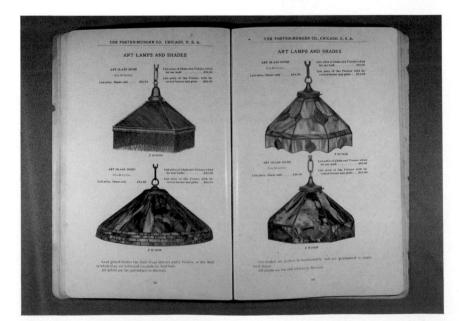

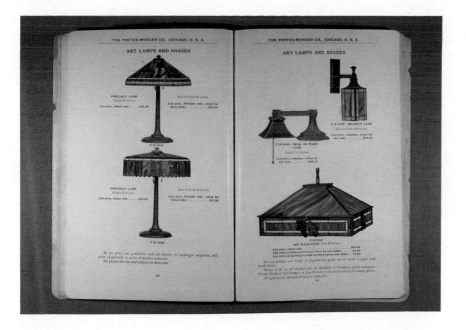

Postcard Views in Color

C. Dorflinger and Sons Glass Factory, White Mills, Pennsylvania (1908)

Water Tank - C. Dorflinger & Son's Glass Plant, Capacity of tank 75,000 gallons, White Mills, Pennsylvania

A very warm thank you to Louise Heiser, a most gracious lady. Louise consented to share with the reader views of the interiors and exteriors of 32 glasshouses. Her extremely advanced postcard collection has made this section of the book a revelation for the majority of glass collectors. Generally most glass enthusiasts I spoke with were not aware that postcards of this type ever existed. The dates indicated are the postmarks, and important messages have been quoted. Earl and Louise Heiser deal in postcards, china and glass and may be visited every Sunday of the year at their booth in Renninger's Market, Adamstown, Pennsylvania.

Office of C. Dorflinger & Sons, White Mills, Pennsylvania.

Macbeth-Evans Glass Company, Charleroi, Pennsylvania

Next 7 photos Consolidated Lamp and Glass Company, Coraopolis, Pennsylvania

Blowhouse

Cutting Room #1 (1908)

Cutting Room #2

Cutting Room #4

Decorating Room

Frosting Room

Testing Room

Sandwich Factory (1908), "This is the old glass factory at Sandwich."

Corning Glass Works, Corning, New York (1908)

Corning Glass Works, Wellsboro, Pennsylvania

203

Empire Cut Glass Factory, Flemington, New Jersey
(1908)

Glass Furnace, Morgantown, West Virginia

Smethport Cut Glass Works, Smethport, Pennsylvania
(1909)

H.C. Fry Glass Company, Rochester, Pennsylvania (1907)

Eygabroat, Ryon Cut Glass Company, Lawrensville, Pennsylvania (1908)

The Silk Mill and Glass Cutting Factory, East Hawley, Pennsylvania (1913)

The Glass Blowing Factory, West Hawley, Pennsylvania (1912)

Whitall Tatum Company, Upper Works, Millville, New Jersey (1913)

A.H. Heisey and Co.'s Glass Factory, Newark, Ohio

Louden Glass Factory Fostoria, Ohio (1909) " I am still working in the glass factory. This is the factory I work in. We have a fine time down here. We can go to a show every night or a dance on Friday night or Saturday. From a good friend, Geo L."

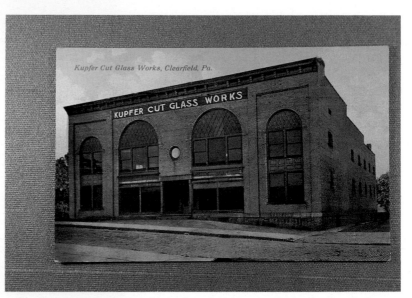

Kupfer Cut Glass Works, Clearfield, Pennsylvania

Cambridge Glass Company, Cambridge, Ohio

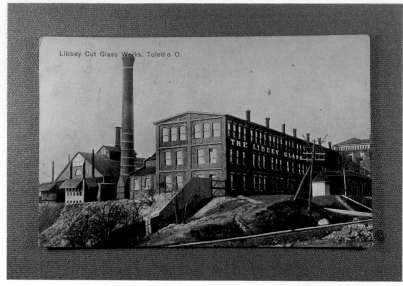

Libbey Cut Glass Works, Toledo, Ohio (1910)

Peerless and Lafayette Glass Factories, Clarksburg, West Virginia

Dugan Glass Company, Indiana, Pennsylvania (1911)

Glass Factory, Vineland, New Jersey

Glass Works, Swedesboro, New Jersey (1907)

Brookville Glass Plant, Brookville, Pennsylvania (1912)

U.S. Glass Company, Glassport, Pennsylvania (1912)

Fenton Art Glass Company, Williamstown, West Virginia

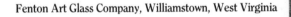

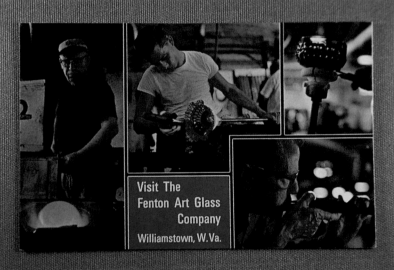

Blenko Glass Company, Milton, West Virginia

Lippencott's Glass Works, Alexandria, Indiana (1908)

Making of Steuben Glass, Corning Glass Center, Corning, New York. A "Gaffer," or master glass blower, fashions a crystal bowl by the ancient free-hand method.

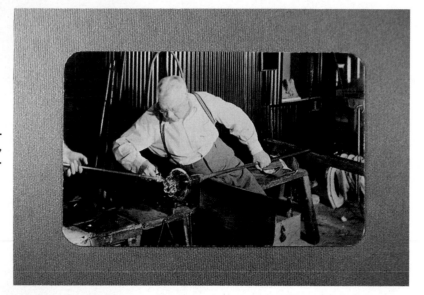

Making of Steuben Glass. Skilled master glass blowers fashion Steuben Crystal at the factory.

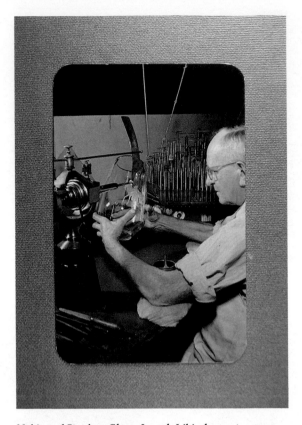

Making of Steuben Glass. Joseph Libisch, master copper wheel engraver, skillfully carves a crystal vase to reproduce in shallow intaglio, a design by the sculptor, Sidney Waugh.

Engraving of Steuben Glass. A master copper wheel engraver, working from an artists's design, carves a shallow intaglio design on a Steuben vase.

Advertisements in Color and Other Views

Left and above, views of the Sandwich Glass Factory (1938) taken from original photographs, courtesy of Mary Yuhasz.

A view of the Sandwich Glass Works in 1835.

Niagara Cut Glass Company. Factory and salesrooms: 506-508 East Genesee Street, Syracuse, New York

Imperial Glass Corporation, Bellaire, Ohio (1965). The great internationally known factory, established in 1903, Imperial Glass is today's version of our nation's oldest industry and employs over 400 skilled craftsmen.

A view of the Libbey Glass Works at the World's Columbian Exposition, held in 1893 in Chicago. This was one of the few American exhibitions on the Midway Plaisance. The processes of glass making, from the first, when oxide of lead, lime and sand are mixed, to the last, when the polishing of the finished articles is executed, were demonstrated for the public. In addition to glass blowing, there was glass spinning. The threads were drawn out so fine that they could then be woven into strong and beautiful napkins, dresses, etc.

A division of Tiffany and Company, Forest Hill, Newark, New Jersey (1912).

An assortment of American Art Glass in the Bennington Museum, Bennington, Vermont. Shown from the collection of Mr. and Mrs. Joseph W. Limric are bottom row, Amberina, Crown Milano, Wheeling Peach Blow, Mount Washington Peach Blow, Plated Amberina, Royal Flemish and decorated Burmese. Top row, from left to right, Aurene, Quezal, Kew Blas, Burmese, Mount Washington Cameo, New England Peach Blow and Agata.

A closer view of American Art Glass on display in the Bennington Museum. Left to right, Mount Washington Peach Blow, Burmese, Agata, Tiffany, Plated Amberina, decorated Mount Washington Peach Blow, and a satinized Wheeling Peach Blow vase in an amber griffin holder.

Selections from the Bennington Museum in Vermont include a red, white and blue epergne made by Nicholas Lutz for his wife in 1876, and rare canary triple dolphin candleholders with clear shades, made in Sandwich about 1840.

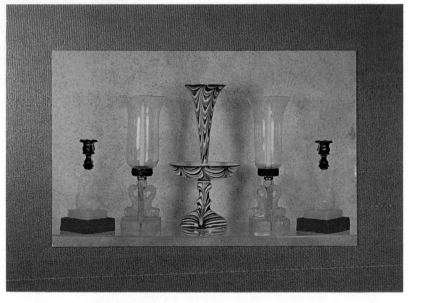

A window in the Deming Jarves Memorial Wing of the Sandwich Museum featuring assorted overlay made at the Boston and Sandwich Glass Factory between 1825 and 1888.

Iridescent gold vase with intaglio floral cutting, signed "L.C. Tiffany Favrile," 9¾" high, courtesy of the Lightner Museum, St. Augustine, Florida.

Iridescent gold vase with applied gold handles, signed "L.C. Tiffany Favrile," 11¾" tall, courtesy of the Lightner Museum, St. Augustine, Florida.

Fabricated from Steuben Glass at the Corning Glass Center.

Leaded glass lamp with hanging dragonfly shade and adjustable base, Tiffany Studios, New York City, circa 1890-1930, courtesy of the Lightner Museum, St. Augustine, Florida.

Steuben Glass vases designed by Bruce Moore showing engraved figures of Huckleberry Finn and Tom Sawyer.

The Merry-Go-Round Bowl designed by Sidney Waugh, elaborately engraved to depict a carousel in motion. The bowl was presented to Her Majesty, Queen Elizabeth II, on the occasion of her marriage in 1947. The then President of the United States and Mrs. Truman bestowed the gift.

The Explorers, designed by Bruce Moore, illustrates delicately engraved figures of three early adventurers, Himilco, Marco Polo and Christopher Columbus.

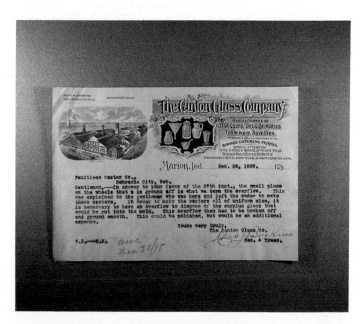

Broadside of John C. Kirkpatrick, 72 and 74 Third Street, Pittsburgh, Pennsylvania, dated July 13, 1860. Note the fancy carbon and coal oil lamps that this firm sold.

Very ornate letterhead of The Canton Glass Company, Marion, Indiana, dated December 29, 1898. Note the furnace chimneys on the two buildings.

An elaborate broadside of the Phoenix Glass Company, Beaver County, Phillipsburgh, Pennsylvania, dated November 22, 1882. This letter was written on heavy paper marked "Antique Flax" showing a rampant lion facing to the left centered within a shield. The letter was an answer to Mr. J.L. McCulloch, ℅ Southern Glass Works, Louisville, Kentucky, who wished to serve as a representative to the Phoenix Glass Company in the South and the West. Both positions had already been filled. Phoenix advertised that they were the sole makers of the Dithridge lamp chimney, their general manager was E.D. Dithridge. They also manufactured XX flint glass oil polished chimneys, opal shades and globes, silvered reflectors, engraved globes, and engraved and etched flint gas and kerosene globes.

A four sectioned pamphlet advertising Fry's transparent oven glass, manufactured by H.C. Fry Glass Company, Rochester, Pennsylvania. Illustrated here are examples of their ware.

The interior of the pamphlet showing many different shapes available to the buying public. They are numbered starting with 1916 and ending with 1952. Some examples were made in one size, while other more popular items in the line could be had in up to seven sizes.

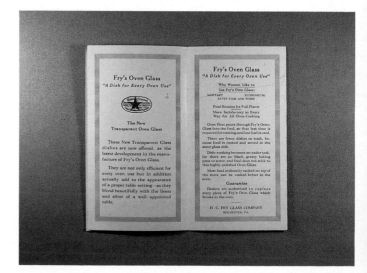

The back of the pamphlet shows the oval seal stating "Tested and Approved by the Good Housekeeping Institute", 1919. This ware was advertised as adding to the appearance of a table set with silver and linen, was sanitary, economical to use, saved time and work since food would not stick to the glass, and also aided in retaining the full flavor of any food properly stored and covered.

218

Original Handel Lamp Ads

This ad depicts Number 6778 constructed of "durable materially fashioned."

The lamp illustrated is Number 6785. "The beauty, dignity, and rich coloring of Handel Lamps are the inspiration of artists who glory in creating. Look for the Handel name on every lamp. A dealer near you has them. His name on request."

Shown in this colored sketch is Handel Lamp Number 6688.

"Richness of color, grace of form, and beauty of design are embodied in every Handel Lamp. And the delight which the possession of one brings, is a lasting one; for a Handel Lamp becomes a permanent part of your home - treasured as your oriental rugs and first editions." Pictured is lamp Number 6852.

TOP LEFT: "Nowhere will you find such a wealth of original and lovely lamps as in the Handel Lamps. There are designs to harmonize with every type of furnishings; designs for living room, sun parlor and porch, for vestibule or bedroom. There is a grace of line, a harmony between shade and standard, an individuality in the colorful shade decorations of Handel Lamps that is most unusual and artistic. Each is the work of master craftsmen, skilled in the art of creating beautiful things. All Handel Lamps are made for permanence. With ordinary care, they will last a lifetime." The top illustration shows Lamp Number 7010 and pendant Number 7007. At the bottom are smaller lamps for dressing table, piano or for decorative use. From left to right, numbers 6919, 7011, 6989 and 7008.

TOP RIGHT: "During the long, bleak evenings of winter, the soft, colorful beauty of a Handel Lamp adds a warm glow of friendly welcome to every room. So skillfully are the rich colors blended that there is a perfect harmony between shade and standard - between lamp and the most thoughtfully selected interior draperies and furnishings." This lamp is Number 7026. The advertisement also shows the newest Handel creations fashioned after the rarest of Colonial models. Illustrated are Mantel Lamps Numbered 7080, 7082, and 6879. This is an ad that appeared in *The House Beautiful,* November 1923.

RIGHT: This is a 1927 ad showing assorted Handel Lamps. The top illustration is Number 7202 featuring an 18″ hand-painted shade with a polychrome gold standard on a black marbleized base. At the bottom are Boudoir Lamp, Number 7169 finished in ivory, Boudoir Lamp, Number 7177 in black and gold, and Night Lamp Number 7093, adjustable to dim, medium and bright light. On the right is Floor Lamp, number 7099, 62″ high. It features a 10″ adjustable Fabrikon shade, polychrome gold standard, and marbleized base.

TOP LEFT: This very attractive ad by The Duffner & Kimberly Company, 11 West 32nd Street, New York, appeared in the December 1906 issue of *Country Life In America,* page 215. Shown from top to bottom, left, Louis XIV; right, Italian Renaissance; bottom, left, Viking; and right, Roman. These electric lamps represented all periods from Classic to Modern and were carried by 20 major representatives throughout the United States. Morgan and Allen Company were sole agents for the Pacific Coast.

TOP RIGHT: Shown is Macbeth-Evans Iridile Portable Lamp, Number 4515. The firm located in Pittsburgh, also had sales and showrooms in New York, Chicago, Philadelphia, St. Louis, Boston and Toronto. By requesting catalogue number 42, you would be shown "fine examples of artistic illuminating glassware." This ad appeared in January 1915.

BOTTOM LEFT: This full page ad from Macbeth-Evans Glass Company was run in the July, 1922, issue of *Pictorial Review.* Their advertisement noted that they were "Makers of Scientific and Art Glassware for Illuminating Purposes." Mentioned were the facts that they were America's oldest and largest makers of fine illuminating glassware. This promotional ad was for Macbeth Candle Shades, made in various shapes and designs, individually decorated in rich colors. They were furnished with a metal holder that would fit any standard candle-type fixture, thus in the evening the lighted shade provided a glowing warmth. Other unshaded lamps produced by their competitors were said to give off a monotonous white glare.

TOP LEFT: Appearing in *Good Housekeeping*, September, 1928, this wonderful Heisey ad tells the story of a nobleman and his beautiful lady coming to a glassworks to view the creation of a hot bubble of glass with a blowpipe. This invention revolutionized the industry, it is still used today to fashion hand-blown articles. Mentioned in the Heisey ad are the popular colors Flamingo, Hawthorne and Moon Gleam. The first is a subtle rose, the second a royal amethyst and the third a cool green. This Heisey ad gave their address as 301 Oakwood Avenue, Newark, Ohio.

TOP RIGHT: This illustration, another in the Heisey series, appeared in the May 1928 issue of *Good Housekeeping*. The story tells how Marietta Beroviero betrayed her father's trust. Angelo Beroviero owned the Sign of the Angel, one of the most famous glass houses in 15th century Venice. He possessed the priceless secret of giving glass color, thus this was a source of wealth and power for him. He kept the secret formulae hidden—only his daughter knew where they were hidden. Giorgio, a skillful Beroviero artisan wished to gain the secrets for himself. Whispering endearments to win Marietta's heart, he succeeded in stealing them. Later they would be passed on to future generations so that they too might enrich their glass creations.

BOTTOM RIGHT: Cool colors and quaint contours are the themes of this Steuben Glass ad where the forms and sizes harmonize with flowers, summer dinner parties, luncheons and teas. Types of glass pictured are translucent Jade Green, an etched Pomona Green vase with Rose foot, a Celeste Blue vase, "two quaint pieces," and a boater urn with the bowl in Rose and the base in Pomona Green. The ad states "No matter what your choice in decorative glass, you will want only honest glass, hand-blown and hand-modeled, as fine glass has been made since history began, and just as Steuben Glass is made today."

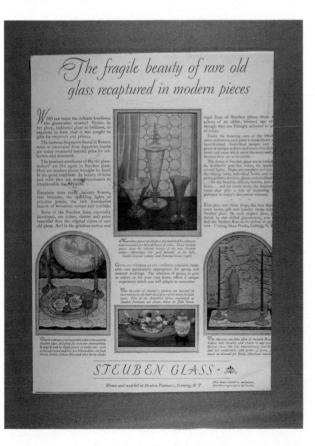

TOP LEFT: "Every piece in the Steuben collection is designed by an artist glass-maker (Frederick Carder) honored on two continents for his masterly achievements. Under his direction, craftsmen with that rare delicacy and sureness of touch which distinguish the worker in the arts from other men, fashion by hand each lovely piece." Mentioned are the hues sapphire blue, amethyst, sunshine yellow, bubbly Spanish green, rosy grenadine, soft old green, crystal with black reeding, flame and onyx black, jade, amber and ruby red.

TOP RIGHT: "All these lovely things, and others equally useful, are blown and modeled by honest handcraft, in graceful shapes and rare colorings Each original Steuben piece bears the signature "Steuben", which identifies it to the purchaser." "Aurene Glass by Steuben takes full heed of the decorative principle that if texture's the thing, then form had best be simple. The iridescent splendor of Aurene is so cunningly achieved, that each piece is unique in its striking color sheen." Note the Cerise Ruby console set at the top of the page.

BOTTOM LEFT: "The fragile beauty of rare old glass recaptured in modern pieces" is the message conveyed in this Steuben ad. Interesting colors mentioned are rose hued Grenadine combined with crystal, Jade Green, Amber, Celeste Blue, Moonlight (pale lavender), Smoke Crystal (pale pink), Pomona Green and Bristol Yellow. Note the covered Jade Green Acid Cutback jar, and Bristol Yellow blown fish vase in the Venetian tradition.

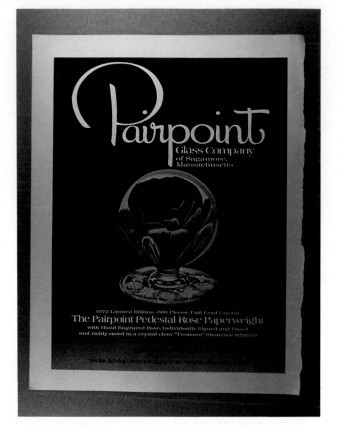

Pictured in this advertisement are an unusual three piece velvety set consisting of two bowls and a central covered jar, a crystal cut bird, a crystal goblet with mirror-black reeding, a rare "Rouge flamme" plate with wide black border, and two amethyst-shaped lotuses, suitable as bookends. "Each piece is individually wrought by workers adept in the handicraft of glass. Exquisite forms take shape at the end of the master's blow pipe! Delicate vases, goblets, compotes as perfect in their contours as orchids, and as marvelously tinted . . . large bowls with a rich clarity of color and a cool hard smoothness of surface perfect to the touch. For the collector's trained fingers quickly learn to judge the quality of glass by the feeling of it."

The Pairpoint Glass Company, Sagamore, Massachusetts, advertised in 1972 a limited edition of their Pedestal Rose Paperweight. Three hundred pieces in full lead crystal were fabricated, each had a hand-engraved base, and was individually signed and dated. The cost including a crystal clear showcase was $200.00 each.

Glass Dictionary of Terms

Acid Cutback (ACB): A two-layered art glass of contrasting colors that looks like cameo glass. This process was developed about 1906 by Frederick Carder at the Steuben Glass Works. A design was transferred to the piece. Areas not to be cut with acid were protected with wax.

Acid Etched: The glass object is covered with wax and a design is cut through by submerging the article in acid. The desired effects are thus achieved.

Air Traps: The controlled entrapment of bubbles within a glob of glass. A pleasing decorative technique.

Annealing: The cooling of hot glass gradually in a furnace known as a lehr.

Application: Attaching hot rods of glass on blown or pressed wares to form handles, bases or other desired additions.

Art Deco: The use of geometric designs, back to nature themes, massive shapes and contrasted colors. (1920s-1930s).

Art Glass: 1. A variety of forms and surface textures incorporated to form both fancy colored and clear glass from the 1880s. Made, in many cases, by hand. 2. The Arts and Crafts Movement of the 1860s, where artists renewed artistic standards. Much of the indusry was flooded with pressed glass and gaudy Victorian examples.

Art Nouveau: A reaction to the Industrial Age; extravagant details and flowing lines derived from plant life. (1890-1910).

Ball Stopper: A glass ball with a neck used to plug the mouth of cruets, perfumes and decanters. Popular in the mid-1800s in the United States.

Batch: A mixture of the necessary ingredients that are liquid at around 2500 degrees Fahrenheit to form molten glass.

Battledore: A wooden paddle used to shape or flatten the bottoms of glass objects.

Black Glass: Glass colored black by including oxide of manganese blended with oxide of iron. Some glass in reality is purple but is so dark that it appears to be black.

Blank: Any undecorated glass form intended to be ornamented at a later time.

Blister: A broken surface bubble that leaves a pit mark.

Block: A wooden dipper used in the shaping of molten glass.

Blowpipe: A hollow iron tube used by the glassmaker to expand glass freely or into a mold. The trick is in learning just the right amount of gathering on the end of the tube to make a certain sized object.

Bobeches: Disks serving as a catchall for hot candle wax drippings.

Brilliant Cut: Deep and complicated patterns that are highly polished. Developed during the second half of the 1800s; now highly prized and widely collected. This glass has a beautiful resonance and radiates a hue of rainbow colors when held to the bright sunlight.

Cased: Also referred to as plated glass. Any blown object having successive layers of glass incorporated into one over an inner core.

Cast: By pouring molten glass into this form, the precise shape may be obtained.

Chair: The specially designed bench where the gaffer rolls his iron as he shapes the glass.

Clam Broth: A grayish white semi-opaque glass. The name is often associated with examples manufactured at Sandwich. The color of this glass appears much like clam juice.

Clay Pot: A very carefully constructed clay lining placed in the pot which is fired at white heat within the furnace. This pot holds the batch, its life varies with usage.

Compasses and Calipers: Compasses were used to check the uniformity and heights of objects, while calipers aided in measuring the diameters.

Copper Wheel: Abrasive copper disks operated at high speeds to engrave both shallow and broad outlines.

Cowl Board: A wooden face mask used by the furnace tender to protect him from the intense heat.

Cracking-Off: The removing of a glass object such as a wine glass from the blowpipe requires that a line be circumscribed about the glass. A sharp tap should then permit the glass to break away cleanly.

Crackle Glass: First made in Venice in the 16th century, and then revived in a mold-blown form in the 19th century. It is also called "ice glass," "Venetian Frosted Glass," and "Craquelle." The expanded gather is dipped into cold water, while extremely hot, producing a crazing or fractured surface. Sandwich; Reading; Mt Washington; and Hobbs, Brockunier are some firms that produced this glass type.

Crimper: A wooden form that is used to give a bowl or pitcher a crimped rim.

Crucible: The pot used to melt the glass.

Crystal: Clear and colorless fine flint approaching the purity of rock crystal.

Cullet: Purchased by all glasshouses, this broken glass was used in mixtures to produce new objects.

Cutting: Fine quality faceted glassware which was quite elegant in the 1800s to the 1900s. This decorative technique dates to the Greek and Roman civilizations.

Decay: The separation of a glass surface into fine thin films. These refract the rays of light, giving a prismatic effect, thus causing a pleasing iridization. This look is very evident in ancient glass that has been buried.

Diamond Point: Engraving tools that are stylus-like that aided in engraving and etching designs on glass.

Dip Mold: A one-piece mold that is open only at the top to allow for the imprinting of a design.

Disintegration: Thick hot glass that is cooled too rapidly, creating an undue tension in the molecular structure. This glass is easily affected by temperature changes, the weather and vibrations.

Enameling: Vitrifiable enamels artistically applied like paint to glassware are then fired to create a fusion with the object.

Engraving: This ancient decorating process utilizes the diamond point and the wheel to create an aesthetic effect.

Fake: A genuine example of glassware either altered or added to for the purpose of increasing its value.

Fire Polishing: The final reheating in a small furnace to remove any unnecessary marks and give the glass brilliance.

Flashing: Decorative stains and thin glass coatings that are fixed by heat.

Flint: Any glass which has a beautiful brilliance and resonance. A combination of sand, potash, niter, black oxide of manganese, and oxide of lead are used.

Flux: A substance added to the batch to aid in the fusion of the silica. Additions to the silica included potash, carbonate of soda and oxide of lead. It is also added to enamel colors thereby lowering their fusion point during firing to below that of the glass on which they were applied. Some softening of the glass occurs for proper adhesion.

Foot: The base of any object.

Forgery: A copy of any old and valuable glassware, made expressly to deceive and offered as genuine for a high price.

Free-Blown: No molds are used in creating this artistically blown glass. Tools may be employed to shape the article.

Frigger: Inferior pieces made by beginners learning glass making techniques.

Gaffer: The master glassblower or foreman in a shop.

Gilding: The artistic application of gold to glass to increase its appeal.

Glory-Hole: A hole in the side of a glass furnace, used to withdraw small amounts of molten glass; for reheating the blowpipe and punty; to fire-polish the ware, and to check melting and remove impurities. It is also called the Bye-Hole, Spy-Hole and Bocca.

Hooked Decor: Threading applied to glass which is pulled with a hooked-shaped device to form feathers and other decorative motifs.

Hydrofluoric Acid: A volatile, colorless and highly corrosive acid used as an agent to etch glass. Pure acid dissolves glass leaving a bright surface. Mixed with sulphuric acid, it produces a high gloss on lead glass; mixed with ammonia, the neutralized acid leaves a frosted finish.

Inclusions: Decorative particles of a substance placed within glass such as metallic flecks in Spangle or Aventurine.

Iridescent: A glass form reflecting an array of rainbow-like colors from its surface.

Jack-in-the Pulpit: Any vase with a narrow neck and a widely exaggerated top, produced in colored and iridescent glass. Generally it was made to resemble this American woodland flower.

Lehr: A Leer or glass furnace used to cool hot glass gradually so it does not shatter.

Marver: A metal or stone-polished surface upon which the gathered molten glass is rolled to form an even surface before blowing commences.

Metal: Any gathering of glass in either a viscous or a hardened state.

Metallic Oxide: An oxide of a metal used as a pigment to color glass; it is also used in the making of enameled colors.

Mold-Blown: Glass that is blown into a mold to give it a shape and a pattern.

Muffle: An oven where articles are heated so that the enameling or applied decoration permanently adheres to the body.

Opal: Milk-white opalescent glass having the fiery properties of an opal gem.

Opalescent: Glass reflecting a bluish milky iridescent light. This characteristic was obtained through the use of heat-sensitive minerals placed in the batch.

Opaque: Glass not penetrated by rays of light. Possibly the first glass made, also known as milk white and containing tin oxide.

Overlay: Superimposed shapes applied to the body of glass using a multitude of colors and techniques.

Overshot: A novelty ware at Sandwich and the Reading Artistic Glass Works in Pennsylvania. The glass has a sharp ice-like crystal finish achieved by rolling the molten objects in a bed of crystalline bits of clear or colored glass.

Padding: A process where glass pads are applied to the glass article. They are then cut in relief to complete the floral and/or other designs. This technique is seen on advanced examples.

Parison: A blow or globule of hot glass gathered on the end of the blowpipe.

Pontil: A rough indentation on the bases of objects indicative of where the object was held with the pontil rod. On finer and expensive pieces this mark is usually ground or polished.

Pressed: The process where molten glass is pressed into a mold by a plunger. This was the beginning of mass produced glass.

Prunt: Applied glass globs which aid in the identification of various glass types. Application, tooling and impressed seals were sometimes employed.

Pucellas: Pincher-like iron tongs used in manipulating and shaping blown glassware.

Pumice: A light, powdered volcanic glass used in polishing.

Punty Rod: A long and solid iron rod which aids in holding an object after it has been released from the blowpipe.

Reactive Glass: This art glass inlaid with many colors and sometimes iridescent was made by Louis C. Tiffany. The pieces suggest an underwater effect; some patterns include: "Poppies," "Morninglory," "Gladiola," and "Rainbow."

Reproduction: A fairly close copy of a genuine glass object, but not made to deceive. Often these objects are copied after one-of-a-kind or rare museum examples.

Resonance: The quality, bell-like sound created when lead glass is tapped lightly on its top edge.

Reverse Painting: Designs or highlights painted on the interior of glass complimented by the rest of the view appearing on the exterior. A difficult and scarce example to find; Mt. Washington used this process on their "Napoli" glass.

Seam Mark: The seams appearing in the glass where molten glass seeped through parts of a worn mold. On most worthy examples the seams are smoothed or fire-polished.

Servitor: The main assistant to the gaffer.

Shaft: A candlestick's column between the base and its nozzled top.

Shop: A collective term designating the crew that produces a completed glass object.

Sick Glass: Any abused glassware that has become cloudy and/or checked. Chemicals in water can ruin a vase, or it may come about as a result of a poor glass mixture when the object was manufactured.

Signature: The mark(s) or label used by a manufacturer for the expressed purpose of identification.

Silica: An essential ingredient in the making of glass. The most common form is sand (an impure silica) derived from inland beds, underground deposits and the seashore. All clay and organic material must be removed before it can be used successfully.

Threading: The application of glass threads either by hand or with the aid of a machine. This was a popular technique at Sandwich.

Tooling: A decorative technique that allows for the application of glass to an object in a specific shape.

Tools: The following tools are used in glass-making: compass, caliper, block, blowpipe, crimper, purcellas and punty rod.

Translucent: This glass admits light, but diffuses it so that objects cannot be distinguished through it.

Transparent: Any glass which allows light to penetrate and pass through so that objects can still be seen.

Viscosity: A state of glass between liquidity and solidity. At this point, it is ductile and is adapted best to the processes of manufacture.

Waffle Pontil Mark: A small gather of glass attached to the base of an object permitting the pontil to be separated from the glass object easily. Some Steuben glass has such a mark.

Glass Making Tools

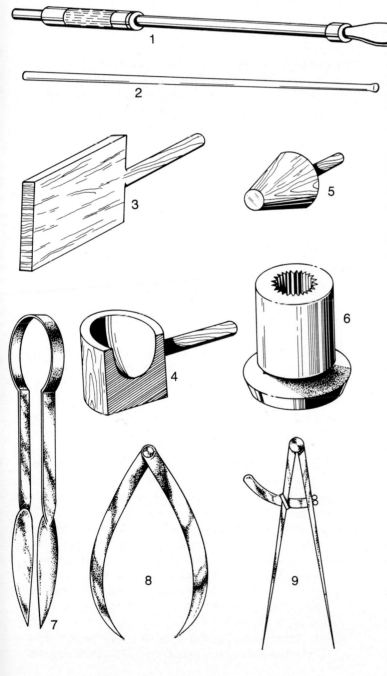

1. A hollow iron, bronze or brass tube varying in length from 2½′ to 6′ feet. Known as the blowpipe, the mouthpiece end was insulated with wood in this example. Others used heavy twine. The tube is thicker at the gathering end than at the blowing end.

2. The pontil or punty rod is usually the same length as the blowpipe and may be hollow or solid iron. The rod has a slight bulge on one end to hold the object while it was being shaped after it had been whetted and knocked from the blowpipe.

3. The battledore, constructed of wood and shaped like a paddle, was used to flatten the bottoms of objects.

4. A wooden block was used in the early stages of fabrication. Dipped first in water so that the intense heat from the glass metal would not char the surface, it was then used to give the parison form.

5. This small tapered wooden device is known as a lipper and was used to form the wide lips on pitchers.

6. The metal dip mold in this illustration is a one-piece mold; it aided in giving the glass a pattern. Some molds were part size while others were full size.

7. This specialized iron tool is the pucellas, also called a steel jack and simply—the Tool. It was essential in shaping and elongating stems, spreading the tops of bowls and reducing diameters when necessary.

8. Steel calipers aided the workers in measuring the diameters of objects while they were being fabricated. In this way, all pieces of the same type would be uniform in their measurements.

9. The steel compass made in a variety of sizes assisted in providing uniform heights on drinking vessels and other objects.

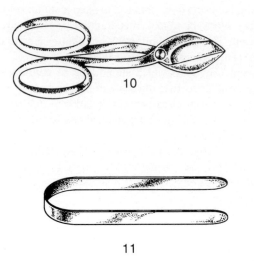

10

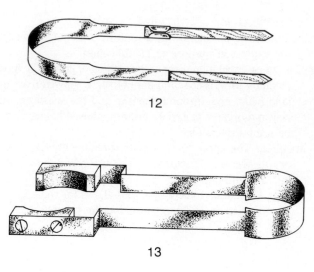

12

11

13

10. Shears in assorted sizes were used to cut the glass while in a soft plastic state, similar to pliable leather. Larger sizes could help in the forming of handles and stems, or even to cut blobs from a gather.

11. The metal tongs or spring tool was a simple device used as a pincer and in applying handles.

12. The wood jack was introduced about the mid-1800s and was used to form the glass surfaces while they were still plastic.

The wooden prongs were less likely to mar the glass; they could easily be replaced when they became badly burned. This tool was a metal spring type.

13. Holding tongs are a type of carrying tool invented in the 19th century. They enabled the worker to carry the completed object to the leer. The metal holding tongs had semi-circular wooden ends. When closed, the tips formed an opening in which a glass object could rest without being marked or deformed.

Principal Glass-Coloring Agents

Good judgment and ingenuity figures largely in producing colored glass. The basis for creating the prominent colors has been outlined. Much can be determined by experimentation and exacting formulas. All materials used play a very important role in the final product.

Other hues and colors may be produced by blending the existing colors; thus, hues and densities may be modified or intensified into new colors. Intense colors may be toned down by adding clean flint glass cullet of the same composition.

Gold: Produces a red or ruby color. The batch must be of great purity with the gold well incorporated in the batch. The gold will only be well distributed when the temperature of the furnace is very high.

Silver: Oxide of silver yields a color from light yellow to orange. Chloride of silver applied to the glass with a brush will reveal a tinted or stained pigment. The glass must be exposed to a moderate heat in a muffle. Silver is rarely introduced with the batch.

Copper: The black oxide creates green; red oxide forms red or ruby; the furnace temperature must be regulated carefully. Generally, copper colors glass deeper than gold since it has a greater fusibility.

Iron: Colors derived from iron are green, yellow and red. Pure

oxide imparts an orange-red to the glass. Protoxide of iron will create a green color that lacks brilliance. An orange yellow is obtained by mixing iron, antimony and oxide of lead.

Manganese: In proportionate quantities the colors may vary from rose to violet, purple, brown and black.

Cobalt: Oxide of cobalt is exceedingly easy to handle and provides a rich blue. Nickel and zinc help to brighten the blue.

Uranium: Expensive to use and only incorporated in the finest glassware. The peculiar yellow coloration is best known as canary.

Chromium: The oxide produces emerald yellow passing into a grass green.

Minium: Oxide of lead used in excess will give a pale yellow color.

Antimony: Antimonious acid melted with 3% to 5% of undecomposed antimony sulphide produces a fine yellow.

Selenium: Added directly to the pot ingredients, Selenium gives a rose tint to glass. Soft glass will assume a tint of greater depth and intensity than hard glass. Combining cadium sulphide with the selenium will result in an orange-red color.

Nickel: Tints imparted by the oxide of nickel are constant. A bluish tint is given to potash glass; a hyacinth tinge to soda glass. If used in excess with soda glass, a violet tint will appear.

Zinc: Oxide of zinc hues glass, giving a yellow color.

Carbon: Occurring in many forms (oats, corn, burned animal hoofs, birch bark, coke, cannel coal, anthracite and powdered charcoal), carbon colors glass in varying degrees from a straw color to a dark amber.

Calcium Phosphate: Bone ash gives opacity to glass. In moderate quantities, it imparts opalescence to colored glass when used proportionately with lime.

Cryolite: A mineral found in Greenland, used sometimes to create opal glass. Objectionable since it attacks the melting pot.

Sodium Seleniate: About two pounds mixed with 1,000 pounds of sand will produce a very fine red color. Also used to replace oxide of gold when ruby colored glass is desired.

Feldspar, Fluorspar: Used as substitutes in manufacturing opal glass. Both materials tend to erode the clay of the pot; yet the glass can be melted at a lower temperature than cryolite glass. The proportions of ingredients used are 20 feldspar to 100 pounds of sand; 40 fluorspar to 100 of sand.

Tin Oxide: Expensive, but used to impart a white opacity to glass.

Guano: Imparts a white opacity to glass, is economical and has little effect on the pots.

Borax: Used in colored glass to intensify the color.

Planning An Interesting Itinerary

The collectors of glass, in their quest to view new examples, are often caught up in the travel dilemma. Do not wait until arriving in an area to ask the perplexing question, "Where are the museums?" Carry the handy list provided below, plus your camera, note pad and extra pens. The various examples one is privileged to view will provide the answers to many questions. Make your vacation travel time both fun and rewarding!

United States Glass Displays
Brunnier Gallery, Ames, Iowa
Yale University, New Haven, Connecticut
The Walters Art Gallery, Baltimore, Maryland
The Museum of Modern Art, New York City
Degenhart Museum, Cambridge, Ohio
W.H. Stark House, Orange, Texas
The Art Insititute of Chicago, Chicago, Illinois
Heisey Glass Museum, Newark, Ohio
Thomas County Museum, Colby, Kansas
New Jersey Historical Society, Newark, New Jersey
Mercer Museum, Doylestown, Pennsylvania
Winterthur Museum, Winterthur, Delaware
Seneca County Museum, Tiffin, Ohio
New Jersey State Museum, Trenton, New Jersey
Freer Gallery of Art, Washington, District of Columbia
Duncan and Miller Glass Museum, Washington, Pennsylvania
Fenton Glass Museum, Williamstown, West Virginia
Jones Gallery, East Baldwin, Maine
Beauport Museum, Gloucester, Massachusetts
Margaret Woodbury Strong Museum, Rochester, New York
Greentown Glass Museum, Greentown, Indiana
Mark Twain Museum, Hannibal, Missouri
William Penn Memorial Museum, Harrisburg, Pennsylvania
Hershey Museum, Hershey, Pennsylvania
The Wine Museum of San Francisco, San Francisco, California
The Currier Gallery of Art, Manchester, New Hampshire
Tuthill Museum, Middletown, New York
Everhart Museum, Scranton, Pennsylvania
Valentine Museum, Richmond, Virginia
The Bennington Museum, Bennington, Vermont
The Sandwich Historical Society Museum, Sandwich, Massachusetts

Corning Museum of Glass, Corning, New York
Henry Ford Museum, Dearborn, Michigan
Museum of Art, Carnegie Institute, Pittsburgh, Pennsylvania
The Smithsonian Institute, Washington, District of Columbia
Mansion Museum, Oglebay Institute, Wheeling, West Virginia
The Toledo Museum of Art, Toledo, Ohio
Rockwell Galleries, Corning, New York
The Morse Gallery of Art, Rollins College, Winter Park, Florida
The Metropolitan Museum of Art, New York City
The Milan Historical Museum, Milan, Ohio
The Brooklyn Museum of Art, Brooklyn, New York
Alfred University Museum, Alfred, New York
Dorflinger Glass Museum, White Mills, Pennsylvania
Egon and Hildegard Neustadt Museum for Tiffany Art, New York
Wayne County Historical Society, Honesdale, Pennsylvania
The Historical Society of Western Pennsylvania, Pittsburgh, Pennsylvania
Philadelphia Museum of Art, Philadelphia, Pennsylvania
Houston Antique Museum, Chattanooga, Tennessee
Chrysler Museum, Norfolk, Virginia
Old Sturbridge Village, Sturbridge, Massachusetts
Portland Museum of Art, Portland, Maine
Wadsworth Atheneum Museum, Hartford, Connecticut
Wheaton Village, Millville, New Jersey
The Morgan's Museum of Art Glass, Groveland, California
Cooper Union Museum, New York City
New Bedford Glass Museum, New Bedford, Massachusetts
Boston Museum of Fine Arts, Boston, Massachusetts

European Glass Displays (*)
Bethnal Green Museum, London, England
Haworth Art Gallery, Accrington, England
British Museum, London, England
Mus'ees royaux d'Art d'Histoire, Brussels, Belgium
Ulster Museum, Belfast, Ireland
Bristol City Art Gallery, Bristol, England
Fitzwilliam Museum, Cambridge, England
American Museum in Britain, Claverton Manor, Bath, England
Yorkshire Museum, York, England
National Museum of Ireland, Dublin, Ireland

Staatliche Kunstsammlugen, Kassel, West Germany
Badisches Landemuseum, Karlsruhe, West Germany
Kunstindustrimuseet, Oslo, Norway
Museum Stuck-Villa, Munich, West Germany
Victoria and Albert Museum, London England
KunstmuseumderStadtDusseldork, Dusseldorf, West Germany
Osterreichisches Museum fur angewandte Kunst. Vienna, Austria
Royal Scottish Museum, Edinburgh, Scotland
Stourbridge Council House, Stourbridge, England

Stevens and Williams Limited, Brierley Hill, England
Mus'ee des Arts D'ecoratifs, The Louvre, Paris, France
Musee de L'Ecole de Nancy, Nancy, France
Brierley Hill Library, Brierley Hill, England
Hessisches Landemuseum, Darmstadt, Germany

(*) Although there is not a great profusion of American Art Glass in any of these museums, it is often interesting to compare the output of various factories in Europe with the known wares of American manufacturers.

Some Contemporary Glass Manufacturers and Sellers

The names listed are just a small portion of those either manufacturing and/or selling contemporary and reproduction glass items. Be on the lookout, and be aware; learn to differentiate between what is old and what is new! Markings vary from engraving and acid stamps, to paper labels, or no identification at all. Many hand crafted items cost as much, or more, as their antique counterpart. Many objects are exceedingly beautiful and finely crafted. Possibly some of the finest contemporary glass on the market today is indicated by a star. (*)

A. A. Importing Company
4244-48 Olive Street
St. Louis, Missouri

Alfredo Barbini
Murano, Italy
(Ceramics and Glass)

Anchor Hocking Glass Corporation
Lancaster, Ohio

Atlantis
Full Lead Crystal
Portugal

Avitra Corportion
New York City

*Baccarat - Compagnie des Cristalleries de Baccarat
France (since 1764)
The glass of kings, czars, popes, and presidents

Balboa
Italy
(Venetian Glass)

Bavarian Bristol
Hand Blown, Hand Fired, Blown
Western Germany

Berkeley Art Glass
2 Kansas Street
Suite 408
San Francisco, California 94103

Bibi and Company
New York City

Blenko Glass Company
Milton, West Virginia
(Hand Craft)

Bohemian Crystal
Made in Czechoslovakia

Brockway Glass Company
Clarksburg, West Virginia

*Caithness Glass Limited, Wick
Scotland
Master Designer, Colin Terris
(Fine glass paperweights)

Castle
Murano, Italy
(Cut Crystal)

Chardavogue Glass
Glenwood, New Jersey

Clamborn Glass Company, Incorporated
Box 266
Yachats, Oregon

Colony
Handcrafted in Romania

Correia Art Glass
711 Colorado Avenue
San Monica, California 90401

Cristal d' Argues
Made in France

Cristalli
Italy

Crystal Art Glass
1203 Morton Avenue
Cambridge, Ohio

Crystal Brook
Germany
(Lead Crystal)

Crystal Clear Importing Company
Made in Romania

Crystal Import Corporation
New York City

*Daum Crystal
France

Doris Lechler
1388 Turell Road
Columbus, Ohio
(Heirlooms of Tomorrow)

*Edinburgh Crystal
Scotland

Fenton Art Glass Company
Williamstown, West Virginia

Fostoria Glass Company
Moundsville, West Virginia

Franconia Crystal
Germany

Genuine Crystal and Silver Plate
By Leonard
Italy

George Good Corporation
City of Industry, California
(Made in Taiwan)

Guernsey Glass Company
Cambridge, Ohio

Hand Made Crystal
Taiwan

Henry's Collectible Art Glass
3416 Raymond Street
Fort Wayne, Indiana

Hoya Crystal
Japan

Hunter Collectable Art Glass
Post Office Box 5140
Akron, Ohio

Imperial Glass Company
Bellaire, Ohio

Imperlux Crystal
Germany

Indiana Glass Company
Dunkirk, Indiana

Javit Badash
Hollis, New York
(Hand Cut Crystal)

John E. Kemple Glass Works
Kenova, West Virginia

Josh Simpson
Shelbourne Falls, Massachusetts 01370

K.R. Haley Glassware Company
Greensburg, Pennsylvania

Kanawha
Dunbar, West Virginia
(Hand Crafted Glassware)

*Lalique
Made in France

L.E. Smith Glass Company
Mount Pleasant, Pennsylvania

Lenox
(Hand Blown Crystal)

L.G. Wright Glass Company
New Martinsville, West Virginia

Libbey (Owen-Illinois, Incorporated)
Toledo, Ohio

Lotus Glass Company, Incorporated
Barnesville, Ohio

Louis Glass Company, Incorporated
Weston, West Virginia

Mann
Taiwan

Marcel Franck
Paris
(Objects D'Art)

Mary Angus
777 E. Main Street
Branford, Connecticut

Mats Jonasson Signature Collection
Sweden
"Wildlife" Sculptures
(Full Lead Crystal)

Medina Glass
Malta

Metropolitan Museum of Art
New York City

Mosser Glass
Route 22, East
Cambridge, Ohio

Mountaineer Glass Company
Western, West Virignia

Murmac Importing Corporation
New York City
(Hand Cut Lead Crystal)

National Glass Manufacturing Company
Buffalo, New York
(Murray's Rock Crystal)

Nick Del'Matto
32201 Logan Horns Mill Road
Logan, Ohio 43138

N.O. Phelps and Son
Rochester, New York
(Hand Cut Glass and Crystal)

North Hill Gift Shoppe
255 East Tallmadge Avenue
Akron, Ohio

Nourot Glass Studios
Bencia, California

*Orrefors Crystal
Sweden

*Pairpoint Glass Works
Sagamore, Massachusetts

Peter Breck Corporation
New York City
(Notsjoe Crystal)

Philadelphia Museum of Art
Benjamin Franklin Parkway
Philadelphia, Pennsylvania

Phoenix Studios
Los Angeles, California

Pilgrim Glass Corporation
Ceredo, West Virginia

R.E. Hansen
Mackinaw, Michigan

R.J. LaTournous
471 Welwood Avenue
Hawley, Pennsylvania 18428
(Specializes in Cut Glass)

Rainbow Art Glass Incorporated
Huntington, West Virginia

Reha Glass Company
Chicago, Illinois

Riedel Glass
Austria

Riekes Crisa
Turkey
(Crystal/Hand Crafted)

Royal Castle
England
(Hand Cut Lead Crystal)

Royal Netherland
Holland
(Fine Crystal)

Saint-Louis-les-Bitche, France
(Handcrafted crystal since 1767)

Sasaki Crystal
Japan

Seneca Glass Company
Morgantown, West Virginia

Silver City Glass Company
Meriden, Connecticut
(Sterling on Crystal)

Smithsonian Institute
The National Museum of American History
Division of Ceramics and Glass
Washington, D.C. 20560

St. Clair Glass Works
Elwood, Indiana

Star Crystal Company
West Englewood, New Jersey

*Steuben Clear Lead Crystal
Contemporary Glass Showroom
Corning, New York 14831
(Since 1933)

Stuart Crystal
England

Summit Art Glass Company
2236 Hartville Road
Mogadore, Ohio

Susquehanna Glass Company
Columbia, Pennsylvania

Swarovski Silver Crystal
Austrian Crystal - (32% Lead)

The Crystal Mirage At The Court
King of Prussia, Pennsylvania
Audrey and Bob Leavitt

The Jeanette Glass Company
Jeanette, Pennsylvania

Tiffin Glass Company
Tiffin, Ohio
(Subsidiary of Continental Can Company)

Touch of Glass Limited
4116 West 214th Street
Cleveland, Ohio

United China and Glass Company
New Orleans, Louisiana

*Val St. Lambert Cristalleries
Belgium
(Since 1825)

Viking Glass Company
New Martinsville, West Virginia

Vintage Art Glass Collectibles
Post Office Box 28464
Columbus, Ohio

Vistra Crystal
By Wiesenthal
West Germany

Waterford Glass Limited
Republic of Ireland

Westmoreland Glass Company
Grapeville, Pennsylvania

West Virginia Glass Specialty Company
Weston, West Virginia

For the Record

1. What is the difference between an antique and a semi-antique?

Objects are legally antique, under the new U.S. statue, if manufactured prior to 1866. In recent years, collectors, for the most part, have ignored this legality and are now acquiring semi-antiques (less than 100 years), collectibles, limited editions and anything that is in vogue.

2. How can I learn more about glass?

The study of glass is a lifetime endeavor. Go to your local library and avidly read many books on the subject. Take a course on antique glass; attend museums and historical societies viewing selected examples. Talk to intelligent dealers; attend auctions, shows and extravaganzas.

3. Should antique glass be used?

Of course, that was its original intent. Many people feel that this glass can no longer be used. Enjoy your acquisitions, whether they be purchased or inherited. Antique glass, treated with care, makes a beautiful and impressive table setting. It is especially nice when used on festive occasions, at Christmas and Thanksgiving for example. Even lovely vases can hold your favorite flowers, if the same water is not left in the vessels for several days.

4. What are some acceptable ways to display glass?

Glass needs space to breathe in order to be viewed properly. Lighting also enhances each object. Cupboards, curios, tables, wide window ledges, cases with sliding glass doors, and the well of a dry sink are just some of the interesting ways to exhibit glass.

5. Name some antique publications that could help me with my collection.

First, get your name on the mailing list(s) of reputable auction firms, and periodically attend these sales, to handle, study and purchase examples. Also consider subscribing to any of the following: *Americana, The Antiquarian, Antique Monthly, The Antique Trader Weekly, Hobbies, Antiquing Houston, Collector Editions Quarterly, Collectors News, Joel Sater's Antiques and Auction News, Tri-State Trader, The Magazine Antiques,* and *Art and Antiques.*

6. Is there one right or wrong way to photograph glass?

Glass is probably one of the most difficult subjects to capture because of its myriad of textures. A light table is acceptable; flood lights and an electronic flash properly balanced are also used. An excellent camera is absolutely essential—cheap cameras will give inferior results. Backdrops which provide a contrast make interesting shots. Observe depth of field, use a tripod, and work with film that is not too grainy. Slides stored in boxes and plastic sleeves, in a cool place, out of bright light, heat and dust will keep for years.

7. Is antique glass a good investment and a hedge against inflation?

Art and cut glass was relatively expensive when it was first made. Usually it was possessed by the wealthy. The law of supply and demand prevails. In recent years, collectors have elevated this field to one for sound investors. Do not follow trends, recognize quality for what it was, and what it remains today.

8. How do I determine the authenticity of a piece of glass from a reproduction?

Study, observe and read! Antiques have a grace about them; learn about shapes, colors, textures and manufacturing. Many of the manufacturing techniques have become a lost art form. Reproductions should not fool anyone!

9. Is it possible to restore a glass object that has been damaged?

Small rim chips can be ground down; roughness can be polished out. Long cracks are in the glass forever. Broken pieces are sometimes glued in place with a clear waterproof adhesive. Occasionally, missing pieces are built up and replaced with resins. Each example must be properly evaluated before a commitment is made. It seldom pays to restore an inferior glass object.

10. Are there suitable ways to protect a glass collection from theft?

Some people catalog their collection with photographs, accurate descriptions, and measurements. Many types of insurance are now available; a binder may be placed on your present policy. There is also a fine arts type, where objects are appraised annually. Do not advertise the fact that you are going away. Make your home or apartment appear like someone is living there. Have a friend collect the newspapers, shovel the snow, cut the grass. Timers which turn off and on throughout the day, and especially at night, are an excellent idea. Reinforce doors and windows with secure, quality locks. Many excellent alarm systems are on the market; one installed at your residence may give you complete peace of mind. For an aditional monthly fee, such a system may be hooked into the police station. It is always better to be safe than sorry.

11. What is meant by a "bastard" or "orphan" piece of glass?

Unfortunately, there are many types of American and European glass that cannot be properly identified. This is due to lack of records, and the fact that some firms copied the successes of others but modified, to a degree, to escape legal rights and lawsuits. Classic examples are the many forms of European iridescent glass imitating Tiffany's tremendous success.

12. How do pattern glass and cut glass differ?

There are literally thousands of patterns in these two types of glass. Pattern glass is made in three ways: 1. block molding, the earliest and simplest; 2. split molding, the mold having several divisions; and 3. font molding, each item identical in every aspect. Since it was mass produced, everyone could afford this type of glass manufactured in clear, frosted, etched, gilded, in flint and non-flint, flashed, in milk glass, opalescent and in a variety of colors. The pattern could be on both sides of the object or just on one surface. It was stocked by many of the cheaper novelty stores. Cut glass was expensive and time consuming to produce. Most of the outstanding factories manufactured this form in many shapes, illustrating it in their advertisements. The blanks were blown, marked off in their appropriate patterns, and then cut. Some of the early blanks are a full ¾" in thickness. The cutting is deep and sharp to the touch. Cut glass is usually much heavier than its pressed glass counterpart. Sunlight makes cut glass sparkle; this is not true with pressed glass, which has a flat feel when touched. The finer jewelry stores throughout the country patronized the cut glass firms. The bulk of the glass in vogue was made from the 1880s to 1910.

13. What are the dangers of sunlight and temperature changes to glass?

They are critical to most delicate art glass forms, especially cut glass. Glass brought in from the cold must be warmed gradually in its packing box before it can be unpacked and placed under hot lights at an antique show. Prolonged sunlight can break the finest art glass or cut glass. Places in the home where there are extremes in temperatures, like the cellar and attic, are not very likely locations to store glass when it is not being used or shown.

14. Why is one type of glass more valuable than another?

The quality and notoriety of the glass caught on; then the glass was recognized. Some very valuable glass today was not widely acclaimed when it was made; its scarcity today has driven the price upward. Lava and Royal Flemish are examples of this.

15. Is contemporary glass worth collecting?

There are many contemporary artists throughout the United States and Europe (see the list provided) that excel in creativity. Be selective when buying. As time progresses, some of these items will continue to escalate in value.

16. How is iridescence achieved on a glass surface?

This was an attempt to create the allusion of ancient buried glass. It was utilized on even the finer art glass types, and later on Carnival Glass. The surface coloration, which is multi-hued was achieved when glass was coated with a sprayed-on metallic chloride stain. Numerous other successful methods were used, which include: exposing glass to pressurized and heated water mixed with 15% hydrochloric acid, sulphurous fumes placed on the glass body, and introducing glass to tin crystals placed in a muffle, where the oxidizing crystals would attack the glass surface.

17. Is there any significance when a piece of glass is tapped and possesses resonance?

This characteristic comes about when certain ingredients are blended into the batch. The glass is soft to the touch, cuts easily and fuses at low temperatures. It was manfactured in clear, transparent and colors. Some collectors prefer this type. There is a tendency to use the terms flint and lead glass interchangeably; this is not considered correct.

18. What is meant by a "sleeper?"

Sometimes you are able to find a bargain by paying far less than the going price guide rate. Dealers often purchase complete estates; it is very challenging for them to "be on top" of all commodities. Be on the lookout, study and read about specific types of glass in which you are interested. Do not be fooled; however, there are many reproductions on the market!

19. How can an ultra-violet or black light be a helpful aid?

This light may be purchased from a supplier for a nominal fee. It is especially valuable for identifying cracks, flaws or mends on china and porcelain. Colored glass, which is opaque and translucent, may have damage not detected by the naked eye; an ultra-violet light used in dim surroundings then proves invaluable.

20. What are suitable ways to dispose of a collection?

You may sell privately, go through an auction house which charges a commission (usually 15%), do a flea market, or advertise a garage sale. Some choice objects should, perhaps, be passed on in your will. Some individuals loan objects to historical societies and museums for display. Others donate pieces so that they may be preserved, viewed and enjoyed for future generations.

21. Could there be more information available on specific types of glass?

There is much misinformation about glass. Some factories may have used only numbers for identification in their catalogs; later, dealers and other individuals assigned names to various unknown types. Publishers look for books that will yield volume sales and appeal to the masses; antique books, unfortunately, do neither of these. Therefore, many excellent manuscripts are never published, and books are taken out of print, remaindered, or shredded to avoid strict tax laws. Refer to the Supreme Court decision of January 1979; Thor Power Tool Company vs. Commissioner of Internal Revenue.

22. What is the significance of colors in glass?

People are usually partial to certain colors that appeal to them; this is often what they collect. Some people decorate entire rooms by coordinating the colors of glass objects with the drapes, rugs, wallpaper and paintings. The basic ingredients in the glass will determine the hue that the completed object will have. This called for very technical skills on the parts of workers as they tried to control temperatures and precise batch measurements. See the section which refers to coloring agents.

23. Is it permissible to place antique glass objects in a dishwasher?

Some householders do this with no detrimental results. However, when a piece breaks loose and tumbles about, each clink represents a sizable monetary loss. It is best to wash antique glass by hand. Take your time washing each piece. Carefully dry with a lint-free cloth and return it to its original location.

24. What are some ways of accumulating a glass collection?

Individuals on occasion are fortunate enough to inherit examples. Others attend sales and shows, which can become an obsession. Many people enjoy exercising and the flair and fascination that a large flea market brings. Often you can buy privately, deal through the mail, or look in shops in different localities as you travel to and from work, or while on vacation. The yellow pages in a telephone book or a library will prove of assistance when you are visiting an area for the first time.

25. Is all antique glass marked in some manner?

Unfortunately, most of it is not marked. Enameling, cutting, etching, acid-stamping, and raised logos incorporated in the original mold are just a few identifying insignias. Many pieces are found with spurious signatures; most having been forged with an electric engraving needle. By learning a manufacturer's styles, shapes and colors, it is then no longer necessary; to seek just signed examples. Acid signatures turn up on pieces (especially Lalique) that were never made by that firm; this is also becoming very prevalent in the cut glass field.

26. Why has not legislation been passed forcing manufacturers to mark all contemporary produced glass?

There have been numerous efforts to require that all glass be permanently marked as to its origin. The law has never been passed and enacted. Most contemporary glass has only a gummed paper label affixed to it. Once these labels are removed, the item becomes an "instant antique." Too much of this is being done by dealers. Be on guard so you are not fooled into thinking that you have purchased a sleeper!

27. Have all types of antique glass beeen reproduced?
Practically every type, at one time or another, has been duplicated. Many ventures have been dismal failures, others have met with very profitable successes. Some firms possess the original molds and formulas; then it becomes exceedingly difficult to differentiate the old from the new. A few art glass types, like Pomona, have not been copied because of the time, labor and technical knowledge needed.

28. How were the names for types of antique glass derived?
In many instances, the names were assigned to describe a particular pattern that was incorporated, a specific color, a technique, or a type of stone. Some were derived from Latin and Greek words. The name for Frederick Carder's Steuben "Aurene" came from "aureus," meaning golden. This aptly describes the particular iridescence found on this glass. The output of some glasshouses is often referred to by the location where it was made or the maker's name. Some names were assigned to suggest wealth, quality, nobility and elaborateness. Examples of each type are as follows: Lion Pattern Glass, Cranberry, Overlay, Onyx, Honesdale and Webb. Names that seem to suggest royalty are Crown Milano, Royal Flemish and Queen's Burmese.

29. What is the proper way to store glass?
Glass should be cleaned, then carefully wrapped in plastic bubble paper, tissue paper, styrofoam chips, newspaper, or some other material that will properly cushion it. Heavy cardboard fruit boxes with separate box lids are very suitable. Heavy objects should go in the bottom of the box first. Label all boxes and place them where the temperature is fairly constant throughout the year. Sixty to seventy degrees are ideal temperature ranges.

30. You often see examples of ancient glass excavated after being buried for centuries; sometimes these pieces have an iridescence. Did these cultures have the technology to produce such a glass?
Absolutely! Most of the techniques that we come across in glass, including iridescence, were known by the ancients. Early glass that has been buried takes on an "incandescent" look, since the outer glass surface has fragmented and fissured. These tiny particles, in turn, pick up the varying hues in the rainbow, giving a very pleasing illusion.

31. Was glass invented or discovered by accident?
It is not positively known how glass originated. There are many references to glass in early literature, and we know that originally, it was owned by nobility and the wealthy. It has been speculated that lightning striking a sandy beach generated enough heat to create globules of glass. Pliny, an ancient historian, relates the story of how a ship carrying niter was stranded on the banks of a river in Syria. The merchants supported their cauldrons with lumps of this material, since no stones were available. The combination of fire, niter and sand was said to produce an unknown liquid. The Venetians tried to prevent their formulas from being discovered by other countries. Any glassmaker who tried to escape from Murano was given the death penalty. Many cultures looked upon the glass artisans as magicians, since they were able to manipulate and conjure from red hot molten masses useful objects in all sizes, colors and shapes.

32. What does the term "mold mark" mean?
These are the raised delineations found on glass surfaces indicating the point at which the mold would open and close. The number of marks, or seams, signifies the number of molds used to make the piece.

33. Do etched or enameled numbers mean anything on a piece of glass?
Sometimes yes and sometimes no. An etched or enameled number seven, for example, might be found on the base of a cruet, cologne or boudoir bottle. The matching stopper (if it fits properly) usually has the same number marked on the flat portion of the neck. Manufacturers often incorporated metal with glass in some of their production items. These might include lamps, vases, sugars and creamers, condiment sets, brides' baskets, jewel and trinket boxes, and perfumes. Impressed or etched numbers on the metal surfaces might assist in determining where these parts were fabricated. A variety of metals, including silver, brass, quadruple plate, and base metals, may be found on various items. Undoubtedly, the numbers found on glass items always have a meaning. However, without the proper knowledge, you will be unable to discover their significance. Firms such as Kimble and Tiffany frequently used numbers on their glass to indicate heights, batch numbers, colors and shapes.

34. What do the terms "crown glass" and "bull's-eye" glass mean?
Crown glass is a form of early window glass. An entire crown, or wheel, of glass was made when a large parison of glass was whirled around as it was attached to the pontil. Spinning forced the bubble to explode and expand into a "wheel" of glass. The glass was then cut to size to fit a particular window opening. Pieces with the pontil mark became the "bull's-eye" and were originally said to be inferior; today they are highly sought.

35. Did glass manufacturers advertise their products?
Yes, especially in the eighteenth and nineteenth centuries. Advertisements were placed in newspapers, magazines, and city directories—to name a few. Letterheads and original factory catalogs are sometimes discovered leading to new and valuable facts concerning these firms.

Artistic renderings found on silver plate and cut glass were drawn from an actual piece that possessed this mark. This research was for the purpose of aiding in identifying the great variety that exists in these fields.

Silver Plate Accompanying Art Glass

Victorian glass manufacturers further embellished their wares with the addition of quadruple plate. Some noteworthy shapes found with this aesthetic addition are cookie and cracker jars, bride's baskets, pickle castors, condiment sets, covered jars (some with side handles), ice water pitchers, bowls, vases, carafes, sugars and creamers, and atomizers and colognes.

Glasshouses ordered the necessary attachments from numerous competing silver plate firms. More often than not, a mark of manufacture is found stamped on the underside. In sets, one or several parts could be found marked with a popular logo. The list provided gives the pictorial names, locations and dates of manufacture for many establishments.

Mismatches are common today. Carefully observe the fit of all pieces. Note that the pattern follows through on the metal pieces. Is the lid too loose or too snug? Does the diameter of the cruet, salt and pepper or bride's basket fit properly? Are the glass and metal complimentary to each other, or do they clash as a mismarriage?

You are fortunate indeed to find an outstanding glass example trimmed in well-cared-for silver plate. What appears to be a hopeless case can readily be remedied many times with a little planning. Dents can be removed, pieces can be made if they are missing, a break can be resoldered, dingy surfaces can be polished, and old worn plate can be replated. Make certain that all restoration work is completed by a reputable concern and that an accurate appraisal of costs is given in writing before the refurbishing commences.

The home enthusiast is capable of some minor restorations. Detached tops are common on covered jars and cookie containers. Soak the edge of the glass in equal solutions of warm water and vinegar until the residue is released without applying undue pressure. Do the same for the metal portions. Cautiously remove the hardened plaster without scratching or gouging. A sharpened wooden popsicle stick or a metal screw driver with its tip covered works very well. After the parts have been cleaned and dried, you are ready to reattach them. Mix a batter like consistency of plaster-of-Paris and apply carefully in the well of the lid. Now join the metal and the glass, wipe off the excess with a damp sponge and set aside to dry thoroughly overnight.

Britannia, generally, was the base metal for wares of this type. An alloy of copper, tin, zinc and antimony was mixed and cast into ingots. The ingots were rolled into sheets and then submitted to a hydraulic press which exerted over 650 tons of pressure. Patterns created by artists were transferred to steel dies to create elaborate embossed designs.

All parts were soldered and cleaned before they were coated with silver by means of electrolysis. Some portions were also ornamented by gold plating.

Finishes included burnished articles, some done by hand and others by machinery. Others were given satin finishes. High speed wire brushes produced this roughened appearance.

Special orders had initials and other designs engraved by hand. Today these items are widely collected and cherished. As long as the glass portion remains intact, one might consider the merits of a fine quadruple-plated example for his/her collection.

Some Silver Plate Marks

725

Acme Silver Plate Co. (1885)
Boston, MA

Adelphia Silver Plate Co.
(1890-1920)
New York, NY

Albany Silver Plate Co. (1890-1904)

The American Silver Co. (1853-1899)

Crown Silver Plate Co.
Sterling Plate

◁B▷

Eastern Silver Co.

H. & T. Mfg. Co.

New England Silverplate Co.

Pequabuck Mfg. Co.

Royal Plate Co.

Welch Silver

1857 Welch-Atkins

Ames Mfg. Co.
(1870-1885)
Chicopee, MA

Aurora Silver Plate Manufacturing
Co. (1869-1904).
Aurora, Ill.

Barbour Silver Co. (1882-1898)
Hartford, CT

Albany Silver Plate Co.

Sterlin **E**

James E. Blake Co. (1904)
Attleboro, MA

(East Haddam, Comm.)
L. Boardman & Son
(1884-1904)

Brown & Bros.
(1884-1904)
Waterbury, CT

Columbian Quadruple Plate
(1893) - New York, NY

J.F. Curran & Co.
(1860-1900)
New York, NY

Yukon Silver
(Cattaraugus Cutlery Co.)
1904-1922
Little Valley, NY

Derby Silver Co.
(1873-1898)
Birmingham, CT & Derby, CT

Empire Silver Plate Co.
(1890-1922)
Brooklyn, NY

FILLEY

Harvey Filley & Sons (1859-1884)
Philadelphia, PA

ALBERT G. FINN SILVER CO.
CRESCENT SILVER CO.

TRADE MARK

Albert G Finn Silver Co.
(1904-   )
Syracuse, NY

Forbes Silver Co.
(1890-1898)
Meriden, CT

Gem Silver Co.
(1899-   )

B. Gleason & Sons (1860-1870)
Dorchester, MA

Gorham Manufacturing Co.
(1863-present)
San Francisco, CA
Chicago, IL
New York, NY

Hartford Silver Plate Co. (1884-1887)
Hartford, CT

H.B. & H.A.7.
Sheffield Plated Co.
Union Silver Plate Co.
Homes, Booth & Haydens
(1853-1920)
Waterbury, CT

EDWARDS

The Holmes & Edwards Silver Co.
(1851-present)
Bridgeport & Stratford, CT

Homan & Co.
(1847-1900)
Cincinnati, OH
Homan Silver Plate Co.
(1900-1922)
Cincinnati, OH
Became Homan Manufacturing
Company
in 1922

Lyons Silver Co (1890-   )
Lyons, NY

David H. McConnel & Co.
(1895-1915)
New York, NY

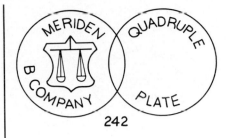

242

Meriden Brittannica Co. (1852-1898)
Meriden, CT

MERIDEN
BRITᴬ CO.

The Meriden Silver Plate Co.
(1869-1898)
Meriden, CT

The Middletown Plate Co.
(1864-1899)
MIddletown, CT
New York, NY

S.F. Myers & Co.
(1860-1920)
New York, NY

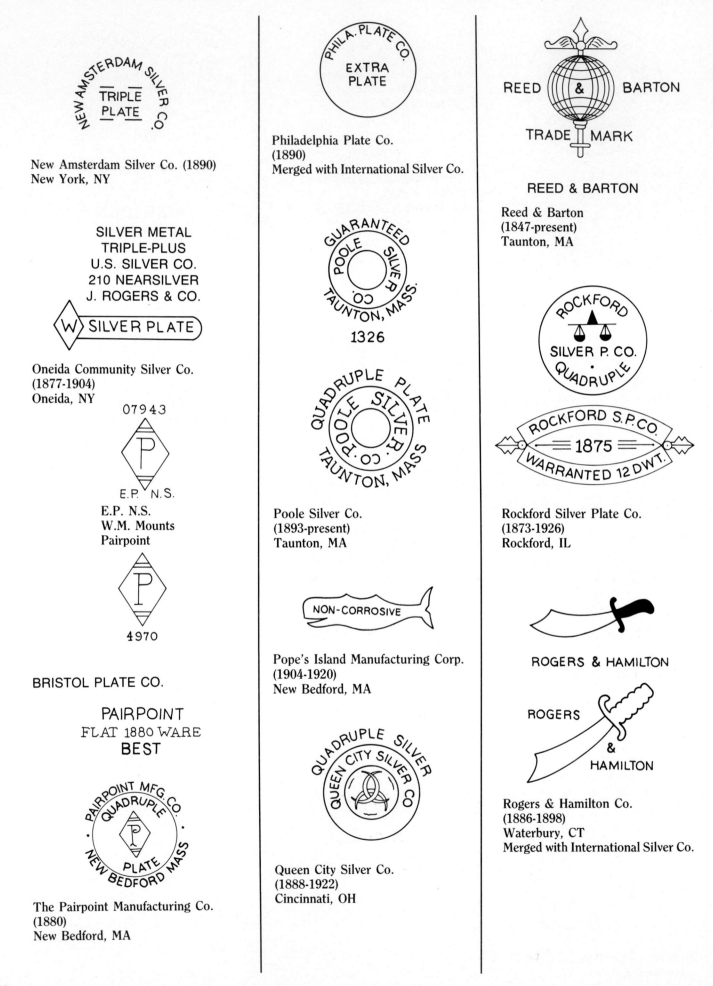

New Amsterdam Silver Co. (1890)
New York, NY

SILVER METAL
TRIPLE-PLUS
U.S. SILVER CO.
210 NEARSILVER
J. ROGERS & CO.

Oneida Community Silver Co.
(1877-1904)
Oneida, NY

07943

E.P. N.S.
W.M. Mounts
Pairpoint

4970

BRISTOL PLATE CO.

PAIRPOINT
FLAT 1880 WARE
BEST

The Pairpoint Manufacturing Co.
(1880)
New Bedford, MA

Philadelphia Plate Co.
(1890)
Merged with International Silver Co.

1326

Poole Silver Co.
(1893-present)
Taunton, MA

NON-CORROSIVE

Pope's Island Manufacturing Corp.
(1904-1920)
New Bedford, MA

Queen City Silver Co.
(1888-1922)
Cincinnati, OH

REED & BARTON

Reed & Barton
(1847-present)
Taunton, MA

Rockford Silver Plate Co.
(1873-1926)
Rockford, IL

ROGERS & HAMILTON

Rogers & Hamilton Co.
(1886-1898)
Waterbury, CT
Merged with International Silver Co.

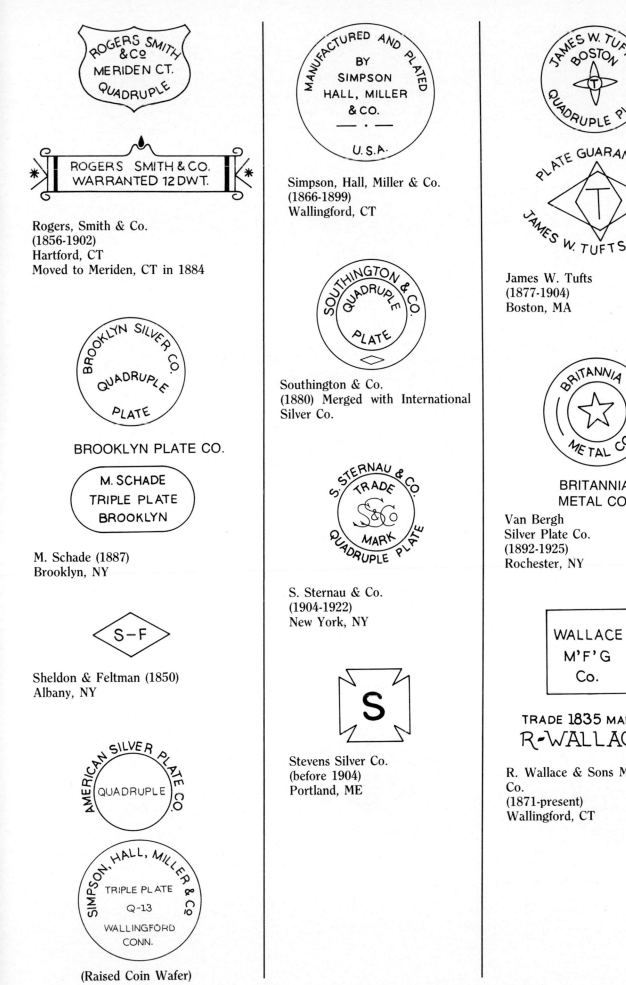

Rogers, Smith & Co.
(1856-1902)
Hartford, CT
Moved to Meriden, CT in 1884

BROOKLYN PLATE CO.

M. Schade (1887)
Brooklyn, NY

Sheldon & Feltman (1850)
Albany, NY

(Raised Coin Wafer)

Simpson, Hall, Miller & Co.
(1866-1899)
Wallingford, CT

Southington & Co.
(1880) Merged with International
Silver Co.

S. Sternau & Co.
(1904-1922)
New York, NY

Stevens Silver Co.
(before 1904)
Portland, ME

James W. Tufts
(1877-1904)
Boston, MA

BRITANNIA
METAL CO.

Van Bergh
Silver Plate Co.
(1892-1925)
Rochester, NY

R. Wallace & Sons Manufacturing
Co.
(1871-present)
Wallingford, CT

SILVER SOLDERED

Waltrous Mfg. Co.
(1896-1898)
Wallingford, CT

E.G. Webster & Son
(1886-1928)
Brooklyn, NY

West Silver Co.
(1883-1904)
Taunton, MA
Became F.B. Rogers Silver Co.
before 1922

Wilcox Britannia Co. (1865)
West Meriden, CT
Became Wilcox Silver Plate Co.
Meriden, CT
(1867-   )

Wilcox Silver Plate Co.
(1867-1898)
Meriden, CT

William Wilson & Son
(Est. ;1812; Incorp. 1883)
Philadelphia, PA

The logotypes listed are a random
sampling from literally hundreds of
factories, small shops and general
distributors that existed throughout
the United States.

Cut Glass Marks

1. Abraham and Straus Inc.

2. C.G. Alford & Co.

3. Almy & Thomas

4. T.B. Clark & Co.

5. J.D. Bergen Co.

6. Maple City Glass Co.

7. George L. Borden & Co.
(KK-Krystal Krafters)

8. George Borgfeldt & Co.

9. Corona Cut Glass Co.

10. Burley and Tyrrell Co.

11. Crown Cut Glass Co.

SILVART

12. Deidrick Glass Co.

13. Diamond Cut Glass Works

14. C. Dorflinger & Sons

15. O.F. Egginton Co.

16. H.C. Fry Glass Co.

17. T.G. Hawkes & Co.

18. A.H. Heisey & Co.

19. L. Hinsberger Cut Glass Co.

20. J. Hoare & Co.

21. Hobbs Glass Co.

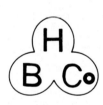

22. Hobbs, Brockunier & Co.

23. Honesdale Decorating Co.

24. Hope Glass Works

25. Hunt Glass Co.

26. Irving Cut Glass Co.

27. Jewel Cut Glass Co.

28. Edward J Koch & Co.

29. Lackawanna Cut Glass Co.

30. Laurel Cut Glass Co.

31. W.L. Libbey & Son

32. Joseph Locke & Sons

Joseph Locke

33. Lowell Cut Glass Co.

34. William H. Lum

35. Luzerne Cut Glass Co.

36. McKanna Cut Glass Co.

PRESCUT

37. McKee-Jeannette Glass Works

38. Majestic Cut Glass Co.

39. Maple City Glass Co.

40. Meriden Cut Glass Co.

41. Signet Glass Co.

42. H.P. Sinclaire & Co.

43. Standard Cut Glass Co.

44. Sterling Glass Co.

45. Steuben Glass Works

46. L. Straus & Sons

47. Taylor Brothers Co.

48. Thatcher Brothers & Co.

Tuthill

49. Tuthill Cut Glass Co.

50. U.S. Glass Co.

51. Newark Cut Glass Co.

52. Pairpoint Corporation

53. Pitkin & Brooks

54. P.X. Parsche & Son Co.

UNGER
BROS

55. Unger Brothers

Wright

56. Wright Rich Cut Glass Co.

Locations of Cut Glass Houses

The numbers correspond to numbers accompanying the cut glass marks.

1. Brooklyn, New York
2. New York, New York
3. Corning, New York
4. Honesdale, Pennsylvania
5. Meriden, Connecticut
6. Hawley, Pennslvania
7. Trenton, New Jersey
8. New York City, New York
9. Toledo, Ohio
10. Chicago, Illinois
11. Pittsburgh, Pennsylvania
12. Monaca, Pennsylvania
13. New York City, New York
14. White Mills, Pennsylvania
15. Corning, New York
16. Rochester, Pennsylvania
17. Corning, New York
18. Newark, Ohio
19. Brooklyn, New York
20. Corning, New York
21. Wheeling, West Virginia
22. Wheeling, West Virginia
23. White Mills, Pennsylvania
24. Providence, Rhode Island
25. Corning, New York
26. Honesdale, Pennsylvania
27. Newark, New Jersey
28. Chicago, Illinois

29. Scranton, Pennsylvania
30. Jermyn, Pennsylvania
31. Toledo, Ohio
32. Mt. Oliver, Pennsylvania
33. Lowell, Massachusetts
34. New York City, New York
35. Pittston, Pennsylvania
36. Honesdale, Pennsylvania
37. Jeannette, Pennsylvania
38. Elmira, New York
39. Hawley, Pennsylvania
40. Meriden, Connecticut
41. Address Unknown
42. Corning, New York
43. New York City, New York
44. Cincinnati, Ohio
45. Corning, New York
46. New York City, New York
47. Philadelphia, Pennsylvania
48. Fairhaven, Massachusetts
49. Middletown, New York
50. Tiffin, Ohio
51. Newark, New Jersey
52. New Bedford, Massachusetts
53. Chicago, Illinois
54. Chicago, Illinois
55. Newark, New Jersey
56. Anderson, Indiana

Ads

The list of original advertisements which follows should prove a valuable and definitive aid to the collector, dealer, historical society and museum in identifying many examples according to shape, pattern number and price. The artistic renderings are beautifully executed and the verbage used is fascinating. Dates when the ads ran are recorded in most instances.

Sources include: *The Review of Reviews, Scribner's, Home Journal, Country Life in America, The Jewelers' Circular, The Cosmopolitan, Everybody's Magazine, McClure's, The Century Magazine, Munsey's Magazine, The Sketch Book, Good Housekeeping, Harper's Magazine, The House Beautiful, Pictorial Review, Life, The Literary Digest, Christian Herald,* postcards, original catalogs, patent records, etc.

All examples shown are from the author's private collection.

TIFFANY FAVRILE GLASS

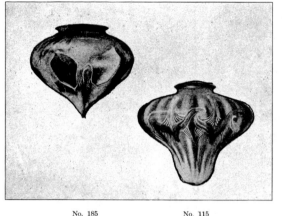

No. 185   No. 115

STALACTITES FOR ELECTRIC LIGHTING

No. 185 8¼ in. high 10½ in. diameter, for 5 in. fitter

No. 115 8½ in. high 10 in. diameter, for 4½ in. fitter

TIFFANY FAVRILE GLASS
LEGION D'HONNEVR-GRAND PRIX = PARIS, 1900.

MADE AT THE
TIFFANY FVRNACES
CORONA, LONG ISLAND, N.Y.

TIFFANY FAVRILE GLASS

TIFFANY FURNACES
CORONA, LONG ISLAND, NEW YORK

TIFFANY FAVRILE GLASS

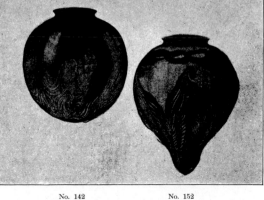

No. 142   No. 152

GLOBES AND STALACTITES FOR ELECTRIC LIGHTING

No. 142 8 in. high 8 in. diameter, for 3¼ in. fitter
         10 "   "   10 "   "   " 3¼ " "
         12 "   "   12 "   "   " 3¼ " "

No. 152 11 in. high 5½ in. diameter, for 3¼ in. fitter
         13 "   "   9 "   "   " 4½ " "
         16 "   "   13 "   "   " 7 " "

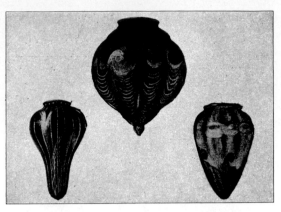

No 125   No. 127   No. 116

STALACTITES FOR ELECTRIC LIGHTING

———————

No. 125   10½ in. high   5 in. diameter   3¼ in. fitter

No. 127   14 in. high.   12 in diameter   5 in. fitter

No. 116   11 in. high   6 in. diameter   4½ in. fitter

T HIS book is presented for the purpose of illustrating Tiffany Favrile Glass. This glass, which was first produced in 1893, is the result of research, and development of possibilities in glass-making, by Mr. Louis C. Tiffany. It differs radically from all glass heretofore produced, and occupies a position in decorative art that is individual. Its individuality lies in its diversified radiance of iridescence, and in the use of glass of various colors and metal combinations, to produce design as an integral part of the structure of the object decorated, all of which is accomplished in the actual making of the article in the furnace, and not by any subsequent treatment.

Tiffany Favrile Glass is made only at the Tiffany Furnaces, at Corona, L. I., N. Y., under the direction of Mr. Tiffany. Some imitations

of Tiffany Favrile Glass have been made in America and Europe, and represented to be the genuine. Each piece of Tiffany Favrile Glass is marked " L. C. T." or " Louis C. Tiffany." The name " Tiffany Favrile Glass" is a Registered Trade-Mark, and the use of either of the words " Tiffany" and " Favrile," or words of the same import, describing any glass not made at the Tiffany Furnaces, is an infringement.

Tiffany Favrile Glass was awarded the Grand Prix at the Exposition of Paris 1900, St. Petersburgh 1901, Turin 1902, the Gold Medal of the Pan American Exposition 1901, and it has been shown at the Paris Salons since 1895. The glass has attracted such attention in the art world that many museums, of which a list is given on succeeding pages, have purchased collections for permanent exhibition.

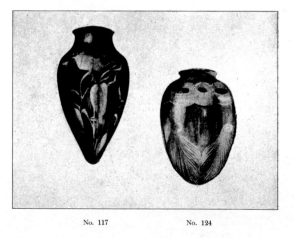

No. 117   No. 124

STALACTITES FOR ELECTRIC LIGHTING

———————

No. 117   15 in. high   6 in diameter, for 4½ in. fitter
            20 "   "   7 "   "   " 4½ "   "

No. 124   8½ in. high   6½ in. diameter, for 3¼ in fitter
            10½ "   "   7 "   "   " 4 "   "

"MOORISH" DESIGN

STALACTITE FOR ELECTRIC LIGHT

7 in. high   3¼ in. fitter
12 " "   5 " "

COLLECTIONS OF TIFFANY FAVRILE GLASS
HAVE BEEN PURCHASED AND ARE EXHIB-
ITED BY THE FOLLOWING ART MUSEUMS

National Museum, ... Washington
Metropolitan Museum of Art, . . New York
Art Institute, ... Chicago
Field Columbian Museum, . . . Chicago
Cincinnati Museum of Art, . . . Cincinnati
Pratt Institute, ... Brooklyn, N. Y.
Worcester Art Museum, ... Worcester, Mass.
South Kensington Museum, . . . London
Museum of Science and Art, . . . Glasgow
Museum of Science and Art, . . . Dublin
The National Art Gallery of Victoria, Melbourne
Musée du Luxembourg, . . . Paris
Musée des Arts décoratifs, . . . Paris
Musée du Conservatoire des Arts et
    Métiers, ... Paris
Musée Galliéra, ... Paris
Musée de la Manufacture de Sèvres, Sèvres
Musée des Arts décoratifs, . . . Limoges
Kunst Gewerbe Museum, ... Berlin
Museum für Kunst und Gewerbe. . Hamburg
Museum of Decorative Arts, . . . Dresden
Kestner Museum, ... Hanover

Nordböhmisches Gewerbe Museum, Reichenberg
Museum für Kunst und Industrie, . Vienna
Museum of Decorative Arts, . . . Budapest
Musée des Arts decoratifs, . . . Bruxelles
Musée de l'Ecole Central de Dessin, St. Petersburgh
National Museum, ... Stockholm
Nordenfjeldske Kunstindustri Mu-
    seum, ... Trondhjem
Museum of Copenhagen, ... Copenhagen
Imperial Museum of Japan, . . . Tokio, Japan
Museum of the Fine Arts Society, . Tokio, Japan
The Victoria and Albert Museum, . London
Regio Museo Industriale, ... Turin
Kunst Gewerbe Museum, ... Leipzig
Kaiser Wilhelm Museum, ... Crefeld
Musée Stieglitz, ... St. Petersburgh
Pennsylvania Museum of Industrial
    Art, ... Philadelphia, Pa.
Musée des Arts Decoratifs, . . . Bergen
Musée des Arts décoratifs, . . . Prague
Musée des Arts Industriels, . . . Christiania
Imperial Commercial Museum, . . Tokio
An die Grossh. Centralstelle für die
    Gewerbe, ... Darmstadt
Musée de Mulhouse, ... Mulhouse

TIFFANY FAVRILE GLASS

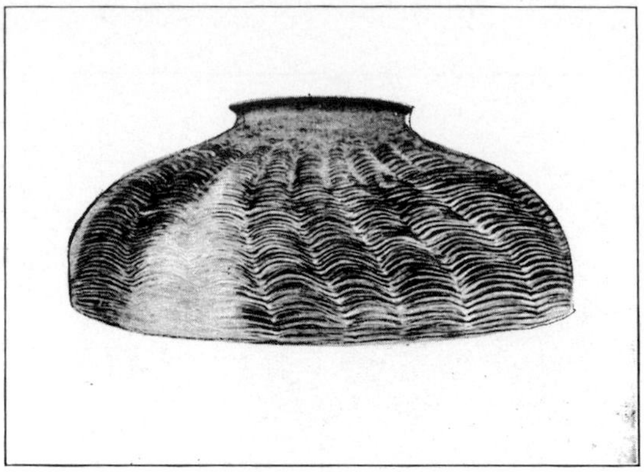

"WAVE" DESIGN

DOME SHADES

Green Opalescent, Gold Decoration, Lined with White or Ivory Opalescent, Gold Decoration

For Oil and Electric Light

7 in. 10 in. 12 in. 14 in. Diameter

TIFFANY FAVRILE GLASS

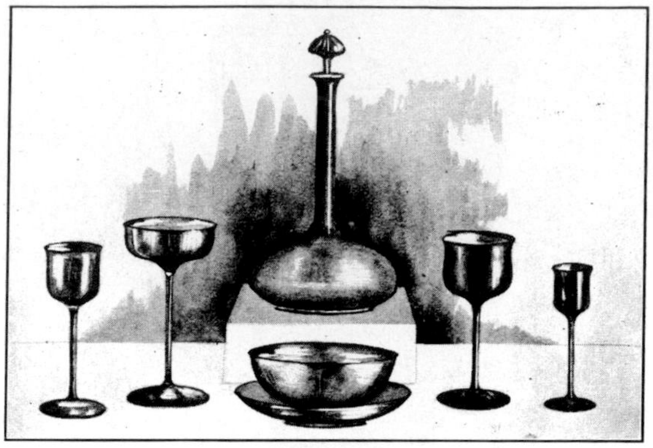

"PRINCE" DESIGN

Rich Golden Lustre Glass

This Suite of Glass comprises Liqueur, Sherry, Claret, Champagne, Sorbet, Decanter, Finger Bowl and Ice Plate

TIFFANY FAVRILE GLASS

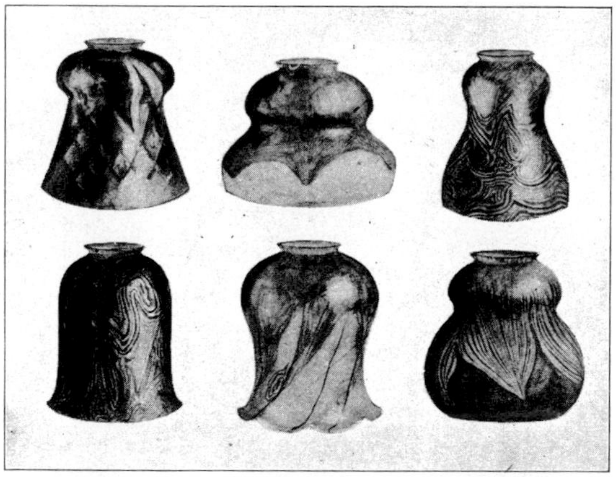

No. 178 No. 110	No. 109 No. 134	No. 111 No. 112

ELECTRIC LIGHT SHADES FOR 2¼ INCH FITTER

No. 178	4⅝ in.	high	3¾ in.	diameter	4¼ in.	opening	2¼ in.	fitter
No. 110	4½ in.	"	3½ in.	"	4 in.	"	2¼ in.	"
No. 109	4 in.	"	5¼ in.	"	4¾ in.	"	2¼ in.	"
No. 134	5 in.	"	4⅜ in.	"	4¼ in.	"	2¼ in.	"
No. 111	5 in.	"	4 in.	"	3½ in.	"	2¼ in.	"
No. 112	4⅜ in.	"	4¼ in.	"	2⅞ in.	"	2¼ in.	"

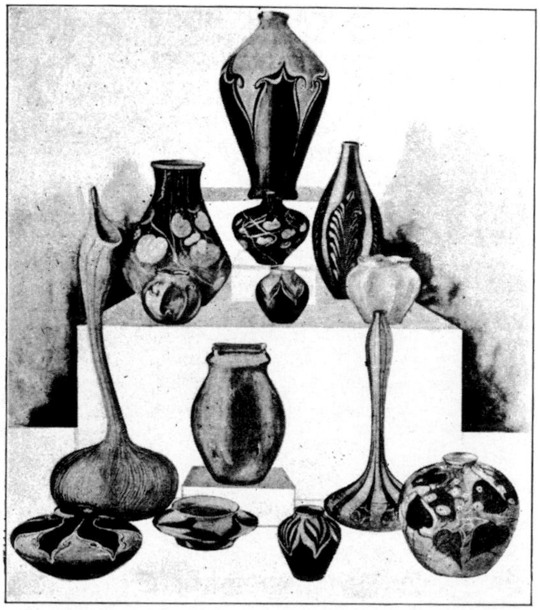

"EARL"

"VICTORIA"   "ASCOT"
"PRINCE"   "QUEEN"

FINGER BOWLS AND ICE PLATES

Light Shaded Gold, with Iridescent Lustre

"DAMASCENE" DESIGN

DOME SHADES

Green Opalescent, Gold Decoration, Lined with White or Ivory Opalescent, Gold Decoration

For Oil and Electric Light

7 in.   10 in.   12 in.   14 in. Diameter

"ETRUSCAN" DESIGN

DOME SHADES

Green Opalescent, Gold Decoration, Lined with White or Ivory Opalescent, Gold Decoration

For Oil and Electric Light

7 in.   10 in.   12 in.   14 in. Diameter

"PRINCESS"   "PRINCESS"   "MANHATTAN"
(Hock)   (Champagne)   (Champagne)
"DOMINION"   "PRINCE"   "ROYAL"   "SAVOY"
(Champagne)   (Champagne)   (Champagne)   (Champagne)

HOCK AND CHAMPAGNE GLASSES

Rich Golden Lustre

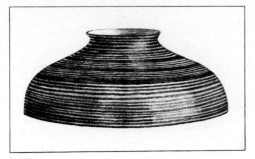

"RIBBON" DESIGN

DOME SHADES

Green Opalescent, Gold Decoration, Lined with White or Ivory Opalescent, Gold Decoration

For Oil and Electric Light

7 in.   10 in.   12 in.   14 in. Diameter

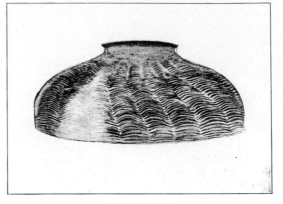

"WAVE" DESIGN

DOME SHADES

Green Opalescent, Gold Decoration, Lined with White or Ivory Opalescent, Gold Decoration

For Oil and Electric Light

7 in.   10 in.   12 in.   14 in. Diameter

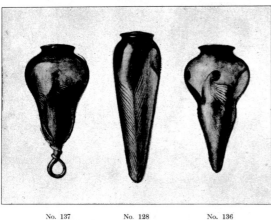

No. 137   No. 128   No. 136

STALACTITES FOR ELECTRIC LIGHT

No. 137	12 in. high	5¾ in. diameter	3¼ in. fitter
No. 128	9 in. high	4½ in. diameter	3¼ in. fitter
	15 in. high	5 in. diameter	3¼ in. fitter
No. 136	11¼ in. high	8½ in. diameter	3¼ in. fitter

F   H   E   G
A   I   B   C   D

COMPORTS, EPERGNES, BON BON DISHES, PLATES AND PIN TRAYS

Light Shaded Gold, with Iridescent Lustre

A—"Queen" Comport, low . . . . . 3 in.   4 in.   6 in. Dia.
B—"Queen" Comport, high . . . . 4 in.   6 in.   8 in. Dia.
C—"Colonial" Comport, low . . . . 3 in.   4 in.   6 in.   8 in. Dia.
D—"Colonial" Comport, high . . . 4 in.   6 in.   8 in. Dia.
E—"Earl" Comport . . . . 4 in.   6 in.   8 in. Dia.
F—"Prince" Epergne . . . . 11 in.   14 in. high
G—"Iris" Epergne . . . . 11 in.   14 in. high
H—"Ascot" Plate . . . . 3 in.   3½ in.   4 in. Dia.
I—"Queen" Bon Bon Dish or Pin Tray 2½ in. 3 in.   4 in.   5 in. Dia.

250

"ROYAL" DESIGN

Rich Golden Lustre

This Suite of Glass comprises Liqueur, Sherry, Claret, Hock and Champagne

"FLEMISH" DESIGN

Light Shaded Gold, with Iridescent Lustre

This Suite of Glass comprises Liqueur, Claret, Sherry, Champagne and Decanter

A Gift from the Tiffany Studios is always appreciated. Exclusive selections are offered in Tiffany Lamps, Desk Sets and the numerous Bronze and Favrile Glass Articles from which appropriate Christmas remembrances may be chosen.

Bronze Articles	From $2.	To	$40.
Candlesticks	" 5.	"	30.
Favrile Glass Articles	" 1.	"	100.
Desk Lamps	" 22.	"	50.
Library Lamps	" 50.	"	350.
Piano & Floor Standards	" 57.	"	500.
Desk Sets	" 28.	"	200.

Suggestions for Gifts Sent Upon Request

TIFFANY STUDIOS
347-355 MADISON AVE. COR.45TH ST.NEW YORK CITY.

TIFFANY FAVRILE BRONZE POTTERY

A unique art product; a combination of Favrile glass, pottery and metal; the result of several years' study in the treatment of porcelain bodies with metals, creating rich color effects, and novel expressions of low relief and other forms of decoration.

"TIFFANY FAVRILE GLASS"

MADE ONLY BY THE TIFFANY FURNACES
LONG ISLAND, NEW YORK

The distinguishing name is Registered in the United States Patent Office, and is also protected by Letters Patent in Great Britain, France, Germany, Austria and Hungary.

Tiffany Favrile Glass exists under no other name.

Importers and Dealers are notified that the use of this name wholly or partly, in connection with any glass not made by the Tiffany Furnaces, is an infringement, and all persons so using it will be prosecuted.

Sold in New York only by
Tiffany & Co., Fifth Avenue
Tiffany Studios, Madison Avenue

TIFFANY FURNACES
LONG ISLAND, NEW YORK

Mutual Lamp Manufacturing Company · Catalog number 15

The Mutual Lamp Manufacturing Company issued catalog number 15 about 1900-1920. Its gray cover with black printing listed their address as 413-415 West Broadway, New York City. The firm designed and manufactured assorted art glass domes for gas, oil and electric. The complete 24 pages are illustrated here, showing leaded and cast metal bent glass domes, some with fringes; leaded glass, and cast lamps with bent and straight panels; indirect shower type lights; a four-light electric candelabra chandelier; and inverted overhead domes suspended from four and five chains. Notice the unique and compact shipping method that Mutual had devised which enabled them to ship five domes in one package.

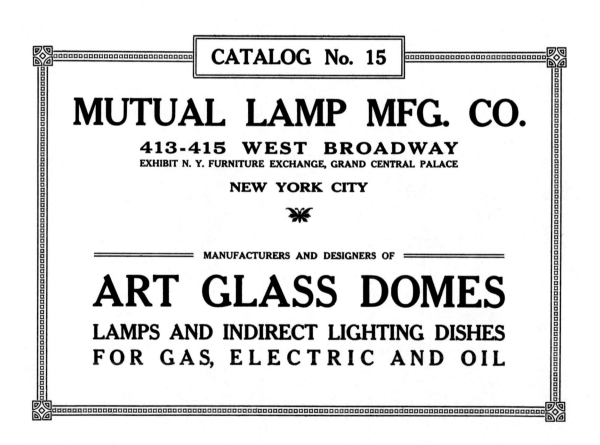

CATALOG No. 15

MUTUAL LAMP MFG. CO.

413-415 WEST BROADWAY
EXHIBIT N. Y. FURNITURE EXCHANGE, GRAND CENTRAL PALACE

NEW YORK CITY

MANUFACTURERS AND DESIGNERS OF

ART GLASS DOMES

LAMPS AND INDIRECT LIGHTING DISHES
FOR GAS, ELECTRIC AND OIL

GENERAL INFORMATION

PRICES IN THIS CATALOG ARE ABSOLUTELY NET, ALL TRADE DISCOUNTS HAVING BEEN TAKEN OFF

ALL PRICES ARE F. O. B. NEW YORK.   WE MAKE NO CHARGE FOR CARTAGE OF DRAYAGE
CRATES, CASES AND BARRELS CHARGED AT ACTUAL COST

We prefer that you send us cash with order.   However, we are also ready to ship by Express C. O. D. or by freight with sight draft and bill of lading attached.   Deposit amounting to 25 per cent of total bill, or enough to cover transportation charges both ways, should accompany each order.

Prices in this catalog are for the following three finishes:

Brush Brass
Brush Brass and Black
and Copper Oxidized

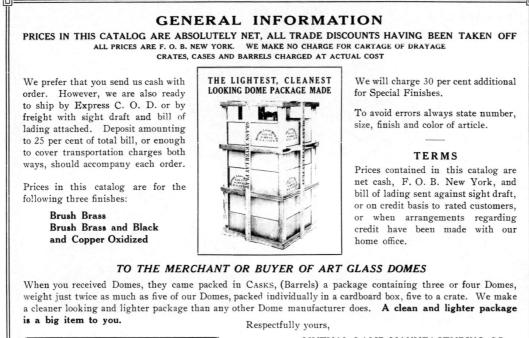

THE LIGHTEST, CLEANEST LOOKING DOME PACKAGE MADE

We will charge 30 per cent additional for Special Finishes.

To avoid errors always state number, size, finish and color of article.

TERMS

Prices contained in this catalog are net cash, F. O. B. New York, and bill of lading sent against sight draft, or on credit basis to rated customers, or when arrangements regarding credit have been made with our home office.

TO THE MERCHANT OR BUYER OF ART GLASS DOMES

When you received Domes, they came packed in CASKS, (Barrels) a package containing three or four Domes, weight just twice as much as five of our Domes, packed individually in a cardboard box, five to a crate.   We make a cleaner looking and lighter package than any other Dome manufacturer does.   **A clean and lighter package is a big item to you.**

Respectfully yours,

References: Bradstreet's, Dun, and Security Bank of New York.

MUTUAL LAMP MANUFACTURING CO.

Dome Stem for Gas No. 25. 36 inches long to lock nut, made of ⅞ inch tube with slip canopy.   Key made of 5/16 inch tube.   Price......**$2.55**

Complete with Inverted Light, consisting of burner, mantle and globe.
Price **$4.05**

Made in Green. Amber or Nile Glass, with new style fancy imported Fringe.
Dome No. 121.   24 in. Diam.   **$16.50**

SPECIAL

Take advantage of these prices and order in bulk.   The three Domes Nos 105, 616 and 121, on this page, at a great saving if ordered together.

$78.00

Colors artistically arranged, consisting of Ruby, Green, Pink, Amber and White Fitted with cross-bar
Dome No. 105.   24 in. Diam.   **$36.00**

Colors artistically arranged, consisting of Ruby, Green, Pink, Amber and White Fitted with cross-bar
Dome No. 616.   24 in. Diam.   **$33.00**

ABOVE PRICES QUOTED ON DOMES ONLY

SPECIAL

Take advantage of these prices and order in bulk. The three Domes No. 152, 629 and 453, on this page, at a great saving if ordered together.

$64.00

Chain Set for Electric No. 30. 42 inch. long, 3 or 4 light cluster 2½ inch. Heavy links, Brass finish. Chain canopy and cluster **$3.00**

Wired with 3 Key sockets **$4.50**

Wired with 3 pull chain sockets **$6.00**

Made in Green, Amber or Nile Glass
With fancy imported Fringe, all colors
Dome No. 152.   22 in. Diam.   **$12.75**

Colors artistically arranged, consisting of Ruby, Green, Pink, Amber and White, fitted with cross bar.
Dome No. 629.   24 in. Diam.   **$24.75**

Colors artistically arranged, consisting of Ruby, Green, Pink, Amber and White, fitted with cross-bar.
Dome No. 453.   24 in. Diam.   **$28.50**

ABOVE PRICES QUOTED ON DOMES ONLY

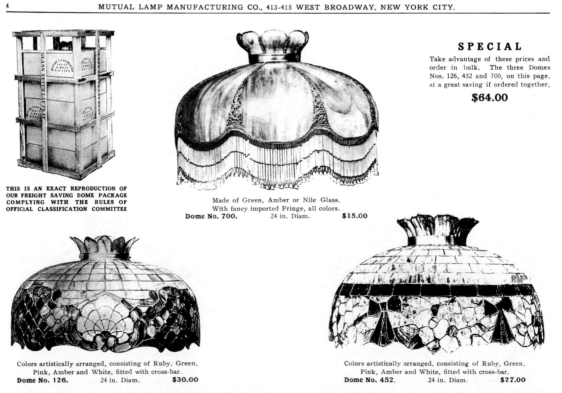

SPECIAL

Take advantage of these prices and order in bulk. The three Domes Nos. 126, 452 and 700, on this page, at a great saving if ordered together,

$64.00

THIS IS AN EXACT REPRODUCTION OF OUR FREIGHT SAVING DOME PACKAGE COMPLYING WITH THE RULES OF OFFICIAL CLASSIFICATION COMMITTEE

Made of Green, Amber or Nile Glass.
With fancy imported Fringe, all colors.
Dome No. 700.   24 in. Diam.   **$15.00**

Colors artistically arranged, consisting of Ruby, Green, Pink, Amber and White, fitted with cross-bar.
Dome No. 126.   24 in. Diam.   **$30.00**

Colors artistically arranged, consisting of Ruby, Green, Pink, Amber and White, fitted with cross-bar.
Dome No. 452.   24 in. Diam.   **$27.00**

ABOVE PRICES QUOTED ON DOMES ONLY

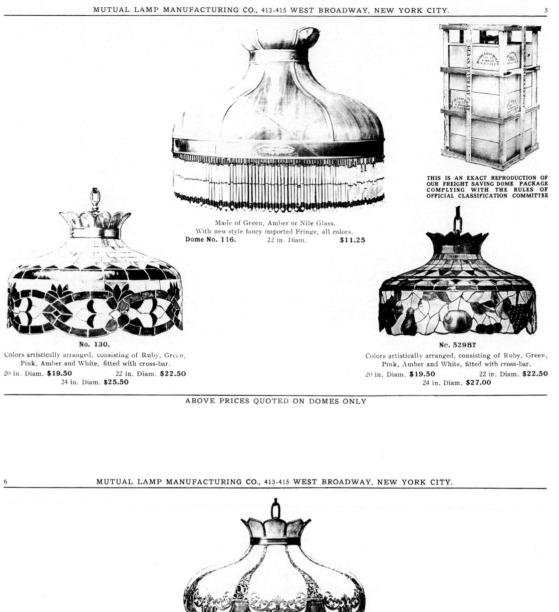

THIS IS AN EXACT REPRODUCTION OF
OUR FREIGHT SAVING DOME PACKAGE
COMPLYING WITH THE RULES OF
OFFICIAL CLASSIFICATION COMMITTEE

Made of Green, Amber or Nile Glass.
With new style fancy imported Fringe, all colors.
Dome No. 116. 22 in. Diam. **$11.25**

No. 130.
Colors artistically arranged, consisting of Ruby, Green,
Pink, Amber and White, fitted with cross-bar.
20 in. Diam. **$19.50** 22 in. Diam. **$22.50**
24 in. Diam. **$25.50**

No. 529BT
Colors artistically arranged, consisting of Ruby, Green,
Pink, Amber and White, fitted with cross-bar.
20 in. Diam. **$19.50** 22 in. Diam. **$22.50**
24 in. Diam. **$27.00**

ABOVE PRICES QUOTED ON DOMES ONLY

Made of Green, Amber or Nile Glass.
With new style fancy imported Fringe, all colors.
Dome No. 602. 22 in. Diam. **$12.75**
" " 24 in. Diam. **$14.25**

No. 111.
Colors artistically arranged, consisting of Ruby, Green,
Pink, Amber and White, fitted with cross-bar.
20 in. Diam. **$19.50** 22 in. Diam. **$22.50**
24 in. Diam. **$25.50**

No. 102.
Made of Amber, Green or Amber and Green mixed
Glass. Border artistically arranged.
20 in. Diam. **$16.50** 22 in. Diam. **$21.00**
24 in. Diam. **$24.00**

ABOVE PRICES QUOTED ON DOMES ONLY

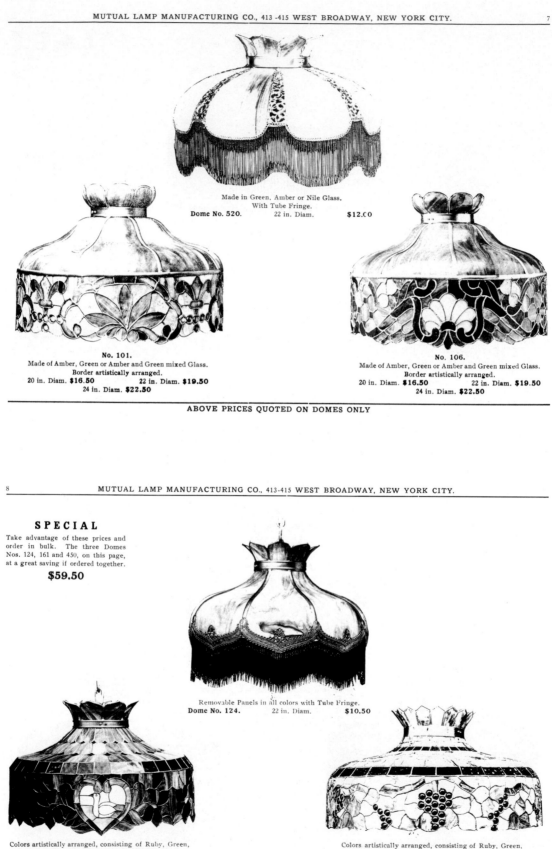

Made in Green, Amber or Nile Glass.
With Tube Fringe.

Dome No. 520.   22 in. Diam. $12.00

No. 101.
Made of Amber, Green or Amber and Green mixed Glass.
Border artistically arranged.
20 in. Diam. **$16.50**   22 in. Diam. **$19.50**
24 in. Diam. **$22.50**

No. 106.
Made of Amber, Green or Amber and Green mixed Glass.
Border artistically arranged.
20 in. Diam. **$16.50**   22 in. Diam. **$19.50**
24 in. Diam. **$22.50**

ABOVE PRICES QUOTED ON DOMES ONLY

SPECIAL

Take advantage of these prices and order in bulk. The three Domes Nos. 124, 161 and 450, on this page, at a great saving if ordered together.

$59.50

Removable Panels in all colors with Tube Fringe.
Dome No. 124.   22 in. Diam. $10.50

Colors artistically arranged, consisting of Ruby, Green, Pink, Amber and White, fitted with cross-bar.
Dome No. 161.   24 inch. Diam. $25.50

Colors artistically arranged, consisting of Ruby, Green, Pink, Amber and White, fitted with cross-bar.
Dome No. 450.   24 in. Diam. $25.50

ABOVE PRICES QUOTED ON DOMES ONLY

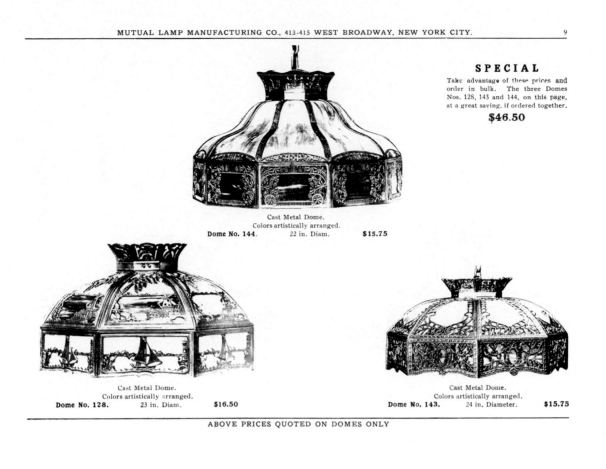

Cast Metal Dome.
Colors artistically arranged.
Dome No. 144.   22 in. Diam.   **$15.75**

Cast Metal Dome.
Colors artistically arranged.
Dome No. 128.   23 in. Diam.   **$16.50**

Cast Metal Dome.
Colors artistically arranged.
Dome No. 143.   24 in. Diameter.   **$15.75**

ABOVE PRICES QUOTED ON DOMES ONLY

Dome Stem for Gas No. 25. 36 inches long to lock nut, made of ⅞ inch tube with slip canopy. Key made of 5/16 inch tube.   Price......**$2.55**

Complete with Inverted Light, consisting of burner, mantle and globe.

Price **$4.05**

Made in all colors of Glass, with Tube Fringe.
Dome No. 525.   22 in. Diam.   **$12.00**

Made in Amber, Green and Nile, with Ruby Diamonds.
Dome No. 600.   22 in. Diam.   **$9.00**
        "   "   24 in. Diam.   **$10.50**

Made in Amber, Green and Nile.
Dome No. 521.   24 in. Diam.   **$13.50**

ABOVE PRICES QUOTED ON DOMES ONLY

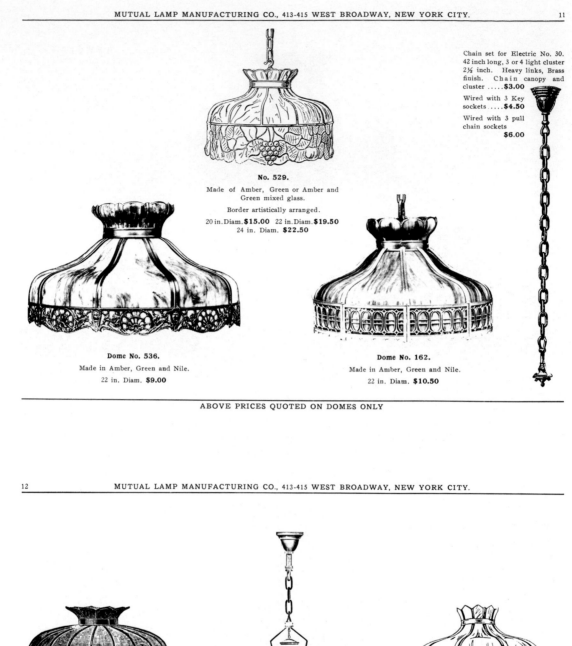

Chain set for Electric No. 30.
42 inch long, 3 or 4 light cluster
2½ inch. Heavy links, Brass
finish. Chain canopy and
cluster **$3.00**

Wired with 3 Key
sockets **$4.50**

Wired with 3 pull
chain sockets
$6.00

No. 529.
Made of Amber, Green or Amber and
Green mixed glass.
Border artistically arranged.
20 in. Diam.**$15.00**   22 in. Diam.**$19.50**
24 in. Diam. **$22.50**

Dome No. 536.
Made in Amber, Green and Nile.
22 in. Diam. **$9.00**

Dome No. 162.
Made in Amber, Green and Nile.
22 in. Diam. **$10.50**

ABOVE PRICES QUOTED ON DOMES ONLY

No. 501.
Sixteen panels made in all colors with
seed fringe
24 in. Diam. **$12.00**

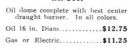

No. 207.
Oil dome complete with best center
draught burner. In all colors.
Oil 16 in. Diam.............**$12.75**
Gas or Electric.............**$11.25**

No. 600 B.F.
With new style Imported fringe
all colors.
22 in. Diam........ ....**$12.00**
24 in. Diam. **$13.50**

ABOVE PRICES QUOTED ON 501-600 B.F. ON DOMES ONLY

SPECIAL

Take advantage of these prices and order in bulk. The three Lamps Nos. 117, 118 and 129, on this page, at a great saving if ordered together.

$72.50

No. 117.
MOSAIC LAMP FOR ELECTRIC.
Wired with two pull chain sockets or for Gas. Complete with Hose, Burner, Mantle and Globe. Colors artistically arranged, consisting of Nile, Amber, Ruby, Pink and White Glass.

18 in. Diam.
Height 25 in.
Price **$24.00**

No. 129.
MOSAIC LAMP FOR ELECTRIC.
Wired with two pull chain sockets or for gas. Complete with Hose, Burner, Mantle, and Globe. Colors artistically arranged, consisting of Nile, Amber, Ruby, Pink and White Glass.
20 in. Diam., Height 25 in.
Price **$30.00**

No. 118.
MOSAIC LAMP FOR ELECTRIC.
Wired with two pull chain sockets or for Gas. Complete with Hose, Burner, Mantle and Globe. Colors artistically arranged, consisting of Nile, Amber, Ruby, Pink and White Glass.

18 in. Diam.
Height 25 in.
Price **$24.00**

SPECIAL

Take advantage of these prices and order in bulk. The three Lamps Nos. 145, 146 and 147, on this page, at a great saving if ordered together.

$54.00

Portable Reading Lamps on this page can be furnished in the following finishes:—Brush Brass and Black, Verdi Green, Rose Gold and Old Ivory.

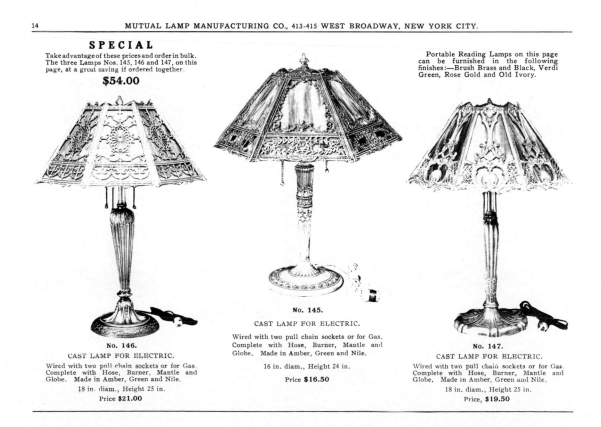

No. 146.
CAST LAMP FOR ELECTRIC.
Wired with two pull chain sockets or for Gas. Complete with Hose, Burner, Mantle and Globe. Made in Amber, Green and Nile.
18 in. diam., Height 25 in.
Price **$21.00**

No. 145.
CAST LAMP FOR ELECTRIC.
Wired with two pull chain sockets or for Gas. Complete with Hose, Burner, Mantle and Globe. Made in Amber, Green and Nile.
16 in. diam., Height 24 in.
Price **$16.50**

No. 147.
CAST LAMP FOR ELECTRIC.
Wired with two pull chain sockets or for Gas. Complete with Hose, Burner, Mantle and Globe. Made in Amber, Green and Nile.
18 in. diam., Height 25 in.
Price, **$19.50**

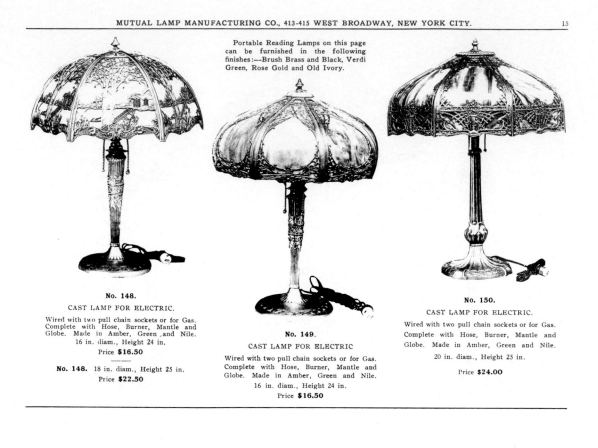

Portable Reading Lamps on this page can be furnished in the following finishes:—Brush Brass and Black, Verdi Green, Rose Gold and Old Ivory.

No. 148.

CAST LAMP FOR ELECTRIC.

Wired with two pull chain sockets or for Gas. Complete with Hose, Burner, Mantle and Globe. Made in Amber, Green ,and Nile. 16 in. diam., Height 24 in.

Price **$16.50**

No. 148. 18 in. diam., Height 25 in.

Price **$22.50**

No. 149.

CAST LAMP FOR ELECTRIC

Wired with two pull chain sockets or for Gas. Complete with Hose, Burner, Mantle and Globe. Made in Amber, Green and Nile. 16 in. diam., Height 24 in.

Price **$16.50**

No. 150.

CAST LAMP FOR ELECTRIC.

Wired with two pull chain sockets or for Gas. Complete with Hose, Burner, Mantle and Globe. Made in Amber, Green and Nile. 20 in. diam., Height 25 in.

Price **$24.00**

Portable Reading Lamps on this page can be furnished in the following finishes:—Brush Brass and Black, Verdi Green, Rose Gold and Old Ivory.

No. 122.

CAST LAMP FOR ELECTRIC.

Wired with two pull chain sockets or for Gas. Complete with Hose, Burner, Mantle and Globe. Made in Amber, Green and Nile.

18 in. diam., Height 25 in.

Price **$24.00**

No. 156.

CAST LAMP FOR ELECTRIC.

Wired with two pull chain sockets or for Gas. Complete with Hose, Burner, Mantle and Globe. Made in Amber, Green and Nile. 10 in. diam., Height 21 in.

Price **$12.00**

No. 151.

CAST LAMP FOR ELECTRIC

Wired with two pull chain sockets or for Gas. Complete with Hose, Burner, Mantle and Globe. Made in Amber, Green and Nile.

18 in. diam., Height 25 in.

Price **$24.00**

SPECIAL

Take advantage of these prices and order in bulk. The three Lamps Nos. 454, 160 and 157, on this page, at a great saving if ordered together.

$58.25

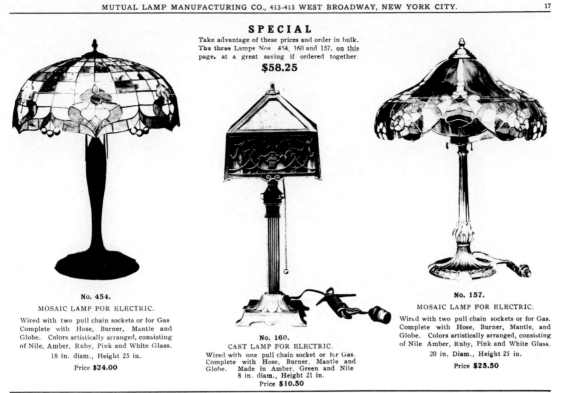

No. 454.

MOSAIC LAMP FOR ELECTRIC.

Wired with two pull chain sockets or for Gas Complete with Hose, Burner, Mantle and Globe. Colors artistically arranged, consisting of Nile, Amber, Ruby, Pink and White Glass.

18 in. diam., Height 25 in.

Price **$24.00**

No. 160.

CAST LAMP FOR ELECTRIC.

Wired with one pull chain socket or for Gas. Complete with Hose, Burner, Mantle and Globe. Made in Amber, Green and Nile

8 in. diam., Height 21 in.

Price **$10.50**

No. 157.

MOSAIC LAMP FOR ELECTRIC.

Wired with two pull chain sockets or for Gas. Complete with Hose, Burner, Mantle, and Globe. Colors artistically arranged, consisting of Nile Amber, Ruby, Pink and White Glass.

20 in. Diam., Height 25 in.

Price **$25.50**

Portable Reading Lamps on this page can be furnished in the following finishes:—Brush Brass and Black, Verdi Green, Rose Gold and Old Ivory.

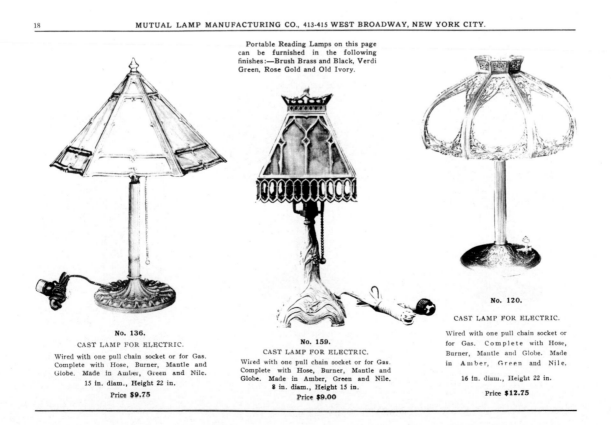

No. 136.

CAST LAMP FOR ELECTRIC.

Wired with one pull chain socket or for Gas. Complete with Hose, Burner, Mantle and Globe. Made in Amber, Green and Nile.

15 in. diam., Height 22 in.

Price **$9.75**

No. 159.

CAST LAMP FOR ELECTRIC.

Wired with one pull chain socket or for Gas. Complete with Hose, Burner, Mantle and Globe. Made in Amber, Green and Nile.

8 in. diam., Height 15 in.

Price **$9.00**

No. 120.

CAST LAMP FOR ELECTRIC.

Wired with one pull chain socket or for Gas. Complete with Hose, Burner, Mantle and Globe. Made in Amber, Green and Nile.

16 in. diam., Height 22 in.

Price **$12.75**

SPECIAL

Take advantage of these prices and order in bulk.
The three Lamps Nos. 200, 201 and 204, on this
page, at a great saving if ordered together.

$30.00

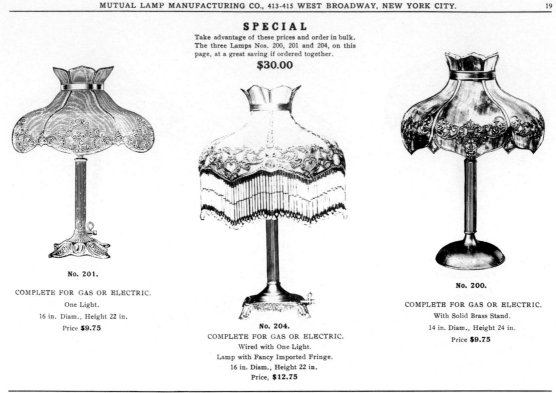

No. 201.

COMPLETE FOR GAS OR ELECTRIC.

One Light.

16 in. Diam., Height 22 in.

Price **$9.75**

No. 204.

COMPLETE FOR GAS OR ELECTRIC.

Wired with One Light.

Lamp with Fancy Imported Fringe.

16 in. Diam., Height 22 in.

Price, **$12.75**

No. 200.

COMPLETE FOR GAS OR ELECTRIC.

With Solid Brass Stand.

14 in. Diam., Height 24 in.

Price **$9.75**

No. 203.

COMPLETE FOR GAS OR ELECTRIC.

One Light.

12 in. Diam., Height 22 in.

Price **$8.25.**

No. 202. Same as 203 less Fringe.

Price, **$6.75**

No. 250.

COMPLETE FOR GAS OR ELECTRIC.

Wired with One Light.

Lamp with Tube Fringe.

14 in. Diam., Height 22 in.

Price **$11.25**

No. 300.

COMPLETE FOR GAS OR ELECTRIC.

One Light.

Fancy Bell Fringe.

12 in. Diam., Height 22 in.

Price **$11.25**

ABOVE PRICES FOR GAS SAME AS FOR ELECTRIC

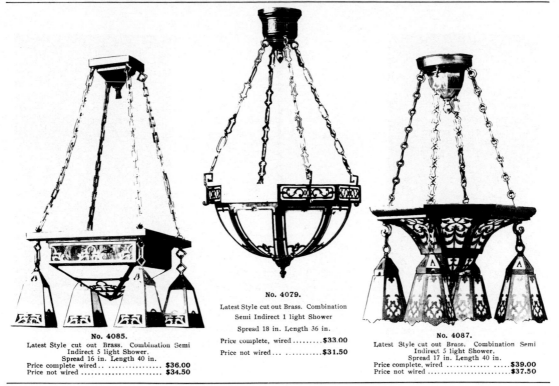

No. 4085.
Latest Style cut out Brass. Combination Semi
Indirect 5 light Shower.
Spread 16 in. Length 40 in.
Price complete wired.. .... $36.00
Price not wired $34.50

No. 4079.
Latest Style cut out Brass. Combination
Semi Indirect 1 light Shower
Spread 18 in. Length 36 in.
Price complete, wired $33.00
Price not wired... .... $31.50

No. 4087.
Latest Style cut out Brass. Combination Semi
Indirect 5 light Shower.
Spread 17 in. Length 40 in.
Price complete, wired $39.00
Price not wired $37.50

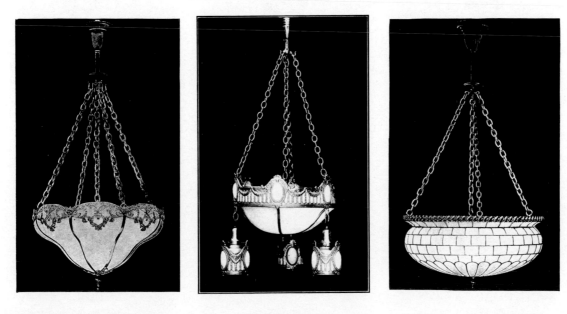

Wired for one light pull chain socket
No. 103   18 in. Diam.   **$19.50**

Wired complete as shown
No. 110   18 in. Diam.   **$33.00**

Wired for one light pull chain socket
No. 132   20 in. Diam.   **$30.00**

ABOVE PRICES FOR GAS SAME AS FOR ELECTRIC

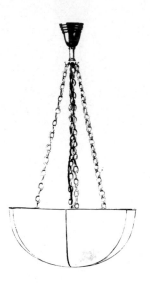

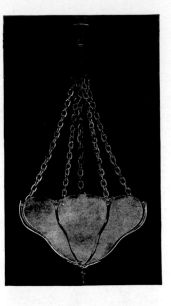

Wired for one light pull chain socket

No. 131   16 in. Diam.   **$18.00**

Wired for one light pull chain socket

No. 158   18 in. Diam.   **$15.00**

Wired for one light pull chain socket

No. 134   18 in. Diam.   **$16.50**

ABOVE PRICES FOR GAS SAME AS FOR ELECTRIC

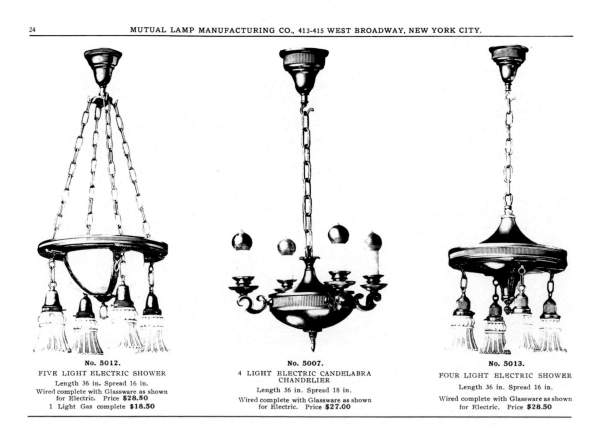

No. 5012.

FIVE LIGHT ELECTRIC SHOWER

Length 36 in. Spread 16 in.

Wired complete with Glassware as shown
for Electric.   Price **$28.50**

1 Light Gas complete **$18.50**

No. 5007.

4 LIGHT ELECTRIC CANDELABRA
CHANDELIER

Length 36 in. Spread 18 in.

Wired complete with Glassware as shown
for Electric.   Price **$27.00**

No. 5013.

FOUR LIGHT ELECTRIC SHOWER

Length 36 in. Spread 16 in.

Wired complete with Glassware as shown
for Electric.   Price **$28.50**

Fine Crystal and Cut Glass

IT is rapidly becoming the vogue to use more fine crystal and cut glass. Families who have always prized their collections are now adding the latest Libbey art creations. These newest pieces are distinguished for their beauty of form and rare design. They breathe an atmosphere of quality possible only as a result of the long years of experience of Libbey artists and master craftsmen.

Exhibitions now being shown by the best dealers in your city

THE LIBBEY GLASS COMPANY, TOLEDO, OHIO

Christmas Gift Suggestions

Vase and flower basket have frost-like engraving.
The bowl is diamond cut, brilliant, and clear.

THE renaissance in the vogue which favors crystal and cut glass provides new pleasure in Christmas gift selection.

For this season, Libbey presents many designs, new and beautiful in form and decoration, the inspiration and handwork of Libbey artists and master craftsmen. The superior quality and finish of this art ware is possible only through the many years of Libbey experience. The gift of Libbey ware will undeniably add a tone of quiet elegance, a touch of the artistic when displayed in the home. The book of Libbey Christmas gift suggestions will be sent on request. Exhibitions are being shown by the best dealers in your city.

THE LIBBEY GLASS COMPANY, TOLEDO, OHIO

The vases above are beautifully varied forms. Sugar bowl and cream pitcher are delightfully quaint. The lower group is suggestive of the rare beauty and exquisite design in the delightful variety of the Libbey collection.

Exclusiveness
Brilliance
Artistic Design
and
Perfect Cutting
make

Libbey

Cut Glass

The World's Standard of Excellence

It has received the highest awards wherever exhibited.

Look for *Libbey* on each piece.
the mark

The leading dealer in each city sells it.

The Libbey Glass Co.
Dept. L   Toledo, Ohio

No. 625—Handle Decanter, 1903 Pattern.

No. 573. Fourteen Inch Punch Bowl "Ellsmere"

Libbey Cut Glass

is the best made in America, and American cut glass is the best in the world. The name

Libbey engraved on every piece.

THE LIBBEY GLASS CO., Dept. E,   TOLEDO, OHIO.

Principal dealer in each city sells it. Book "Things Beautiful" sent on request.

265

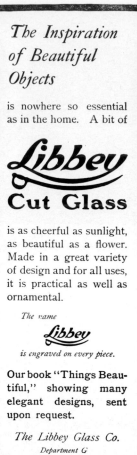

THERE IS pronounced prestige in the ownership of cut glass or engraved crystal which bears the Libbey trade mark — and a lack of it when that trade mark is missing.

Both types of Libbey craftsmanship suggest, at this season, beautiful gift possibilities.

THE LIBBEY GLASS COMPANY, Toledo, Ohio

IN CUT GLASS; in rock crystal; and in engraved crystal glass — nothing but *Libbey* will meet your wants.

It is recognized as the world's best, the world over.

Look for the *Libbey* nameplate engraved on every piece.

A Libbey dealer in each city.

The Libbey Glass Co., Toledo, Ohio

The Proof of Quality
in cut glass is the finding of the mark

Libbey

engraved on each piece. It signifies blue-white purity in the glass itself,
beauty of design, depth of cutting and lasting brilliancy
"The World's Best."

Look for *Libbey* the proof
the mark of quality.

The Libbey Glass Co.,   -   -   Toledo, O.

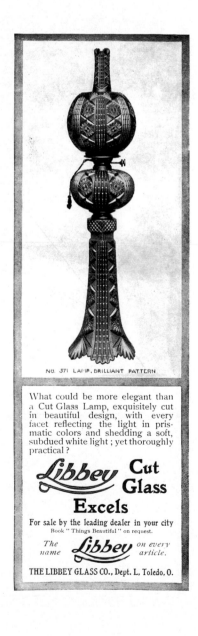

NO. 371 LAMP, BRILLIANT PATTERN

What could be more elegant than
a Cut Glass Lamp, exquisitely cut
in beautiful design, with every
facet reflecting the light in prismatic colors and shedding a soft,
subdued white light; yet thoroughly
practical?

Libbey Cut
Glass
Excels

For sale by the leading dealer in your city
Book "Things Beautiful" on request.

The *Libbey* on every
name article.

THE LIBBEY GLASS CO., Dept. L, Toledo, O.

NO. 211 PUNCH BOWL 15 IN. AZTEC PATTERN

When Buying, Buy for Posterity.

Nothing so dignifies a family as the elegant and valuable articles which descend from generation to generation. The best of its kind is always worthy — always respected, always valuable.

Libbey Cut Glass

is made for all time and will be as elegant a hundred years from now as it is today.

Libbey engraved on every piece.

Send for book "*Things Beautiful,*" which shows many elegant and exclusive Libbey designs.

The Libbey Glass Company, Toledo, Ohio.

The LIBERTY
VIOLET VASE
$1.50
Direct from
The LIBERTY
CUT GLASS WORKS

An exquisite cut glass creation for short stem flowers, designed from the newest French model. A perfect gem, five inches high. Deep, rich cutting. Exceedingly dainty table decoration. This vase cannot be purchased from any dealer for less than $5.00, but to introduce Liberty Cut Glass in the home of every reader of THE JOURNAL, it will be delivered, charges prepaid, to any address in the United States for $1.50.

Over 6000 pieces of the sugar and cream set which we offer for $3.75 have already been sold

Buy Cut Glass Direct from the Works and Save at Least 40 Per Cent.

Illustrated catalogue "A" contains description of many beautiful pieces in rich cut glass at wholesale prices.

Liberty Cut Glass Works
EGG HARBOR CITY, N. J.

Cut Glass—the Gift that Never Fails of a Welcome

¶ Who is it you have in mind— some one just entering upon fresh and rosy young girlhood?

¶ What will appeal to her budding love of beauty so charmingly as a little piece of cut glass for the toilet table?

¶ Is it one with whitening hair— your mother, or some dearly loved old friend?

¶ Again—cut glass.

¶ The young wife and mother; the fiancee; the man of affairs; the boy at college—in dining room, library, boudoir or den, there is a vacant place waiting to be beautified by a piece of cut glass.

¶ Cut glass never wearies the eye;

never loses its first charm; never diminishes in lustre and loveliness.

¶ It is eminently practical—and still a source of aesthetic satisfaction.

¶ The more you study its possibilities for gift-purposes—the more numerous will be your cut glass purchases for Christmas.

¶ And this will inevitably lead you to insist that the glass you choose shall have the name Libbey 'graven in the glass.

¶ Because Libbey Cut Glass is in very fact "the world's best."

¶ One store in each city sells Libbey cut glass and no other.

The Libbey Glass Company, Toledo, Ohio

Tuthill
Cut Glass

IT APPEALS to those whose knowledge of cut glass approaches or attains that of the connoisseur.

Its beauty and brilliance are underlaid by a precision and fineness of cutting peculiar to Tuthill.

Each piece is full-cut from blown blanks and throughout is the handiwork of an artist. The designs comprise facet cutting, intaglio cutting and engraving — pure and in combination.

Your city's best dealer in cut glass probably has Tuthill. The name is on each piece.

We send upon request without charge a little book that makes its every reader a qualified judge of cut glass and an expert in its care.

TUTHILL CUT GLASS COMPANY,
MIDDLETOWN, NEW YORK

Tuthill
Cut Glass

Any woman would be charmed with this exquisite glass as a Christmas gift. Every piece shows a collaboration of artist with artisan. Inherently and distinctively beautiful.

Ask your city's best dealer for it.

TUTHILL CUT GLASS CO.
Middletown, N. Y.

Tuthill

Tuthill
etched on each piece

THE cut glass that shows a collaboration of artist with artisan. Inherently and distinctively beautiful.

A postal for our booklet will make you a qualified judge of all cut glass. . . .

TUTHILL CUT GLASS CO.
Middletown, New York

Tuthill Cut Glass

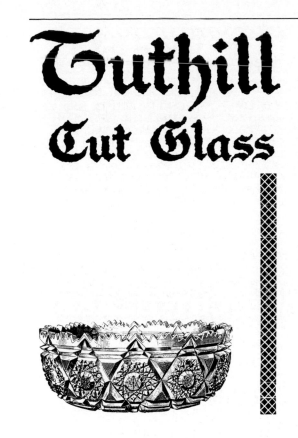

JUNE suggests weddings— weddings suggest cut glass for the bride. The choice of Tuthill bespeaks discrimination and highest taste on the part of the giver; insures fullest appreciation on the part of the recipient. Tuthill Cut Glass has a crystalline brilliancy, a jewel-like accuracy of cutting, an exclusive artistry of design.

Your city's best dealer in cut glass probably has Tuthill. We send upon request without charge a little book that makes its every reader a qualified judge of cut glass and an expert in its care.

 The name as it appears etched on each piece.

TUTHILL CUT GLASS COMPANY,
MIDDLETOWN, NEW YORK

Tuthill etched on each piece

Tuthill Cut Glass

ARTISTIC combinations of intaglio and facet cuttings. The most beautifully finished glass.

Write for the Connoisseur Book.
TUTHILL CUT GLASS CO., Middletown, N. Y.

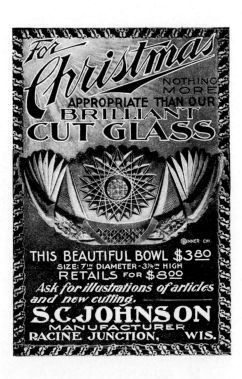

For **Christmas** NOTHING MORE APPROPRIATE THAN OUR **BRILLIANT CUT GLASS**

THIS BEAUTIFUL BOWL $3.80
SIZE: 7 IN DIAMETER - 3¾ IN HIGH
RETAILS FOR $8.00
Ask for illustrations of articles and new cutting.
S.C. JOHNSON
MANUFACTURER
RACINE JUNCTION, WIS.

273

THE COSMOPOLITAN.

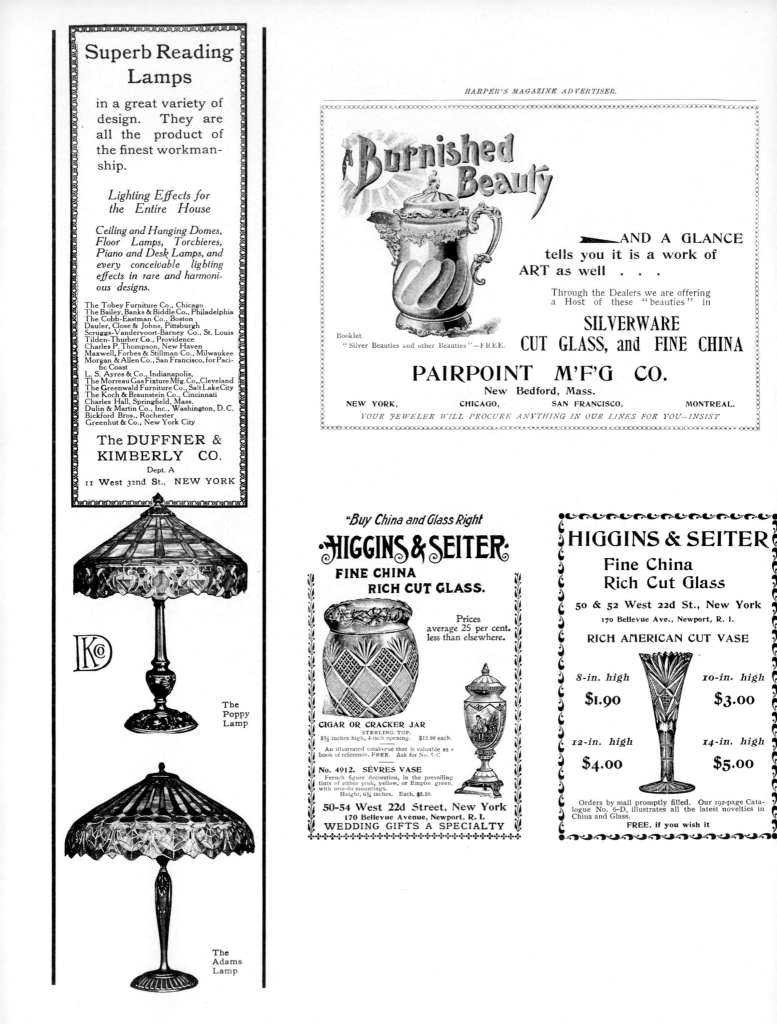

HIGGINS & SEITER

ILLUSTRATE their "¼ Less than Else-where" policy by pricing these exquisite specimens of genuine American Cut Glass (Sugar and Cream) at $3.00—both pieces (see illustration top and bottom of this advertisement). For thousands of other offerings equally attractive, see Catalogue 14 Z with delicately tinted pictures of Choicest China—free to all interested in purchasing; as also artistic brochure on "Serving a Dinner" by "Oscar" of the Waldorf Astoria. Address

West 21st and West 22nd Street
NEAR SIXTH AVENUE, NEW YORK

"BUY CHINA AND GLASS RIGHT"

HIGGINS & SEITER

To those interested in China or Glass we will mail free our large illustrated Catalogue No. 12 (B) showing China in exact color and shape and containing thousands of illustrations, prices always averaging

"¼ Less than Elsewhere"

Our new book, "Serving a Dinner," by "Oscar," of Waldorf-Astoria fame, is ready, and a limited number will be mailed on request only.

51-55 West 21st St.
50-54 West 22d St.
NEW YORK CITY

"BUY CHINA AND GLASS RIGHT"

HIGGINS & SEITER

Fine China   Rich Cut Glass
EXCEPTIONAL VALUE

is offered in this beautiful silver mounted fern dish. It will make an unusually attractive gift. Every detail is wrought with the utmost care and precision and for equal value you would undoubtedly be asked to pay at least 25 per cent more elsewhere.

3¾ inches high. 7¾ inches in diameter. Polished silver plated mountings. White metal satin finished inner.

SPECIAL—H. & S. PRICE **$6.75**

We charge nothing for packing and assume all risk of loss or breakage in transit.
The advantage is always *yours*.   The risk always ours.

Send for complete catalogue (15M) of china and glass.

West 21st and West 22nd Streets, near Sixth Ave., New York.

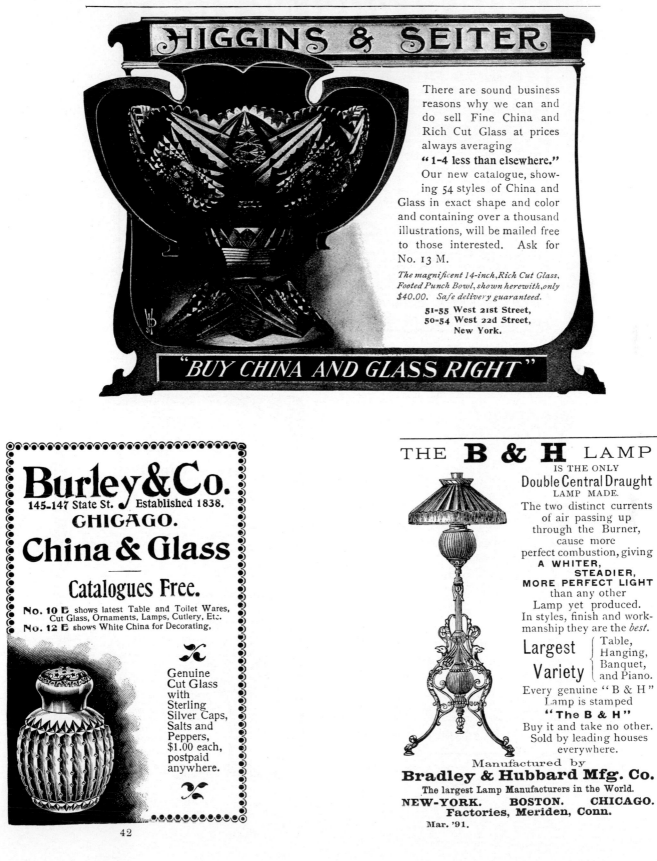

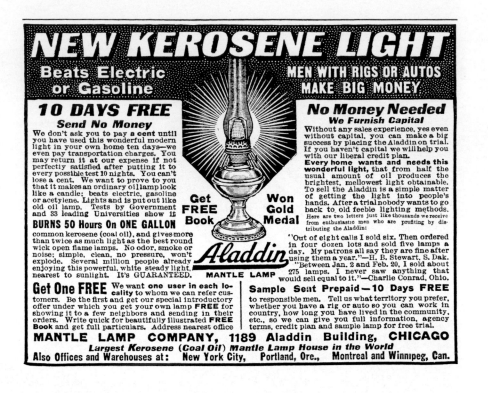

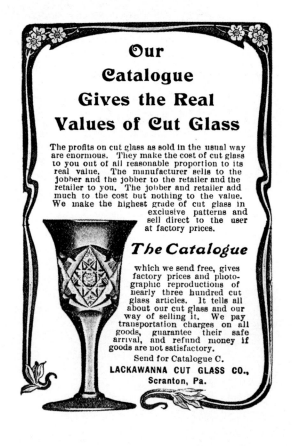

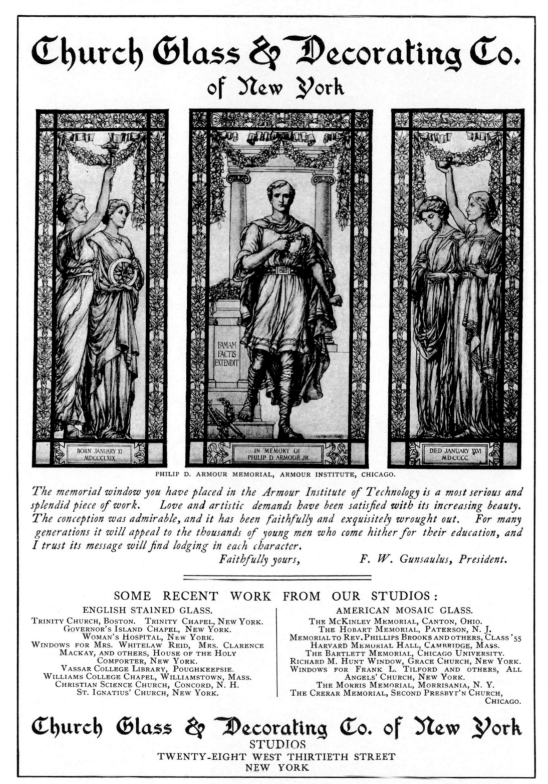

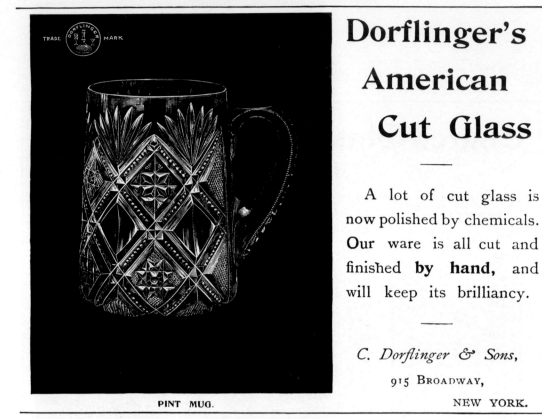

Dorflinger's American Cut Glass.

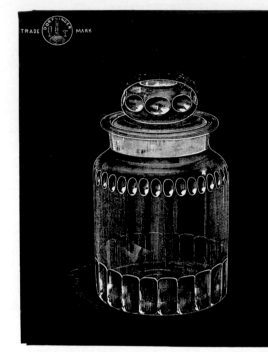

Cigar Jar

All Glass—Air Tight.

To hold 50 Cigars.

PLAIN	- - -	$2.25
LIKE ILLUSTRATION		4.50
RICHLY CUT	- -	10.50

Also made in sizes for Cigarettes, Tobacco and Bon-Bons.

C. Dorflinger & Sons,
915 BROADWAY,
Near 21st St.   NEW YORK.

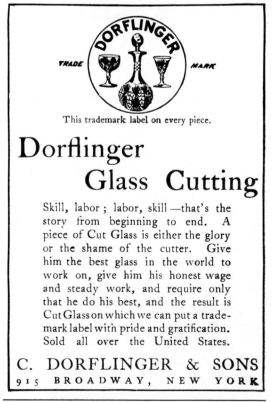

This trademark label on every piece.

Dorflinger Glass Cutting

Skill, labor; labor, skill —that's the story from beginning to end. A piece of Cut Glass is either the glory or the shame of the cutter. Give him the best glass in the world to work on, give him his honest wage and steady work, and require only that he do his best, and the result is Cut Glass on which we can put a trademark label with pride and gratification. Sold all over the United States.

C. DORFLINGER & SONS
915 BROADWAY, NEW YORK

; desirable that you mention MUNSEY'S MAGAZINE.

For Christmas

NOTHING MORE APPROPRIATE THAN OUR BRILLIANT CUT GLASS

THIS BEAUTIFUL BOWL $3.80
SIZE: 7 IN. DIAMETER—3¾ IN. HIGH
RETAILS FOR $8.00
Ask for illustrations of articles and new cutting.

S.C. JOHNSON
MANUFACTURER
RACINE JUNCTION,   WIS.

Honesdale, Pa.

A copy showing the Krantz and Sell Company letter head, manufacturers of rich cut glass, located in Honesdale, Pennsylvania. John E. Krantz and John H. Smith operated a cutting shop from 1893-1932, under the name Krantz-Smith and Company. They had showrooms in New York City and Chicago.

George W. Sell joined the firm in 1899, and Krantz sold his interest in the company to Sell in 1920. The company then became known as G. Sell and Company The factory was destroyed by fire in 1932. Facsimile courtesy of Wayne County Historical Society, Honesdale, Pennsylvania.

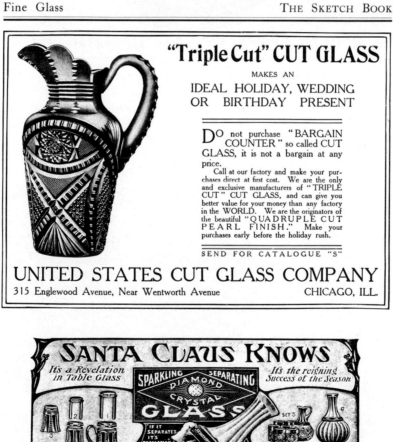

The Beauty of *Clark* Cut Glass

Among dealers and connoisseurs, "Clark" Cut Glass has been famed for over 25 years. It has been *standard* in high-grade stores. It has always been notable for beauty and variety of patterns and pure water color.

To-day every article of "Clark" cut glass bears the trade mark "Clark." An arrow points it out. Look for it so that you can readily identify it from other brands.

Whether purchased for service or ornamental purposes, "Clark" Cut Glass affords the greatest satisfaction.

"Clark" glass has always been foremost in designs of marked originality. The newest—"Rose"—is a wide departure. It is of exquisite grace and workmanship, and so brilliant, so attractive in design, that it at once commands attention.

In selecting gifts it is always good judgment to buy the "Clark" goods. Then you are certain you have the best made.

"Clark" Cut Glass is sold by principal dealers everywhere. Send for catalogue of designs.

T. B. CLARK & CO., Inc. Honesdale, Pa.

Exclusive Cut Glass
FOR CHRISTMAS GIFTS

"Clark" Cut Glass has for 25 years been noted among high class dealers for its grace and delicacy of design and high polish, giving an unusually rich effect.

Every article of cut glass bearing the trade mark

Clark
(An arrow points it out.)

will be found distinctive in the depth of cutting and water color.

The "Clark" imprint is a guarantee of the highest quality, both in appearance and craftsmanship.

"Clark" Cut Glass is famed throughout the country for the exclusiveness of its patterns, of which a large variety is offered for choice.

The newest pattern, "Rose," has won immense popularity. It is of striking beauty.

"Clark" Cut Glass is sold by leading dealers. Be sure to ask for it by name—"Clark"—and see that name and arrow are on the glass.

If your dealer does not sell it, write for illustrated booklet, showing all designs.

T. B. CLARK & CO., Inc., Honesdale, Pa.

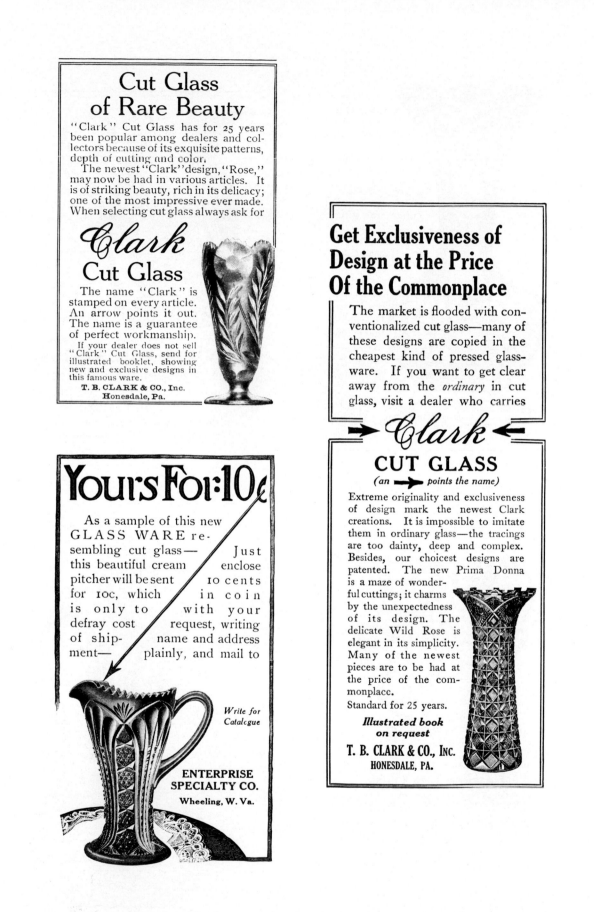

Cut Glass of Rare Beauty

"Clark" Cut Glass has for 25 years been popular among dealers and collectors because of its exquisite patterns, depth of cutting and color.

The newest "Clark" design, "Rose," may now be had in various articles. It is of striking beauty, rich in its delicacy; one of the most impressive ever made. When selecting cut glass always ask for

Clark Cut Glass

The name "Clark" is stamped on every article. An arrow points it out. The name is a guarantee of perfect workmanship.

If your dealer does not sell "Clark" Cut Glass, send for illustrated booklet, showing new and exclusive designs in this famous ware.

T. B. CLARK & CO., Inc.
Honesdale, Pa.

Yours For: 10c

As a sample of this new GLASS WARE resembling cut glass— this beautiful cream pitcher will be sent for 10c, which is only to defray cost of shipment—

Just enclose 10 cents in coin with your request, writing name and address plainly, and mail to

Write for Catalogue

ENTERPRISE SPECIALTY CO.
Wheeling, W. Va.

Get Exclusiveness of Design at the Price Of the Commonplace

The market is flooded with conventionalized cut glass—many of these designs are copied in the cheapest kind of pressed glassware. If you want to get clear away from the *ordinary* in cut glass, visit a dealer who carries

➡ *Clark* ⬅

CUT GLASS

(an ➡ points the name)

Extreme originality and exclusiveness of design mark the newest Clark creations. It is impossible to imitate them in ordinary glass—the tracings are too dainty, deep and complex. Besides, our choicest designs are patented. The new Prima Donna is a maze of wonderful cuttings; it charms by the unexpectedness of its design. The delicate Wild Rose is elegant in its simplicity. Many of the newest pieces are to be had at the price of the commonplace.

Standard for 25 years.

Illustrated book on request

T. B. CLARK & CO., INC.
HONESDALE, PA.

Hawkes Cut Glass ranks with silver and gold articles which have name and reputation for intrinsic value, artistic designs and faultless execution, for gifts.

Hawkes Cut Glass

is for sale by dealers known to keep the best of everything.

Hawkes Cut Glass has this trade-mark engraved on each piece. Intending purchasers who find it on pieces of cut glass they examine are able to buy with all the assurance of connoisseurs.

HAWKES

HAWKES
No piece without this trademark engraved on it is genuine.

Hawkes Cut Glass

articles, although in daily use, are a joy forever, because artistic, beautiful and distinctive.

Dealers everywhere who keep the best of everything, sell Hawkes Cut Glass.

Any beverage will appear well and taste better in this pitcher of
Hawkes Cut Glass.

Cut Glass and Hawkes Cut Glass are different. Hawkes Cut Glass is unique.

No piece without this trade-mark engraved on it is genuine. If your dealer **HAWKES** does not sell Hawkes Cut Glass, please write us for address of dealer who does.

T. G. HAWKES & Co., Corning, N. Y.

Hawkes Cut Glass.

No piece is genuine without this trade-mark.

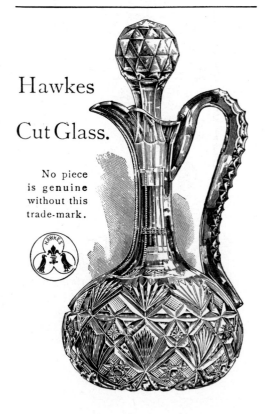

Lemonade Bowl

This cutting varies from a hair's depth to a *full inch*. It requires such absolutely accurate skill the ordinary glass worker couldn't even attempt it. Every piece of

Hawkes Cut Glass

is, by its unusual cutting, always distinguishable at a glance as being above the ordinary.

No piece without engraved upon it your dealer Hawkes Cut Glass name of one this trade-mark is genuine. If does not sell write us for the who does.

T. G. Hawkes & Co.   **Corning, N. Y.**

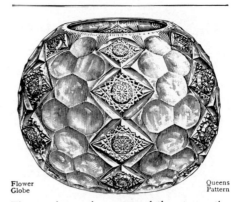

Flower Globe   Queens Pattern

Flower tints—the green of the stems, the delicate blossom tones—bring into vivid relief the distinctive beauty of

Hawkes Cut Glass

Glittering like some great jewel, in color the sought-for perfect white, in design an expression of the finest art—a piece of Hawkes Cut Glass is indisputably the welcomest gift to brides.

At the best dealers. No piece without this trade-mark engraved on it is genuine. If your dealer does not sell Hawkes Cut Glass, write for address of one who does.

T. G. Hawkes & Co., Corning, N. Y.

Hawkes Cut Glass   Hawkes Cut Glass

The clear pure of Hawkes i s i t s f e a t u r e it a brilliant nized by judges as the highest the glass worker's quality skillfully Hawkes designs beauty table. pleasing   transparent quality Cut Glass distinctive which gives clarity recog- of artistic value achievement of art. Glass of this cut in the artistic adds grace and to every Makes gifts.

No piece without this trade-mark engraved on it is genuine. If your dealer does not sell Hawkes Cut Glass, please write us for address of dealer who does.

T. G. HAWKES & Co., Corning, N. Y.

Hawkes Cut Glass

In form, color and cutting Hawkes Cut Glass is distinctive.

No piece without this trade-mark engraved on it is genuine. If your dealer does not sell Hawkes Cut Glass, please write us for address of one who does.

T. G. HAWKES & CO., Corning, N. Y.

Hawkes
Cut Glass

articles, being artistic, useful, distinctive and not likely to be dupli-cated, make ideal

Wedding Presents

Be sure to see that this trade-mark is engraved on the piece you buy, as no piece without it is genuine. The best dealers every-where sell Hawkes Cut Glass. **HAWKES**

Hawkes Cut Glass ranks with silver and gold articles which have name and reputation for intrinsic value. artistic designs and faultless exe-cution, for gifts.

Hawkes
Cut Glass

is for sale by dealers known to keep the best of every-thing.

Hawkes Cut Glass has this trade-mark engraved on each piece. Intending purchasers who find it on pieces of cut glass they examine are able to buy with all the assurance of connoisseurs. **HAWKES**

Articles of cut glass make acceptable and appropriate wedding presents. In order that there may be no question as to their intrinsic value they should be

Hawkes Cut Glass,

Without this trade-mark no piece is genuine.

Grand prize, Paris 1889.

Hawkes Cut Glass.

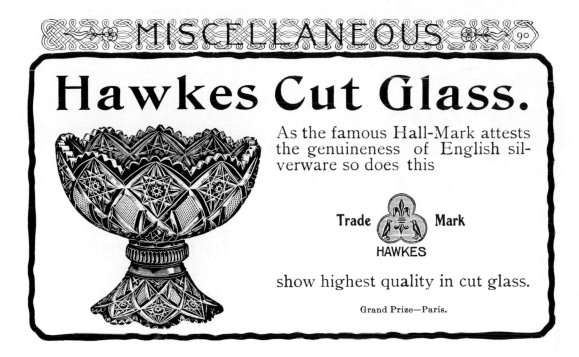

As the famous Hall-Mark attests the genuineness of English silverware so does this

Trade Mark

HAWKES

show highest quality in cut glass.

Grand Prize—Paris.

Oil or Vinegar

Taste *in* Tableware

has no purer expression than

Hawkes Cut Glass

Delightful studies in grace are the newer shapes, while the luminous *white* of the glass itself gives to the simplest piece a beauty.

At the best dealers. No piece without this trade-mark engraved on it is genuine. If your dealer does not sell Hawkes Cut Glass, write for address of one who does.

T. G. Hawkes & Co., Corning, N. Y.

Jardiniere with Lining

A symphony in cut glass which in design and workmanship expresses in the highest degree the glass workers art.

Hawkes Cut Glass

is famous the world over for its rare perfection in quality, its individuality of pattern and its crystalline clarity.

At the best dealers. No piece without this trade-mark engraved on it is genuine. If your dealer does not sell Hawkes Cut Glass, write for address of one who does.

T. G. Hawkes & Co., Corning, N.Y.

291

Steps In Glass Manufacturing

Sand for Glass Manufacture

Weighing the raw materials

Filling pots in furnace

Hand blowing: starting the bubble

Removing pot from furnace

Shaping the foot

Hand blowing in carbon-lined molds

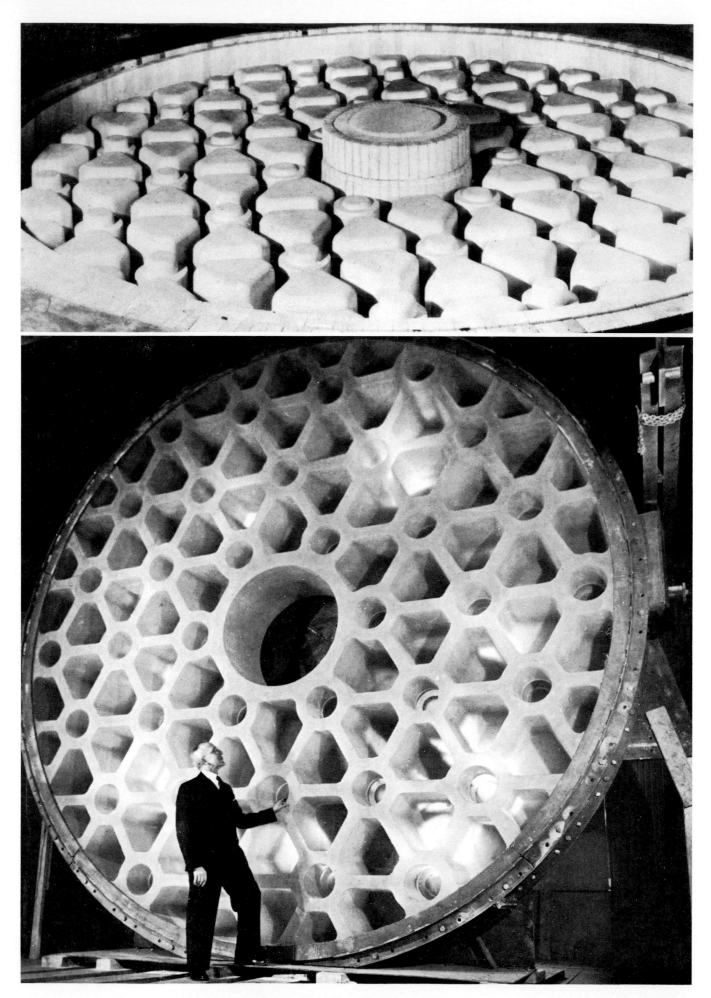

Mold for Palomar Observatory reflecting mirror (upper)
Palomar Observatory reflecting mirror (lower)

Historical Time Line

The foundings of numerous American glasshouses have historical significance for the collector. Their dates (*) of origin are listed and we are reminded of America's varied productivity through each factory's creative wares. Other milestones in literature, politics, inventions and important discoveries have also been recorded. All of this information assists the reader with a better understanding of the era in which a particular glass firm was producing.

1492 Columbus discovers America
1539-1542 De Soto explores North America; discovers the Mississippi River
1607 Jamestown, Virginia settled
*1608 Jamestown establishes the first glasshouse in America
1620 Mayflower Compact; landing at Plymouth
1636 Roger Williams founds Providence
1639 First printing press, Cambridge, Massachusetts
1704 First newspaper in America, Boston - *News-Letter*
1732-1757 Benjamin Franklin, *Poor Richard's Almanac*
1765 Stamp Act
1770 Boston Massacre
1773 Boston Tea Party
1774 First Continental Congress
1775 Patrick Henry Speech, Virginia Convention
1775-1783 Revolutionary War
1776 Declaration of Independence
1788 Constitution Ratified
1789 Washington Inaugurated
1790-1850 Industrial Revolution
1793 Eli Whitney invents the cotton gin
1796 George Washington's Farewell Address
1800 Washington, D.C. named the U.S. Capital
1804-1806 Lewis and Clark's Northwest Expedition
1807 Robert Fulton's steamboat a success
*1818 New England Glass Company
1821 *Saturday Evening Post* founded
*1825 Boston and Sandwich Glass Company
1828 First steam locomotive
1834 McCormick's mechanical reaper
*1837 Mount Washington Glass Works, South Boston, Massachusetts
1844 Samuel B. Morse's telegraph
1850 Nathaniel Hawthorne, *The Scarlet Letter*
*1851 Herman Melville, *Moby Dick*; Union Glass Company
1854 Henry David Thoreau, *Walden*
1855 Walt Whitman, *Leaves of Grass*
*1857 *Atlantic Monthly* founded; Boston Silver Glass Company
*1858 Cape Cod Glass Company
1859 First oil well drilled in the United States
1861-1865 Civil War
*1863 Emancipation Proclamation; Abraham Lincoln's *Gettysburg Address*; Hobbs, Brockunier and Company
*1865 Beginning of westward expansion; Abraham Lincoln assassinated; Dorflinger Glass Works
*1867 Gillinder and Sons
1869 Union Pacific Railroad completed; Bret Harte, "*The Outcasts of Poker Flat;*" Mount Washington Glass Works, New Bedford, Massachusetts
*1872 Rochester Tumbler Company
*1874 Smith Brothers
*1876 Alexander Graham Bell's telephone; Mount Washington Glass Company
1879 Thomas Alva Edison's incandescent light bulb
*1880 Pairpoint Manufacturing Company; Thomas G. Hawkes and Company
*1881 Phoenix Glass Company
*1884 Mark Twain, *Huckleberry Finn*; Reading Artistic Glass Works
*1885 Tiffany Glass Company
*1887 Fostoria Glass Company; Northwood: Union Glass Works, Martins Ferry, Ohio
*1888 Libbey Glass Company; Dalzell, Gilmore and Leighton Company
*1890 Northwood: Union Glass Works, Elwood City, Pennsylvania
*1891 Locke Art Glass Company
*1892 C.F. Monroe Company; Vineland Flint Glass Works
*1893 First gasoline-powered automobile; Handel and Company
*1894 Jointure Mount Washington Glass Company/Pairpoint Manufacturing Company; Indiana Tumbler and Goblet Works
*1895 Motion picture projector developed; Stephen Crane's *The Red Badge of Courage*; A.H. Heisey Glass Company; Northwood: Union Glass Works, Indiana, Pennsylvania
1898 Spanish-American War
*1901 First transatlantic radio communication; Cambridge Glass Company; Quezal Art Glass and Decorating Company; Honesdale Decorating Company; Imperial Glass Company; H.C. Fry Glass Company; New Martinsville Glass Company; Northwood: Union Glass Works, Wheeling, West Virginia
*1903 Wright Brothers' plane; Jack London, *The Call of the Wild*; Steuben Glass Works
*1904 Helmschmied Manufacturing Company
*1905 Fenton Art Glass Company
1906 Upton Sinclair, *The Jungle*
*1907 Alton Manufacturing Company
1914 Robert Frost, *North of Boston*
1914-1918 World War I
1915 Edgar Lee Masters, *Spoon River Anthology*
1919 Sherwood Anderson, *Winesburg, Ohio*
*1920 League of Nations founded; Womens' Suffrage Amendment (19th); First Commercial radio broadcast; Sinclair Lewis, *Main Street*; Lustre Art Glass Company
*1922 Blenko Glass Company
*1924 Durand Art Glass
1925 F. Scott Fitzgerald, *The Great Gatsby*
1927 First talking motion picture
*1928 A. Douglas Nash Corporation
1929 Stock market crash; Thomas Wolfe, *Look Homeward, Angel*
1930 Sinclair Lewis receives Nobel prize
*1931 Pearl Buck, *The Good Earth*; Kimble Glass Company
1936 Eugene O'Neill receives Nobel prize
1938 Pearl Buck receives Nobel prize
*1939 First commercial television; John Steinbeck, *The Grapes of Wrath*; Gundersen Glass Works
1939-1945 World War II
1945 United Nations founded; first atomic bomb dropped
1949 Arthur Miller, *Death of a Salesman*
1950 William Faulkner receives Nobel prize
1950-1953 Korean War
1952 Ernest Hemingway, *The Old Man and the Sea*; first hydrogen bomb tested
1954 Ernest Hemingway receives Nobel prize
*1957 First man-made satellite; Pairpoint Glass Company, Incorporated
1961 First manned space flight
1962 John Steinbeck receives Nobel prize
1963 Atomic test ban with U.S.S.R. and Great Britain; John F. Kennedy assassinated
1964 Civil Rights Act

Bibliography

Arwas, Victor. *Glass*. New York: Rizzoli International Publications, Incorporated, 1977.

Arwas, Victor. *Tiffany*. New York: Rizzoli International Publications, Incorporated, 1979.

Avila, George C. *The Pairpoint Glass Story*. Massachusetts: Reynolds-De Walt Printing, Incorporated, 1978.

Barrett, Richard Carter. *A Collectors Handbook of American Art Glass*. Manchester, Vermont: Forward's Color Productions, 1971.

Bastow, Harry. *American Glass Practice*. Pittsburgh: The Glassworker, 1920.

Biser, Benjamin F. *Elements of Glass and Glassmaking*. Pittsburgh: Glass and Pottery Publishing Company, 1920.

Boggess, Bill and Louise. *American Brilliant Cut Glass*. New York: Crown Publishers, 1977.

Boston and Sandwich Glass Company (catalogue reprint of 1874), Wellesley Hills, Massachusetts: Lee Publications, 1968.

Brahmer, Bonnie J. "Custard Glass." The *Antiques Journal*, August 1968, pp.12 and 34.

Brahmer, Bonnie J. *Custard Glass*. Privately published, Springfield, Missouri, 1966.

Burns, Mary Louise. *Heisey Glassware of Distinction*. Mesa: Triangle Books, 1974.

Butts, Sheldon. "Joseph Locke's Artistry on Glass." *Hobbies*, February 1979, pp. 156-157.

Christie, Manson and Woods International, Incorporated, Catalog, Fine Art Nouveau and Art Deco, Sculpture (1850-1930), and Animalier Bronzes, September 22 and 23, 1978, 502 Park Avenue, New York City.

Cole, Ann Kilborn. *Golden Guide to American Antiques*. New York: Golden Press, 1967.

Columbia Exposition Album, Chicago, 1893, New York: Rand McNally and Company, 1893.

Copper, Kenneth F. "Question and Answer Department." The Magazine of *Old Glass*, March, 1940. p.16.

Cowie, Donald and Keith Henshaw. *Antique Collector's Dictionary*. New York: Gramercy Publishing Company, 1962.

Daniel, Dorothy. *Cut and Engraved Glass 1771-1905*. New York: M. Barrows and Company, 1950.

Davidson, Marshal B., ed. *The American Heritage History of Colonial Antiques*. New York: American Heritage Publishing Company, 1967.

Di Bartolomeo, Robert E. "Hobbs Brockunier's Fancy Glass." The Magazine *Antiques*, March, 1975, pp. 494-501.

Di Noto, Andrea. "Art Glass Victorians Fanciful Ware." *The Encyclopedia of Collectibles*, pp. 54-69.

Drepperd, Carl W. *ABC's of Old Glass*. New York: Doubleday and Company, 1968.

Drepperd, Carl W. *A Dictionary of American Antiques*. New York: Doubleday and Company, 1968.

Ericson, Eric E. *A Guide To Colored Steuben Glass* (1903-1933). 2 volumes. Colorado: the Lithographic Press, 1963.

Fauster, Carl U. "Libbey's Famous Glass Menagerie." *Hobbies*, February 1972, pp. 120-121, 124, 95.

Fauster, Carl U. *Libbey Glass Since 1818*. Ohio: Len Beach Press, 1979.

Frazer, Margaret. "Colored Glass." *Discovering Antiques*, volume 8, New York: Greystone Press, 1973, pp. 904-907.

Freeman, Larry. "The Dorflinger Glass Works at White Mills." The Magazine of *Old Glass*, March 1940, p. 11.

Gaddis, James H. "Custard Glass." The *Antiques Journal*, August 1969, pp. 15-16.

Gaines, Edith. "American Glass." *Woman's Day*, August 1961, pp. 19-34.

Gaines, Edith. "Sandwich Glass." *Woman's Day*, August 1963, pp. 21-32.

Gaines, Edith. "Seventy years of Steuben glass." The Magazine *Antiques*, August 1975, pp. 234-245.

Gaines, Edith. "Victorian Art Glass." *Woman's Day*, August 1964, pp. 23-33.

Gardner, Paul V. *The Glass of Frederick Carder*. New York: Crown Publishers, 1971.

Garner, Philippe. "Tiffany Glass." *Discovering Antiques*, volume 2, New York: Greystone Press, 1973, pp. 220-224.

Grover, Ray and Lee. *Art Glass Nouveau*. Vermont: Charles E. Tuttle, 1967.

Hammond, Dorothy. *Confusing Collectibles*. Iowa: Mid-American Book Company, 1969.

Hammond, Dorothy. *More Confusing Collectibles*. Kansas: C.B.P. Publishing Company, 1972.

Heacock, William. "Phoenix/Consolidated Copies and Look-Alikes" *Collecting Glass* (Volume 2), 1985, pp. 33-40.

Heacock, William. "Phoenix Glass Company Catalogue Reprint (circa 1942)." *Collecting Glass*. (Volume 2), 1985, pp. 33-40.

Hogrefe, Jeffrey, ed., *The Antiques World Price Guide*, Doubleday and Company, Incorporated, 1982.

Hollister, Paul. "The Kahila Dig at Mount Washington." The Magazine *Antiques*, September 1972, pp. 455-459.

Horton, Christine. "Giants In Glass Houses." *American Antiques*, September 1976, pp. 26-33.

Hoskins, Dorothy M. "Designs and Decorations on Pomona Glass." *Spinning Wheel*, May 1957, p.12.

Hotchkiss, John F. *Art Glass Handbook*. New York: Hawthorn Books, 1972.

Hotchkiss, John F. *Carder's Steuben Glass Handbook and Price Guide*. New York: Hawthorn Books, 1972.

Hudgeons III, Thomas E., ed., *Official 1985 Price Guide To Glassware*. Florida: The House of Collectibles, Incorporated, 1985.

Innes, Lowell. *Pittsburgh Glass 1797-1891*. Massachusetts: Houghton Mifflin Company, 1976.

Janse, Rose and Richard C. Rolfe. "BURMESE...New Bedford's Interpretation of the Victorian Era." The Magazine of *Old Glass*, June 1939, pp. 17-18.

Jordan, Donn Marsh. "Finger Bowl by Nicholas Lutz." The Magazine of *Old Glass*, May 1939, p. 17.

Koch, Robert. *Louis C. Tiffany, Rebel in Glass*. New York: Crown Publishers, 1964.

Koehler, Ethyl May. "Cambridge's Crown Tuscan Glass." *National Antiques Review*, June 1976, pp. 24-25.

Koehler, Margaret H. "Pairpoint Glass." The *Antiques Journal*, January 1975, pp. 18-21.

Kovel, Ralph and Terry. *The Complete Antiques Price List*. New York: Crown Publishers, 1973, 1976, 1980, 1981, 1982, 1985, 1986.

Kovel, Ralph and Terry. *Know Your Antiques*. New York: Crown Publishers, 1967.

Kovel, Ralph and Terry. "A New Discovery: Star Holly," *Hobbies*, December 1959, pp. 70-71.

Lagerberg, Theodore and Viola. *Collectible Glass*. Volumes 1, 2, and 4. Privately published, New Port Richey, Florida, 1963-1968.

Lagerberg, Theodore and Viola. *Durand Glass*. Book 3. Des Moines: Wallace-Homestead Book Company, 1978.

Lee, Ruth Webb. *Nineteenth Century Art Glass*. New York: M. Barrows and Company, 1952.

Lee, Ruth Webb. *Sandwich Glass*. Wellesley Hills, Massachusetts: Lee Publications, 1966.

Lee, Ruth Webb. *Victorian Glass Handbook*. Wellesley Hills, Massachusetts, 1946.

Lindsey, Bessie M. *American Historical Glass*. Vermont: Charles E. Tuttle, 1967.

Mackay, James. *Glass Paperweights*. New York: Facts on File, 1973.

Manchee, Kathryn Hait Dorflinger. "Dorflinger Glass." (Part I), The Magazine *Antiques*, April 1972, pp. 710-715.

Manchee, Kathryn Hait Dorflinger. "Dorflinger Glass." (Part II), The Magazine *Antiques*, June 1972, pp. 1006-1011.

Manchee, Kathryn Hait Dorflinger. "Dorflinger Glass." (Part III), The Magazine *Antiques*, July 1972, pp. 96-100.

Manley, Cyril. *Decorative Victorian Glass*. New York: Van Nostrand Reinhold Company, 1981.

McKearin, George and Helen. *American Glass*. New York: Crown Publishers, 1966.

Measell, Dr. James S. "Golden Agate: Greentown's Glory Glass." *Spinning Wheel*, July-August 1979, pp. 40-43.

Mebane, John and Catherine Murphy. *The Antique Trader Price Guide To Antiques and Collectors' Items*. Iowa: The Babka Publishing Company, Spring 1972, Fall 1972, Spring 1973, Spring 1974, Fall 1974, Winter 1974, Fall 1976.

Mehlman, Felice. *Glass*. Oxford: Phaidon Press, Limited, 1982.

Miller, Robert W. *Mary Gregory and Her Glass*. Iowa: Wallace-Homestead Book Company, 1972.

Miller, Robert W. *Price Guide to Antiques and Pattern Glass*, Iowa: Wallace-Homestead Book Company, 1975, 1977, 1978, 1979, 1981, 1982, 1983.

Moore, Hudson N. *Old Glass - European and American*. New York: Tudor Publishing Company, 1944.

Murphy, Catherine. *The Antique Trader Antiques and Collectibles Price Guide*. Iowa: The Babka Publishing Company, 1984, 1985, 1986.

Neustadt, Dr. Egon. *The Lamps of Tiffany*. New York: The Fairfield Press, 1970.

The New England Glass Company (1818-1888). The Toledo Museum of Art.

Newman, Harold. *An Illustrated Dictionary of Glass*. London: Thames and Hudson, 1977.

Oliver, Elizabeth. *American Antique Glass*. New York: Golden Press, 1977.

Padgett, Leonard E. *Pairpoint Glass*. Iowa: Wallace-Homestead Book Company, 1979.

Parke-Bernet Galleries Catalog, *Collection of the Louis Comfort Tiffany Foundation*, September 24-28, 1946, 30 East 57th Street, New York City.

Pearson, J. Michael and Dorothy T. *American Cut Glass for the Discriminating Collector*. Miami, Florida: The Franklin Press, 1965.

Revi, Albert Christian. *American Art Nouveau Glass*. Tennessee: Thomas Nelson, 1968.

Revi, Albert Christian. *American Cut and Engraved Glass*. Tennessee: Thomas Nelson, Incorporated, 1972.

Revi, Albert Christian. *Nineteenth Century Glass*. New York: Galahad Books, 1967.

Revi, Albert Christian, ed., *The Spinning Wheel's Complete Book of Antiques*. New York: Grosset and Dunlap, 1972.

Richard A. Bourne Company, Incorporated catalog, *Art Glass*, February 26, 1972, Corporation Street, Hyannis, Massachusetts.

Richard A. Bourne Company, Incorporated catalog, *Rare Art Glass*, May 5, 1973, Corporation Street, Hyannis, Massachusetts.

Richard A. Bourne Company, Incorporated catalog, *Rare Art Glass*, October 21, 1972, Corporation Street, Hyannis, Massachusetts.

Rolfe, Richard Carman, ed., "Aurene," The Magazine of *Old Glass*, March 1940, p. 18.

Rolfe, Richard Carman, "Florette Blown Ware." The Magazine of *Old Glass*, April 1940, pp. 11-12, 14.

Rosenblatt, Sidney, "Frederick Carder's Venetian Style Glass" *Hobbies*, August 1973, pp. 105, 129.

Sandwich Glass. The Sandwich Historical Society, 1981.

Schwartz, Marvin D. *American Glass: Blown and Moulded*. New Jersey: The Pyne Press, 1974.

Shields, Harriet I. "The Story of Mercury Glass." The Magazine of *Old Glass*, March and April 1939, pp. 17-21 and 23.

Shuman III, John A. *Art Glass Sampler*. Des Moines: Wallace-Homestead Book Company, 1978.

Shuman III, John A. and Susan W. *Lion Pattern Glass*. Boston: Branden Press, 1977.

Spillman, Jane Shadel. *Glass Tableware, Bowls and Vases*. New York: Alfred A. Knopf, 1982.

Warman, Edwin G. *Ninth Antiques and their Current Prices*. Uniontown, Pennsylvania: E.G. Warman Publishing, Incorporated, 1968.

Warman, Edwin G. *Eleventh Antiques and their Current Prices*. Uniontown, Pennsylvania: E.G. Warman Publishing, Incorporated, 1972.

Warman, Edwin G. *Thirteenth Antiques and their Current Prices*. Uniontown, Pennsylvania: E.G. Warman Publishing, Incorporated, 1976.

Whitlow, Harry H. *Art, Colored and Cameo Glass*. Privately published, Riverview, Michigan, 1967.

Wiener, Herbert and Freda Lipkowitz. *Rarities In American Cut Glass*. Houston: The Collector's House of Books Publishing Company, 1980.

Ziegfeld, Edwin; Faulkner, Ray; and Hill, Gerald. *Art Today*. New York: Holt, Rinehart and Winston, 1965.

Zimmerman, Philip D., ed., *Turn of the Century Glass*. New Hampshire: The University Press of New England, 1983.

Index

Price Guide to American Art Glass Types Plus Other Glass

The values listed in this guide are intended as an aid to pricing perfect glass specimens. Art Glass in mint condition will have no cracks, missing portions, parts reground and polished, chips, undesirable stains and discolorations, and only a very minimum of scratches, other than on the bases of articles. Should an object not merit inclusion in the above category, its selling price will be altered to a degree, depending upon the nature of the problem.

Minor flaws in the making, such as a burst internal bubble; a heat check from an applied handle; a rough broken off pontil; or slight variations in enameling, cutting, etching, or glass application, will reduce the value up to 15%. Items with nicks, scratches, and chips that can not be remedied by grinding and polishing should sell for 25% less than the price listed. Objects with stains, discolorations, cracks, bumps, bruises, and missing portions will be cut to 50% of their intended worth. The overall shape and color should also be carefully considered. Poorly conceived objects lacking grace, beauty, and vivid color representation should not be considered for purchase if they do not possess outstanding traits unique to a particular classification. Objects of an imperfect nature in any respect should be glossed over, unless, of course, they are exceedingly rare and not likely to be encountered again.

The reader, perhaps, has noted objects of a similar nature being bought or sold for more or less than the prices stated. Additional factors which create varying price ranges are: 1) the availability or scarcity of the object (common to museum quality), 2) authentic signatures (labels, acid stamps, artists' signatures, etchings, mold marks, impressed marks in metals, etc.), 3) the geographic area where it was bought or sold (regional or universal interest item), 4) the manner by which it was bought or sold (privately, garage or house sale, auction firm), 5) the sentiments of the crowd (money available, specific collectors present) and 6) the weather (numbers in attendance, inclement situations, and unforeseen emergencies).

Use the price guide as just that, a guide. Be knowledgeable about the specific type(s) of glass that you buy or sell. Read widely on the subject; frequent museums, historical societies, and quality shows. Above all, buy those items which you can afford, enjoy, and care for properly. If you are a dealer, strive to advertise and sell, consistently, quality merchandise at a fair price, backed by a written guarantee that you will honor.

Every effort has been made to assure accuracy of prices listed in the guide and those that also refer to the colored examples shown in the book. All prices have been double checked, however, neither the author or the publisher can assume any responsibility for losses, should they occur as a result of consulting this book.

AMBERINA

Bowl, footed, melon ribbed with 4 amber feet, polished pontil, 7" tall, $504.00.

Bowl, rose, 6", Hobnail pattern, $380.00.

Bowl, scalloped rim, 2¾" high x 5⅜" diameter, $266.00.

Champagne, 6", hollow stem, scarce, $324.00.

Cruet, attributed to New England Glass Company, 7¾", Inverted Thumbprint, original stopper, outstanding color, $367.00.

Cup, punch, excellent fuchsia shading, 2½" high, Inverted Thumbprint, amber reeded handle, $173.00.

Dish, canoe shape, pressed Daisy and Button, Amberina, 8" long, $1,008.00.

Glass, whiskey, Diamond Quilted Amberina, 2⅝" high, $144.00.

Mug, barrel shaped, Baby Thumbprint, ribbed applied handle, 2½" high, $209.00.

Pitcher, square top, 7" high, Inverted Thumbprint, amber reeded handle, New England Glass Company, $310.00.

Pitcher, water, Craquelle, applied reeded handle, $468.00.

Pitcher, water, 9½", applied amber handle, Mount Washington, circa 1880s, enameled Apple blossoms, leaves, buds, and branches, rare, $828.00.

Spittoon, ruffled edge, hourglass form, $410.00.

Shakers, salt and pepper, Mount Washington, 1880s, original tops, Inverted Baby Thumbprint, $432.00 pair.

Shakers, salt and pepper, Quilt pattern, $266.00 set.

Shaker, salt, Reverse Amberina, pewter top, Inverted Baby Thumbprint, $252.00.

Spooner, Mount Washington, square top, Diamond Quilted, $497.00.

Toothpick holder, tri-cornered, Baby Thumbprint, deep fuchsia, $396.00.

Tumbler, Inverted Baby Thumbprint, $108.00.

Tumbler, Swirl pattern, $130.00.

Vase, celery, cylinder with square top and scalloped rim, 6½" high, Mount Washington, Diamond Quilted, $396.00.

Vase, Reverse Amberina, Swirl pattern, satinized, 9¼" x 4½", lacy gold flowers, enameled, rare, $1,728.00.

Vase, trumpet shaped, vertical ribs and wavy flaring rim, narrow stem joins circular foot, polished pontil, 7½" high, $570.00.

C. F. MONROE

Ashtray, 4½" diameter, ormolu rim, applied twisted bar with flowers, Robin's egg blue, white dotted scrolls, pink apple blossoms, $324.00.

Box, glove, signed "WAVE CREST," hinged lid, Embossed Scroll, pink florals on blue, 8½" long x 4½" wide, $972.00.

Box, hinged, hexagonal, 4" diameter, deep blue and tan, white beading, signed "NAKARA," $468.00.

Box, hinged, hexagonal shape, 4" high, Robin's egg blue, tan accents, white raised beading, signed "NAKARA," $468.00.

Box, hinged, red and white roses, pink and green ground, blue and white beading, signed "NAKARA," 6" diameter, $634.00.

Box, hinged, round, woman's portrait on the lid, signed "NAKARA," embossed rococo, pink and peach ground, 5½" high x 8¼" diameter, $1,174.00.

Box, hinged, signed "KELVA," octagonal mold, moss green, pink florals and daisies, $814.00.

Box, jewel, off-white, pastel flowers, 7", Wave Crest, $324.00.

Box, ring, double shell, blue with beading and small flowers, 3½", signed "WAVE CREST," $238.00.

Box, signed "NAKARA," olive green, cartouche of 2 women in a garden among flowers and birds, 8½" wide rare, $1,008.00.

Box, trinket, Robin's egg blue and cream background, pink clover, signed "NAKARA," $288.00.

Box, with hinged lid, floral decor on white, Embossed Scroll mold, marked in gold "Collars and Cuffs," ormolu collar and base, lion masks above the feet, signed "WAVE CREST," $1,404.00.

Dish, hairpin, molded fan shaped pattern, enameled flowers, 3¼" diameter, signed, $158.00.

Ewer, melon ribbed, Victorian children in a garden, 15½" tall, $288.00.

Ewers, scenic decor, 14" tall, $396.00 pair.

Fernery, violets, raised gold tracery on white, Egg Crate mold, 7" wide, ormolu rim, unsigned Wave Crest, $425.00.

Holder, cigarette, hexagonal, red banner mark, outdoor scene, raised pink scrolling, "Spider Webbing," raised blue and white forget-me-not, $576.00.

Holder, letter, Embossed Scroll, flowers painted on white, ormolu footed base and collar, unsigned Wave Crest, $425.00.

Holder, whisk broom, Embossed Scroll, signed "WAVE CREST" on back plate, 8½", florals on white, ormolu trim, $936.00.

Jar, biscuit, Wave Crest, Swirl pattern, light blue ground, delicate floral decor, 10" to top of bail handle, $648.00.

Jar, blown-out, covered, 3" double shell, red banner Wave Crest mark, blue enameled flowers, $418.00.

Jar, toothpowder, signed "WAVE CREST," red banner mark, blue forget-me-nots with raised white dotted centers, original brass embossed lid, $540.00.

Jar, unusual tobacco, metal lid, signed "NAKARA," 6¾" high, frog reading newspaper, blue ground, lettered "Tobacco," $1,044.00.

Lamp base, rare Wave Crest, blown out, embossed scrolls on sides and collar, old crystal frosted shade, base has tiny pink and blue flowers, 17" with shade, $936.00.

Lamp, table, signed "WAVE CREST," mint, $504.00.

Pitcher, syrup, Helmschmied swirl, blue background, enameled pink wild roses, silverplated top and handle, $684.00.

Planter, signed "WAVE CREST," daisies and beaded brass rim, 7½", $504.00.

Receiver, hair, covered, signed "NAKARA," diamond shape, enameled children at tea, blue on pale blue ground, white beading, $576.00.

Set, sugar and creamer, swirl pattern, roses, blue background, silver-plated mounts, $360.00.

Shakers, salt and pepper, spiked pewter tops, "WAVE CREST," Artichoke pattern, $504.00 pair.

Tray, bon bon, signed "NAKARA," ormolu collar, diamond swirl mold, geometric scrolling and beading, pink outlined in white, blue ground, $504.00.

Vase, cabinet size, ormolu top, bronze footed holder, embossed, blue with flowers, 5" tall, $238.00.

Vase, hexagonal, signed "KELVA," 13" tall, Robin's egg blue, marbled background, pink roses, white dotted rim, $792.00.

Vase, signed "KELVA," green background, pink flowers, 14" high, silverplated ormolu feet, $972.00.

Vase, signed "WAVE CREST," iris on a blue ground, 12" high, 9" widest diameter, ormolu feet, handles, and collar, $842.00.

CHOCOLATE

Bowl, berry, Chocolate Wild Rose and Bow Knot, $122.00.

Bowl, Chocolate, Fenton Vintage, $281.00.

Bowl, master berry, Cactus, 9¼" diameter, $115.00.

Bowl, master berry, Leaf Bracket, 8" diameter, $158.00.

Bowl, oval, Geneva, 8¼" x 5¼" $101.00.

Bowl, sugar, covered, Cactus, $209.00.

Bowl, sugar, covered, Chrysanthemum Leaf, $511.00.

Bowl, sugar, covered, Leaf Bracket, $158.00.

Compote, Cactus pattern, Greentown, 7¼" diameter, $144.00.

Compote, Geneva, 4½" diameter, x 3½" high, $209.00.

Compote, jelly, Cactus, 5¼" diameter x 5" high, $202.00.

Compote, Large, 8¼" diameter, Chocolate, Cactus pattern, $298.00.

Creamer, Cactus, $122.00.

Creamer, Leaf bracket, $108.00.

Creamer, Shuttle pattern, $101.00.

Creamer, tankard, Strigil pattern, 6" tall, $115.00.

Cruet, Chocolate, Cactus, original stopper, $266.00.

Cruet, Chocolate, Leaf Bracket, original stopper, $252.00.

Compote, scalloped rim, Melrose, 6", $410.00.

Dish, butter, covered, Cactus pattern, $274.00.

Dish, butter, covered, 4" diameter, Dewey patter, $216.00.

Dish, butter, covered, on a pedestal, Cactus, Greentown, $540.00.

Dish, sauce, Cactus, $65.00.

Dish, sauce, Geneva, $65.00.

Dish, covered, Greentown Dolphin, $432.00.

Dish, sauce, Teardrop and Tassel, $223.00.

Dish, sauce, Wild Rose and Bowknot, $144.00.

Fernery, 3 feet, Vintage, Fenton, $252.00.

Hamper, Amber tall cat, original label on the base, $324.00.

Hatpin holder, Orange Tree pattern, $367.00.

Lamp, kerosene, Wild Rose with Festoon patter, $324.00.

Mug, Cactus, $101.00.

Mug, Herringbone Buttress, $94.00.

Mug, Shuttle pattern, $122.00.

Nappy, handled, Masonic, $137.00.

Nappy, handled, triangular, Leaf Bracket, $79.00.

Pitcher, water, Chocolate Ruffled Eye, superior color, $468.00.

Pitcher, water, Greentown Chocolate, Wild Rose pattern, good coloration, $540.00.

Pitcher, water, Heron, $324.00.

Pitcher, water, Indiana Feather, $864.00.

Pitcher, water, Racing Deer and Doe, $504.00.

Pitcher, water, Squirrel patter, $490.00.

Pitcher, syrup, original top, Cactus pattern, $144.00.

Pitcher, syrup, original top, Cord Drapery, Greentown. $360.00.

Relish, oval, 8" x 5", Leaf Bracket, $101.00.

Set, master berry, 8" diameter, 6 sauces, Leaf Bracket, $432.00.

Shaker, salt, Chocolate, Leaf Bracket, $158.00.

Spooner, Cactus, $137.00.

Spooner, child's, pedestal, Austrian pattern, $252.00.

Spooner, Chocolate Wild Rose and Bow Knot, $209.00.

Spooner, Dewey, $137.00.

Spooner, Leaf Bracket, $137.00.

Spooner, Wild Rose with Bowknot, $180.00.

Stein, Drinking Scene Indoors, 8½" high, $331.00.

Stein, Outdoor Drinking Scene, $238.00.

Sweetmeat, covered, Cactus pattern, $540.00.

Toothpick holder, Cactus, $122.00.

Toothpick holder Geneva, $180.00.

Toothpick holder, picture frame model, $1,008.00.

Tray, celery, 11" long, Leaf Bracket, $166.00.

Tray, oval, Chocolate Leaf Bracket, 5½" x 10¾", $137.00.

Tray, Serpentine, Amber Dewey, $58.00.

Tumbler, Chocolate, Cactus, $86.00.

Tumbler, Chocolate, Cord Drapery, rare, $360.00.

Tumbler, Chocolate, Leaf Bracket, $86.00.

Tumbler, Chocolate, Shuttle, $122.00.

Tumbler, Chocolate, Uneeda Biscuit $245.00.

Tumbler, Chocolate, Wild Rose with bowknot, excellent color, $166.00.

Tumbler, sawtooth pattern, $108.00.

Vase, Celery, Fleur-de-lis pattern, 5¾" high, $288.00.

Vase, Scalloped Flange pattern, $86.00.

COIN

Bowl, frosted coins, oval, 8", $367.00.

Bowl, sugar, covered, frosted coins, $598.00.

Champagne, frosted dimes, $490.00.

Compote, frosted dimes and quarters, open, 5½" diameter x 5½" high, $338.00.

Compote, covered, dollar finial, 6" x 9½", $554.00.

Compote, covered, frosted coins, 8" diameter x 11½" high, $806.00.

Compote, covered, frosted coins, 9" diameter, $770.00.

Compote, covered, high standard, 6⅞" high, frosted coins, $713.00.

Compote, covered, high pedestal, frosted 1892 quarters and half dollars, 8" diameter, $540.00.

Compote, frosted U.S. Coin, 11¼" tall, 8" diameter, $792.00.

Compote, frosted dimes and quarters, open, 6½" diameter x 8" high, $331.00.

Compote, open, frosted dimes and quarters, 7" diameters, 5¾" high, $598.00.

Cruet, original stopper, 5½" tall, frosted coins, $763.00.

Dish, butter, dollars, half dollars, $756.00.

Dish, pickle, 7½" x 3¾", clear coins, $302.00.

Dish, sauce, 4" diameters, frosted quarters, $252.00.

Epergne, frosted dollars, scarce, $1,800.00.

Goblet, frosted dimes, $410.00.

Lamp kerosene, clear quarters in base, round font, handled, $526.00.

Lamp, kerosene, frosted quarters, round font, pedestal base, $720.00.

Lamp, milk glass, Columbian Coin, 8" tall, $482.00.

Mug, frosted coins, $526.00.

Pitcher, water, frosted dollars, $720.00.

Relish, frosted coins, $302.00.

Shaker, salt, original top, $194.00.

Spooner, frosted quarters, $468.00.

Stand, cake, 10" diameter, clear dollars, $353.00.

Stand, cake, frosted dollars, 10" diameter, $540.00.

Toothpick holder, clear coins, $274.00.

Tray, bread, dollars, half dollars, $482.00.

Tumbler, frosted dollar in base, $259.00.

Vase, celery, clear dimes, $209.00.

Vase, celery, clear quarters, $360.00.

Vase, celery, frosted quarters, $410.00.

Wine, frosted half dimes, rare, $670.00.

CONSOLIDATED

Bowl, sugar, covered, Guttate pattern, Cranberry, $202.00.

Butter, covered, Florette pattern, pink satin, mint, $238.00.

Candlestick, flat stem, Hummingbird, Martele, $108.00.

Candlesticks, orange tinge, Poppy, Martele, $86.00 pr.

Creamer, pink satin, Florette, $137.00.

Cruet, all original, Guttate, white, $252.00.

Cruet, pink satin Florette with clear stopper, $202.00.

Dish, butter, covered, Guttate, white, gold trim, $115.00.

Jar, Cookie, pink satin, Florette, original silverplate, $288.00.

Lamp, miniature, enameled pink, blue, and yellow flowers, the Daisy, $360.00.

Lamp, miniature, milk glass, raised designs enameled green, the Kitty, $396.00.

Lamp, miniature, number 390, 7" high, cased pink glass, melon ribbed base and shade, which is an umbrella type, $864.00.

Lamp, miniature, raised scrolls and leaves in pink and orange, the Leaf, $432.00.

Lamp, miniature, the Star, $396.00.

Lamp, oil, rare quilt pattern, Florette, cased yellow font on clear quilted base, 10" tall, $468.00.

Pitcher, Pigeon Blood, gold Aventurine throughout, bulbous, clear ribbed handle, ruffled top, ground pontil, $324.00.

Pitcher, syrup, original top, dated, pink satin, Guttate pattern, $302.00.

Pitcher, syrup, squat, original silverplated top, pink satin Florette, $302.00.

Pitcher, water, 7¼" blue satin, florette, white lining, applied camphor handle, $396.00.

Pitcher, water, glossy blue, Florette, 7¼" high, $324.00.

Pitcher, water, Guttate pattern, yellow cased in clear, scarce, $410.00.

Pitcher, water, Guttate pattern, white, $115.00.

Pitcher, water, Guttate,, white, gold trim, $137.00.

Pitcher, water, pink satin, Florette, 7¼" high, $338.00.

Tumbler, Guttate pattern, pink cased in clear, $65.00.

Toothpick holder, yellow, glossy, florette, $108.00.

Set, condiment, 3 pieces, salt, pepper, and mustard, original tops, pink satin, florette, handled holder, $216.00.

Set, table, 4 pieces, pink satin, Florette, sugar, creamer, spooner, and covered butter, $713.00.

Set, water, 7 pieces, pitcher and 6 tumblers $432.00.

Shakers, salt and pepper, original tops, Guttate, pink cased in clear, $137.00 pair.

Shakers, salt and pepper, Pigeon blood, original tops, $180.00.

Shaker, sugar, original top, Guttate, pink cased in clear, $238.00.

Shaker, sugar, pink satin finish, Florette, original top, $187.00.

Vase, fan, Cockatoo, Martele, amethyst, 8" high, $122.00.

Vase, frosted grasshoppers on green background, 8¼" $108.00.

Vase, milk glass, florentine, painted decor, scarce. $101.00.

Vase, Pine Cone, light blue opaline, $115.00.

CORALENE

Mug, amber satin ground, applied turquoise handle, orange seaweed design, 2" high, $137.00.

Pitcher, orange satin, amber neck rigaree and applied amber handle, green leaves and white water lily decoration, 6¼" high x 4" diameter, $310.00.

Pitcher, water, shaded blue satin, white interior, square top, applied blue reeded handle, yellow seaweed design, $886.00.

Toothpick holder satin background, shades from yellow to white, applied and fired yellow seaweed, $346.00.

Tumbler, straight sided, 4" tall, shaded pink satin glass, yellow seaweed decor, $252.00.

Tumble-up, cranberry background, 2 pieces, carafe and fitted tumbler lid, snowflake and swag decorations, $374.00 set.

Vase, blue satin, 8½" high, flared top rim, yellow seaweed embellishment, $432.00.

Vase, cocoa hued satin, 5" high, yellow and green hued coralene design, $288.00.

Vase, cranberry, 10¼" high x 4⅝" diameter, 3 clear applied reeded and scrolled feet, scalloped gold edged rim, green leaves, pink and blue beaded florals, $468.00.

Vase, tapered and ruffled top, white lining, 6" tall, pink satin ground, floral and leaf beading, $194.00.

Vase, tapered neck with ruffled rim, white lining, deep rose satin at the top, shading to a pink base, left hand swirled snowflake design, $626.00.

Vase, white interior, shaded pink satin exterior, 4 applied clear frosted feet, branched yellow seaweed beading, 5½" tall, $670.00.

CRANBERRY

Basket, ruffled rim, clear twisted handle, $209.00.

Basket, vertical ribbing, wide scalloped top, clear applied handle and circular foot, 6" high, $202.00.

Bell, smoke, $108.00.

Bottle, barber's, square shaped, vertical ribbing, 8½" high, $137.00.

Bottle, perfume, enameled flowers and leaves, original stopper, 3⅛" tall, $94.00.

Bowl, enameled flowers, clear rigaree on the top lip, 7½" diameter, $194.00.

Bowl, finger, amber threading on the ruffled rim, $122.00.

Bowl, rose, threaded body, ruffled rim, 3" high, $94.00.

Box, round, hinged and enameled lid, 4" diameter, $180.00.

Castor, pickle, Cranberry glass in fancy Forbes #250 silvered footed frame, with lid and tongs, $360.00.

Castor, pickle, signed Pairpoint silverplated frame, footed, original tongs, $432.00.

Chalice, covered, enameled girl, also gilded, 16" tall, $266.00.

Creamer, clear applied handle, rigaree at the neck, shell feet, ruffled top, 4¼" high, $130.00.

Cruet, Craquelle, cut stopper, clear applied handle, $238.00.

Cup, punch, enameled flowers applied clear handle, $50.00.

Decanter, floral enameling, footed, 10", amber berry prunt, $281.00.

Decanter, Inverted Thumbprint, clear stopper and applied handle, 11" high, $266.00.

Epergne, single trumpet, 12" high, crystal rigaree, $209.00.

Ewer, floral decor, clear applied handle, 8½" x 4¼", $266.00.

Glass, liqueur, Cranberry bowl, gold panels, 4" high, $65.00.

Hat, silverplated brim, 2⅝" high, $173.00.

Jar, powder, silverplated lid, $137.00.

Lamp, hanging, all original brass, clear glass insert, Hobnail shade, $655.00.

Mug, Inverted Thumbprint, clear applied handle, 4" high, $101.00.

Pitcher, square top, Bull's Eye pattern, $382.00.

Pitcher, Swirl pattern, 9" high, enameled forget-me-nots, $281.00.

Pitcher, tankard, applied handle, 8½" high, Inverted Thumbprint, $454.00.

Pitcher, water, Inverted Thumbprint, bulbous body, 8" high, $194.00.

Plate, 8" diameter, $50.00.

Set, sugar and creamer, floral enameling, silverplated holder, $281.00.

Set, water, 5 pieces, Inverted Thumbprint, bulbous pitcher, 4 tumblers, $324.00.

Set, water, pitcher, 4 tumblers, Inverted Thumbprint, enameled flowers, $360.00.

Shade, 4" x 6" x 8 ", Diamond Quilted, $266.00.

Shade, fluted, 7¾" diameter, Hobnail pattern, $94.00.

Shakers, salt and pepper, floral enameled decor, original tops, $194.00 pair.

Shaker, sugar, Drape pattern, silver top, 6½" high, $122.00.

Syrup, 6¾", silverplated handle and spout, $396.00.

Toothpick holder, satin finish barrel shaped, Inverted Baby Thumbprint, $166.00.

Tumbler, Inverted Thumbprint, 4¼" high, $58.00.

Vase, 8½" tall, enameled flowers outlined in gold, $166.00.

Vase, cylinder, straight sides, clear spiral rigaree, applied ruffled feet, $180.00.

Vase, enameled white lilies of the valley, gold leaves, 7½", $122.00.

Vase, trumpet, ruffled top, clear circular foot, applied spiral rigaree, 7½" high, $180.00.

CUSTARD

Bowl, berry, Ring Band, $180.00.

Bottle, cologne, original stopper, Northwood Grape, $756.00.

Bottle, cologne, original stopper, Winged Scroll, $374.00.

Bowl, master berry, Maple Leaf, $562.00.

Bowl, master berry, ruffled, footed, 11" diameter, Northwood Grape, $641.00.

Bowl, punch, footed, Inverted Fan and Feather, $3,816.00.

Bowl, sugar, covered, Argonaut Shell, $223.00.

Bowl, sugar, covered, Chrysanthemum Sprig, $252.00.

Bowl, sugar, covered Maple Leaf, $259.00.

Bowl, sugar, covered, Victoria, $252.00.

Compote, jelly , Everglades, $526.00.

Compote, jelly, Inverted Fan and Feather, $598.00.

Compote jelly, Maple Leaf, $554.00.

Creamer, Fan, $158.00.

Creamer, Fluted Scrolls, $94.00.

Cruet, Chrysanthemum Sprig, creamy background, brilliant gold, coral and green highlights, original stopper, $454.00.

Cruet, Louis XV, excellent gold, original stopper, $458.00.

Cruet, original stopper, Beaded Circle, $958.00.

Cruet, original stopper, Everglades, $1,102.00.

Cruet, original stopper, Georgia Gem, $382.00.

Cruet, original stopper, Intaglio, gold and green decor. $482.00.

Cruet, original stopper, Maple Leaf, $1,728.00.

Cruet, original stopper, Ring Band, $454.00.

Cruet, original stopper, Winged Scroll, $266.00.

Dish, butter, covered, Beaded Circle, $353.00.

Dish, butter, covered, Cherry and Scale, $338.00.

Dish, butter, covered, Diamond With Peg, $302.00.

Dish, butter, covered, Grape and Gothic Arches, $310.00.

Dish, butter, Louis XV, domed cover, gilted scroll finial, raised flowers and sprigs, circular plate with scalloped edge, 4 scrolled and gilded feet, height 6¼", plate diameter 8", Northwood, $238.00.

Dish, butter, covered, Ribbed Drape, $396.00.

Dish, pickle, Beaded Swag, $382.00.

Dish, sauce, Fan, $94.00.

Dish, sauce, Fluted Scrolls, $65.00.

Humidor, covered, Northwood Grape, $814.00.

Mug, souvenir, Punty Band, $72.00.

Nappy, ruffled, 6½" diameter, Prayer rug, $86.00.

Pitcher, syrup, original top, Winged Scroll, $497.00.

Pitcher, water, Argonaut Shell, $482.00.

Pitcher, water, Cherry and Scale, $482.00.

Pitcher, water Grape and Gothic Arches, $425.00.

Pitcher, water, Louis XV, $252.00.

Pitcher, water, Northwood Grape, $569.00.

Pitcher, water, Ribbed Drape, $518.00.

Pitcher, water, tankard, Diamond With Peg, $554.00.

Pitcher water, Victoria, $526.00.

Ring, napkin, souvenir, Diamond With Peg, $230.00.

Set, table, chrysanthemum Sprig, excellent gold, 4 pieces, $958.00.

Set, table, covered butter and covered sugar, creamer, and spooner, Louis XV, $641.00.

Set, berry, 6 sauces, master bowl, Fan, $814.00.

Set, table, 4 pieces, Fan, $821.00.

Set, tankard pitcher and 4 tumblers, Beaded Swag, $742.00.

Set, water pitcher and 6 tumblers, Argonaut Shell, $1,116.00.

Set, water, beaded Circle, scarce, good gold, excellent enameling, 5 piece set, $1,346.00.

Set, water, pitcher and 6 tumblers, Fluted Scrolls, $612.00.

Set, water pitcher and 6 tumblers, Chrysanthemum Sprig, $1,130.00.

Set, water pitcher and 6 tumblers, Louis XV, $864.00.

Shakers, salt and pepper, original tops, Geneva, $187.00 set.

Shakers, salt and pepper, Custard, pink and gold trim, pewter tops, Inverted Fan and feather, $626.00 pair.

Spooner, Intaglio, $144.00.

Spooner, Inverted Fan and Feather, good color and gold trim, $180.00.

Spooner, Ring Band, $158.00.

Spooner, Argonaut Shell, $166.00.

Spooner, Beaded Circle, $180.00.

Spooner, Everglades, $180.00.

Spooner, Fluted Scrolls, $86.00.

Spooner, Geneva, $101.00.

Table set, 4 pieces, Geneva, $598.00.

Table set, 4 pieces, Georgia Gem, $576.00.

Toothpick holder, Inverted Fan and Feather, $684.00.

Toothpick holder, Ribbed Drape, $209.00.

Toothpick holder, "Wild Bouquet," rare, excellent color, $540.00.

Tumbler, Everglades, $173.00.

Tumbler, Intaglio, $94.00.

Tumbler, Louis XV, excellent gold, $86.00.

Tumbler, Prayer Rug, $130.00.

Tumbler, Victoria, $94.00.

Vase, celery, Georgia Gem, $259.00.

Vase, celery, Winged Scroll, $425.00.

Vase, ruffled hat shape, Grape and Gothic Arches, $86.00.

Vase, souvenir, 5½" high, Punty Band, $122.00.

Wine, Diamond With Peg, $86.00.

CUT

Basket, 14" high, 10" diameter, bottom cut in honeycomb, top intaglio sprays of daisies and leaves, signed "Hunt," $792.00.

Bottle, perfume, 3" high, cut green to clear, $252.00.

Bowl, Brilliant period, shallow, scalloped and serrated rim, 8¼" diameter, 2½" high, 8 spaced oval miters, 6 rows of hobstars between the ovals, marked "J. HOARE & CO./1853/CORNING," $720.00.

Bowl, centerpiece, rare, 5" tall, 4" diameter, base flares to 9" diameter, 24 point hobstar bottom, hobstar set into scalloped rim, signed "Hawkes," $648.00.

Bowl, cut, 8" diameter, Rose pattern, Tuthill, $468.00.

Bowl, engraved punch, bell shaped, deeply engraved grape clusters and leaves, scalloped rim, band of alternating X-cuts and hobstars, bowl's disk fits into conical foot, polished pontil, "Tuthill" written in script, 13" diameter, height 16", $6,912.00.

Bowl, finger, green overlay to clear, honeycomb cutting, multi-rayed base, 2" high, 4¼" diameter, $36.00.

Bowl, rose, pedestal, wide ribbed pattern around sides, signed "Libbey" in circle, 6½" tall, 4½" top opening, $158.00.

Bowl, signed "Taylor Brothers Company, Incorporated, " 9" x 4½" stars, hobstars, and ferns, $382.00.

Butter pat, cut signed "Hoare," hobstar and crossed ovals, $43.00.

Candlesticks, paneled stem with teardrop, rayed base, faceted ball, signed "Hawkes," $648.00 pair.

Carafe, water, Drape pattern, signed "Straus," $274.00.

Celery, Encore pattern, signed "Straus," $238.00.

Celery, Harvard pattern, signed "Hoare," 11¼" long, $216.00.

Celery, Libbey's Harvard pattern, 11", $180.00.

Centerpiece, bowl spherical, scalloped and swirled leaf panels alternate with strawberry-diamonds, clear, rim curves inward, 11½" diameter, 5½" high, J.Hoare and company, $1,260.00.

Centerpiece, canoe shape, Brilliant cut, high pointed ends, scalloped rims, Quarter Diamond pattern 12½" long, 4" high, J.Hoare and Company, $1,224.00.

Charger, 12½" diameter, signed "Tuthill," intaglio strawberry leaf and vine, $526.00.

Cheese, covered, Brilliant cut, American shield pattern, $576.00.

Cologne, bell shaped, original stopper deep all over gravic cutting, signed "Hawkes," $216.00.

Compote, heavy, fine cutting, hobstars, 6", signed "Clark," $360.00.

Compote, signed "Clark," 5½" high, 5" diameter, Leicester pattern, $382.00.

Compote, signed "Tuthill," 14½" x 6½", Intaglio Vintage pattern, $238.00.

Cup punch, Tuthill, vintage pattern, 3½" high, 3" diameter, bell shaped, flaring rim, short stem, circular foot ear handle, $144.00.

Decanter, blown out 6 lobed base, applied cut Cranberry handle, Cranberry 6 lobed stopper, sterling collar, polished pontil, 9½", $252.00.

Decanter, handled, Primrose pattern, 12" high, signed "Tuthill," $612.00.

Decanters, pair, Dorflinger's Renaissance, $468.00 pair.

Dish, oblong, 5⅞" x 4½", signed "Tuthill," Rosemere pattern, $302.00.

Fernery, signed "Pitkin and Brooks," 7¾" diameter, florals and X-cut diamonds in panels, $158.00.

Flask, overall cutting, sterling top, $238.00.

Glass, champagne, shallow saucer shaped bowl, flint glass, deeply cut hobstars between miter cuts, hollow hour glass stem with flutes and notches, circular foot, sunburst underneath, 5", J. Hoare and Company, $86.00.

Glass, juice, Russian cut, 4", $101.00.

Glass, wine, clear, bucket-shaped bowl, large engraved iris design, straight button knob stem, circular foot with flower wreaths, 5½" tall, T.G. Hawkes Gravic trademark, $94.00.

Glass, wine, oval bowl, etched flowers and leaves, double knob stem, circular foot, polished pontil, clear, 5¾", signed "Locke Art," $137.00.

Glass, wine, Russian cut, $72.00.

Goblet, signed "Bergen," star base, three 16 pointed hobstars, fans and strawberry diamond vesicas, $86.00.

Goblet, signed "Hawkes," 5¾" high, gravic florals, $137.00.

Goblet, signed "Hawkes," 6¾" high, intaglio Three Fruits, $202.00.

Humidor, Brilliant cut, zipper, bull's eye, full hobstar bottom, 9½" high x 4½" diameter, $756.00.

Jar, tobacco, signed "J. Hoare and Company," 7⅛" high, fitted lid, hobstars, swags, faceted cuttings, $785.00.

Jug, whiskey, original stopper, Cranberry to clear, $720.00.

Lamp, with prisms, Brilliant cut, Harvard pattern, 18" $1,728.00.

Nappy, handled, engraved flowers between hobstars, 6", signed "Hawkes," $79.00.

Nappy, signed "Pitkin and Brooks," double handled, Crete pattern, $194.00.

Pitcher, Brilliant cut, corset-shaped, cut geometric pattern of sunbursts and x's, scalloped rim, high lip has notched prism cuts, ear shaped handle with rings and notches, 10", Dithridge and Company, Cambridge, Massachusetts, $410.00.

Pitcher, Brilliant cut, vase-like, narrow corset-shape, high serrated pouring lip, cut vertical rows alternating with hobstars, larger hobstars at the base, notched ear shaped handle, 14½" high, Ideal Cut Glass Company, Canastota, New York, $936.00.

Pitcher, cylindrical, flared at the bottom, large hobstars below scalloped rim, notched prism on lower body, 9¼" tall, small lip, ear shaped handle, cut sunburst base, signed "J. HOARE & CO./1853/CORNING" on the base, $540.00.

Pitcher, globe-shaped, clear, cut strawberry diamonds and fans below the neck, vertical cut panels at the neck, scalloped lip, notched ear shaped handle, cut sunburst base, 8½" high, C. Dorflinger and Sons, $454.00.

Pitcher, syrup, well cut, silverplated top, small, $122.00.

Pitcher, water, Triple Square pattern, signed "Clark," $576.00.

Plate, Brilliant cut, clear with scalloped rim, flat in shape of 8 pointed star, cut 8 pointed star covers the plate, 13½" diameter, acid stamped "Hawkes," $1,584.00.

Salt and pepper shakers, Russian pattern, Canterbury sterling tops, $238.00.

Set, pitcher, 4 tumblers, signed "Egginton," Thistle pattern, $612.00.

Set, sugar and creamer, signed "Keystone Cut Glass Company," double handles, double spout on creamer, rare, $1,116.00.

Tray, Brilliant cut, ice cream, oval cut hobstar center with fans on each side, hobstars and strawberry diamonds on the border, scalloped rim, 13" long, marked "J. Hoare and Company," $972.00.

Tray, celery, cut, signed "Clark," pinwheel plus other varied cutting, $266.00.

Tray, celery, signed "Tuthill," 11" x 5", intaglio primrose, hobstar vesicas, $504.00.

Tray, ice cream, cut hobstar, cane, fan, strawberry diamond, signed with maple leaf mark, Maple City Glass company, 14½" x 8", $792.00.

Vase, Gracia pattern, 4½" x 9", bands of fine lines, 3 engraved medallions, signed "Hawkes," $252.00.

Vase, pedestaled with large faceted ball, Queen's pattern, hobstar base, 18" tall, $1,872.00.

Wine, Monarch pattern, Hoare, $86.00.

CUT VELVET

Bottle vase, rose-pink, 7¼" high, Diamond Quilted, white lining, $238.00.

Bowl, finger, sky blue, white lining, Diamond Quilted, 2½" high, $216.00.

Bowl, rose, Diamond Quilted, globular with peaked scalloped rim, 4½" high, $252.00.

Bowl, rose, Swirled blue ribbon, 4" diameter, $216.00.

Bowl, square top, 4¼", pink to white, Diamond Quilted, $252.00.

Creamer unique pinks and whites, L shaped opalescent handle, Diamond Quilted, 3½", $360.00.

Cup, punch, white lining, pink, Diamond Quilted, $122.00.

Ewer, applied handles, rose to white, 11" Diamond Quilted, $396.00.

Pitcher, rosy pink, white lining, Honeycomb, applied amber handle, 4½" high, $497.00.

Set, water, rare, pitcher, 6 tumblers, butterscotch, Quilted Diamond, $1,224.00.

Tumbler, yellow to white, rose lining, scarce, $122.00.

Vase, blue, vertical ribs, 8", $266.00.

Vase, cranberry red over white, Diamond Quilted, bulbous, flared ruffled rim, 9¼", $216.00.

Vase, Diamond Quilted, white lining, green, 6¼" $180.00.

Vase, pink Herringbone pattern, bulbous base, 11" $310.00.

De VILBISS

Bottle, perfume, 5" high, signed, gold trim, 3 etched panels and foot, $194.00.

Bottle, perfume, 7" high, signed, gold crackle, Art Deco, black trim, $144.00.

Bottle, perfume, black shiny glass with chrome neck, $108.00.

Perfume, atomizer, black and gold decoration, 9¼", $180.00.

Perfume, atomizer, blue glass, black enameled designs, $108.00.

Perfume, atomizer, Durand, orange iridescence, graceful shape, 7¾" tall, signed "De Vilbiss," $360.00.

Perfume, atomizer, green, cut leaf design, signed, $194.00.

Perfume, atomizer, gilded with black enameling, $122.00.

Perfume, atomizer, signed, mesh bulb and cord, amber iridescence, $288.00.

Perfume, atomizer, tapered top, amber jewel set in the cap, allover exquisite gold decor, $346.00.

Set, dresser, 7 pieces, signed, gold trim, enameled flowers, $1,008.00.

Set, perfume atomizer, lidded box, round tray, iridescent and gilded, $367.00.

DORFLINGER

Bowl, finger and underplate, Picket Fence, $93.00.

Bowl, Prince of Wales, Plumes pattern, 7" high, 9" diameter, knob stem, hobstar foot, $554.00.

Bowl, punch, Marlboro pattern, twelve 8 pointed hobstars in a chain, 24 point hobstar center, strawberry diamond and fan, 24 point hobstar base, 2 pieces, 11½" high, 14⅛" diameter, $2,160.00.

Bucket, ice, Marlboro pattern, tabs on handles, underplate, $2,016.00 set.

Carafes, pair, 8¼" high, cut oval and Split pattern, $497.00 pair.

Dip, salt master, Parisian pattern, paperweight style, $130.00.

Fernery, Picket Fence pattern, cut, $79.00.

Glass, juice, Parisian pattern, 3⅞" high, $216.00.

Jar, cookie, Sussex pattern, cut, hobstar base, sterling cover marked "Gorham," repousse with roses, shells, daisies, buds and leaves, 6¼" high, $540.00.

Nappy, 6½" diameter, cut, Cramberry to clear, cross-cut diamonds, strawberry diamond and fan, $684.00.

Perfume, green cut to clear, 7¾", attributed to Dorflinger, faceted stopper, Montrose pattern, clear thumbprints alternate with Harvard pattern, variant, $612.00.

Perfume, original stopper, cut, hobstar base, Marlboro pattern, $230.00.

Pitcher, water, Colonial pattern, 7½" high, $281.00.

Pitcher, water, cut, bulbous, 8", Colonial pattern, $324.00.

Plate, 7½" diameter, cut, American pattern, scalloped and serrated rim, $86.00.

Plate, 6¼" diameter, cut, Picket Fence pattern, $50.00.

Set, salad, 3 pieces 10" square bowl, sterling fork and spoon, cut handles, Parisian pattern, $2,376.00.

Tumbler, Old Colony pattern, 3¾" high, $187.00.

Vase, 7½" high, cut, Kalana Geranium pattern, $122.00

Vase, 6" high, Kalana Pansy pattern, $108.00.

Cruet, cut, fan and star cutting, pattern number 80, $180.00.

Wine, circa 1893, knobbed stem, Colonial pattern, $86.00.

DURAND

Bowl, rose, bulbous, iridescent peacock blue, 7½" diameter, signed, $1,080.00.

Bowl, rose signed, blue and silver, King Tut pattern, $756.00.

Bowl, rose, Moorish Crackle, cranberry and white, 2¾" high, $288.00.

Bowl, signed, orange and iridescent gold, 4" high x 10" diameter, $648.00.

Box, covered, green luster and gold, King Tut pattern, 3¼" x 2¾", $1,404.00.

Compote, signed and numbered, 6¾" high x 7" diameter, gold iridescent, $540.00.

Cup and saucer, signed, iridescent gold, $468.00 set.

Jar, covered, green pulled feather on finial shaped lid and jar, white iridescent ground, 11", signed "V DURAND 1994-8," $1,584.00.

Jar, covered, green triple overlay, 11", vertical ribs, signed "DURAND," rare, $3,168.00.

Jar, covered, rare, 7" high, silver marvered threads on red iridescent, $3,888.00.

Lamp, electric, signed, 7½", calcite ground, gold loops, $936.00.

Light, wrought iron night mount with berries, iridescent cylindrical form, green King Tut pattern, 9¾" tall, $770.00.

Perfume, original stopper, 6" tall, gold with gold iridescent threading, $828.00.

Plate, white pulled feathers on ruby, pink circle over the feathers, "Bridgeton Rose" by Charles Link engraved on reverse side, $468.00.

Shade, 5½" high, gold lining, blue and gold hearts, gold threading on white, $180.00.

Shade, 5½", gas, scalloped, gold interior, white, blue, and gold leaves, $180.00.

Sherbet and underplate, King Tut pattern, $497.00 set.

Sherbet, signed, green, white feathering, $360.00.

Tazza, gold iridescence, signed, 6¾" x 7¾", gold spider webbing, $1,073.00.

Tumbler, amber, signed, $144.00.

Vase, blue feathering on ivory, overlay threading, gold calcite interior, 9¼", $1,080.00.

Vase, blue iridescent on gold crackle, signed "V DURAND," 12" $828.00.

Vase, bulbous, 16" tall, tapered neck, signed, iridescent blue, $1,116.00.

Vase, bulbous body, narrow neck and base, intaglio cut, 4 layers, 10¾", signed "V DURAND 1911-70," $1,224.00.

Vase, bulbous form with flaring rim, deep blue iridescence, silver threading, signed "DURAND" in a "V," numbered "1710-6," 6⅛" high, $1,080.00.

Vase, bulbous, silver King Tut on iridescent green, signed, 8" $1,728.00.

Vase, clear crystal cased with red, intaglio flowers and pulled feathers, 10" high, signed "DURAND," $1,058.00.

Vase, covered, white hearts and clinging vines on iridescent blue, 7½" tall, $1,584.00

Vase, crackle, blue and white overlay on frosted clear glass, 10½" high, signed "DURAND" in a large "V," $1,058.00.

Vase, cylinder shaped with bulbous body near the circular base, raspberry coloring silvered King Tut pattern, gold interior, 12½", silvered "DURAND" signature, $1,440.00.

Vase, cylindrical body, iridescent gold ground, silver green whorls, King Tut pattern, marked "DURAND 1910," 10", $936.00.

Vase, Egyptian Crackle, spherical body, opal glass with gold and green overlay, lustered, 5½", $936.00.

Vase, gold iridescence, bulbous with thin neck, turned down collar, 8" signed "V DURAND 20161-8," intaglio cut florals between bands, $1,404.00.

Vase, gold King Tut, green ground, pink and lavender highlights, signed, 12½", $1,440.00.

Vase, gold luster background, green Heart and Clinging vine design, classical shape, 6¼", $648.00.

Vase, iridescent baluster form, muted yellow ground, striated yellow feathers edged in blue, rare twin applied yellow handles, gold latticed threading, inscribed "DURAND 1302," 8" high, $1,584.00.

Vase, iridescent, bulbous, long tapered neck, 15½" tall, ivory King Tut pattern on gold, signed "DURAND" in a "V" number "1974-15," $1,224.00.

Vase, iridescent gold lining, 6" high, green pulled loops on platinum, $1,130.00.

Vase, King Tut pattern, 9", green and gold, circular pedestal, $972.00.

Vase, King Tut pattern, green background, silver swirls, white interior, signed, $1,440.00.

Vase, red to clear overlay, cut vertical design, 9¾", $1,044.00.

Vase, signed, 7", iridescent blue, $540.00.

Vase, swollen cylindrical shape, short inverted rim, iridescent, golden yellow translucent glass, air bubbles in a Raindrop pattern, 6" high, inscribed "DURAND 1968-6," $828.00.

Vase, urn-shaped, flarin grim, 9¼" high, yellow gold interior, opaque white exterior, Blue Feather pattern, overlaid with horizontal gold threading, polished pontil, signed "V DURAND," $842.00.

Vase, urn shaped, signed, 8" tall, King Tut pattern, green to apricot gold, $1,152.00.

Vase, white feather design, cranberry collar and foot, 9¾", $1,320.00.

Vase, white ground, heart shaped leaves, orange and gray, 10", signed, $756.00.

Vase, 3 engraved thistles on iridescent amber, signed, 4" high, $216.00.

Vase, 7" tall, signed, oiled luster, opal leaf and vines, $540.00.

Vase, 7" high, intaglio cut, signed "V DURAND," $2,016.00.

Vase, 11½" tall, blue luster exterior, silver luster interior, signed, $1,116.00.

FENTON

Basket, wicker handle, turned down sides, opaque royal blue, 1930s, 5" diameter at base, $137.00.

Vase, cobalt blue, 7⅝", paper label reads: "Fenton Art Glass," mottled red, orange, green, and yellow, applied ear handles, black Spider Web threading, $648.00.

Vase, footed, circa 1925, "Karnak Red," entwining vines and heart shaped leaves, $626.00.

Vase, green, Dancing Ladies pattern, 9" $302.00.

Vase, "Mosaic," 9" cobalt blue body, mottled red, orange, and yellow, marvered Spider Webbing, lustre finish, $504.00.

Vase, oriental Ivory ground, "Hanging Hearts" decor, circa 1925, $288.00.

Vase, Peking blue, covered, 12" high, "Dancing Ladies," $770.00.

Vase, periwinkle blue, 9" high, "Dancing Ladies" pattern, $288.00.

FOSTORIA

Bowl, rose, Iris glass, no neck, small opening, opal glass body, gold lustre leaf design runs horizontally around the ovoid body, $238.00.

Decanters, clear, American pattern, in metal holder, metal chain, tabs engraved "Scotch" and "Rye," $302.00 set.

Lamp, vase shaped pedestal, flared foot, domical shade, rests on 3 brass spiders, opal glass, horizontal pulled threaded design in green and gold lustre, 15" high, $1,296.00.

Shade, bell-shape, gold interior, gold stylized leaves and vines, perpendicular designs on pearly white, $245.00.

Shade, gold and green leaf and vine design, heavy random gold threading, gold liner, $266.00.

Shade, gold lining, ruffled edge, open flower shape, Festoon pattern, pulled gold design on white, $195.00.

Shade, green and gold leaf and vine on opal glass, 4 sided, $230.00.

Shade, green ground, platinum King Tut pattern, $518.00.

Shade, heavy, 7", green festoons on opal glass, $230.00.

Shade, larger parlor type, pearl white ground, gold lustre tendrils and heart-shaped leaves touched with green run perpendicular, gold lustre lining, $324.00.

Shade, opal ground, gold zipper design over green, $252.00.

Shade, opalescent, pulled green feathers, outlined in gold, $216.00.

Vase, clear pedestal base, ribbed bowl, rim turned down, acid etched acorns and oak leaves, $180.00.

Vase, gold lustre, Iris glass, 4½" high, footed, 3 pinched in sides, short narrow neck, $216.00.

FRY

Basket, 7½" high x 7¼" wide, white opaline, Delft blue handle, $432.00.

Bowl, cut, Chain Hobstars, Fans, Rayed base, 9" signed "Fry," $302.00.

Candlesticks, 12" high, white opaline, Delft blue diagonal threading, blue wafers, Foval, $324.00 pair.

Creamer, blue Delft handle, Foval, opaline with blue loopings, scarce, $216.00.

Cruet, opaline Foval, cobalt applied handle, cobalt stopper, $425.00.

Cup and saucer, Foval, jade green handle on opaline, $144.00 set.

Cup, custard, ovenware, dated 1919, $14.00.

Cups, bouillon with underplates, Foval, 12 double handles in deep opaque blue, scarce, $792.00 set.

Dish, casserole, covered, oval, blue finial, 1½ qts, marked "Fry OVENGLASS 1925-6 PAT, 5-8-17 PAT. 5-27-19," $65.00.

Dish, tri-cornered, cut, signed, 9¾" wide, flaring notched prism, $828.00.

Nappy, opaline, handled, $72.00.

Pan, bread, opalescent ovenware, $29.00.

Pitcher, lemonade, clear Craquelle, covered, jade green handle, $158.00.

Plate, pie, ovenware, $29.00.

Plate, 7" square, cut, Brighton pattern, $223.00.

Reamer, juice, opaline, marked, $65.00.

Set, creamer and sugar, opaline, Foval, Delft blue handles, $288.00.

Set, tea, opaline pot, 5 cups and saucers, $648.00.

Sherbet, Foval, opaline, applied blue stem and foot, $115.00.

Teapot, covered, Foval, opaline, green spout, handle, and lid's finial, $252.00.

Toothpick holder, 2¼" high, opaline, Foval, applied blue handles, $72.00.

Tumbler, cut highball, 5½" tall, cylindrical glass, elaborate cut pattern, pinwheel central motif, plan rim, flat base had cut hobstar underneath, marked "Fry," $122.00.

Vase, clear Craquelle, amethyst applied rosettes, $72.00.

Vase, jack-in-the-pulpit, 11" high, foval, opaline, blue spiral twist, 3 rows of Delft blue at rim, $252.00.

Vase, tall, opaline, Foval, applied blue pedestal base, $396.00.

GILLINDER

Bowl, covered, Classic, 7", hexagonal open log feet, $194.00.

Bowl, covered, oblong, Frosted Lion, collared base, 6⅞" x 3⅞", $166.00.

Bowl, covered, oblong, Frosted Lion, collared base, 7½" x 4¾", $173.00.

Bowl, covered, oblong, Frosted Lion, collared base, 9" x 5½", $194.00.

Bowl, open, Classic, 8" hexagonal, open log feet, $79.00.

Bowl, sugar, covered, Classic, collared base, $230.00.

Bowl, sugar, covered, Classic, open log feet, $266.00.

Bowl, sugar, covered, rampant lion finial, $122.00.

Bowl, sugar, covered, Westward Ho, $223.00.

Bowl, sugar, open, Classic, log feet, $187.00.

Bowl, sugar, open, Frosted Lion, $72.00.

Bust, Abraham Lincoln, opaque white, 6" high, $612.00.

Bust, George Washington, 5" high, $382.00.

Child's miniature table set, all clear Lion, 4 piece, $612.00 set.

Compote, covered, Classic, 6½" diameter, collared base, $230.00.

Compote, covered, Classic, 6½" diameter, open log feet, $360.00.

Compote, covered, collared base, rampant lion finial, oval, 6¾" x 7" high, $202.00.

Compote, covered, 6" diameter x 12" high, Westward Ho, $296.00.

Compote, covered, 8" high x 7½" diameter, Classic, open log feet, $331.00.

Compote, covered, 8" diameter x 14" high, Westward Ho, $432.00.

Compote, covered, 8½" diameter, Classic, collared base, $266.00.

Compote, covered, 12½" diameter, Classic, collared base, $482.00.

Compote, covered, low standard, 8" diameter, Westward Ho, $425.00.

Compote, covered, lion's head finial, 7" diameter x 11" high, $144.00.

Compote, covered, low standard, 6" diameter, Westward Ho, $223.00.

Compote, covered, oval 7¾" high, rampant lion finial, $194.00.

Compote, covered, oval 10" x 6½", low standard Westward Ho, $253.00.

Compote, covered, oval, 12" high, 8" x 5½", Westward Ho, $432.00.

Compote, covered, oval, Westward Ho, 6¾" x 42", $238.00.

Compote, covered, rampant lion finial, 8" diameter x 13" high, $209.00.

Compote, open, 7¾" diameter, Classic, open log feet, $137.00.

Compote, open, 8" high, Westward Ho, $108.00.

Compote, open, 9" high x 9" oblong, Frosted Lion, $122.00.

Compote, open, high standard, 7¾" diameter, Frosted Lion, $115.00.

Compote, open, low standard, 8" oblong, Frosted Lion, $151.00.

Creamer, Classic, $194.00.

Creamer, Frosted Lion, $94.00.

Creamer, low pedestal circular foot, handled, Westward Ho, $166.00.

Creamer, open sugar bowl, Westward Ho, 2 pieces, $266.00 pair.

Dip, salt, master, rectangular, Frosted Lion, collared base, $518.00.

Dish, butter, covered, Classic collared base, $194.00.

Dish, butter, covered, Classic, open log feet, $266.00.

Dish, butter, covered, rampant lion finial, $144.00.

Dish, cheese, covered, scarce, rampant lion finial, $468.00.

Dish, butter, covered, Westward Ho, $274.00.

Dish, duck cover, amber, $79.00.

Dish, pickle, oval, Westward Ho, $72.00.

Dish, sauce, 5" diameter, Frosted Lion, $36.00.

Dish, sauce, Classic, $58.00.

Dish, sauce, footed, Westward Ho, $50.00.

Egg cup, Frosted Lion, $108.00.

Figurine, Buddha, amber, 6" high, $65.00.

Figurine, Buddha, orange, 5¼" high, signed "GILLINDER," $130.00.

Goblet, Classic, scarce, $302.00.

Goblet, Frosted Lion, $108.00.

Goblet, Westward Ho, $128.00.

Jar, marmalade, covered, rampant lion finial, $130.00.

Paperweight, faceted, attributed to Charles Challinor, pink and blue canes surround a red and white cane within a large white cane, concentric rings of pink, blue, white, and blue-green, 3" diameter, $382.00.

Paperweight, Frosted Lion, $194.00.

Paperweight, Ruth the gleaner, $166.00.

Paperweight, slab type, intaglio portrait, Abraham Lincoln, 1876 circa date, $128.00.

Pitcher, Frosted Lion, $324.00.

Pitcher, milk, Classic, open log feet, scarce, $756.00.

Pitcher, milk, 8" high, Westward Ho, $382.00.

Pitcher, water, Classic, $396.00.

Pitcher, water, hexagonal, 6 Gothic arches, Classic, alternating draped women, Daisy and Button panels, 9¼", feet and handle are barklike, $504.00.

Pitcher, water, Westward Ho, $310.00.

Plate, 10" diameter, "Blaine," signed Jacobus, $281.00.

Plate, 10" diameter, "Cleveland," $274.00.

Plate, 10" diameter, "Logan," $338.00.

Plate, 10" diameter, "Warrior," signed Jacobus, $202.00.

Plate, bread, handles, Frosted Lion, rope edge, 10½" diameter, $94.00.

Platter, bread, Westward Ho, $144.00.

Platter, lion handles, 10½" x 9", oval, $128.00.

Relish, Frosted Lion, $58.00.

Set, berry, 5 pieces, Classic pattern, 4 sauces and master bowl, $410.00.

Shakespeare, frosted bust, marked, 5" high, $266.00.

Slipper, lady's clear glass, marked "Gillinder & Sons Centennial Exhibition" 3" x 6" long, $58.00.

Spooner, Classic, $166.00.

Spooner, Frosted Lion, $94.00.

Spooner, Westward Ho, $115.00.

Toothpick holder, "Just Out" chick, $144.00.

Vase, celery, 6½" high, Classic open log feet, $281.00.

Vase, celery, collared base, Classic, $180.00.

Vase, celery, Frosted Lion, plain, $108.00.

Vase, celery, Westward Ho, $180.00.

Vase, celery, stitched, Frosted Lion, $158.00.

Vase, hand, frosted, impressed "Gillinder Centennial," $65.00.

Vase, white ferns and other leaves, collar rings, blue background, cameo, medium size, extremely rare, ovoid shaped body, straight neck, $2,448.00.

Vase, ivy vines, ruffled collar ring, ruby ground, cameo, large size, extremely rare, ovoid shape, tapers to a joined foot, tapered neck, $2,736.00.

Vase, white stylized leaves and vines, yellow background, cameo, small size, extremely rare, pear shape, flared rim, $2,160.00.

GUNDERSEN

Basket, applied thorn handle, Burmese, circa: 1955, $353.00.

Bottle, banjo, Peach blow, 6¾", $194.00.

Bowl, rose, Peach Blow, 3½", applied leaves, $86.00.

Bowl, rose, pinched ruffled top, 3½", $94.00.

Compote, floriform, acid finish, 7" diameter x 6" high, $554.00.

Creamer, acid finish, applied handle, $367.00.

Cup and saucer, Peach blow, rich coloration, Peach Blow handle, satin finish, $266.00 set.

Ewer, Peach Blow, 6", $209.00.

Goblet, enameled forget-me-nots, 6¾", $158.00.

Hat, glossy, Burmese, 2" whimsey, $137.00.

Hat, Peach Blow, Diamond Quilted, excellent color, 2⅞", whimsey, $122.00.

Plate, 8" diameter, $108.00.

Tumbler, 5" high, $180.00.

Tumbler, shiny, 4" tall, $122.00.

Vase, celery, acidized, Hobnail pattern, Burmese, 7", $324.00.

Vase, enameled, glossy, 3", $540.00.

Vase, Peach Blow, trefoil shape, 9¼", $432.00.

Wine, satin finish, $209.00.

HANDEL

Candlesticks, Dutch windmills and enameled landscapes, baluster shape, flared foot, frosted, artist signed, 8½" high, $1,728.00 pair.

Holder, cigars, hinged top, bear design at bottom and top, 3¼" x 6", $310.00.

Humidor, cover has fez and the word "Cigars," Shriner's emblem, jeweling, star, man riding a camel, brown and green with gold and white trim, $864.00.

Humidor, ornate metal lid, opalware, owl on a pine branch, 5" high, signed and numbered, $504.00.

Humidor, pewter top, pipe finial, horse and dog decor, browns and greens on opal, signed "Braun," $540.00.

Humidor, silverplated collar and cover, Indian chief on russet to green ground, signed, $504.00.

Lamp, Boudoir, #5853, windmill scene, rare glass base, $1,548.00.

Lamp, Boudoir, conical leaded shade, white panels with purple band, metal base, $684.00.

Lamp, desk, green chipped ice shade, bronze base, signed and numbered, $1,368.00.

Lamp, double student, green and yellow chipped ice shades, bronze base, 24", $1,728.00.

Lamp, lilies and buds in green and white, bronze base, 16" x 22", signed, $7,200.00.

Lamp, piano, leaded poppies on a rose background, bronze stand, 14" tall, $1,152.00.

Lamp, shade, chipped ice, tree design, 14", base signed, $15,840.00.

Lamp, table, 15" diameter, autumn hued reverse painted shade, amber to blue, round foot, baluster shaped metal standard, 21½" high, $1,296.00.

Lamp, table, amber, green, and carmel leaded shade, 19" diameter, metal base, $1,080.00.

Lamp, table, birds flying in a tropical setting, 16" diameter, $3,600.00.

Lamp, table, blue and green Wisteria, carmel geometrics, 25" high, $5,040.00.

Lamp, table, chipped ice shade painted in reverse, parrots in tropical trees, blue, yellow and green background, Chinese urn shaped base, 24½" to the finial, $11,520.00.

Lamp, table, cupola shaped leaded glass, yellow daffodils, green leaves, pale green and white ground, bronze base with overlapping lily pads, 25" tall, impressed "HANDEL," $2,376.00.

Lamp, table, domical shade, bright and olive green stylized oak leaves, opaque yellow ground, chipped grey-green stippling, painted signature "Handel #5351," bronze base, original Handel cloth label, 20½" high, $1,224.00.

Lamp, table, domical leaded shade, 20" diameter, apple blossoms and leaves, cast floral bronze base, 29½", $4,608.00.

Lamp, table, leaded shade, Chinese bronze urn shaped base, 20" tall, $4,320.00.

Lamp, table, reverse painted domical shade, yellow moonlit scene with tepee and trees, bronze base with leaves, 22½" high, $1,080.00.

Lamp, table, scene of lake and trees painted in reverse, 18" diameter shade, grey, black, green, 22" high, metal base, $7,200.00.

Lamp, table, windmill scene painted on reverse side of shade, 14" diameter, patinated metal base, $2,376.00.

Lamp, wall globe, 18" diameter, cobalt Bluebird on floral ground, $648.00.

Pitcher, Limoges blank, pink roses and white carnations, 9½" $360.00.

Plate, cake, 2 handles, pink florals, gold edged, 10 diameter, $115.00.

Shade, hanging leaded, colorful scrolls and rosettes, bronze plated, signed, 25" diameter, $8,640.00.

Vase, "Teroma" woodland scene, artist signed, 10" high, $2,160.00.

Vase, floral decor, beaded brass top, raised scroll design, 12" tall, signed, $864.00.

HEISEY

Bookends, Angel Fish, clear, 7", $259.00 pair.

Bookends, horse, rearing, clear, 7¾", $281.00.

Bookends, Scottie Dog, 5" high, 1941-46, $288.00.

Bottle, cologne, original stopper, Winged Scroll, $382.00.

Bowl, Cornucopia, 11", cobalt blue, Warwick, $432.00.

Bowl, fruit, Winged Scroll, 8½" diameter, $266.00.

Bowl, master berry, Ring Band, Custard, $173.00.

Bowl, master berry, Winged Scroll, boat shaped, 11" long, $158.00.

Bowl, sugar, covered, Ring Band, $194.00.

Bowl, sugar, covered, Winged Scroll, $274.00.

Bucket, ice, dolphin feet, grape and leaf sterling silver overlay, $108.00.

Bull, clear, 4" high, 1948-52, $1,872.00.

Candlesticks, Flamingo pink, 6" high, dolphin feet, $266.00 pair.

Candlesticks, frosted, Flamingo, cherub, $842.00 pair.

Candlesticks, Lariat, $310.00 pair.

Candlesticks, petticoat dolphins, flamingo pink, $374.00 pair.

Candlesticks, Saraha yellow, chintz etching, $144.00 pair.

Candlesticks, Sahara yellow, dolphin footed, Empress pattern, $324.00 pair.

Centerpiece, tropical fish, large and small with coral, 12", $1,584.00.

Champagne, tangerine, plain stem, Spanish pattern, $446.00.

Clydesdale horses, clear, 8" high, 1942-48, $720.00.

Compote, 10", Fandango pattern, $137.00.

Compote, jelly, Ring Band, $223.00.

Compote, Saturn pattern, Limelight, $194.00.

Cordial, Alexandrite (orchid) bowl, short stem, Carcassone pattern, $137.00.

Cornucopia, footed, marked, cobalt blue, $396.00.

Creamer, Ring Band, $130.00.

Creamer, Winged Scroll, $137.00.

Cruet, green, gold trim, Pineapple and Fan, $360.00.

Cruet, original top, Ring Band, $468.00.

Cruet, original stopper, Winged Scroll, $266.00.

Cup, Custard, Winged Scroll, $72.00.

Decanter, Carcassone pattern, Alexandrite, $576.00.

Dish, butter, covered, Ring Band, $338.00.

Dish, butter, covered, Winged Scroll, $238.00.

Dish, olive, Winged Scroll, $72.00.

Dish, pickle, Beaded Swag, Custard, $396.00.

Dish, pickle, Winged Scroll, $72.00.

Dish, sauce, 4½" diameter, Winged Scroll, $50.00.

Dish, sauce, Ring Band, $72.00.

Dish, sauce, souvenir, Beaded Swag, $72.00.

Dog, Airedale, clear, 6" high, 1948-49, $835.00.

Donkey, clear, standing, 6½" high, 1944-53, $259.00.

Elephant, 4½" high, trunk up, 1944-53, $230.00.

Gazelle, clear, 11" high, 1927-49, $1,872.00.

Giraffe, head straight, clear, 11¼", 1942-52, $216.00.

Giraffe, head turned, clear, 11", 1942-52, $223.00.

Goblet, Beaded Swag, $79.00.

Goblet, souvenir, Beaded Swag, $115.00.

Goblet, 10 ounce, Spanish, cobalt blue bowl, $115.00.

Goose, wings down, clear, 5¾", 1942-53, $454.00.

Goose, wings half up, clear, 6½", 1942-53, $115.00.

Goose, wings up, clear, 6½", 1942-53, $137.00.

Hen, clear, 5½", 1948-49, $598.00.

Holder, cigarette, emerald green, Winged Scroll, $216.00.

Holder, match, fish, clear, $115.00.

Holder, match, Winged Scroll, $238.00.

Holder, toothpick, Winged Scroll, $194.00.

Jar, cigar, Winged Scroll, $252.00.

Jar, cigarette, Winged Scroll, $194.00.

Jar, powder, covered, Winged Scroll, $130.00.

Jar, powder, covered, souvenir, Winged Scroll, $86.00.

Mug, Ring Band, $72.00.

Nappy, Winged Scroll, 6", folded, side handle, $86.00.

Pheasant, ringneck, clear, 4¾" high, 1942-53, $209.00.

Pig, mother, 3 piglets, 1948-49, set of 4, $864.00 set.

Pigeon, pouter, clear, 6½", 1947-49, $734.00.

Piglet, sitting, clear, 1", 1948-49, $115.00.

Pitcher, syrup, original top, Winged Scroll, scarce, $526.00.

Pitcher, water, bulbous, Winged Scroll, 9" high, $360.00.

Pitcher, water, Ring Band, $353.00.

Pitcher, water, tankard, Winged Scroll, $360.00.

Plug horse, Sparky, 4¼" tall, cobalt blue, 1941-46, $1,188.00.

Pony kicking, 4" high, clear, $245.00.

Pony standing, 5" high, clear, 1940-52, $115.00.

Receiver, hair, Winged Scroll, $187.00.

Rooster fighting, clear, 8½", 1940-46, $194.00.

Set, berry, 7 pieces, Beaded Swag, $425.00 set.

Set, berry, Winged Scroll, Custard, 6 sauces, master bowl, 7 pieces, $770.00.

Set, condiment, tray, salt and pepper, toothpick holder, compote, 5 pieces, Ring Band, $648.00.

Set console, marked center fishbowl, 8½", candlesticks, $1,044.00.

Set, console, 4 pieces, Sahara yellow, oblong swan handled bowl, oblong flower frog, pair swan handled candlesticks, $936.00.

Set, ice cream, 7 pieces, signed, Sunburst, $166.00.

Set, table, 4 pieces, Winged Scroll, $900.00.

Set, 7 pieces, water pitcher, 6 tumblers, Ring Band, $864.00.

Set, water, 7 pieces, tankard pitcher, 6 tumblers, Winged Scroll, $1,022.00.

Set, water, 5 pieces, tankard pitcher, 4 tumblers, Beaded Swag, $792.00.

Shaker, cocktail, signed, cobalt blue, 4 Roly Poly, $310.00.

Shaker, cocktail, 3 pieces, cut, pheasants, forest scene, $425.00 set.

Shakers, salt and pepper, all original, Ring Band, $180.00 set.

Shakers, salt and pepper, original tops, Winged Scroll, $266.00 set.

Sparrow, clear, 2¼" high, 1942-45, $115.00.

Spooner, Beaded Swag, $122.00.

Spooner, Ring Band, $158.00.

Spooner, Winged Scroll, $130.00.

Swan, baby, clear, 2¼" high, 1947-49, $252.00.

Syrup, original top, Ring Band, $432.00.

Toothpick holder, 2½" high, Ring Band, $137.00.

Toothpick holder, Beaded Swag, $223.00.

Toothpick holder, souvenir, Ring Band, $86.00.

Tray, condiment, Ring Band, $266.00.

Tray, dresser, Winged Scroll, $238.00.

Tub, ice, cut and handled, Flamingo pink, $158.00.

Tumbler, Ring Band, $86.00.

Tumbler, souvenir, Ring Band, $65.00.

Tumbler, souvenir, Beaded Swag, $86.00.

Tumbler, Winged Scroll, $122.00.

Vase, celery, Ring Band, scarce, $454.00.

Vase, celery, Winged Scroll, $425.00.

Wine, souvenir, Beaded Swag, $108.00.

Wine with advertising, Beaded Swag, $122.00.

Wood Duck, clear, 5½" high, $864.00.

HOLLY AMBER

Bowl, berry, 3½" high, 8½" diameter, $936.00.

Bowl, oval, 7⅜" x 4 ⅝", $576.00.

Compote, covered, 6½" diameter, $1,728.00.

Compote, covered, 12½", $1,944.00.

Compote, covered jelly, 4½" diameter, $1,512.00.

Creamer, 3" high, $1,152.00.

Cruet, original stopper, $2,232.00.

Cup, with handle, 5", $720.00.

Dish, covered butter, $1,584.00.

Dish, dolphin covered, 7", $1,440.00.

Dish, relish, oblong, 7½", $828.00.

Dish, sauce, $382.00.

Jug, syrup, original tin lid, $1,130.00.

Mug, handled, 4" tall, $619.00.

Mug, handled, 4½" tall, $684.00.

Parfait, 6" high, $670.00.

Pitcher and 6 tumblers, rare, $5,472.00.

Plate, round cake on pedestal stand, rare 9¼", $2,016.00.

Plate, round, 9¼", $3,024.00.

Set, condiment, 4 pieces on serpentine shaped tray, $1,800.00.

Set, table, 4 pieces, spooner, creamer, covered butter and sugar, $3,888.00.

Toothpick holder, 2½", $432.00.

Toothpick, rare pedestal base, 5", $864.00.

Vase, footed, 6", $828.00.

Tray, pickle, 2 handles, 6½" x 4", $554.00.

Tumbler, 4" high, $554.00.

HONESDALE

Glass, cocktail, colorful enameled fighting roosters, $50.00.

Plate, amethyst, narrow gold border band, Wild Laurel pattern, $122.00.

Plate, crystal, gold decorated border, St. Regis pattern, $108.00.

Tumbler, gold decorated border, crystal, St. Regis pattern, $65.00.

Tumbler, narrow gold decorated border, crystal, Cataract pattern, $50.00.

Vase, Art Nouveau flowers, gold gilding, emerald green background, 14", $216.00.

Vase, basketweave design, 4 single stars in a square are crisscrossed, clear ground, gold tracery, 17½" high, $1,224.00.

Vase, black glass, 14½", etched and gilded, Versailles pattern, $266.00.

Vase, bulbous, green cameo scrolls, gold tracery, 9" high, $504.00.

Vase, cameo, carved and enameled trees, hunters and foxes, royal blue, 11" high, signed, $1,152.00.

Vase, cameo, cased topaz over frosted crystal, etched and gilded decoration, $864.00.

Vase, cameo cattails and wild geese in green cameo, gold outline, 12", $756.00.

Vase, cased amethyst on crystal, stylized floral buds and leaves, etched and gilded decoration, 11" $504.00.

Vase, cased green on frosted crystal, tinted, gilded and etched leaves, landscape and rising sun design, signed "Honesdale," 10¾" high, $648.00.

Vase, cased green on clear crystal, tinted, yellow flowers, gold decoration, 13⅝", $468.00.

Vase, cylindrical, flares at rim and base, clear crystal, gilt decorated flowers and leaves, polished pontil, signed in gold "Honesdale," 14", $396.00.

Vase, green acid cutback, crane and rushes on clear acid etched ground, gold trim, signed, 9" tall, $540.00

Vase, green leaves, purple and red poppies outlined in gold, clear glass background, gold beaded rim, signed, 8½", $540.00.

Vase, red cameo on etched and frosted crystal, flared top, designs outlined in gold, 12", $792.00.

Vase, topaz over frosted crystal, 12½", etched border, floral and scroll designs, stylized, outlined in gold, signed "Honesdale," $864.00.

Vase, yellow cameo scrolls, iridescent crystal, 4" high, $396.00.

IMPERIAL

Bowl, footed, Amberina, Lustre rose, old iron cross mark, $252.00.

Bowl, rose, Jewels, amethyst, signed, $158.00.

Dish, candy, Jewels, covered, pink, $50.00.

Jar, sweetmeat, Jewels, covered, sapphire blue, $137.00.

Vase, bulbous base, long neck, Free Hand, drag loops in blue on opaque white, 10" high, $310.00.

Vase, fan shape, 8½" high, blue threads on Cranberry, $144.00.

Vase, flared top, Free Hand, iridescent orange interior, light blue and cobalt ground, $194.00.

Vase, Free Hand ware, 7" high, iridescent white calcite ground, gold drag loops, $346.00.

Vase, Free Hand, 8" high, frosted ground, iridescent blue random designs, $194.00.

Vase, Free Hand, blue loops on opaque white, 10 high, $310.00.

Vase, Free Hand, drag loop in green on opal, 9" high, $410.00.

Vase, Free Hand, glossy, green, 10" high, iridescent orange interior, $180.00.

Vase, Free Hand, heart shaped leaves and vines in orange on cobalt blue, $324.00.

Vase, Free Hand, iridescent blue ground, 6" high, white leaves and vines, $281.00.

Vase, Free Hand, orange lustre interior, iridescent burgundy drag loops on white, 8½", scarce, $648.00.

Vase, Free Hand, white leaves and vines on green, orange throat, 9" high, $202.00.

Vase, gourd shape, Free Hand, 11¼" high, orange lustre interior, lustred green leaves marvered in white opalescent, scarce, $497.00.

Vase, iridescent dark green ground, silver lily pads and lattice of marvered trails, pear shaped, flaring rim, applied flat foot, 7¾" high, $504.00.

Vase, Jewels, amethyst, 6" high, $194.00.

Vase, Jewels, orange lustre, $115.00.

Vase, orange lustre interior, 9½" high, Free Hand, 3 applied handles, green hearts and vines marvered in opal iridescent, $432.00.

KEW BLAS

Bowl, cup-shaped, flaring rim, domed foot, polished pontil, 3⅞" high, interior reddish orange, exterior opaque white with green feather like pattern on bowl and foot, signed "Kew Blas" in script, $468.00.

Bowl, rose, 4½", signed, butterscotch ground, shaped base, iridescent gold and green Zipper pattern, $864.00.

Candlesticks, iridescent gold, 8", signed, swirled stems, $698.00.

Compote, footed base, 3½" x 4½", baluster support, $576.00.

Creamer, signed, 3¼", gold iridescent, $540.00.

Cup and saucer, signed, applied ornate handle, feather design, iridescent green, gold and ivory, $792.00.

Cuspidor, lady's, signed, pulled green feathers, fluted top, rare, $1,944.00.

Tumbler, iridescent gold, 4 pinched in sides, 3½" tall x 3" diameter, $540.00.

Vase, Kew Blas, amber iridescent Fishscale pattern, wide base, flared out ruffled top, 3¾", signed, $576.00.

Vase, Kew Blas, gold iridescence, double gourd shape, 8½" tall, 5½" diameter, $396.00.

Vase, signed, iridescent gold interior, white top with pulled iridescent gold feathering, 5½", $576.00.

Wine, 4¾", gold iridescence, twisted stem, signed, $216.00.

KIMBLE

Bowl, globe shaped, cluthra, small top opening, blue ground, orange and brown streaks, signed and numbered, $288.00.

Vase, blue, Cluthra, bulbous, signed, 10", $382.00.

Vase, Cluthra, 3 hues, bulbous, flared rim, 6½", $792.00.

Vase, Cluthra, 18", blue ground with yellow spattering, signed, $670.00.

Vase, Cluthra, white, 6", signed, $202.00.

Vase, Cluthra, 4 colors, yellow, white, orange, and green, rare, bulbous, 6½", signed, $1,188.00.

Vase, Cluthra, light blue and orange, signed, 4¼", $288.00.

Vase, 12", Cluthra, signed and numbered, jade and white, baluster shape, $468.00.

Vase, gourd shape, 7¾", cylindrical, white, signed, $266.00.

Vase, green to white, white lining, cluthra, numerous bubbles, 5" high x 3" diameter, $410.00.

Vase, pedestal foot, 8½", orange and white, Cluthra, $281.00.

LAMPS

Candelabrum, 6 branched, green glass cabochons set in each nozzle, oval base has Tiffany Studios circular mark, central handle encloses a snuffer, 15", $4,320.00.

Chandelier, rare convex Alamander leaded glass, pink, orange and yellow flowers, green leaves, 6 beaded chains set in a ceiling mount, overhanging arms support 6 iridescent gold Favrile shades, each shade marked "L.C.T.," 50" high, $33,120.00.

Fixture, circular ceiling mount, 6 iridescent gold shades, bell shaped, interspersed by and on chains with bronze spheres, shades inscribed "L.C.T.," height 17", $3,600.00.

Lamp, bronze floor, "Roman" pattern leaded glass domical shade, 64½", mottled ellipses, lozenges and scallops, uniform cylindrical column with circular foot raised on 4 feet, base impressed "TIFFANY STUDIOS NEW YORK 387," $11,952.00.

Lamp, bronze table, domical leaded Peony shade, delicate pink and blue flowers, yellow centers, raised bronze base on 4 feet, base impressed "TIFFANY STUDIOS NEW YORK 849," shade with impressed tag "TIFFANY STUDIOS NEW YORK 1475-13", height 26½", $28,080.00.

Lamp, bronze table, Dragonfly leaded glass conical shade, 7 dragonflies, olive-green, red eyes, green wings with bronze filigree, bronze base on 5 ball feet, shade and base both stamped "TIFFANY STUDIOS NEW YORK," height 23¼", $11,520.00.

Lamp, bronze table, leaded Acorn glass shade, orange acorns on streaked green panels, buttlet nosed base on 4 raised feet, both marked "TIFFANY STUDIOS NEW YORK", 21¼" high, $2,880.00.

Lamp, bronze table, Poinsettia leaded glass hemispherical form, red flowers, blue and orange centers, bright green leaves, rope twist bronze base with leaf decor, base numbered 366, shade numbered 558, both impressed "TIFFANY STUDIOS," 26" high, $13,680.00.

Lamp, bronze table, Wisteria leaded glass domical shade, irregular lower border, mottled dark and light blue flowers, bright green/yellow leaves, greenish patina bronze tree-form base, 27½" high, both signed "TIFFANY STUDIOS NEW YORK," $61,920.00.

Lamp, cut, signed "Straus and Sons," 18½" high, clear bulbous base, spherical shade, fan, crescent, and hobstar cutting, $3,168.00.

Lamp, desk, bronze, turtleback tiles, emerald green, adjustable oval sade, twin curved arms, domed circular cast foot, stylized leaves and green glass cabochons, impressed "408 TIFFANY STUDIOS NEW YORK" 14½" high, $2,880.00.

Lamp, double gooseneck, Quezal, calcite exterior, gold interior, pearlized base with claw feet, $684.00.

Lamp, Frank Art, girl with raised knee gazes into green Craquelle globe, original wiring, $238.00.

Lamp, Gone with the Wind, ball shade, matching base, opaline glass with green wash, enameled dogwood blossoms, 23" high, brass font signed "Royal," dated "1895," $936.00.

Lamp, Gone with the Wind, enameled jack-in-the-pulpit, 10" ball, 21" high, leaf footed, $792.00.

Lamp, Gone with the Wind, red satin, ball sade, inverted pear shaped base, Baby Face pattern, $1,440.00.

Lamp, Gone with the wind red satin, 24½", circa 1890, brass font marked "Pittsburgh Lamp and Glass Company," puffy ball shaped shade, matching base, $1,080.00.

Lamp, Gone with the wind, signed "TIFFANY STUDIOS," bronze base and glass shade both signed, shade has freeform orange feathers and off-white satin background, 15" tall, $4,320.00.

Lamp, hall, Peach Blow shade, polished and lacquered brass frame, mint, $1,656.00.

Lamp, hanging, H. J. Peters, slag glass, scenic design with cottage and trees, $288.00.

Lamp, kerosene, hanging fixture, domical milk glass shade, painted bluebirds, clear font, original brass frame with chains, glass prisms, $1,224.00.

Lamp, kerosene, hanging fixture, pull down, swirled cranberry shade, brass frame, $468.00.

Lamp, library, double row prismed, ornate frame, embossed font and font holder signed "Miller," 14" shade, apple blossoms on both sides, $1,080.00.

Lamp, Pairpoint, signed, 13¾" high, quatrefoil shade, metal tree base, enameled apples and apple blossoms, $6,624.00.

Lamp, Pairpoint, signed, frosted dome, painted sunset and desert scene, 15¾" high, $3,312.00.

Lamp, signed "Bradley and Hubbard," 22" high, 14" diameter, 6 panels, domed, orchre stained, floral metal border, $1,224.00.

Lamp, signed "Duffner and Kimberly," 73" high, domed, multi-hued flowers and leaves, leaded, gilded bronze base, $18,360.00.

Lamp, signed "Eclipse Lamp company," 20" high, bronze urn base, poppy decor, green and orange slag, $2,124.00.

Lamp, signed "Handel" bronze base, 28" high, domed blue leaded, Sphinx and Egyptian design, $12,528.00.

Lamp, signed "Handel," 22½" high, green domed shade, stormy sea, painted in yellow, salmon, and brown, $3,816.00.

Lamp, signed "Handel," 29" high, domed, blue leaded, tree shaped metal base, wisteria and leaves, $16,920.00.

Lamp, signed "Jefferson," 23¼" high, conical, multicolored, lake scene painted in reverse, etched exterior, $1,584.00.

Lamp, signed "Moe Bridges," 23" high, painted winter scene on the shade, multi-hued, brass base, urn-shaped, $2,232.00.

Lamp, signed "Pairpoint," red domed shade, black and green blossoms in high relief, 24¼" high, $2,016.00.

Lamp, signed "TIFFANY," favrile glass, iridescent amber, blue and green, cabochon jewels, dragonfly border, 28" high, 22" diameter, $48,240.00.

Lamp, signed "TIFFANY," gilded bronze base, concial blue and green leaded shade, yellow fish design, $69,840.00.

Lamp, table, 10 feather green and white shades, lily pad base marked "TIFFANY STUDIOS NEW YORK 381," shades inscribed "L.C.T.," 20¼" tall, $9,360.00.

Lamp, table, Fostoria, circa 1912, cased domical shade, baluster base, white opalescent ground, pulled green feathers edged in amber, 15¼" high x 6⅝" wide, $1,368.00.

Lamp, table, signed "Bradley and Hubbard," bulbous brass base, 12" diameter, domical shade, clear with frosting and floral etching, $396.00.

Lamp, Tiffany bronze twin shaded student lamp, olive-green hemispherical damascene shades, bronze base, adjustable twin columns, gravity feed fuel canister, 29½" high, $3,600.00.

Lamp, Tiffany table, conical yellow Daffodil leaded shade on signed urn-shaped "Grueby" base, rare mottled sky-blue ground shading to turquoise green shade, cucumber green glazed base, molded yellow flowerheads at the shoulder, overall height, 22", $18,720.00.

Lamp, Tiffany, Venetian, gold iridescent Favrile glass and gilt-bronze, torchere form, tapering cylinder, shade housed in open-work bronze mount, rare, circa 1904, shade singed "L.C.T.," 17¾" high, $3,600.00.

Lamp, Tiffany, signed, 16½" high, green and amethyst dome leaded shade, white and yellow roses and butterflies, $97,920.00.

Lamp, Tiffany, signed, 32" high, 22" diameter, bronze base, 6 feet, domed blue leaded shade, red peonies and leaves, $128,160.00.

Shade, chandelier, 9 sided leaded glass, 26½" diameter, green and white mottled panels, floral border in green, red, and yellow, $432.00.

Shade, Duffner-Kimberly, 900 pieces of glass in amber, white, carmel, 28" diameter, fish scale design, 3 vertical decorative columns, perfect, $6,480.00.

LIBBEY

Basket, rare, Amberina, applied amber handle, signed "Libbey," 7½" high, $2,232.00.

Bottle, perfume, original stopper, Amberina, signed $1,008.00.

Bottle, water, cut, Imperial pattern, signed, $281.00.

Bottle, whiskey, cut, matching stopper, 14", signed, intaglio cut sheaves of rye, $281.00.

Bowl, cut, 10" diameter, fluted, Kimberly pattern, $432.00.

Bowl, cut, 10" diameter, Sultana pattern, 16 point hobstar base, signed "Libbey," $425.00.

Bowl, cut, 10⅛" diameter, Stratford pattern, $684.00.

Bowl, cut, 7" diameter, signed, Colonna pattern, $252.00.

Bowl, cut, fruit, Thistle pattern, hat shaped, signed "Libbey," $626.00.

Bowl, Eulalia pattern, cut, fan and hobstars, $569.00.

Bowl, finger, floral etched, signed, $137.00.

Bowl, finger, Grape and Leaf intaglio, 5" x 2½", signed, $216.00.

Bowl, Geometrics, black cut to clear, 12" x 4", signed, $698.00.

Bowl, Maize, white opaque with green leaves, 4" high x 8¾" diameter, $266.00.

Bowl, punch, cut, 2 pieces, signed, Spillane pattern, $4,320.00.

Bowl, rose, 4¼" high, cut, signed, flared ruffled top, foliage and florals, $216.00.

Bowl, signed, cut, Glenda pattern, 2" high x 9" diameter, $497.00.

Bowl, sugar, Peach Blow, enameled "World's Fair 1893," $684.00.

Bowl, Swirl pattern, flared rim, trapped bubbles, dusty pink, 1930s, signed, $324.00.

Box, cream colored satin, signed "Libbey Cut," 4¼", enameled Shasta Daisies, marked "World's Fair 1893," $468.00.

Box, powder, cut, hinged lid, 6" diameter, Florence pattern, $670.00.

Candlestick, air twisted stem, 8" high, signed, $238.00.

Candlestick, clear crystal stem and foot, opalescent cup with pulled pink feather design on the interior surface, signed "Libbey," 6" tall, $1,044.00.

Candlesticks, cut, teardrop stems, plain fluted, 6" high, signed, $468.00 pair.

Candlestick, signed, silhouette of opalescent camel on stem, clear bowl, $372.00.

Carafe, signed, cut, hobstar, fan, and mitre, $209.00.

Champagne, cut, signed "Libbey," engraved ferns and florals, $50.00.

Champagne, squirrel stem, signed "Libbey," $216.00.

Claret, high stem cut, 1920s, Royal Fern pattern, $324.00.

Cocktail, clear, crow silhouetted stem, $108.00.

Cocktail, crystal with opalescent kangaroo stem, signed "Libbey," $180.00.

Compote, Amberina, 5" diameter, signed, $864.00.

Compote, deep color, 6½" high x 4¼" diameter, fluted rim, hollow swirled and ribbed stem, $1,872.00.

Compote, signed, cut, 10½" diameter, knobbed stem with teardrop, geometric cutting, $936.00.

Cordial, cut, signed, Harvard pattern, fluted stems, faceted knobs, 24 ray base, $108.00.

Cordial, signed, cut, long stem, Embassy pattern, $94.00.

Cordial, signed, cut, Princess pattern, $94.00.

Cup and leaf shaped saucer, marked "World's Fair 1893," camphor, $166.00 set.

Cup and saucer, lettered "World's Exposition 1893," vaseline, $209.00 set.

Decanter, handle on the side, cut, Corinthian pattern, $446.00.

Dipc salt, signed, cut overall, pedestal base, $180.00.

Dish, covered butter and underplate, cut, Gloria pattern, domed lid, hobstar and strawberry diamond, $785.00.

Dish, cut, round relish, 6" x 2½", signed "Libbey," $238.00.

Dish, ice cream, cut, Sonora pattern, 17½" long, diamond shaped, $1,440.00.

Dish, square, cut, Eulalia pattern, 10⅞" square, $382.00.

Glass, crystal footed, dark green applied prunts, 3" tall, signed "Libbey," $180.00.

Glass, water, cut, signed, cut in a strawberry diamond, $79.00.

Goblet, controlled bubble stem, signed, 5¼" etched bowl, $86.00.

Goblet, cut, 7¼" high, Cornucopia pattern, $65.00.

Goblet, cut stem, signed "Libbey," $216.00.

Goblet, monkey silhouette, 1930s, $151.00.

Jug, milk, clear with peridot green threading, signed, circa 1930s, $245.00.

Nappy, 7" diameter, signed, cut, Heart pattern, $202.00.

Nappy, signed, cut, hobstars, strawberry diamond and fan, $115.00.

Paperweight, signed, "Columbian Exposition 1893," frosted lady's head, $396.00.

Paperweight, woman's head, 1893 World's Fair, $130.00.

Pitcher, Reverse Amberina, Inverted Thumbprint, melon ribbed, applied handle, 7½" high, signed "Libbey," $900.00.

Pitcher, syrup, Maize, pewter top, iridescent gold cob, blue husks, 6" tall, $576.00.

Plate, cut, 6¾", signed with saber mark, Ellsmere pattern, $187.00.

Plate, cut, signed, 11½" diameter, thistles on 6 panels, $396.00.

Plate, cut, signed, 11¾" diameter, Sultana pattern, $857.00.

Plate, sepia hues, 7¾" diameter, signed, "Santa Maria" ship, $576.00.

Set, Amberina, water pitcher, reeded handle, 4 tumblers, Thumbprint pattern, signed "Libbey," $886.00.

Set, ice cream, 10 dishes, 17" x 10" tray, cut, Jewel pattern, $2,160.00.

Set, lemonade, cut, Scotch Thistle pattern, pitcher and 6 tumblers, $792.00.

Set, salt and pepper, signed, "1893 Exposition," egg on side, blue, $281.00.

Set, stemware, signed, cut, Embassy pattern, 24 pieces, 8 of each, wines, champagnes, and goblets, $2,304.00.

Set, sugar and creamer, Amberina, shallow bowls, vertical ribs, hollow knobbed stems, ribbed circular feet, signed "Libbey" near the polished pontils, amber ear shaped handles, creamer 4¾" high, sugar bowl 4½" high, $2,880.00.

Set, sugar and creamer, signed, cut, strawberry diamond and hobstars, $324.00.

Set, water, cut, pitcher and 6 tumblers, Scothch Thistle pattern, $792.00.

Shakers, salt and pepper, Maize, original brass tops, white creamy corn, blue husks with gold edges, $288.00.

Shaker, sugar, Maize, original top, pearlized lustre, yellow husks, 5½" high, $245.00.

Sherry, signed, Moonbeam cut, $43.00.

Tankard, signed, cut, 11½" high, hobnail notched prism and other cutting, $864.00.

Tazza, signed, crystal stem, opalescent foot, shallow opalescent bowl, marvered blue swirled threading, 6" tall, $1,008.00.

Toothpick holder, "Little Lob" inscribed in gold, pink shading to white, blue flowers and green leaves, $144.00.

Toothpick holder, Maize, Custard hued, green leaves outlined in gold, $504.00.

Toothpick holder, white satin, Little Lob pattern, $180.00.

Tray, celery, cut, 12" x 4⅜", Gem pattern, eight 12 pointed hobstars, diamond and fan cross-cut, radiant fan center, $202.00.

Tray, cut, Wisteria and Lovebird's, 2" high, 11¼" x 4½", $1,728.00.

Tray, ice cream, cut, signed "Libbey," Ivernia pattern, cut flowers in 4 sections, flashed, 16" x 9¾" $1,260.00.

Tray, ice cream, cut, Kimberly pattern, 14" x 7½", $396.00.

Tray, ice cream, cut, 12" diameter, Somerset pattern, $252.00.

Tray, ice cream, 18" diameter, Princess pattern, $756.00.

Tray, round, cut, 12" signed, Senora pattern, $792.00.

Tray, signed, cut, 12" diameter, scalloped rim, 6 clear panels for a star on a diamond point ground, $1,296.00.

Tumbler, Amberina, signed "Libbey," $252.00.

Tumbler, juice, cut, signed, Corinthian pattern variant, $65.00.

Tumbler, Maize, iridescent gold ear, blue leaves, $281.00.

Tumbler, Maize, white body, green leaves outlined in gold, $194.00.

Vase, Amberina, signed 9½", 2 handles, $864.00.

Vase, Amberina, signed, 11" tall, flower form, $1,368.00.

Vase, Brilliant cut, 12", signed, corset shaped, $713.00.

Vase, bulbous, tapered amber stem, 11¼", circular foot, signed "Libbey," $770.00.

Vase, celery, Maize, opaque white, green husks, $216.00.

Vase, celery, Maize, opaque white, green husks, $216.00.

Vase, opalescent base in form of a rabbit, 10 high, $259.00.

Vase, cutting with roses, 16" tall, signed, $238.00.

Vase, footed, clear, applied green prunts, signed, $180.00.

Vase, lily, Amberina, classic form, signed, 7½" high, $684.00.

Vase, mushroom shaped, ribbed, 4½" high, signed "Libbey," $1,044.00.

Vase, signed, cut, 16" high, Star and Feather pattern, $1,440.00.

Vase, 12" high, cut, Radiant pattern, $432.00.

Vase, 12½", ribbed, circular foot, signed "Libbey," $1,073.00.

Wine, opalescent monkey stem, clear bowl, signed, 5" $137.00.

Wine, opalescent polar bear stem, clear bowl, signed, $144.00.

Wine, silhouetted kangaroo, signed "Libbey," $216.00.

LOCKE ART

Champagne, 6" Poppy pattern, $122.00.

Cup, ice cream, signed, footed, etched Kalana Poppy, $173.00.

Cup, punch, Poppy pattern, signed, "Locke Art," $86.00.

Glass, brandy, rare paper sticker, 3¼", etched flowers and leaves, $144.00.

Goblet, etched Poppies, signed, $130.00.

Goblet, signed, etched Ivy, $144.00.

Pitcher, Amberina, engraved characters of Otus and Ephialtes holding Mars captive, title panel below, signed "J. LOCKE," height 12", $1,224.00.

Pitcher, 8", signed, etched Rose pattern, $324.00.

Pitcher, tankard, 13½", etched Vintage pattern on clear crystal, signed, $1,368.00.

Plate, 7" diameter, signed, etched Poinsettias, $252.00.

Salt, signed, 2¼" x 1¼", pedestal foot, Vintage pattern, $94.00.

Sherbet, multi-fruit etched, signed, $259.00.

Sherbet, signed, Ivy pattern, $259.00.

Sherbet, signed, saucer base, Vintage design, $266.00.

Sherbet, signed, 3½", etched Grapes and Vines, $94.00.

Tray, ice cream, 16" x 8", engraved flowers, $425.00.

Tumbler, signed, Grape and Vine decor, $101.00.

Tumbler, 2¾", engraved sheaves of wheat, $158.00.

Vase, cylindrical, Rose pattern, flowers tinted rose and leaves gold, signed "Locke Art - Mount Oliver, Pennsylvania," 10¾", $1,224.00.

Vase, ruffled top, 5", signed, etched Peonies, $792.00.

Vase, signed, 6¼", flared top, etched Rose design, $648.00.

Vase, signed, 5" flared, Buds and Poppies, $576.00.

Vase, 6" high x 3" wide, engraved Poppies, clear glass, $252.00.

MERCURY

Ball, witches with stand, 18", scarce, $216.00.

Bottle, 7½" high, 4½" diameter, bulbous with flashed amber cut neck, etched grapes and leaves, $238.00.

Bowl, sugar, knob finial on domed cover, low foot, floral decor, 6¼" high x 4¼" diameter, $50.00.

Bowl, 3 clear applied feet, 9½" diameter, 4¾" high, $115.00.

Candlesticks, children's, circa 1850, $122.00 pair.

Candlestick, doomed base, 6¼", gold wash effect, stem teardrop shape, $65.00.

Candlesticks, raised round bases, balaster shaped stems, white enameled floral decor, 12" hgih, $266.00.

Centerpiece, baluster shaped stem, round base, spherical top, 10", $94.00.

Compote, interior bvowl has gold-amber washed effect, 8¼" high, knobbed stem, $137.00.

Compote, white floral effect, 6¼", cylindrical stem, $86.00.

Dip, salt, master size, 1½" high, 3" diameter, flat, $58.00.

Dip, slat, pedestal base, master size, 3" high, amber interior bowl, etched florals, signed "N.E.G.," $238.00.

Doorknobs, pair, $65.00.

Drawer pulls, matching set of 6, 1¼" diameter, $72.00 set.

Flower holders, pair for an automobile, $79.00.

Goblet, amber interior, white enameled floral band, 5⅛" high, $36.00.

Holder, match, $66.00.

Lamp, 10" high, pewter connections, Vintage design on the bowl, $288.00.

Mug, clear applied handle, 3" high, $36.00.

Perfume, original amber glass dauber, striped design, 2¾" high, $65.00.

Pitcher, water, clear applied handle, bulbous, engraved lacy florals and leaves, circa 1840s, scarce, $324.00.

Rolling pin, $108.00.

Rose bowl, melon ribbed, 2½" high, $94.00.

Stand, wig, 10" high, $108.00.

Tiebacks, curtain, etched vines and grape clusters, original pewter shanks, 3½" diameter, $36.00 pair.

Tiebacks, curtain, pewter shanks, etched grape vines and fruit, marked "New England Glass Co., patented January 15, 1855," 3½" diameter, $144.00 pair.

Toothpick holder, $43.00.

Urn, gold lining, 3" high, pedestal base, $122.00.

Vases, baluster shaped, 7" high, light blue deer and foliage, enameled, $101.00 pair.

Vase, bird decor, 7½" high, $65.00.

Wine, enameled decor, etched, stemmed, $58.00.

MOTHER-OF-PEARL

Basket, ruffled rim, frosted and twist applied handle, pink, Herringbone pattern, 5½" high, $288.00.

Bottle, cologne, apricot, Drape design, chased silver top, 4½" high, $238.00.

Bowl, blue, ribbon pattern, 4" high, applied frosted feet, ruffled top, $554.00.

Bowl, bride's Amberina, Diamond Quilted, wide scalloped top, deep melon ribbing, gold flowers and leaves, 10" diameter, $1,080.00.

Bowl, bride's, butterscotch, Herringbone pattern, pink interior, melon ribbed, enameled insects and cherry blossoms, oblong with ruffled edge, probably Mount Washington, 12¼" long x 7" wide x 5¼" high, $540.00.

Bowl, bride's pink, Herringbone design, ruffled edge, gold scrolls, tiny blue and white flowers, gold highlights, possibly Mount Washington, 11" diameter, 4" high, $511.00.

Bowl, rose, 2½" x 3", white Ribbon, Mother-of-Pearl, $734.00.

Box, hinged lid, brass bail handle, lavender-pink, white lining, enameled leaves and scrolls, 4¾" high, $324.00.

Creamer, blue, with blue frosted and reeded handle, white lining, Raindrop pattern, 4½" high, $353.00.

Cruet, Diamond Quilted pattern, cased pink to white, straight sided body, original stopper, $202.00.

Cruet, swirled shades of pink, frosted handle and stopper, silky sheen, 5½" tall, 3" diameter, $684.00.

Ewer, Rainbow, frosted hdls, Herringbone pattern, 9¾" h, $1,404.00.

Jar, cookie, green, enameled chrysnathemums, silverplated handle, cover, and rim, $216.00.

Lamp, kerosene, hanging fixture, brass frame and chain, 16½" high, pink Mother-of-Pearl shade, 8" diameter, Diamond Quilted with white lining, $1,332.00.

Lamp, miniature, 8", number 601, white Mother-of-Pearl Satin, raindrop pattern, ball shaped base, applied frosted feet, fluted and upturned shade, $936.00.

Pitcher, bulbous, oval top, frosted handle, blue enameled with flowers and foliage, $353.00.

Pitcher, cream, Rainbow Satin, Herringbone pattern, ruffled top, frosted handle, 5½" high, $504.00.

Pitcher, syrup, original top, red Beaded Drape pattern, $540.00.

Salt and pepper, Diamond Quilted pattern, original pewter tops, deep rose to white, $382.00 pair.

Set, sugar and creamer, apricot, Raindrop pattern, frosted handled creamer, dome lidded sugar, $410.00.

Tumbler, pink, Diamond Quilted pattern, enameled daisies and leaves, 3⅞" high, $310.00.

Vase, 8" high, Raindrop design, apple green, crimped top, $468.00.

Vase, rare Acorn pattern, 5¾" high, American Beauty Rose, $612.00.

Vase, blue, ruffled top, 13" high, Herringbone pattern, $353.00.

Vase, celery, lemon yellow, white lining, ruffled top, enameled florals, silverplated holder with ribbon handles, 9" high, $353.00.

Vase, chartreuse green, Diamond Quilted design, ruffled top, white lining, 10" high, ormolu base with flowers, $662.00.

Vase, Drape pattern, deep pink, 7¼" tall, $288.00.

Vase, Hobnail pattern, yellow gold shaded to white, 6" high, $900.00.

Vase, Raindrop pattern, butterscotch, bulbous melon ribbed, ruffled top, 7¼" tall, $324.00.

Vase, Ribbon pattern, gold bows and garlands, white ground, 6½" high, $1,332.00.

MOUNT WASHINGTON

Basket, bride's, cameo, pink to white florals and winged griffins, gold washed silverplated holder, 8" square, signed "Reed and Barton," $1,296.00.

Basket, bride's cameo, yellow to white, square bottom with ruffled top, griffins and florals, silverplated angel holder supports the glass, 14½" high, $1,368.00.

Basket, bride's, cameo cut, pink to white casing, wavy flaring rim, classical profile, silverplated basket with handle, on 4 feet, 14" tall, $1,440.00.

Basket, bride's, Crown Milano, signed, square bowl with rounded corners, ruffled rim, yellow finish, enameled flowers and leaves, ornate silverplated stand, 4 feet, birds on handles, 14¼", $1,130.00.

Bottle, perfume, ribbed, Peach Blow, original stopper, enameled apple blossoms, $2,736.00.

Bowl, bride's ruffled, cased pink and white melon ribbed, florals inside and out, 4 legged holder in heavy triple plate, $504.00.

Bowl, bride's, cameo, deep rose over white, Winged Griffins and floral design, exceptional, $1,224.00.

Bowl, Butterfly and Daisy pattern, pierced sterling silver rim, impressed "WSW," Wilcox, 8½" diameter, $684.00.

Bowl, cameo, pink and white with cameo heads, $1,188.00.

Bowl, clear acid finish, rosaria overlay at the lip, Peppermint Stick, cut picket fence design, 24 pointed star base, 2⅝" high x 8¾" diameter, $288.00.

Bowl, ovid, very rare opalescent Rainbow, ornate ormolu footed holder, interior ribbed swirl, 20½" diameter, $713.00.

Bowl, Peach Blow, ruffled rim, 3 scalloped feet, raspberry prunt, 4½" diameter, 3" high, pink to gray-blue shading, $1,440.00.

Bowl, rose, Burmese, gold applied handles, Charles Dickens' verse, ivy decor, $2,808.00.

Bowl, rose, large, Lusterless, colorful cherub decoration, $396.00.

Bowl, rose, 5¼" high x 6" wide, Lusterless, enameled blue and pink daisies, $338.00.

Bowl, 3 sections, cut, Strawberry Diamond and Fan, $180.00.

Bowl, sugar, 2½" high, original label, Peach blow, open, applied handles, $2,520.00.

Candlesticks, ribbed column opalware, peach and white ground, peach florals and ribbons, silver footed bobeches, silver footed Pairpoint holders, dated August 22, 1893, $648.00 pair.

Champagne, 5" high, cut, Hobstar base, diamond and Star pattern, $122.00.

Creamer and covered sugar, Crown Milano, shiny white with molded ribs, gold embellishments on the glass, metal has burnished gold finish, creamer, 3¼", sugar, 6" to top of bail handle, signed with a crown and wreath and #"2040," $1,116.00.

Creamer, classic shape, Peach blow, loop handle, $3,312.00

Cup and saucer, Burmese, satin shading, $432.00 set.

Epergne, double Burmese circular bowls on silverplated stand with 4 feet, matte, ruffled rims, enameled flowers, polished pontils, stand by Simpson, Hall, Miller, & Company, Wallingford, Connecticut, bowls 4" high, stand 23½" high, rare, $4,032.00.

Ewer, Crown Milano, decorated with church, brook, and shepherd with his flock, $3,744.00.

Goblet, 6⅛" high, star base, cut Angular ribbon pattern, fluted stem, $122.00.

Goblet, Rose Amber, Amberina, $238.00.

Hat, Amberina, rough pontil, 6" across, $86.00.

Holder, hatpin, Lusterless, mushroom shaped, satin finish, enameled forget-me-nots and ferns, $324.00.

Jar, biscuit, Burmese hued ground, oak leaves and acorns, barrel shaped body, quadruple plated top, original paper label, $1,368.00.

Jar, biscuit, Crown Milano, gold with Thistle decor, signed twice, on base and in lid, $1,872.00.

Jar, biscuit, Crown Milano, square form, white glass painted in pastel colors, desert scene, travelers at the pyramids, #3910/530," silvered foliated top inscribed "A.L. from Friends" plus Pairpoint stamp, 8¼" high, $1,332.00.

Jar, cookie, Lusterless, melon shape, silverplated handle, rim and lid, gold outlined thistles, signed, $936.00.

Jar, cookie, Royal Flemish, large, Rose decor, $2,160.00.

Jar, covered, ovoid shape, Burmese acidized, applied handles and small lid, 6½" high, $1,404.00.

Jar, cracker, Albertine, leaves outlined in pink and lavender, pastel florals, $792.00.

Jar, cracker, biscuit colored ground, gold and green foliage and gold tracery, signed, Crown Milano, $670.00.

Jar, cracker, clear crystal, enameled Brownies, scarce, signed "Napoli," 6" high, $1,152.00.

Jar, jam, cut, Strawberry Diamonds and Hobstars, quadruple plated top with handle and hinged lid marked "M.W.," $454.00.

Jar, pickle, silverplated frame, labeled "ALBERTINE," globe shaped insert, blue/white florals, domed cover, matching tongs, jar 5", frame 9¼", $1,008.00.

Jar, powder, Crown Milano, ribbed and lidded, bulbous, enameled bouquets and blossoms, red laurel wreath and crown signature, 3" tall, $720.00.

Jar, sweetmeat, gold washed, Crown Milano, embossed, 5", signed, $864.00.

Jug, creamer, Burmese, glossy finish, 4" high x 3½" diameter, applied handle and wishbone feet, $1,404.00.

Jug, syrup, tan florals, bouquets of roses and buds with green leaves, rust and blue daisies outlined in gold, original collar and lid, $2,160.00.

Lamp, banquet, Royal Flemish, aqua and blue, shields and lions in gold with red accents, crystal glass shade, electrified, 42" to top of chimney, $7,920.00.

Mustard, covered, fig mold, pink to white background, typical leaf decor, ornate pagoda hinged cover, $367.00.

Lamp, kerosene, Lava glass, rare, $2,304.00.

Lamp, kerosene table, matte shade in opaque white glass, pink and yellow narcissi, globular glass base has matching floral design, base festooned with shells and rams' head feet, 19¾" high, $2,088.00.

Paperweight, "Rose" shaded blue and white, yellow, white and aventurine center, long green stem, surrounded by 5 serrated green leaves, rare, 4⅛" diameter, $31,680.00.

Pitcher, acidized, Burmese, 9" applied handle, gold outlined oak leaves and vines, $2,304.00.

Pitcher, acidized, excellent color, Peach Blow, vase shaped, square neck, applied reeded yellow handle, $3,168.00.

Pitcher, Burmese, acidized, 6¾", ivy decor with verse: "Creeping where/no life is seen/A rare old plant/is the ivy green," Charles Dixon, $4,032.00.

Pitcher, tankard, Burmese, glossy, 9", $1,152.00.

Plate, Burmese, pansy design, acid texture, $382.00.

Plate, cut, Butterfly and Daisy pattern, 8" diameter, $194.00.

Plate, pansies enameled, 10" diameter, Lusterless, $79.00.

Plate, woman's portrait, 12" diameter, Lusterless, $137.00.

Pot, mustard, Burmese, acid finish, ribbed, silver tops, pair, $540.00 set.

Pot, mustard, handled, open top, cut, Wheeler pattern, $338.00.

Salt, open, shiny finish with ribs, 4 feet, pink and yellow pansies, gold highlights, $252.00.

Set, Burmese castor, vertical ribbed, matte, cylindrical salt and pepper with metal tops, globe-shaped cruets, high lips, ear handles, pointed stoppers, good color, silverplated stand, 4 embossed feet, loop handle, frame 9¼" high, $3,168.00.

Set, water pitcher and 6 tumblers, satin, Burmese, $3,600.00.

Shade, Burmese, 5¼" x 3¾", satin finish, $288.00.

Shakers, Burmese salt and pepper, satin finish, barrel shaped, pewter tops, deep coloration, $526.00.

Shakers, egg-shaped salt and pepper, opaque white, enameled floral design, push-on pewter tops, 2½" tall, $504.00 pair.

Shakers, Ribbed Pillar salt and pepper, in a handled holder, original collars and lids, $410.00.

Shaker, salt, metal chick's head, egg shaped, glossy white, orange peel textured, sprays of roses and foliage, scarce, mint, $518.00.

Shaker, sugar, fig, pink/blue enameled flowers, creamy ground, $482.00.

Shaker, sugar, melon ribbed with purple violets, $281.00.

Shaker, sugar, cut, Strawberry Diamond and Fans pattern, egg shaped, $554.00.

Syrup, barrel ribbed, floral decor, ornate metal lid and handle, 7½" high, $497.00.

Toothpick holder, Burmese, round base, square top, finely enameled flowers, $626.00.

Toothpick holder, Burmese, shaped like a small rose bowl with hexagonal top, satin finish, excellent shading, $360.00.

Toothpick holder, Peach Blow, pink to blue/white at the base, rare, enameled daisies and foliage, gold rim, 2¾" tall, $4,104.00.

Toothpick holder, white Lusterless, enameled leaves, hat shape, 2⅛" high, $367.00.

Top hat, Burmese, shiny finish, extremely rare, peaches 'n cream coloration, 1⅜" tall, 3" across, $684.00.

Tray, turned up rim, cut, 12" diameter, Ox Bow pattern, $792.00.

Tumbler, Burmese, Thomas Hood verse, excellent condition, $1,800.00.

Tumbler, shiny Crown Milano, heavy raised blossoms beneath ribbons and bow, red enameled wreath and number "1026," $1,152.00.

Urn, Crown Milano, signed, crown shaped lid, blossoms and foliage decoration, 16½" high, $4,464.00.

Vase, acid finish, 6¼" high x 2½" diameter, Peach Blow, trumpet shape, excellent coloration, $1,728.00.

Vase, apricot with white lining, Mother-of-Pearl, clear thorn handle, $670.00.

Vase, bottle form, Burmese, 11¾", enameled scrolls and florals run vertically in left handed swirled ribbons, acid finish, $2,520.00.

Vase, bulbous, Burmese, long neck, 11¾" high, enameled butterflies and daisies, verse by James Montgomery, $3,024.00.

Vase, Burmese, enameled pink and yellow flowers, lemon yellow handles, 5" tall, $2,160.00.

Vase, Burmese, glossy, 12", Jack-in-the-pulpit form, $1,584.00.

Vase, Burmese, lily shape, 6", original label, $878.00.

Vase, Burmese, 10¾", poetic verse, butterfly and spray of daisies decor, $2,880.00.

Vase, Burmese, James Montgomery verse, butterflies and daisies decoration, 12" tall, $3,600.00

Vase, Burmese, 12" high, sacred Ibis in flight near pyramids, rare, $5,040.00.

Vase, cabinet, acid finish, Burmese, unique, ruffled top, reverse acorn shape, strawberry pontil, silverplated, 4 legged holder, body has tinted and enameled leaves, 4", $936.00.

Vase, celery, Diamond Quilted, Amberina, $569.00.

Vase, conical, 6" high, opaque white glass, pink ground, enameled bird on a branch, gilded rings, $144.00.

Vase, Crown Mialno, bulbous with long thin neck and applied snail handles, Spider Mums, leaves, buds, background is Burmese yellow, 14" tall, extremely fine, $1,512.00.

Vase, Crown Milano, original label, acorn decor, gold border, scroll handles, $1,800.00.

Vase, Crown Milano, 10½", ducks in flight on back and front, attributed to Frank Guba, rare, $3,600.00.

Vase, Crown Milano, 17" tall, flying Mallard Ducks, signed "Frank Guba," very choice, $5,616.00.

Vase, dusty rose, 16" high, formally dressed page boy on front, blossoms and foliage on reverse, very rare, signed "Verona," $1,224.00.

Vase, Lava, acid finish, 4½" x 5", 2 applied handles, very scarce, $2,304.00.

Vase, Lava, shiny finish, 6½" tall, varied colors of irregular glass imbedded in surface, original paper label with patent date - 1878, extremely rare, $4,320.00.

Vase, Lusterless, 10½", enameled dragonflies and floral sprays, $864.00.

Vase, Napoli, clear crystal, frog design on the interior, gold outlined on the exterior, $1,188.00.

Vase, Peach Blow, 10½", footed ruffled top, pink to blue-grey coloration, $4,752.00.

Vase, Peach blow, ruffled lily form, 3 turned down sides, $5,040.00.

Vase, pear shape, elongated neck, acid finish, excellent color, rare decoration, flowers, stems and leaves plus "Progressive/Fuchre/November 16, 1886," 8¼" high, $2,160.00.

Vase, Rose Amber, 5¼", rolled rim, Venetian diamond, polished pontil, enameled floral decor, $684.00.

Vase, Royal Flemish, 7¼" x 5¾", pansy decoration, gold tracery and border, $2,664.00.

Vase, Royal Flemish, winged gargoyle with scaly tail, stylized florals and panel dividers outlined in heavy gold, tan and brown shaded panels, rare, 8" tall, 6¾" diameter, $3,888.00.

Vase, satin finish, enameled forget-me-nots, ovoid shape, 4¾", original paper label, $720.00.

Vase, signed, Crown Milano, 3 frolicking cherubs on a white tableau, 13" high, bulbous base, slim tapered neck, $2,880.00.

Vase, signed "Napoli - 811," clear crystal glass, rich floral decor, $1,224.00.

Vase, tan and red panels, Royal Flemish, bulbous, 10½", falcon and gold serpent, on front and obverse sides, red top, gold beads at the top and base, $5,256.00.

Vase, tapered baluster shape, glossy finish, Crown Milano, signed, delicate applied gilted handles, pictured is "The Courting Couple" surrounded by scrolled ribbons, 11" high, rare, $2,592.00.

NASH

Bottle, cologne, clear stopper, 5", Chintz, green and blue alternating stripes separated by clear, $720.00.

Bowl and underplate, signed and numbered, iridescent gold and platinum, $504.00.

Bowl, signed, 4", Chintz, red with silver stripes, $648.00.

Candlesticks, Blood Red with gray Chintz pattern, ball stem, 4" tall, $720.00 pair.

Chalice, signed and numbered, 4½" high, fluted, pink, gold, and platinum, $720.00.

Compote, signed, green Chintz, 4½" x 7¼" diameter, $360.00.

Cordial, 4" high, blue and green, Chintz, $101.00.

Dish, signed, 1¼" x 4", ruffled step, gold iridescence, $324.00.

Goblet, applied pedestal foot, signed, 5" Chintz, blue and silver, $158.00.

Goblet, signed "Libbey-Nash," pink threaded bowl, twisted stem, wafer foot, $180.00.

Plate, Chintz, 6½" diameter, clear, orchid and chartreuse spirals from center to the outside edge, $216.00.

Salt, signed, 4" diameter, iridescent bronze, blue and purple highlights, $281.00.

Vase, signed "Nash-544" 4¼", flared lip, iridescent amber, $587.00.

Vase, Chintz, signed, 5¾", red ground, silver stripes, $936.00.

Vase, Chintz, trumpet shape, signed, green and blue, 10", $612.00.

Wine, 6" tall, Chintz, signed, green and lavender, $101.00.

NEW ENGLAND

Bowl, finger, Amberina, 10 folded in pleats, rich amber base, 2½" high, 5⅜" diameter, $238.00.

Bowl, finger, Peach Blow, "Wild Rose," 10 pleated sides, shiny finish, excellent color, 2½" tall, 5½" diameter, $432.00.

Bowl, Green Opaque, 3⅜" high x 9" diameter, $2,268.00.

Bowl, Plated Amberina, circular, 5 lobes curved inward, scalloped rim, glossy, excellent color, white lining, 7½" diameter, 3½" high, paper label "Aurora/NEGW," $3,312.00.

Bowl, Plated Amberina, ruffled top, creamy lining, 5¼" diameter, $2,448.00.

Bowl, Pomona, large with ruffled top and amber rim, 2nd, grind, $230.00.

Bowl, sugar, Agata, rare, flares from the base and at the squared neck, 2 applied handles, excellent mottling, 4" high, $1,872.00.

Bowl, sugar, Pomona, 2nd grind, 2 handles, band of leaves and berries throught the center in gold, 3" tall, $468.00.

Celery, New England Peach Blow, scalloped edge, square top, 4¾" high, $705.00.

Compote, Diamond Quilted, Amberina, crimped rim, 7" high x 4¼" diameter, $792.00.

Cruet, Agata, globe-shaped body, ruffled spout, pink ear handle, white spherical stopper, good color and satin, 5½" high, $2,880.00.

Cruet, Green Opaque, original stopper, $1,800.00.

Cup, punch, acid, New England Peach Blow, $468.00.

Cup, punch, Amberina, Diamond Quilted, $396.00.

Cup, punch, Plated Amberina, $2,340.00.

Cup, punch, shiny, New England Peach Blow, $468.00.

Dish, covered cheese, Amberina, 8" high, cover has large depressed circles, round cut knob, circular flared rim, 9½" diameter, $698.00.

Glass, champagne, Amberina, scarce, hollow stem, $302.00.

Glass, parfait, Plated Amberina, excellent coloration, circa 1886, $1,728.00.

Lemonade, amber handle, Plated Amberina, $1,728.00.

Paperweight, 10 petaled pink Poinsettia, white cane center, stem with green leaves, in a concave white latticino basket, 2¾" diameter, $914.00.

Paperweight, apple with slice cut, clear circular base, extremely rare, by Francois Pierre, circa 1850s, 2¾" high, 3" diameter, $3,600.00.

Paperweight, faceted "Bouquet," red flower, white and red center, 3 buds with millefiori canes, green leaf tips, swirling latticino ground, 2⅝" diameter, $3,744.00.

Pitcher, cream, Agata, rare deepest color and mottling, square top, white applied reeded handle, 4¼", $1,584.00.

Pitcher, square top, Pomona, Cornflower decor, good color on rim and flowers, 6¼", $540.00.

Pitcher, mold-blown, colorless, pear-shaped, spaced vertical cleats below the waist, high lip, horizontal rib underneath, ear shaped handle, 10" high, $216.00.

Pitcher, Pomona, Cornflower decor, 2nd grind, bulbous, amber top, $360.00.

Pitcher, syrup, Amberina, original pewter top, Inverted Thumbprint pattern, $482.00.

Pitcher, syrup, original top, Plated Amberina, circa 1886, $8,352.00.

Pitcher, tankard, Amberina, Diamond Quilted, applied amber handle around the collar, 7" high, $482.00.

Pitcher, water, Plated Amberina, tri-cornered spout, 7" high, amber handle, $8,640.00.

Punch set, Pomona, 9¼" tankard and 6 punch cups, amber trim, excellent condition, $1,728.00.

Salt, pressed floral, rectangular box, bowl of flowers on each side, alternating scallops and points around the rim, 4 feet, transparent light green, 2⅛" high x 3" long, base inscribed "N.E. GLASS COMPANY BOSTON," rare, $281.00.

Set, castor, Amberina, 2 cruets, amber handles and faceted stoppers, salt and pepper shakers, original pewter tops, silverplated frame with embossed handle, 9½" to top of handle, $1,728.00.

Set, creamer and open sugar, squat shape, Plated Amberina, 2½" high, $8,208.00.

Shade, lamp, Plated Amberina, 14" hanging variety, rare, $4,320.00.

Spooner, Green Opaque, 4½" high, very good mottling and gold band, $1,152.00.

Spooner, square mouth, Amberina, scalloped top, round body, Venetian Diamond, $641.00.

Toothpick holder, New England Peach Blow, satin finish, tri-cornered top folded in, raspberry red to pink shades, ground pontil, 2¼" high, $720.00.

Toothpick holder, nice Amberina shading, square rim, round body, 2½" high, Diamond Quilted, $144.00.

Toothpick holder, Peach Blow, cylindrical container, square rim, matte finish, pink to white near the base, in rectangular plated silver frame with Kate Greenaway figure holding the glass, circa about 1886, glass 2½" high, stand 5½" high, $900.00.

Toothpick holder, Pomona, 1st grind, gold stained rigaree collar, $410.00.

Tray, ice cream, Pomona, 1st grind, 12½" long x 7½" wide, ruffled gold rim, Cornflowers and Leaves stained, $936.00.

Tumbler, Agate, 3¾" tall, perfect, $864.00.

Tumbler, Amberina, fuchsia, Exp Diamond pattern, 4" $288.00.

Tumbler, Amberina, Swirl pattern, deep red to gold amber, 3¾" tall x 2½" diameter, $180.00.

Tumbler, Green Opaque, 3¾" high, excellent mottling and gold band, $1,116.00.

Tumbler, Green Opaque, 3¾" high, thick walled, good mottling and gold band, $972.00.

Tumbler, Green Opaque, 3¾" high, thin delicate walls, good mottling and gold band, $1,044.00.

Tumbler, Peach blow, deep raspberry red color to pinkish white, 3¾" high, $720.00.

Tumbler, Plated Amberina, excellent color, $2,448.00.

Tumbler, Pomona, Cornflower decor, 1st grind, amber top, 3¾" high, $194.00.

Tumbler, whiskey, Amberina, Diamond Quilted, 2⅝" high, $223.00.

Vase, Amberina, pressed Stork pattern, 4⅝" high, square, scalloped top, $698.00.

Vase, lily form, Plated Amberina, 6¼" tall, $2,664.00.

Vase, lily, tri-cornered top, ground pontil, Amberina, 7", $540.00.

Vase, Plated Amberina, 4⅛" high, $3,168.00.

Vase, trumpet, Agata, 6" high, gauffered rim, circular foot, superb color with some black mottling, original circular label printed in red "NEGW" in a semicircle at the top, "Agata" in stylized Victorian print "Pat.d" on the bottom in a semicircle "MCH. 2,86," very rare, $2,880.00.

Water carafe, Amberina, ruffled 3 corner top, glass trim 2" from top, 6¾" tall plus tumbler, both are in excellent condition and have excellent coloration, $504.00 set.

NEW MARTINSVILLE

Basket, bride's, elaborately ruffled rim, large, silverplated frame with handle, marked "Homan Brothers," $756.00.

Bear, baby, clear, $65.00.

Bookends, gazelle, clear, 8½" high, $101.00 pair.

Bookends, Russian Wolfhound, clear, 7¼" high, circa 1920s, $180.00 pair.

Bookends, squirrels, clear, on a base, 5¼" high, $144.00 pair.

Bookends, starfish, clear, 7¾" high, $144.00 pair.

Bookends, tigers, clear, 6¾" high x 5¾" long x 3¼" base, $324.00.

Bowl, ruffled rim, Peach Blow, 8" diameter, $166.00.

Bowl, "Sunburst," ribbed body, crimped and ruffled rim, 5" diameter, $209.00.

Bowl, 10¾" diameter, bride's, fluted rim, Peach Blow, $252.00.

Bunnies, clear, 1", ears up, back, or down, $72.00 each.

Chick, baby, clear, 1", $50.00.

German Shepherd, bookends, clear, circa 1937-1950, $144.00 pair.

Hen, clear, 5" high, $72.00.

Mama Pig, 3¾" high, $360.00.

Papa Bear, clear, 4¾" high, $418.00.

Piglet, clear, 1¼" high, $72.00.

Pony, long-legged, oval base, 12" high, $108.00.

Rabbit, clear, 3" high, $72.00.

Rooster, clear, 8" high x 8" long, $79.00.

Seal, baby, candlestick, clear, 4¾" high, $72.00.

Seal with bulb, clear, 7¼", $86.00.

ONYX

Bowl, 2¾" high x 8" wide, creamy ivory ground, raised platinum designs, $1,145.00.

Creamer, raspberry ground, white raised opalescent design, $1,296.00.

Dish, covered butter, off-white background, platinum decor, rare, 4½" tall x 6" diameter, $1,944.00.

Paperweight, pig, rare, Findlay, completely intact, $238.00.

Pitcher, syrup, original silverplated top, marked "Aug 26, '81 - Mar 28, '82" on metal handle, ivory with silver design, $648.00.

Pitcher, water, Findlay Onyx silver, 8", mint, $1,224.00.

Shaker, salt, 2¾", original top, cinnamon ground, silver flowers, $504.00.

Shaker, salt, creamy ivory with raised silver flowers, original top, 2¾", $396.00.

Shaker, sugar, creamy ivory with silver flowers and leaves, original top, 5¾" high, $576.00.

Spooner, creamy ivory with silver, $598.00.

Spooner, raspberry red ground, opalescent white florals, $1,008.00.

Sugar, covered, cream with platinum flowers, knob finial, 6" tall x 4½" diameter, $742.00.

Sugar, covered, raspberry ground, white opalescent flowers, $900.00.

Toothpick holder, raised silver design on ivory, $310.00.

Tumbler, 3¼" high x 2⅞" diameter, barrel shaped, creamy ivory with silver design, $468.00.

Vase, celery, creamy ivory with silver decor, $770.00.

Vase, globe shape, cylindrical neck with 6 lobes, cream-colored ground, raised silver flowers, flat base, 6½" tall, Dalzell, Gilmore and Leighton Company, $770.00.

PAIRPOINT

Bottle, whiskey, 10", cut, 1 quart, Old English pattern, original stopper, $1,872.00.

Bowl, bride's, daisies and bluebells, silverplated, signed "Pairpoint" holder, $864.00.

Bowl, bride's, satin, "peppermint stick" cut rim, footed silver plate frame, Greek medallion warrior heads, 9" diameter, $353.00.

Bowl, centerpiece, amber, silver overlay, turned down rim, $353.00.

Bowl, covered, fish, finial, 2 ornate handles, chrysnathemum decoration, 6½" tall, 8" diameter, signed "Pairpoint Limoges 2502/50," $1,008.00.

Bowl, green, clear swan handles, Gundersen-Pairpoint, $158.00.

Bowl, green, tapered sides, footed, Gundersen-Pairpoint, large, clear swan handles, rare, $396.00.

Box, hinged, oval shape, cream ground, heavy gold decor, flowers and leaves, signed, $648.00.

Box, hinged, scalloped, oval shape, cream ground, heavy gold decor, signed, $670.00.

Candlesticks, emerald green, 16" tall, $720.00.

Candlesticks, emerald green, clear cut prisms, clear ball connector, $432.00 pair.

Compote, amber, controlled clear bubble in stem, 7¼" high x 6¼" diameter, $194.00.

Compote, amber, 6½" high x 12" diameter, controlled bubble paperweight base, $194.00.

Compote, amber, 7½" diameter, clear bubble ball stem, $173.00.

Compote, Aurora, 4" high x 6" diameter, $137.00.

Compote, black silver overlay, 7½" high, scarce, $425.00.

Compote, covered, light green, clear flame finial and bubble ball connector, $144.00.

Compote, dark green, clear bubble connector, $144.00.

Compote, green bowl, clear controlled bubble in stem, 6½" high x 10½" diameter, $187.00.

Compote, green, clear ball stem, silver overlay, floral, marked "Rockwell," 8" high x 8" diameter, $324.00.

Candlesticks, green, mushroom tops, controlled clear bubble stems, 4½" high, $180.00 pair.

Compote, large, light green, Colias design, clear ball connector joins upturned foot, $338.00.

Compote, ruby, clear controlled bubble in stem, 4¼" high x 6" diameter, $130.00.

Compote, ruby, controlled bubble stem, 5" high, $266.00.

Compote, small, light green, engraved grapes, clear ball connects stem to bowl and base, $216.00.

Console set, bowl and 2 compotes, Aurora, scarce, $504.00 set.

Cordial, Amberina, Gundersen-Pairpoint, $50.00.

Dish, candy, covered, Canaria, engraved "Dew Drops," bubble ball finial, $223.00.

Goblet, Canaria, engraved grapes, $144.00.

Jar, cracker, overall gold tracings on melon ground, jar signed "Pairpoint," lid marked "M.W.," $540.00.

Jar, powder, 6" diameter, hinged lid, clear, Viscaria pattern, $288.00.

Lamp, boudoir, signed, puffy Rose Bouquet shade, 5" diameter, tree trunk base, $2,736.00.

Lamp, floor, signed shade painted on the reverse, "Garden of Allah," metal base, $5,544.00.

Lamp, miniature, 9¼" high, kerosene, signed "Delft," blue painted windmill on white, $504.00.

Lamp, puffy, Venice shade, 14" diameter, melon shaped, red roses and green leaves on a soft yellow and white pattern background, brass base, $5,040.00.

Lamp, table, 21" high, brass base, puffy Papillon pattern shade, flowers and butterflies on 14" diameter shade, signed, $5,328.00.

Lamp, table, puffy, Grape pattern, reverse painting with multi-colored leaves, rare gilt-metal base with matching grape vines, shade stamped "The Pairpoint Corp.," 21" high, $4,032.00.

Lamp, table, signed, brass base, puffy shade, 8" diameter, Dogwood Blossom Border, $2,880.00.

Paperweight, Bryden-Pairpoint yellow rose in clear, cut base, $216.00.

Paperweight, clear fish, controlled bubbles, 7" high, $58.00.

Pitcher, deep purple, decorated in white, 3" high, paper label, Pairpoint-Bryden, $108.00.

Plate, cut, 8" diameter, clarina pattern, $79.00.

Swan, Amberina, Pairpoint-Bryden, 5" high, $65.00.

Swan, large, Rosaria, clear neck, $684.00.

Set, sugar and creamer, cut, domed based, Colias pattern, $180.00.

Tumbler, whiskey, Butterfly and Daisy pattern, cut, $65.00.

Vase, amethyst, covered, engraved grapes, 15" high x 5½" diameter, $302.00.

Vase, Canaria, trumpet form, engraved grapes, clear bubble ball connector, $180.00.

Vase, Cobalt Blue spiral on clear, flared rim, 9" diameter, $266.00.

Vase, Cobalt, ruffled top, bubble stem, 5" high, $230.00.

Vase, Cranberry, 12" high, controlled bubble connector, $266.00.

Vase, green cut to clear, 9¾" high, Colias pattern, $324.00.

Vase, green luster, vintage engraved, clear bubble ball stem, 10 prisms, high, 7" diameter, $324.00.

Vase, jack-in-pulpit, Bryden Burmese, circa 1970s, $108.00.

Vase, light green, bulbous footed, engraved grapes, $252.00.

Vase, Ruby, controlled bubble, rolled rim, 8" tall, $209.00.

Vases, Ruby Cornucopia, controlled bubble, 9" high, $360.00 pair.

Vase, Ruby, flared rim, clear bubble ball connects stem to the base, 12" high, $382.00.

Vase, Ruby, stem has controlled bubble ball, 10" high, $288.00.

Vase, Ruby, trumpet shape, clear controlled bubble stem, $266.00.

Vase, signed "Ambero" rare, 9" tall, peasant and country lane scene, $1,130.00.

Whimsey, hat, 3¼" high, milky, pink to blue, $79.00.

Wine, Flambeau, tomato red cup, black stem and foot, scarce, $94.00.

Wine, Flambeau, tomato red cup with silver overlay, black stem and black silver overlay edge on the foot, rare, $122.00.

PHOENIX

Bowl, centerpiece, crystal/footed, Diving Nudes, $194.00.

Bowl, Diamond Quilted Satin, circular divided into lobes, ruffled rim, gilted florals and leaves, polished pontil, matte finish, opaque pink, $468.00.

Bowl, rose, large, original label, pink ground, sculptured flowers, $194.00.

Box, powder, Hummingbirds, blue, $122.00.

Compote, amber, fish design, $108.00.

Lamp, 14", Foxglove, white, aqua, and orange, $223.00.

Sugar, covered, Lacy Dewdrop, blue decoration, $72.00.

Vase, Bluebells, 7", $115.00.

Vase, dark blue with frosted "Madonna" head, original sticker, 10", $353.00.

Vase, 14½", original label, blue and white, blown-out nudes, $648.00.

Vase, Preying Mantis, pink, 8", $122.00.

Vase, sculptured Dogwood, 11", original paper label, $209.00.

Vase, sculptured Fern, blue, 7" tall, 6" diameter, labeled, $122.00.

Vase, sculptured fish, pillow shaped, deep blue, scarce, 9¼" tall, $223.00.

PIGEON BLOOD

Bowl, 7½" high, lion head prunts, applied clear feet, handles, and rim, $360.00.

Bowl, rose, flowers and gold outlines, 5" diameter, $79.00.

Castor, pickle, silverplated cover, frame, and tongs, Torquay pattern, $418.00.

Creamer, enameled designs, Venecia, $194.00.

Cruet, enameled, original stopper, $158.00.

Dish, butter, enameled, Venecia pattern, 5,340.00.

Jar, cookie, silverplated handle, cover, and rim, Florette pattern, $252.00.

Lamp, Gone with the Wind, Pigeon Blood, $1,116.00.

Pitcher, clear applied handle, 7", $238.00.

Pitcher, milk, melon ribs, $180.00.

Pitcher, syrup, original top, Torquay, $353.00.

Pitcher, tankard, diamond Quilted, 10" tall, $252.00.

Pitcher, water, Bulging Loops pattern, $526.00.

Pitcher, water, glossy, Torquay pattern, $396.00.

Pitcher, water, torquay, acid finish, scarce, $684.00.

Shakers, salt and pepper, original lids, Ada pattern, $194.00 set.

Shakers, salt and pepper, plus original tops, Bulging Loops pattern, $194.00 set.

Shakers, salt and pepper, original tops, Flower Band pattern, $194.00 pair.

Shakers, salt and pepper, original metal tops, Torquay, $180.00 pair.

Shaker, sugar, original metal top, Torquay, $382.00.

Spooner, Torquay, $94.00.

Toothpick, Fine Rib pattern, $79.00.

Tumbler, enameled, internal ribs, $72.00.

Vase, celery, silverplated collar, Torquay pattern, $180.00.

Wine, 6" high, $50.00.

PINK SLAG

Bowl, berry, Inverted Fan and Feather, 6½" diameter, $986.00.

Bowl, sugar, covered, 4" high, Inverted Fan and Feather, $972.00.

Creamer, bucket-shaped bowl, Inverted Fan and Feather pattern, 4 ribbed feet, beaded ear-shaped handle, marbleized pink and white, 4¾" high, $864.00.

Creamer, handled, 3½" high, Inverted Fan and Feather, $792.00.

Cruet, all original, Inverted Fan and Feather, $1,980.00.

Cup, punch, Inverted Fan and Feather, $468.00

Dish, butter, covered, 6" diameter, Inverted Fan and Feather, $1,404.00.

Dish, sauce, inverted Fan and Feather, ball feet, 2½" high, $410.00.

Lamp, miniature, rare, swan base, $1,368.00.

Pitcher, 8" high, Inverted Fan and Feather, $2,448.00.

Set, berry, 7 pieces, 6 sauces and a master bowl, footed, Inverted Fan and Feather, very scarce, $5,472.00.

Set, table, 3 pieces, spooner, creamer, covered sugar, Inverted Fan and Feather, scarce, $3,672.00.

Shaker, salt, original top, Inverted Fan and Feather, $360.00.

Spooner, Inverted Fan and Feather, $432.00.

Toothpick holder, Inverted Fan and Feather, $612.00.

Tumbler, 4" high, Inverted Fan and Feather, $576.00.

QUEZAL

Compote, gold iridescent, thin stem, excellent color, signed, $432.00.

Cup, curved body, scroll handle, excellent gold iridescence, fine Quezal signature, rare, $396.00.

Lamp, miniature, gold iridescence, paneled shade and base, bronze footed pedestal, signed "Quezal, - number 240 - The Twilight," $1,944.00.

Salt, open master, gold, signed "Quezal," 2¾" across, $288.00.

Sconce, 2 branched wall, gilt metal, twin arms issue from an oval mount, bell-shaped shades with latticed gold, trails on an alabaster ground, shades 5" high, $576.00.

Shade, 6¾" high, King Tut pattern, iridescent green, gold lining, $1,102.00.

Shade, blue and purple highlights, 6" high, iridescent gold, $230.00.

Shade, bullet shaped, 7¾" high, edged in gold, opal with pulled green feathers, $662.00.

Shade, calcite, gold lining, gold feathering, $158.00.

Shade, calcite, pulled feathering and gold threading, gold lining, bell shaped, scalloped edge, $238.00.

Shade, gold lining, chartreuse with orange drape, green edge, $252.00.

Shade, green and gold leaves, gold threading and lining, opal ground, $166.00.

Shade, iridescent, baluster form with flaring lip and ribbed sides, golden yellow glass, signed "Queal," 7" high, $288.00.

Shade, iridescent, gold trellis and lining, 7" diameter, opal ground, $1,044.00.

Shade, iridescent gold with multicolored highlights, 10 ribbed, 4¾", $158.00.

Shade, opal, 4½" diameter, gold lining, yellow, Zipper patttern, $374.00.

Shade, opal Craquelle, iridescent gold, green flared border, $194.00.

Shade, pear shaped, 8⅜" high, opal, yellow hooked feathering, $806.00.

Shade, pulled feather, iridescent white with gold and green pull ups, $180.00.

Spittoon, lady's, bulbous body, frilled lip, gold mouth, pulled gold feather exterior on a latticed white and green ground, marked "Quezal S 813," 3½" high, $576.00.

Vase, baluster form, gold collared rim, 2 straited hands of silver feathers, avocado-green ground, alabaster neck, signed "Quezla 12," 7¾" high, $1,512.00.

Vase, green iridescence with pulled gold feather, gold lined with stretched and ruffled top, signed, 8¾" high, $1,476.00.

Vase, iridescent floriform, bulbous foot, flaring cylindrical stem, fluted and crackled rim, amber glass decorated with green edged striated white leaves, "Quezal 167," 7", $1,260.00.

Vase, Jack-in-the-pulpit, broad overhanging rim, tapering cylinder, bulbous foot, decorated with striated yellow leaves on an iridescent gold ground inscribed "Quezal," 8½" high, $1,404.00.

Vase, ribbed trumpet form, bright gold interior, latticed gold exterior on ivory white ground, marked "Quezal 6, 11" high, $972.00.

READING

Bowl, rose, Craquelle finish, green, 5", 4 pinched in sides 3¼" across, $288.00.

Cane, ribbed opalescent, ruby ends, 27½" long, $216.00.

Carafe, spouted, rose hued, clear glass spout, 12" high, $288.00.

Ewer, wine, pale rose, domed foot, dark rose lip, clear glass handle, 14½" high, $288.00.

Ewer, wine, rose colored, ice pocket, clear glass spout, 11" high, $288.00.

Pitcher, 10", bulbous, clear overshot, clear reeded handle, $360.00.

Pitcher, bulbous, opalescent Coin Dots, 11½" high, clear applied handle, $396.00.

Pitcher, 9¼" bulbous, pink opalescent, applied opalescent reeded handle, $396.00.

Pitcher, opalescent vertical Ribbed pattern, bulbous, 11½" high, clear handle, $396.00.

Pitcher, 9½" high, pink with white mottling, raised Thumbprint pattern, opalescent base and rare 2-piece reeded handle, $432.00.

Pitcher, 12" white opalescent with overshot effect, $360.00.

Shade, gas, ruffled top, Hobnail pattern, shades from red at the top to opalescent white at the base, $86.00.

Shade, gas, 8 sides, Cranberrry, Diamond Quilted, 4" opening, $94.00.

Vases, baluster shape, opalescent dusty rose, white opalescent neck ring on each, 14" high, $756.00 pair.

Vase, pale yellow, domed foot, applied clear glass handles, 14½" tall, $288.00.

Vase, 14", baluster shape, rare black with applied black neck ring, $432.00.

Vase, 14" baluster shape, frilled top, black with spattered vertical white mottling, very rare, $576.00.

Vase, 13¾" high, white opalescent with overshot, opalescent neck ring, $396.00.

RUBINA CRYSTAL

Basket, small, circa 1880, candy ribbon rim, twisted handle, $137.00.

Bon bon, tri-cornered, 6" wide, pie crust edge, Diamond Quilted, $130.00.

Bottle, perfume, cut body, faceted stopper, 5⅜" high, $137.00.

Bowl, finger, 4½" diameter, Inverted Thumbprint, $94.00.

Bowl, fruit, Royal Ivy, frosted rubina crystal, 9" diameter, $158.00.

Bowl, rose, 6" x 5", overshot, $180.00.

Bowl, rose, Royal Ivy, frosted rubina crystal, $137.00.

Bowl, rubina crystal, 8" diameter, Royal Ivy, $144.00.

Bowl, sugar, covered, Royal Oak, rubina crystal, $223.00.

Bowl, sugar, Royal Ivy, frosted rubina crystal, $194.00.

Box, sterling silver lid, 2" x 1½", paneled, $166.00.

Bucket, ice, silver bail handle, enameled decoration, $122.00.

Butter, covered, Royal Ivy, frosted, $302.00.

Castor, pickle, Northwood's Panelled Sprig, original silverplated holder with tongs, enameled decoration, $324.00.

Castor, pickle, original frame, clear and frosted, Royal Ivy, $216.00.

Castor, pickle, Royal Oak, original silverplated frame and cover, frosted rubina crystal insert, $382.00.

Compote, 4" x 8½", footed, Honeycomb pattern, $230.00.

Creamer, Royal Ivcy, frosted rubina crystal, $266.00.

Creamer, Royal Oak, frosted rubina, $374.00.

Creamer, Royal Oak, rubina crystal, $158.00.

Cruet, clear cut stopper, clear applied reeded handle, overshot, $281.00.

Cruet, clear faceted stopper, clear reeded handle, Inverted Thumbprint, $238.00.

Cruet, Royal Ivy, frosted rubina, $468.00.

Cruet, Royal Oak, original stopper, frosted rubina crystal, $490.00.

Cruet, Royal Oak, original stopper, rubina crystal, $648.00.

Cup, punch, reeded handle, $50.00.

Decanter, original stopper, 8" high, threaded, signed "Northwood," $281.00.

Dip, salt, 6 sided petal rim, clear rigaree around center, silverplated stand, 2" high x 3" high diameter, $180.00.

Dish, butter, 7" high, signed "Northwood," hexagon, gold on bottom and cover, $209.00.

Dish, cheese, covered, 7" high, 10½" diameter, $216.00.

Dish, covered, butter, Royal Oak, rubina crystal, $374.00.

Dish, jelly, triangular, crimped top, threaded, vaseline rigaree, silverplated holder, $252.00.

Dish, sauce, Royal Oak, rubina crystal, $58.00.

Dish, sauce, rubina crystal, Royal Ivy, $50.00.

Jar, cookie, covered, 9" high, melon ribbed, $360.00.

Jar, jam, Swirl pattern, $187.00.

Jar, mustard, silverplated lid, enameled flowers, Baby Thumbprint, $166.00.

Lamp, hall, large, frosted, $648.00.

Pitcher, bulbous, 7½" high, square top, Inverted Thumbprint, rope twisted clear handle around collar, $259.00.

Pitcher, syrup, original top, Royal Ivy, rubina crystal, $396.00.

Pitcher, syrup, threaded, original tin top, $454.00.

Pitcher, water, Royal Ivy, Craquelle, $684.00.

Pitcher, water, Royal Ivy, frosted Craquelle, $626.00.

Pitcher, water, Royal Ivy, rubina crystal, $288.00.

Pitcher, water, Royal Oak, frosted rubina crystal, $511.00.

Pitcher, water, Royal Oak, rubina crystal, $468.00.

Set, berry, 4 sauces, master bowl, 5 pieces, Royal Ivy, $266.00.

Set, condiment, rectangular salt dip and 2 square bottles, cut and polished, 5¾" high, silverplated holder, $288.00.

Set, table, 4 pieces, Royal Oak, frosted rubina crystal, $914.00.

Set, table, Royal Ivy, 4 pieces, Craquelle, $1,296.00.

Set, table, Royal Ivy, 4 pieces, frosted rubina crystal, $770.00.

Set, water, 7 pieces, Royal Ivy, frosted rubina pitcher, 6 tumblers, $864.00.

Shaker, salt, Northwood threaded, original lid, beautiful coloration. $137.00.

Shakers, salt and pepper, original tops, Royal Ivy, frosted rubina crystal, $158.00.

Shakers, salt and pepper, Royal Oak, original tops, frosted rubina crystal, $238.00.

Shaker, sugar, bulbous, original top, melon ribbed, $158.00.

Shaker, sugar, original top, Royal Oak, frosted rubina crystal, $252.00.

Shaker, sugar, Royal Ivy, original top, frosted Craquelle, $310.00.

Shaker, sugar, Royal Ivy, original top, frosted rubina crystal, $252.00.

Spooner, Royal Ivy, frosted rubina crystal, $122.00.

Spooner, Royal Oak, frosted rubina crystal, $158.00.

Syrup, tapered, Inverted Thumbprint, $238.00.

Toothpick holder, Royal Ivy, frosted rubina, $144.00.

Toothpick holder, Royal Oak, frosted rubina crystal, $216.00.

Toothpick holder, Thumbprint, bulbous base, $108.00.

Tumbler, enameled flowers and leaves, Diamond Quilted, $86.00.

Tumbler, enameled, Inverted Thumbprint, $108.00.

Tumbler, Royal Ivy, Craquelle, $130.00.

Tumbler, Royal Oak, frosted crystal, $122.00.

Tumbler, Rubina Overshot, $137.00.

Vase, celery, enameled flowers silverplated holder, $353.00.

Vase, trumpet shape, 13" high, clear pedestal foot, clear applied threading, branch with pink spattered leaves, $238.00.

RUBINA VERDE

Basket, bride's opalescent Hobnail, $612.00.

Bowl, finger, 4¼" diameter, Hobnail pattern ruffled rim, $108.00.

Bowl, finger, threaded, $122.00.

Creamer, Inverted Thumbprint, bulbous, 5", reeded handle, $410.00.

Cruet, Thumbprint pattern, tri-lipped top with matching stopper, 6¾" high, $504.00.

Dish, sweetmeat, notched edge, 8 sided, Vaseline shell trim, silver-plated holder, 5¾" high x 5¾" wide, $194.00.

Epergne, bowl with central trumpet, hanging baskets, 22" high, $504.00.

Pitcher, water, bulbous, applied Vaseline handle, square top, Hobnail, 8" high, $396.00.

Pitcher, water, bulbous, clear applied handle, tri-corner lip, enameled daisies, 8" high, $468.00.

Pitcher, syrup, Hobnail, original top, $137.00.

Shakers, salt and pepper, original tops, $310.00.

Tumbler, 4" high, Hobnail, $324.00.

Vase, jack-in-pulpit, applied Vaseline feet, $180.00.

Vase, ruffled rim, 11" Drape pattern, applied green rim, $410.00.

Wine, Inverted Thumbprint, 4¼", $144.00.

SANDWICH

Basket, overshot, clear glass with twisted handle, $266.00.

Bowl and underplate, canary with canary threads ruffled edges, 3" high, $137.00.

Bowl, covered punch, clear overshot, globe shape, fruit stem finial, 11", $468.00.

Bowl, Peach Blow, ruffled, exquisite color, $396.00.

Candlestick, Acanthus Leaf, dark blue socket, clambroth stem and base, standard, 9¾", $454.00.

Candlestick, amber, hexagonal, 7" $396.00.

Candlestick, amber, hexagonal, 7½", $425.00.

Candlestick, canary, circular base, petal socket, 7" high, $266.00.

Candlestick, canary, circular diamond point base, petal socket, 7" high, $324.00.

Candlesticks, clambroth and translucent blue acanthus leaves, $1,368.00 pair.

Candlestick clambroth, Petal and Loop, 7", $194.00.

Candlestick, crucifix, canary, 11½", $382.00.

Candlestick, crucifix, green, 11½", $670.00.

Candlestick, frosted madonna, 12" $382.00.

Candlestick, dark blue, hexagonal, 7" high, $468.00.

Candlestick, dolphin, clambrothe, single step base, 10¼", $497.00.

Candlestick, dolphin, double step base, clambroth, 10¾", $432.00.

Candlestick, dolphin, green, single step base, 10¼", $756.00.

Candlestick, dolphin, hexagonal base, 6¾", $540.00.

Candlestick, dolphin, single step base, gilded, rare, blue socket, clambroth fish, $814.00.

Candlestick, green socket, hexagonal clambroth stem and foot, 7¼", $756.00.

Candlestick, hexagonal, large base, 7½", amethyst, $540.00.

Candlestick, light blue, hexagonal, 9¼", $396.00.

Candlestick, miniature, clear, 1⅞" tall, $50.00 pair.

Candlestick, sand finish, dark blue petal socket, clambroth column, 9", $238.00.

Celery, clear overshot, scalloped top, hour-glass shape, 8½", $108.00.

Charger, tortoise shell, polished pontil, 11¼", $180.00.

Claret, canary with canary threading, 5" high, $180.00.

Claret, clear with craquelle finish, ruby threading, 4½", $79.00.

Cologne, clear overshot, square bottle, ball stopper, 8", $180.00.

Dish and underplate, oval, clear overshot, 4", $238.00.

Dish, covered cheese, clear overshot with stretch marks, 8", $281.00.

Dish, ice cream, ruby threads on clear, cased in white, supported on clear pedestal and circular base, 4¼" high x 4¼" diameter, $202.00.

Epergne, clear, ruby threading on trumpet and ruffled bowl, supported on a round cut mirror, 12", $281.00.

Fishbowl, clear bowl, etched with fish and underwater vegetation, sits on frosted Dolphin's tail, clear ruffled base, 16½" high, $756.00.

Glass, lemonade, canary with canary threads, needle etching appears like Craquelle, 5½", $194.00.

Glass, lemonade, clear with blue threading, clear handle, 5½", $108.00.

Glass, lemonade, megaphone shape, blue with blue threading, 5½", $194.00.

Glass, lemonade, 6", clear cylindrical shape, copper wheel engraved flowers and leaves on upper body, lower portion has cranberry threading with applied handle, polished pontil, $122.00.

Glass, sarsaparilla, clear with ruby threading, engraved lilies and cat-tails, 3¾", $108.00.

Jug, clear barrel shape, ruby threads at top and bottom, etched wheat, ferns, and bees on the central ground, 6¾" high, $180.00.

Jar, pomade, muzzled bear figure, deep opaque blue, 3½" $468.00.

Lamp, kerosene, circa 1860, jade green, white overlay, $5,616.00.

Paperweight, candy canes fill the entire weight, 2⅞" diameter, $194.00.

Paperweight, clear, blue dahlia on latticino basket, 12 ribbed petals with center yellow cane, emerald green stem, 5 "jeweled" leaves, 2¾" diameter, $410.00.

Paperweight, clear faceted, attributed to Sandwich or New England, blue cornflower with 3 green leaves, signed "DD M/7 1861," honeycomb faceting, concave window in the top, 3" diameter, $281.00.

Paperweight, clear, sulfide bust of Jenny Lind, jasper ground, 3" diameter, $252.00.

Paperweight, deep blue poinsettia, green stem, 3 jeweled leaves on white latticino, 2½" diameter, $936.00.

Paperweight, extremely rare, 5 pears, 4 cherries, 3 emerald green leaves on latticino ground, 2⅜" diameter, $612.00.

Paperweight, multicolored pear with tooled green leaf on small clear base, 2⅛" high, $756.00.

Paperweigh, nosegay of 3 flowers and 4 green leaves on white latticino, circle of blue and white canes, 2⅝" diameter, $468.00.

Paperwieght, pink poinsettia with 5 green leaves on latticino ground, 2⅝" diameter, $324.00.

Paperweight, rare, bouquet of flowers in white latticino basket, central blue flower, 2 pink and 2 white flowers separated by multi-colored canes, bouquet enclosed by 6 emerald green leaves, 2½" diameter, $1,116.00.

Paperweight, sulfide bird in flight, mounted on red, white, and blue ground, 3" diameter, $302.00.

Paperweight, 6 petaled flower with 6 leaves, by Nicholas Lutz, 2¾" diameter, $770.00.

Pitcher, blue overshot, amber lip and handle, 10½" high, $468.00.

Pitcher, bulbous, amber overshot, gr reeded hdl, 6½", $288.00.

Pitcher, champagne, clear crackle glass, pear-shaped, fluted rim, side pocket under rop handle twisted around the neck, flat base, rough pontil, 12", $324.00.

Pitcher, champagne, pink overshot, bladder, clear handle, 11", $540.00.

Pitcher, water, tortoise shell, applied amber handle, 8½", $410.00.

Salt, lacy pressed, 1⅞" x 2⅞", rectangular box with scrolls and stip-ples, ovals and diamonds around the rim, transparent light green, oval knobs around the base, $216.00.

Salt, pressed boat shape, dark blue paddle wheel steamer with "LAFAYET" on each wheel, "B. & S. GLASS CO.," stern, 3½" long, $648.00.

Salt, pressed rectangular box with Gothic arches on 4 feet, 1⅞" high x 2⅞" long, opalescent blue, possibly Sandwich, $216.00.

Serving set, clear overshot, shell 10½" x 9¼", depressions hold a cov-ered sugar and creamer, $396.00.

Set, tea, cranberry with white threading, clear applied petal feet and handle, sugar 2¼", creamer 4", slop bowl 3", $410.00.

Shaker, salt, barrel shaped with threaded rim, pewter screw on top, 4 pronged agitator, marked "patented December 25, 1877," dark blue, base impressed with a sunburst, 2¾" high, $158.00.

Tankard, amber, amber threads, copper wheel engraved lilies and cattails, 7¼" high, $382.00.

Tankard, clear overshot, clear reeded handle, 11½" high, $166.00.

Tankard, clear ruby threads, engraved with a crane, water lilies and cattails, 7½" high, $324.00.

Tankard, dark amber overshot, 9" $670.00.

Tieback knob, cobalt blue to clear, over Mercury, $108.00.

Tieback knob, cranberry red to clear, over Mercury, $108.00.

Tray, ice cream, clear overshot, 13" long, $122.00.

Tumbler, clear with ruby threads, engfraved pond lilies and cattails, 3¼" high, $137.00.

Vase, Bluerina, shades from blue to amber, applied colored leaves and flowers, circa 1880, 6½", $252.00.

Vase, cylinder, enameled roses and leaves, 4" high, $122.00.

Vase, opaque white, conical with flaring rim and 3 scrolled feet, 9¼" high, gilded feet, red enameled leaves, $338.00.

Vases, Peach Blow, ruffled tops, bvarrel shaped, 9", flowers, birds, leaves and insects enameled in gold, black, lavender, and green, $576.00 pair.

Vase, small ring size, white with foliage and bird decor, ornate han-dled food holder, 5½" high, $194.00.

Vase, Trevaise, Alton Manufacturing Company, 3⅝", squat with bul-bous center, green glass pulled and marvered rainbow irides-cent vertical tendrils, raised button pontil, $1,152.00.

Vase, Trevaise, Alton Manufacturing Company, 9⅛" high, greenish iridesence, marvered silver-gold leaves, donut shaped pontil, $1,368.00.

Vase, Trevaise, Alton Manufacturing company, 10½" high, rainbow iridescent background, dark amber leaves edged in green, bul-bous middle, narrow neck and base, raised donut shaped pontil, $1,872.00.

SATIN

Bell, smoke, 8" high, $36.00.

Bowl, Peach Blow exterior, yellow interior, melon-ribbed, ruffled top, 10" diameter, precise enameling and gold mums with gold scrolls, aibuted to Mount Washington, $648.00.

Bowl, 8", ruffled top, rainbow hues, $302.00.

Cruet, 7" high, applied handle, rainbow coloration, $468.00.

Epergne, 18" high, hand enameled birds and florals, $382.00.

Ewer, melon shaped, pedestal foot, 10¾" high, frosted handle, enam-eld berries, $216.00.

Ewer, pink, enameled flower, 9¼" high, frosted handle, $158.00.

Ewer, white casing, acidized, 13" high, applied camphor thorn handle, sham rose to white at the base, $360.00.

Jar, cookie, Florette pattern, pink, silverplated lid, handle, and rim, $302.00.

Lamp, Gone with the Wind, red Satin Bead and Drape pattern, 25½" to the top of the globe, $1,296.00.

Lamp, Gone with the Wind, Red Satin, 2 molded winged Griffins on each globe, reticulated brass foot, electrified, $792.00.

Lamp, miniature, Red Satin glass, 8½", Drape pattern, square base, globe shade, original burner, clear glass chimney, $425.00.

Pitcher, water, square top, applied reeded handle, white liner, $253.00.

Set, creamer and open sugar, blue, New England Glass Company, marked "World's Fair - 1893," $756.00.

Spittoon, ladies, light blue ground, white casing, $144.00.

Toothpick holder, white with enameling, pink casing, $122.00.

Vase, double gourd shaped, robin's egg blue to turquoise, 7" high, $288.00.

Vase, ruffled top, alternating pink and white candy swirls, white lining, Mount Washington, $576.00.

SILVER DEPOSIT AND SILVER OVERLAY

Bottle, clear, pinched sides, floral sterling overlay, $310.00.

Bottle, cologne, corset shape, 7¾" high, clear with silver overlay scrolls/florals, original stopper, $209.00.

Bottle, original stopper, 9¼", cobalt blue, silver overlay, leaf decor, $180.00.

Bottle, perfume, green, bulbous, original stopper sterling overlay, $252.00.

Bottle, perfume, all original, 3½", marked "925," clear with sterling Art Nouveau flowers and vines, $144.00.

Bottle, perfume, 4¼" high, ball stopper, florals and vines in silver deposit, $94.00.

Bottle, perfume, 6" silver overlay stopper and silver design on the bottle, $137.00.

Bowl, clear 12½" diameter, silver deposit and frosted flowers, $94.00.

Cologne, bulbous, original stopper, 6", cranberry with silver overlay, $432.00.

Cruet, all original, 8½", fluted top, sterling overlay on clear, $194.00.

Cup, loving, rare, cranberry with 3 handles, 3½", silver overlay, $878.00.

Jar, candy, covered, 7" diameter, black amehtyst trimming, silver deposit flowers, $79.00.

Jar, honey, covered, clear, marked "Rockwell," bee finial, silver overlay florals, $122.00.

Pitcher, green, sterling silver overlay, grapes and vines, 11½", $1,130.00.

Pitcher, water, clear, 8¼", silver overlay flowers and leaves, $396.00.

Set, console, 3 pieces, low candlesticks and footed bowl, sterling sil ver decoration, $468.00.

Set, liqueur, 11 pieces, decanter with stopper, 10 liqueurs, clear, silver overlay, vines and grapes, marked "Alvin Manufacturing Company," $1,440.00.

Set, water, 7 pieces, cobalt blue pitcher, 6 tumblers, silver overlay, $432.00.

Vase, Art Nouveau, sterling overlay on green, 16", marked "Gorham," $612.00.

Vase, brilliant green, silver overlay tulips, stamped "Alvin Sterling," $1,418.00.

Vase, clear, 14" tall, florals in an Art Nouveau fashion, sterling silver marked "Gorham," $468.00.

Vase, emerald green, silver overlay scrolls and lattice designs, 12" unsigned, $792.00.

Vase, iridescent highlights, green, purple, and gold, sterling overlay, 7½", $612.00.

SINCLAIRE

Bowl, canary yellow, 13", rolled rim, etched florals, $209.00.

Bottle, cologne, original stopper, floral etching, signed, $324.00.

Bowl, cylindrical, scalloped rim, clear, overall diamond and rosette design, 10" diameter, 4" high, $1,224.00.

Bowl, fruit, brilliant cut, 8" x 5", signed, $418.00.

Bowl, Marie border, hexagonal, engraved panels, 9¼", $540.00.

Bowl, pedestal, rolled rim, pale green, 16¾", signed, $144.00.

Box, covered, 3½" square, signed, grapes and bands, $482.00.

Candlestick, light green, swirl ribbed, 10¼", signed, $86.00.

Candlesticks, singles, blue glass with engraved decor, $144.00.

Champagne, Ivy pattern, signed Sinclair, $65.00.

Clock, mantle, signed, cut glass, copper wheel engraved, 8" high, $576.00.

Cologne, signed, cut, 6" high, original stopper, floral designs, $216.00.

Compote, glossy black, Iverene edge, 7", signed, $382.00.

Cordial, clear, cut star base, Greek Key pattern, signed, $50.00.

Cordial, Ivy pattern, signed Sinclaire, $58.00.

Dish, olive, signed, 7¼" x 4", chain of sixteen 12 point hobstars, engraved florals and leaves, $122.00.

Dish, sweetmeat, silverplated top with bail handle, signed, $302.00.

Jug, rock-crystal claret, lead glass, 13½" high, rare, pear-shaped long neck and high pouring lip, raised pillar right hand swirl engraved bees, flowers and birds, ear-shaped handle, 8 sided scalloped foot, acid stamped "S" in laurel wreath, $1,368.00.

Lamp, cut glass, Flower Basket pattern, 17" tall, $1,404.00.

Pitcher, colorless barrel-shape, cut strawberry-daimonds above vertical panels, 8½", notched edge on neck and ear-shaped handle, deeply scalloped rim, leaded glass, $454.00.

Pitcher, 9", pedestal, signed, cut and engraved, $2,880.00.

Plate, cut stars and garlands, 12", signed, $482.00.

Plate, Leaf design, amber, 8½", $50.00.

Plate, signed, cut, star base with 32 points, cross cut diamond, 5½" diameter, $79.00.

Pot, flower, intaglio border, geometric cut, signed, $302.00.

Set, child's cereal, 2 pieces, pitcher and bowl, Queen Louise, 4", signed, $468.00.

Set, compote and candlesticks, etched dark amber, all pieces perfect and signed, $360.00.

Set, console, 2 pieces, yellow-topaz with engraved floral medallions, low candlesticks, 13" rolled rim bowl, signed, $432.00.

Set, sugar and creamer, Queen Louise pattern, signed, $410.00.

Set, water pitcher and 6 tumblers, etched Vintage pattern, apple green tumblers with amber bases, green pitcher has applied amber handle, $626.00.

Set, wines, 6, signed, green to clear, Duchess pattern, $432.00.

Teapot, Rose pattern, signed, $1,332.00.

Tray, card, 7" x 4¾", chain of hobs, engraved border, signed, $151.00.

Tray, celery, signed, 12" x 5", flared ends, scalloped sides, geometric cutting overall with hobstars, $346.00.

Tray, oval, crosscuts, fans and hobstars, 10" x 7", $295.00.

Tray, 13" diameter, signed, Laurel and Greek Key pattern, $353.00.

Vase, amethyst to clear, Lily pattern, 6" high, $288.00.

Vase, clear crystal, 12" high, engraved foliage and flowers, signed, $194.00.

Vase, crystal, 13½" high, etched tulips, $504.00.

Vase, flower center, 6½" high x 8" diameter, cut, Bengal pattern, $1,030.00.

Vase, silver threads and diamonds, 12" high, signed, $1,368.00.

Vase, 16" high, signed, Stratford pattern, $454.00.

Wine, Ivy pattern, signed $58.00.

SMITH BROTHERS

Bottle, cologne, rampant lion stamp, 10¾" x 5¾", $432.00.

Bowl, 2 handled silverplated holder, opaque glass, handpainted flowers, signed, $576.00.

Bowl, melon shape, silverplated rim, 9" diameter, cream ground, white flowers and green leaves outlined in gold, $756.00.

Bowl, rose, inscribed "Compliments of the Season" in gold, signed with rampant lion mark, $432.00.

Bowl, rose, New England Peach Blow, gold decor "World's Fair 1893," $612.00.

Bowl, signed, 3" high x 5½" diameter, melon ribbed, biscuit ground, blue and violet pansies, beaded edge, $432.00.

Box, covered, white ground, bluebells and leaves on pink, 3½" x 4", $360.00.

Dish, sweetmeat, rampant lion trademark, enameled pansies with raised gold, $540.00.

Fernery, melon ribbed, 10" wide, metal rim, 3 shades of pansies, $720.00.

Humidor, signed, 7" high, 5" diameter, painted pansies on cream ground, silverplated cover, florals, molded pipe, $742.00.

Jar, cookie, barrel shaped and melon ribbed, satin cream ground, open-faced pansies with buds, 7¼" tall x 6½" diameter, $900.00.

Jar, cookie, signed, tan background, florals in green, russet, and pink, $1,404.00.

Jar, rose, edge has raised white dots, 4", Shasta daisies, $281.00.

Mustard, signed, handled, pansy designs, $281.00.

Plaque, signed, Pansy decor, 10" diameter, $122.00.

Set, covered sugar and creamer, cream ground, enameled gold flowers, silverplaed lid and handle, $756.00.

Set, creamer and covered sugar, signed, melon shaped, gold florals with multihued leaves, $698.00.

Shaker, sugar, melon ribbed, signed, white ground, purple colum-bines, decorated silverplate top, 3" high x 4" diameter, $713.00.

Tootpick holder, Columned Ribs, white background with exquisite tiny flowers, $158.00.

Vase, cream ground, pinched sides, 5" high x 4" wide, signed, hand painted florals, $253.00.

Vase, flask shape, rare, signed, 8½" high, Santa Maria ship design, $1,440.00.

Vase, heron in reed on pink ground, rings of glass at top and bottom, 10" high, $202.00.

Vase, pinched in sides, 4½", signed, carnation sprays, $526.00.

Vase, ribbed, signed, 2½" high, Season's Greetings in gold, $360.00.

Vase, signed, 2½", melon ribbed, Daisy design, $360.00.

SPATTER

Basket, 8½" high, white lining, blue spatter, applied blue thorn handle, $266.00.

Bowl, rose, 4½" high, pink and blue spatter, $65.00.

Bowl, white lining, 3" high x 5" diameter, green, red, and yellow spatter, clear swirled outer casing, $122.00.

Box, lidded, 7½" high x 4½" diameter, yellow, egg shaped, 3 applied clear gold decorated feet, $324.00.

Candlestick, 9⅜" high, ruffled base, clear with pink spatter, $115.00.

Cruet, rainbow spatter, original stopper, $238.00.

Decanter, 10" tall, pinched sides, faceted clear cut stopper, Cranberry and white spatter, $122.00.

Dip, salt, green and white spatter, clear petal feet, shell rim rigaree, 1¾" high, $108.00.

Jar, covered, clear finial, 6¼" high x 3½" diameter, yellow, blue enameled forget-me-nots, $108.00.

Pitcher, water, 9¼" tall, 5½" diameter, 6 sided top, applied clear reeded handle, blue and white spatter, $180.00.

Tumbler, 3¾" high, Swirl pattern, green and white, $72.00.

Vase, celery, Cranberry with white spatter, $137.00.

Vase, stick variety white and rose on pink, long neck, 10½", $180.00.

Vase, 3¼" high, Cranberry with white spatter, clear applied rigaree at the top, $122.00.

Vase, 9" high, rainbow spatter, clear applied thorn handles, $173.00.

Vase, 8" high, white lining, yellow, green, maroon, and turquoise spattering, $108.00.

STAR HOLLY

Bowl, sugar and underplate, blue, signed, $410.00.

Bowl, 8¾", coral, signed, $288.00.

Creamer, coral with white border, signed, $180.00.

Goblet, water, 6", green jasper, signed, $266.00.

Plate, green, 6" diameter, $137.00.

Sherbet, blue coloration, signed, $158.00.

Spooner, blue patterned, signed, $144.00.

Tumbler, water, 3½" tall, green, signed, $108.00.

STEUBEN

Atomizer, melon ribbed, #1455, Gold Aurene, fiery iridescence, 5", $281.00.

Bookends, gazelles, clear 6¾", $900.00 pair.

Bottled, perfume, square, Bristol Yellow with black threading, signed, $144.00.

Bowl, ACB, 8" high, Plum Jade, $2,736.00.

Bowl, centerpiece, ACB, jade with etched York pattern, $2,880.00.

Bowl, centerpiece, Bristol Yellow, footed, signed with fleur-de-lis, $734.00.

Bowl, centerpiece, Selenium Red, 3½" tall, 13" diameter, signed "STEUBEN," $288.00.

Bowl, centerpiece, Topaz, signed with fleur-de-lis, $504.00.

Bowl, small, Calcite and Gold Aurene, shape 2928, 2" x 4", $158.00.

Bowl, footed, Oriental Poppy, Pomona Green foot, signed "STEUBEN," $1,152.00.

Bowl, grotesque, 4 lobes, wavy rim, molded vertical ribs, green to clear, polished pontil, acid stamped "STEUBEN," $382.00.

Bowl, grotesque, Cranberry to clear, 12" high, 6½" diameter, $410.00.

Bowl, grotesque, Ivory, oval, folded rim, 12" high, 6½" diameter, $338.00.

Bowl, grotesque on pedestal, shape 7307, signed, bubbly spinach crystal, 6" tall, $252.00.

Bowl, Silverina, mica flecks are air trapped, 11" high x 4¾" diameter, $1,037.00.

Candlesticks, ACB, Jade Green on Alabaster, Rose pattern, 6" high, $526.00 pair.

Candlesticks, amber, ribbed, dome foot, double ball stem, #2956, 12" high, $396.00 pair.

Candlesticks, Amethyst Silverina, airtraps, shape 6998, signed, $518.00 pair.

Candlesticks, Gold Aurene, shape 693, signed "Aurene 686," 8", $1,224.00 pair.

Candlesticks, Gold Aurene, signed, 4¾" x 10" wide, $1,174.00 pair.

Candlestick, single shaft, Rosaline cup, Alabaster foot, signed, $173.00.

Candlesticks, Venetian style, Spanish Green, 14" tall, hollow blown swans with paperweight eyes adorn the stems, $216.00 pair.

Candelabra, silverina, shape 8407, 14½" high, $576.00.

Candy dish, covered, Topaz and blue crystal, on a pedestal, signed, 6" $194.00.

Compote, Venetian style, Rose Cintra, iridescent and striped, Spanish green rims, applied prunts, acid-stamped, $223.00.

Chalice, Venetian style, 12" tall, cobalt blue with gold foil and white streaks, applied griffin handles, paperweight eyes, rose du Barry tongues, colors are repeated in the snake encircling the hollow stem, $238.00.

Champagne, Oriental Poppy, 6¼" high, signed, $482.00.

Cologne, iridescent gold Aurene, bell shaped, ovoid stopper, marked "Aurene 1818," 5½" tall, $504.00.

Compote, covered, Venetian style, 12", Topaz, paperweight pear finial, signed "F. Carder - Steuben," $324.00.

Darner, stocking, Blue Aurene, $914.00.

Darner, stocking, Gold Aurene, $684.00.

Decanter, iridescent, Gold Aurene, rounded body with dimples, circular foot, flaring cylindrical neck, matching dimpled stopper, marked "Aurene 2759," 10¾" high, $756.00.

Dip, salt, Gold Aurene, pedestal, signed, $281.00.

Dip, salt, Verre de Soie, $108.00.

Elephant, clear, standing with trunk above its head, 5½" x 7", $648.00.

Glass, wine, green swirl, signed, $158.00.

Glass, wine, Jade and Alabaster, twisted stem, signed, 7¼", $158.00.

Glass, wine, transparent green, oval bowl, slender baluster stem, 2 knobs at the top, circular foot, polished pontil, 8½" tall, marked "STEUBEN," molded bubbles and horizontal threading around the lower bowl, $50.00.

Goblet, clear bowl, Amethyst twist stem, 9" high, $137.00.

Goblet, opalescent, signed, lavender Cintra stem and border, rare, 7⅛", $396.00.

Goblet, Pomona Green, 6" tall, signed, $50.00.

Goblet, Verre de Soie, 6", $79.00.

Jar, powder, Rosa, covered, signed, $108.00.

Lamp base, ACB, Plum Jade, Oriental pattern, 14", $1,728.00.

Lamp, candelabra, signed, 2 arms, rib-swirled flame center finial, Flemish blue, $396.00.

Lamp, Moss Agate, Art Deco, extremely rare, mounted on a marble base with 2 bronze kneeling nudes, $3,600.00.

Mug, Matsu-no-ke, crystal, footed, 6", green decoration and green handle, $338.00.

Perfume, Blue Aurene, #1818, 5⅞" high, flame shaped stopper, $842.00.

Plaque, Thomas Edison, rare, 6½" x 8", $936.00.

Plaque, Pate-de-Verre, rare, square form molded in low relief, bare-breasted woman in mottled flesh tones reclining, mottled green and white ground, 5½", signed "F. Carder 1915," $1,728.00.

Plate, Amethyst cut to clear, intaglio border, 8" diameter. $137.00.

Plate, clear crystal, black threading, 8" diameter, $65.00.

Plate, Marina blue, copper wheel engraved rim, 8¼" diameter, signed, $137.00.

Plate, wide Amethyst rim cut to clear, 8½" diameter, signed, $151.00.

Shade, 6½" x 6", Green Aurene, platinum leaf and vine decor, Calcite interior, $1,390.00.

Shade, bell shaped, Verre de Soie, $115.00.

Shade, acid etched gold design on calcite, $194.00.

Shade, Calcite lining, 4½" high, iridescent Green Aurene, platinum leaf and vine decoration, $1,332.00.

Shade, Calcite lining, iridescent Brown Aurene, blue drape, $540.00.

Shade, gold lining, iridescent Tan Aurene, gold leaves and threading, $266.00.

Shade, gold lining, yellow feathering outlined in green, opal ground, $202.00.

Shade, tulip shaped, Gold Aurene, 4½" tall, signed, $288.00.

Sherbet and underplate, Jade, $115.00.

Sherbet with underplate, Gold Aurene, marked, $454.00.

Tray, ash, Topaz, signed, applied blue leaf handle, $194.00.

Tumbler, amber with Flemish Blue rim, 5" tall, $72.00.

Tumbler, Verre de Soie, rainbow iridescence, 5" tall, $72.00.

Urn, Venetian style, topaz colored, banjo shape, tapered necks, applied feet, 13" tall, $158.00 pair.

Vase, ACB, Alabaster to Jade, shape #1693, 8" high, $792.00.

Vase, ACB, Alabaster with Green Jade ACB rim, original label, 8", shape #1693, variant, $936.00.

Vase, ACB, Black Jade over Alabaster, Pussy Willow design, signed, 6" high, $2,196.00.

Vase, ACB, shape, #1694, 8" tall, $792.00.

Vase, Blue Aurene, mirror lustre, signed 5" tall, $720.00.

Vase, Celeste blue, ribbed, trumpet shaped, domed pedestal foot, 8¼" high, $158.00.

Vase, Cluthra, large bubbles, shaded white to raspberry, flattened oval shape, 10" tall, $1,152.00.

Vase, Emerald Green, silver overlay tulips, signed "Alvin Manufacturing Company," 12" high, $1,346,00.

Vase, flip edge, Calcite and gold Aurene, original paper label, 6¾", $576.00.

Vase, Gold Aurene, white millefiori flowers, green vines and leaves, 5½" high, cylindrical shape, narrow collar, $2,592.00.

Vase, Ivrene, iridescent, ribbed and ruffled oval body on wafer stem and pedestal foot, shape #7564, 6" high, $360.00.

Vase, Ivrene, trumpet shaped, 6", footed, signed, $454.00.

Vase, Ivory, ribbed body with inverted lip, shape #7437, signed, 10¼" tall, $288.00.

Vase, Ivory with black trim, floriform, 12" tall, $1,166.00.

Vase, jack-in-the-pulpit, iridescent Ivrene, signed, 6½", $684.00.

Vase, Marina Blue, optic ribs, folded rim, 16" high, $454.00.

Vase, Moss Agate, 10¾" high, footed, cylindrical, short neck, amber ground, variegated greens and blued, signed, $1,224.00.

Vase, open mouthed fish with curved tail attached to pedestal, Rose colored, signed "Steuben," $180.00.

Vase, Oriental Jade, opaque white swirls, footed, 6½", $266.00.

Vase, pedestal foot, Rosaline, engraved garlands of flowers, 9¼" high x 7½" diameter, $1,008.00.

Vase, Rosaline cut to Alabaster, shape #7007, $3,600.00.

Vase, Rosaline, engraved florals, alabaster foot, 9¼", $1,130.00.

Vase, Selenium Red, signed, 5" high, $223.00.

Vase, signed, Rosaline with Alabaster pedestal foot, trumpet shape, 6" tall, $259.00.

Vase, stick, iridescent Blue Aurene, 6" $554.00.

Vase, stump, 3 pronged, Gold Aurene, 6¼" high, signed, $720.00.

Vase, thorned, 3 pronged, Emerald Green, 7" tall, $353.00.

Vase, trumpet, fluted, Green Florentia, 13" tall, signed, $2,232.00.

Vase, Tyrian, 13½" tall, rare, signed, $11,664.00.

Vase, White Cluthra, scarce, 8" high, signed with fleur-de-lis, $1,512.00.

Vase, 3 pronged stump type, Aurene, number 2744, $756.00.

TIFFANY

Bowl, flares to the top, red, lip turned in, 6" high, 3" deep, $4,320.00.

Bowl, gold ruffled, beautiful iridescence, intaglio, 7" diameter, $936.00.

Bowl, gold iridescence, double flower frogs, 3" high x 10" wide, marvered green ivy and tendrils, $814.00.

Bowl, ruffled edges, blue, 5" diameter, $684.00.

Bottle, cologne, bulbous, 10", signed, double lobed stopper, $1,102.00.

Box, stamp, bronze with green slag glass, 3 compartments, Pine Needle pattern, 4" x 2¼", signed, $281.00.

Box, stamp, Zodiac doré with 3 glass inserts, signed and numbered, "Tiffany Studios," $194.00.

Candlestick, gold Favrile glass, Morovingian pattern bronze base with Lily Pad design, stamped "27466," 20" tall, $1,008.00.

Compote, stemmed, blue stretch glass signed, 12" diameter, $1,368.00.

Cross, Maltese, iridescent gold, 3" across, 3" tall, $612.00.

Dish, bon bon, opalescent foot and stem, butterscotch iridescent stretch edge, 4" diameter, signed, $360.00.

Finger bowl and underplate, signed, ribbed and ruffled, gold iridescence, $72.00 set.

Floriform, Tiffany Favrile, gold ribbing, graceful line, signed "L.C. Tiffany Favrile - 455H," 11¼", $1,188.00.

Flower frog, double, 3¾" high, signed "L.C. Tiffany Favrile - 5678K," $612.00.

Glass, punch, gold, spreading hollow stem 3½" high, signed, $252.00.

Glass, shot, applied lily pads, gold iridescence, signed, $144.00.

Glass, wine, gold foot and bowl, amber faceted stem, signed, 4", $259.00.

Glass, wine, gold lustre cup, clear faceted stem, signed, 4", $324.00

Glass, wine, shallow opalescent pink ribbed bowl, transparent green hollow stem, circular foot, 8" high, marked "L.C. T. Favrile, " $468.00.

Goblet, water, large stemmed, gold Vintage pattern, soft iridescence, 7" tall x 4" wide, signed, $612.00.

Inkwell, bronze and green slag glass, Pink Needle pattern, hinged lid, original insert, 4" x 4", signed, $468.00.

Inkwell, square embossed brass frame, art glass panels, marked "Tiffany Studios, N.Y. 844," $612.00.

Jar, covered, midnight blue iridescent Favrile glass 9¾" high, ovoid body, domed circular foot, conical cover, spire finial, marked "X236 L.C. Tiffany - Favrile," $2,232.00.

Lamp, candle, gold shade and base signed, riser has green feather on opal glass, all original, electic, 15" tall, $1,872.00.

Lamp candle, gold twist candlestick opal glass insert, green Pulled Feathers, gold ruffled shade, 13", signed, $1,584.00.

Lamp, leaded Acorn, 16" diameter, shade green and white, signed, base signed #25877, $4,608.00.

Lamp, signed shade and base, 16", Canterbury bells in shades of red, amber and green richly shaded, genuine and all original, $12,960.00.

Lamp, table, amber linefold, 16" diameter shade, linefold cap, base and shade signed, $3,744.00.

Pedants, round and pierced rectangular forms, lime-yellow Favrile glass, 92 (4" long), 96 (5" long), $396.00 lot.

Perfume, original stopper, gold iridewscence, blud highlights, rare, signed "L.C. Tiffany Favrile - 923OG," 4¼" high, $720.00.

Plate, turquoise pastel, opalescent star-burst design, 11" diameter, $360.00.

Shade, 5" high, opal with green King Tut pattern, $842.00.

Shade, 6¼" high, citron band at base and rim, acid cut iridescent berries and leaves, $338.00.

Shade, green, King Tut pattern, opal lining, iridescent orange, $382.00.

Salt, ruffled, gold and blue iridescence, signed, "Tiffany," $216.00.

Shade, Tulip lamp, ribbed, gold hued, $288.00.

Shade, waisted, domical form, 10" diameter, silver-blue, green, and iridescent amber, damascene, $1,433.00.

Sherbet, butterscotch and opalescent edge, 4¼" diameter, $353.00.

Toothpick holder, gold iridescence, Inverted Dimple design, signed "L.C.T. - #R8844," $360.00.

Vase, blue iridescent urn shape, domed gold foot, applied swollen collar decorated with overlapping blue and amber herringbone bands, gold ground, Tel El Amarne or Egyptian manner, marked around the pontil "5622G L.C. Tiffany - Favrile," 19¼", high, $4,608.00.

Vase, bud, flower-form, gold iridescence, 6" signed and numbered, $756.00.

Vase, bud, gold with green triangles, signed, 8¼", $670.00.

Vase, bulbous with flaring top, gold iridescent, 4" high, signed "1027-883 GM - L.C. Tiffany Favrile," $425.00.

Vase, cabinet, cased urn shape, 2½" high, crimson red exterior, canary yellow interior, signed "1611K L.C. Tiffany Favrile," $1,728.00.

Vase, cameo, ovoid clear glass, rare overhanging iverted rim, applied purple, green and brown glass, intaglio-carved with nasturtiums, interlacing branches, marked "L.C. Tiffany - Favrile 425A," 6¼", $4,464.00.

Vase, cylindrical form, translucent pea-green glass edged with free form swagged silver band beneath creamy white neck, marked "L.C.T. Q4511," 5¼", $936.00.

Vase, Cypriote, teardroip form, waisted, flat circular rim, pitted surface, bright metallic and rainbow lustre, $2,592.00.

Vase, deep blue iridescence, ribbed melon shaped body with dimples, donut shaped collar, 5¼", signed and numbered, $936.00.

Vase, intaglio cut leaves and vines, urn shaped, curving gracefully near the top to a cylindrical neck, iridized gold, deep cut cameo leaves shading to amber, 9" tall, button pontil, signed Louis C. Tiffany Favrile 6368N," $2,664.00.

Vase, Intaglio, gold iridescence, deep overall cut floral, 10 high, signed "1153 - 3643K L.C. Tiffany Favrile," $2,376.00.

Vase, Jack-in-the-pulpit, gold iridescent Favrile glass, 16½" high, slender stem, bulbous foot inscribed "7841B L.C. Tiffany Favrile," frilled and undulating circular mouth, $4,320.00.

Vase, Lava, Tiffany, signed, oviform 4½" high, cobalt overlay, gold trailings, $24,480.00.

Vase, Lava, yellow Favrile, Tiffany, signed, 5" high, irregular, ovoid form, cobalt texture, $16,560.00.

Vase, Millefiori, white flowers (70), green leaves on gold iridescent, 5½" high, $2,160.00.

Vase, paperweight, urn shaped, opalescent white flowers, green leaves and tendrils, gold iridescence, polished pontil, marked "L.C.T. USO99," 4¼" high, 2¾" base, $5,760.00.

Vase, Phantom Lustre exterior, brilliant gold lining, pulled and pinched with square top, 6", signed and numbered, $540.00.

Vase, ribbed with short pedestal, open flower shape, gold with blue highlights, 13" high, signed, $1,872.00.

Vase, trumpet shape, base has ball and pedestal, gold with Leaf and Vine decor, signed, 14½", $2,808.00.

VASA MURRHINA

Basket, bride's, silver mica flecks in cranberry, ornate footed silver-plated holder, $288.00.

Basket, Cranberry with silver mica flecks, clear reeded handle, $288.00.

Basket, deep rose to pink, 9¼" high, clear thorn handle, $360.00.

Basket, flat with ruffled turned up sides, 6" diameter, clear reeded handle, white body, pink edging, silver flecks, $209.00.

Bowl, finger, cranberry and opalescent with silver flecks, $180.00.

Bowl, rose, swirl design, rulled top, pink and maroon splotches, gold flecks, 4¼" diameter x 3¼" high, $266.00.

Bowls, sugar and creamer, cobalt blue, gold flecks, melon ribbed, finials and handles, $288.00 pair.

Creamer, 4½", white lining, clear applied handle, cranberry with Pigeon blood and silver flecks, $137.00.

Cruet, blue with silver flecks, clear stopper and handle, $252.00.

Ewers, ruffled tops, mottled blue, pink, maroon, and yellow with mica flakes, white interiors, clear applied handles, 9¼" high, $410.00 pair.

Handle, letter seal, striped swirls of white, pink, and gold mica alternating on clear glass, 3" high, $158.00.

Jug, syrup, pink mottling with gold flakes, pewter top, clear applied handle, 6½" high, $216.00.

Lamp base, blue glass, spattered gold mica flecks, mounted on a metal base, brass fittings, 5" high x 7" diameter, $410.00.

Mug, amber with gold mica, $144.00.

Pitcher, pink mottling with silver flecks, 4¾" high, $202.00.

Tumbler, multicolored with fold flecks, $252.00.

Vase, blue with gold, white and light blue splotches, rough pontil, 9¼" high x 4" diameter, $216.00.

Vases, orange, yellow, gold, and red mica crystals, fluted tops, 10" high, $396.00 pair.

Vases, Rainbow striped spater, mica flecks, clear spiral rigaree, cased, $360.00 pair.

Vase, yellow on white, silver flecks, white lining, 8½" high, $216.00.

WHEELING

Bowl, berry, satin Peach Blow, deep mahogany to golden cream, interior white lining, 2½" tall, 4½" diameter, $288.00.

Bowl, boat shaped, daisy and Button pattern (Number 101), length 14¼", width 4¾", Hobbs, Brockunier and Company, $540.00.

Creamer, clear Hobnail, amber rim, $79.00.

Creamer, Frances Ware, frosted Hobnail, amber rim, $115.00.

Creamer, Peach Blow, rare and superb, white cased interior, best colors, $590.00.

Cruet, frosted Rubina Hobnail, blown frosted stopper, Hobbs, Brockunier, $468.00.

Cruet, mahogany to pink hues, Peach Blow, amber handle and cut stopper, tri-cornered spout, $1,908.00.

Cup, punch, matte Peach Blow, cylindrical cup, rounded at base and top, amber circular handle, polished pontil, opaque white lining, $504.00.

Dish, Amberina, oval, shallow, pressed Daisy and Button pattern, 7" diameter, Hobbs, Brockunier and Company, $576.00.

Dish, butter, covered, frosted, Frances Ware, $158.00.

Dish sauce, amberina, Daisy and Button, square with shaped corners, 5½", $302.00.

Muffineer, Peach Blow, 5½", $684.00.

Pitcher, Frances Ware, frosted globe shape with spaced hobnails, amber square neck and rim, C-shaped handle, 8½", Hobbs, Brockunier, $324.00.

Pitcher, milk, 5" high, clear Hobnail with amber rim, $252.00.

Pitcher, milk, 5½", frosted Frances Ware, $288.00.

Pitcher, water, Peach Blow, good colors, applied reeded amber handle, ground pontil, 7", $1,224.00.

Set, berry, 13 pieces, 12 sauce dishes, 9" oval bowl, Frances Ware, $576.00.

Set, table, 4 pieces, frosted Hobnail, amber rims, Frances Ware, creamer, spooner, covered butter and sugar, $554.00.

Set, water pitcher and 6 tumblers, glossy Peach blow, $3,960.00.

Shaker, salt, Peach Blow, 3", $770.00.

Toothpick holder, Frances Ware, $79.00.

Toothpick holder, pressed Daisy and Button, $281.00.

Tray, celery, 12" x 7", Frances Ware, $137.00.

Tray, ice cream, frosted, Frances Ware, 14" x 9½", $360.00.

Tumbler, clear Hobnail, amber ribbon, $538.00.

Tumbler, frosted Frances Ware, $72.00.

Tumbler, shiny Peach blow, dark coloration, $432.00.

Vase, classic Morgan Peach Blow, oval with narrow neck, shiny, rests on matte 5 griffin amber holder, 10¼" high, $1,872.00.

Cane, glass walking, clear glass, gold flecked interior, 54½" long, $137.00.

Cane, glass walking, clear glass, bulbous head, tapered shaft, spirals throughout in red, white, yellow, and blue, 54" long, $158.00.

Gavel, uncommon, clear twisted handle, colorful Star Flower design embedded in the clear cylindrical head, 11" long, $180.00.

Hat, top, upside down, Burmese, Bryden, 2¾" x 3½", $122.00.

Pear, blown, New England Peach Blow, shiny, excellent color, curved stem intact, 4½" high, $396.00.

Pear, blown, jet black, extremely rare, applied and tooled leaf and stem, 5¼" high, marked "F. Carder-Steuben," $324.00.

Pipe, clear with white loopings, 15" long, attributed to Sandwich, $468.00.

Pig, miniature, rare, shiny Burmese, Gundersen, ⅞" long, $144.00.

Pig, miniature, Spangled internally with multi-hued body, clear outer casing forms the ears, legs, tail, and snout, 5" long, $122.00.

Shoe, multi-colored Spangle, upturned toe, white lining, clear glass exterior with clear applied glass decorations, 2⅞" high, $122.00.

Vase, Morgan Peach Blow, oval, narrow neck, satin, matte 5 griffin amber holder, 10¼" high, Hobbs, Brockunier and Company, $2,160.00.

Vase, opalescent white hobnails on opalescent pink ground, cylinderical fluted rim, paper label marked "PATENTED 1886." height 7", $410.00.

Vase, Peach blow, fuchsia to honey amber, 6" x 10½", $1,584.00.

WHIMSEY

Bell, 7" high, white cut to Cranberry, gold tracery, $598.00.

Bell, cut glass, Brilliant period, 4½" high, faceted handle, Libbey's Puritana pattern, $576.00.

Bell, hand, Cranberry, clear applied handle, green clapper, 12" high, $288.00.

Boot, Spangled with Aventurine flecks, white lining, clear outer casing with clear applied rigaree, 3¾" high, $144.00.

Button hook, shoes, rare, 6½" long, amber glass, twisted handle, white opalescent knob joins hook and handle, $108.00.

Chain, glass rings and loops, linked together, assorted colors in the links, 9' long, scarce, $94.00.

Cane, glass walking, bulbous head, aqua, tapering shaft, 48" long, $137.00.